Barcode in Back

D1305904

HUMBER LIBRARIES LAKESHORE CAMPUS
3199 Lakeshore Blvd West
TORONTO, ON.   M8V 1K8

RIVER TOURISM

© **Mixed Sources**
Product group from well-managed
forests and other controlled sources
www.fsc.org Cert no. SA-COC-1565
© 1996 Forest Stewardship Council

FSC

RIVER TOURISM

Edited by

Bruce Prideaux

James Cook University
Cairns
Queensland
Australia

Malcolm Cooper

Ritsumeikan Asia Pacific University
Beppu
Japan

www.cabi.org

HUMBER LIBRARIES LAKESHORE CAMPUS
3199 Lakeshore Blvd West
TORONTO, ON.   M8V 1K8

CABI is a trading name of CAB International

CABI Head Office
Nosworthy Way
Wallingford
Oxfordshire OX10 8DE
UK

CABI North American Office
875 Massachusetts Avenue
7th Floor
Cambridge, MA 02139
USA

Tel: + 44 (0)1491 832111
Fax: + 44 (0)1491 833508
E-mail: cabi@cabi.org
Web site: www.cabi.org

Tel: + 1 617 395 4056
Fax: + 1 617 354 6875
E-mail: cabi-nao@cabi.org

©CAB International 2009. All rights reserved. No part of this publication may be reproduced in any form or by any means, electronically, mechanically, by photocopying, recording or otherwise, without the prior permission of the copyright owners.

A catalogue record for this book is available from the British Library, London, UK.

Library of Congress Cataloging-in-Publication Data

River tourism/edited by Bruce Prideaux and Malcolm Cooper.
    p. cm.
  Includes bibliographical references and index.
  ISBN 978-1-84593-468-2 (alk. paper)
1. River tourism. I. Prideaux, B. (Bruce) II. Cooper, Malcolm, 1946 – III. Title.

G156.5.R58R58 2009
338.4 '791091693–dc22

               2008028688

ISBN-13: 978 1 84593 468 2

Typeset by SPi, Pondicherry, India.
Printed and bound in the UK by the MPG Books Group.

The paper used for the text pages in this book is FSC certified. The FSC (Forest Stewardship Council) is an international network to promote responsible management of the world's forests.

Contents

Contributors

Wolfgang Georg Arlt, *Professor Dr, Study Program Director Bachelor and Master Programme in International Tourism Management, Director China Outbound Tourism Research Institute (COTRI), FH Westkueste/West Coast University of Economics and Technology, Fritz-Thiedemann-Ring 20, 25746 Heide, Germany. E-mail: arlt@fh-westkueste.de*

Ralph Buckley, *PhD, Professor, International Centre for Ecotourism Research, Griffith University, PMB 50 Gold Coast, Qld 9726, Australia. E-mail: buckley@griffith.edu.au*

Dean Carson, *PhD, Associate Professor/Principal Research Fellow, Tourism Research Group, School of Tourism and Hospitality, Faculty of Law Business and Arts, Charles Darwin University, Darwin, NT 0909, Australia. E-mail: dean.carson@cdu.edu.au*

Malcolm Cooper, *PhD, Vice President (Research and International Cooperation), Professor of Tourism Management and Environmental Law, Ritsumeikan Asia Pacific University, 1-1 Jumonjibaru, Beppu 874-8577, Japan. E-mail: cooperm@apu.ac.jp*

Patricia Erfurt-Cooper, *Lecturer in Tourism Resource Management, Ritsumeikan Asia Pacific University, 1-1 Jumonjibaru, Beppu 874-8577, Japan; PhD Student, James Cook University, PO Box 6811, Cairns, Australia. E-mail: erfurtp@yahoo.com.au*

Francisco P. Fellizar, *Jr., PhD, Professor of Environmental Management, Ritsumeikan Asia Pacific University, 1-1 Jumonjibaru, Beppu 874-8577, Japan. E-mail: junpfell@apu.ac.jp*

Feng Gequn, *Ningbo University, China.*

Eric Laws, *PhD, Professor, School of Business, James Cook University, PO Box 6811, Cairns, Australia. E-mail: Eric.laws@jcu.edu.au*

Guilherme Lohmann, *PhD, Assistant Professor in Transportation Management, School of Travel Industry Management (TIM), University of Hawaii at Manoa, 2560 Campus Road, George Hall 206, Honolulu, HI 96822, USA. E-mail: glohmann@hawaii.edu*

Giuseppe Marzano, *PhD, School of Tourism, The University of Queensland, 11 Salisbury Road, Ipswich, Australia.*

Ken'ichi Nakagami, *PhD, Professor and Head, Resource Centre for Sustainability (RCS), Ritsumeikan University, Kyoto, Japan. E-mail: Nakagami@ritsumei.ac.jp*

Khin Myat Nwe, *PhD Student, Ritsumeikan Asia Pacific University, 1-1 Jumonjibaru, Beppu 874-8577, Japan.*

Bruce Prideaux, *PhD, Professor of Marketing and Tourism Management, School of Business, James Cook University, PO Box 6811, Cairns, Australia. E-mail: Bruce.prideaux@jcu.edu.au*

Doris Schmallegger, *PhD Student, School of Business, James Cook University, PO Box 6811, Cairns 4870, Australia. E-mail: d.schmallegger@ fh-krems.ac.at*

Noel Scott, *PhD, School of Tourism, The University of Queensland, 11 Salisbury Road, Ipswich, Australia. E-mail: Noel.scott@uq.edu.au*

Peter Semone, *Bangkok 101000 Thailand. E-mail: www.tourism101.org*

Dallen J. Timothy, *PhD, Professor, Program Director, Tourism Development and Management, School of Community Resources and Development, Arizona State University, 411 N. Central Avenue, Suite 550, Phoenix, Arizona 85004, USA. E-mail: Dallen.Timothy@asu.edu*

Preface

Rivers are fascinating places, exhibiting both natural charm and usefulness for a vast array of human activities. Throughout history, rivers have been used as transport routes, as food sources and in more recent times as places to visit and play. Surprisingly, there has been scant recognition of the role of rivers in the tourism industry, a gap which this book was written to fill. In planning this book, Malcolm and I envisaged an end result that would examine the role of rivers as a tourism resource and that would also identify significant issues and trends that later authors may wish to pursue. We hope that this objective has been realized, even if only in part.

When discussing how the book would be structured, we were mindful of the need for a text that not only examined a range of river tourism-related issues, many of which are quite diverse, but also one that went beyond the often shallow background discussions of significant natural resources in the context of tourism to provide the reader with a deeper knowledge of aspects of the underlying science of rivers. To this end, the first chapter spends some time examining the hydrological cycle and basic river biology. We strongly believe that for tourism planners, administrators, scholars and students it is difficult to develop informed views on issues such as suitable planning strategies, sustainability and carrying capacity in the absence of at least a basic understanding of these more science-related elements. We hope that we have been able to achieve this objective along with providing relevant and timely information on existing river tourism.

Rivers are also major spatial elements of the landscape and constitute a significant tourism resource. As the discussion reveals, their use is increasing as people begin to understand the amenity of river views and tourism operators realize the potential for river cruising. Using rather than abusing rivers is important and will become an increasingly important issue in the future as demand for this finite resource rises with growing world population. Tourism has a major impact in this context and should always strive to be wise in its use of resources.

Finally, we hope you enjoy this book, forgive us for any significant omissions and take up the challenge to undertake further research into this fascinating area of tourism.

Bruce Prideaux
Malcolm Cooper

1 Introducing River Tourism: Physical, Ecological and Human Aspects

B. Prideaux,[1] D.J. Timothy[2] and M. Cooper[3]

[1]James Cook University, Cairns, Australia; [2]Arizona State University, Phoenix, Arizona, USA; [3]Ritsumeikan Asia Pacific University, Beppu, Japan

Collectively, the chapters in this book represent the first serious attempt to develop a coherent body of work that examines aspects of river-based tourism, including tourists' use of major riverine systems, aspects of fluvial hydrology, river management and travel writing based on river travel. Rivers have occupied a central place in human history since the dawn of civilization, and before. They provided water and the fertile alluvial plains that sustained the first human settlements, and in so doing helped foster the accumulation of wealth based on agriculture and trade. This allowed the great civilizations of the past to flourish. Early civilizations and their cities flourished on the banks of many of the world's great rivers including the Indus, Nile, Tigris, Euphrates, Mekong, Rhine, Danube, Yangzi and Yellow rivers. In the modern world, rivers continue to be closely associated with great cities and in the contemporary era have become a significant tourism resource. In some regions, cities and their cultural landscapes are interwoven with the fabric of river life to create unique urban environments, while in rural and other less-developed regions rivers have retained their natural characteristics, creating interest in rivers as ecotourism and nature-based resources. Rivers also act as political boundaries for municipal, regional, state and international entities. In North America, for example, the Colorado River divides municipalities, states (California and Arizona, Nevada and Arizona) and countries (the USA and Mexico), while in Europe the Rhine forms parts of the borders of Germany, France, Austria, Liechtenstein and Switzerland.

Although rivers divide when used as boundaries, they also connect through their role as river transport corridors, and they attract onlookers by their inherent beauty. Many major cities are built beside rivers, and it is this area of the urban–river interface that is of most interest to residents and visitors. The Seine River, for example, divides Paris into precincts while providing an attractive backdrop to the business of the city. Rivers exude beauty, serenity and adventure that draw visitors' attention. In cities, hotels seek out riverside locations as do shopping precincts and recreational areas. In the countryside, rivers appeal to people because they retain much of their natural beauty and offer opportunities for fishing, boating and other forms of recreation. In modified riverscapes, tourists also find opportunities for water-centred recreational activities as well as enjoyment of the urban–river cultural landscapes that have emerged. Rivers also provide opportunities for cruising. However, rivers are sensitive to human intervention and in many riverine systems the ecosystems they support are showing considerable stress from irrigation, catchment clearing, pollution, dam construction and other forms of human intervention.

From this brief introduction it is apparent that rivers are an important but surprisingly neglected aspect of the global tourism industry. Yet rivers form the basis for many of the ecosystems that underpin ecotourism and other recreational activities, in addition to providing water to sustain urban growth, farming, agriculture-related experiences such as viticulture and the transport of goods and people. Compared to the research and industry attention that ocean cruising has attracted recently (see Dowling, 2006), rivers have apparently been of little interest to tourism academics, although the same cannot be said for leisure and recreation scholars, who have demonstrated considerable interest in fluvial systems as outdoor recreation resources in recent years (e.g. Herrick and McDonald, 1992; Adams, 1993; Bricker and Kerstetter, 2000; McKean *et al.*, 2005). The aim of this book, therefore, is to explore a number of issues related to river tourism, raise awareness of the roles that rivers play in tourism and identify areas that require further research. The editors realize that not all issues can be covered but recognize the vast potential scope for additional research in this area.

To set the scene for later chapters, this chapter examines various issues associated with the structure and operation of rivers before developing a framework to describe and understand river-based tourism. For this reason the chapter commences with a necessarily brief, but nevertheless important, discussion about aspects of the water cycle and fluvial hydrology (developed further in Chapters 12 and 13, this volume). Following this, the discussion turns to river ecology to create a foundation for understanding how the ecosystems that often form a significant component of tourism use fluvial systems to operate and are affected by human use. The chapter then examines elements of the tourism–river interface before specifically examining issues related to tourism's use of river systems.

The approach taken by the editors of this book is that to contextualize fully the use of rivers by the tourism industry it is first necessary to understand a range of physical factors that govern river functions and to note other major uses of water. Too often the physical world and the associated sciences that explain its biology and other aspects are ignored both by tourism scholars and importantly by administrators and planners. Fresh water is a scarce resource, and in a world where global population numbers continue to rise and where increasing amounts of fresh water are required for food production, electricity generation and other industrial uses, the recreational uses of fresh water may not rank highly on the list of priorities dealt with by the public sector. Future tourism use of rivers cannot therefore be assumed as a given, and in some circumstances tourism uses of rivers may be limited by other demands on river systems.

The Water Cycle

Perhaps the most fundamental issue that needs to be understood when discussing the use of rivers by the tourism industry is the operation of the water cycle. Figure 1.1 illustrates the generalized global hydrological system and shows the flow of water in liquid, vapour and solid forms from oceans and other large water bodies into the atmosphere, and from there into surface and subsurface systems on the land, and eventually back to the oceans or atmospheres. The water

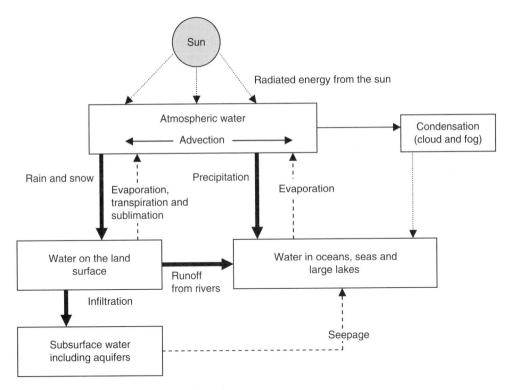

Fig. 1.1. Generalized global hydrological system.

Notes:
1. *Infiltration* – water flows from the surface into the ground where it becomes groundwater;
2. *Advection* – water flows through the atmosphere in solid, vapour or liquid states;
3. *Subsurface flow* – groundwater eventually returns to the surface as a spring, for example, or seeps into oceans;
4. *Condensation* – water vapour transforms into liquid droplets to form clouds and fog;
5. *Sublimation* – solid water (snow and ice) changes directly into water vapour;
6. *Runoff* – water moves across the land surface, entering rivers or lakes, gets stored in reservoirs, evaporates or infiltrates into the ground.

cycle is driven by the energy flux from the sun, which powers the constant movement of water in either solid, liquid or vapour forms between storage areas in the atmosphere, on land (either in surface or subsurface storage areas) and in oceans, seas and lakes. While the total stock of global water is enormous (1500 million cubic kilometres; Howell *et al.*, 1993), much of it is locked in the oceans (97.25%), continental ice sheets and glaciers (2.05%), groundwater (0.68%), lakes (0.01%), soil moisture (0.005%) and the atmosphere (0.0001%). Water for human consumption is drawn from a very small component of the total global volume of water and is located in rivers, lakes, soil and aquifers. Resident time, or the average time a molecule of water will spend in a particular reservoir (ocean, river, ice cap, groundwater, atmosphere, etc.), varies considerably from an average of 3200 years in oceans to 2–6 months in rivers, and 9 days in the atmosphere.

As demand for water has increased in the last few centuries, because of increased urbanization, industrialization and agriculture, and because of the need to reduce the seasonal cycles of abundances and deficiencies, many water-capture schemes using dams have been implemented throughout the world. While increasing the availability of fresh water for human use, dams have had a significant impact on river ecosystems, ocean runoff, evaporation and sediment flows. Driven by the hydrological cycle, the water available for human consumption recycles rapidly, usually through annual cycles of rainfall driven by the seasons. In recent decades, an emerging mismatch has developed between total demand for fresh water and its availability. Demand includes the following:

- farming, including irrigation and animal watering;
- domestic use;
- public uses such as gardens and recreation;
- navigation (canals and locks for example);
- industrial use;
- environmental use (maintenance of river- and lake-related ecosystems);
- hydroelectricity generation;
- flood mitigation.

Globally, the demand for water is increasing, driven by continuing population and economic growth. China is one example of a country where economic growth has created an enormous increase in demand for water, while simultaneously generating increasing pollution of its river systems (Xie *et al.*, 2003; Zhang *et al.*, 2004). The growth in demand for water for industrial use has increased in sectors such as electricity, where water is used for cooling and hydroelectricity generation, factory farming, industrial use, and of course growing domestic demand, particularly in rapidly growing cities. Simultaneously, individual consumption of food measured in calories per person and in increased demand for high-protein foods has generated greater demand for water for farming and to support livestock production. At the same time, deforestation has cleared large areas of river catchments, reducing water quality and increasing the likelihood of downstream flooding (Hofer, 1993; Coulthard and Macklin, 2001). Collectively, this growing demand for water has been met by increasing use of underground aquifers, often in an unsustainable manner, and increased dam construction. In the pursuit of economic development, regulation of the quality of waste-water discharge from factories and urban sewerage systems has not been given a high priority, and in many areas the quality of water has declined. The long-term sustainability of China's current water-use regimes, for instance, is now being questioned and will require enormous investments to improve or restore water quality and satisfy growing future demand.

An examination of global water demand from an economic perspective reveals a highly exploited resource that historically has been treated as a public good available at cost or as a heavily subsidized commodity. In many jurisdictions, the true cost of water capture, treatment and distribution has been disguised by the public sector with the result that demand has grown to levels that are now becoming unsustainable. It has been argued by some authors (e.g. Winpenny, 1994; Gustafson *et al.*, 2000; Garcia and Thomas, 2001) that the undervaluation of water has distorted markets to the extent that the value of the electricity, irrigated crops, industrial outputs where water is used for cooling or other aspects of the manufacturing process, and for household use does not reflect the true cost of water treatment and supply. As global demands increase for what is essentially a finite resource, the economic imbalance between the cost of production of water for human use and the price at which water is sold will have to be corrected, increasing prices in many areas of the global economy.

In the past, the availability of water for recreational purposes created few conflicts with other uses. However, with the industrialization of water supply as an input for factory production commencing with the industrial revolution, the easy coexistence between recreation and other uses such as food production, transportation and industrial use has changed, and today recreational users of water must compete with other consumers. In many jurisdictions this is unlikely to cause problems, but as demand for water grows and the cost of production of water for human and industrial use increases this may change. In sensitive riverine ecosystems the growing popularity of nature-based tourism may create problems with sustainability and capping visitation may become necessary.

Linkages Between the Attributes of River Systems

River systems, rivers and their tributaries can best be described using a systems approach. From a systems perspective, river basins are characterized by size, shape, topography, geology (including soils), climate and ecosystems (Young *et al.*, 2001). Collectively, these attributes determine the hydrology, form and ecological attributes of the river system. To understand how the structure of individual rivers can affect their tourism potential, it is essential to understand the role of the various elements that govern the structure and characteristics of river systems.

The factors that govern the form and structure of rivers, the natural ecosystems they sustain and the uses of rivers may be grouped into three sets of attributes. Primary attributes include geology and derived soils, topography, climate and land cover. Collectively these attributes constitute the river's hydrology. Secondary attributes include material fluxes (organic and inorganic), flow hydraulics and river forms. The third group of attributes includes riverine

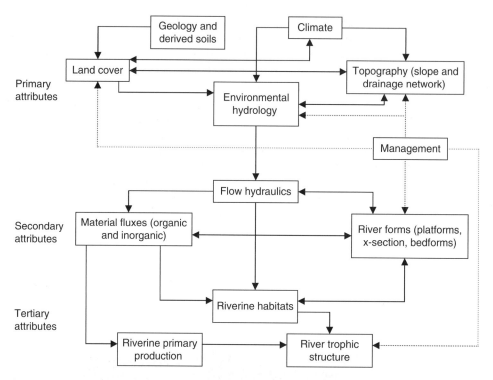

Fig. 1.2. Linkages between major primary, secondary and tertiary attributes of river systems. (From Young *et al.*, 2001, p. 5.)

habitats, riverine primary production and river trophic levels. The relationship of these attributes is outlined diagrammatically in Fig. 1.2. It should be noted that superimposed on this structure, at least where rivers are harnessed for agriculture or other uses, management should occupy a position within the primary set of attributes.

The primary group of attributes collectively describes the hydrological forces that govern shape, size and flow characteristics of the river system. These include climate, which determines water volume; geology, which has a significant influence on the course of the river and its shape; topography, which governs flow rates, and with geology the pattern of the drainage network that feeds the river. Hydrology can be described as the distribution of water in a system including time and space elements (Young *et al.*, 2001). Together with the structure of land cover within the river basin, these factors determine the river systems' environmental hydrology or water cycle including flow rate and the amount of sediment carried. In some circumstances, aquifers (underground bodies of water) may have an effect on groundwater hydrology, particularly in cases where a river has a large flood plain (called the Hyporheic zone). Clearly, hydrology is the key driving force of river systems. Human intervention, through land clearing for agriculture or through the construction of dams, can directly affect river hydrology and requires careful management.

Secondary attributes include the flow regime and sediment load, which together influence, in conjunction with geology, the size of the river channel and its shape, as well as the shape of the river bed. For example, in the Amazon system the high rate of flow and heavy sediment load have created an extensive area of low-lying alluvial islands at the mouth of the river. Hydraulics, which is ultimately governed by hydrology, refers to the forces associated with the movement of water within a system (Young *et al.*, 2001). Hydraulic attributes, including flow velocity and flow depth, influence the shear stresses on river banks and river beds and in this way influence the transport of sediment and the shape of the channel. In mountainous regions, erosion cuts into the under-lying rock strata to create gorges (such as the Grand Canyon in the USA and Mexico's Copper Canyon), rapids and waterfalls (e.g. Victoria Falls in Africa and Iguazu Falls, the world's widest waterfall, located on the border of Brazil and Argentina). Figure 1.3 illustrates the power of waterfalls to create spectacular gorges. In the middle reaches where the land is flatter, and the channel is

Fig. 1.3. The Barron Falls on the Barron River in Cairns, Northern Australia. (Photograph courtesy of Bruce Prideaux.)

surrounded by a flood plain, the river usually creates a series of bends and loops and/or wetlands. At their mouth, rivers may create estuaries, deltas and in some areas fjords or rias. Where precipitation is low, water may flow only part of the year or more infrequently forming intermittent or ephemeral rivers. In other cases, subterranean or underground rivers flow through caves and caverns. These rivers (e.g. the Li River in China) are usually found in limestone regions and are of particular interest to tourists as they help create unique karst landscapes that appeal not only to spelunkers (cavers) but also to the general travelling public.

The rivers' hydraulic profile influences depth and velocity, which in turn determine light, salinity, oxygen and temperature profiles. It is these profiles that govern the river's flora and fauna (Bayley, 1995; Martín-Vide, 2001). Hydraulic variables are the major determinants of the distribution of river species, and the mechanisms they have developed to live in river environments. Changes in river hydraulics through human intervention will often have significant impacts on river ecosystems; in effect, hydraulic variables shape river forms and ultimately govern the structure and operation of river habitats. One element of river hydraulics that is an essential part of the river's ecological health is flooding. While flooding adds fertility to flood plains and is essential for the reproductive processes of many aquatic and terrestrial flora and fauna (Siebentritt *et al.*, 2004), its often adverse impact on human settlement has resulted in considerable re-engineering of river flows via levees, channels and dams to reduce flooding. When this form of intervention occurs, the hydraulic characteristics of rivers are changed, often interrupting the biological processes in riverine ecosystems.

The third set of attributes includes the transport of nutrients and sediments, which combined have an enormous influence on the riverine ecosystem and habitats that the river supports. The transport of nutrients and sediments affects the flow of organic carbon, or energy, throughout the system, the form in which interactions between organisms in the food chain occur, the ecology and adaptations of the flora and fauna within the riverine ecosystem, and ultimately the level of biodiversity found in the river. The types of primary producers in the river ecosystem including plants and algae and the types of primary consumers collectively determine the networks of consumers that occur at higher levels in the food chain. The resulting ecosystems include swamps of the type illustrated in Fig. 1.4, are often unique and, from a tourism perspective, constitute resources that are central to the development of visitor experiences, particularly where nature is a key attraction.

The ecology of the river's aquatic and terrestrial systems is heavily influenced by the downstream transport of nutrients and energy (carbon) as well as the position of the basin or catchment and, importantly, stream discharge. However, the relationship between the biological condition of the riverine system and the physical processes that shape the river is not well understood (see, e.g. Young *et al.*, 2001). What is apparent is that stream discharge which is determined by the condition of the catchment and prevalent weather systems is the major driving force that creates the conditions that sustain

Fig. 1.4. A typical example of a swamp or wetland community. The swamp in this photo is located beside the Murray River in Victoria, Australia. (Photograph courtesy of Bruce Prideaux.)

particular ecosystems. The forces that operate within this system can be described as the longitudinal flow component and the lateral flow component (Young *et al.*, 2001).

The longitudinal flow component consists of the catchment conditions which determine river flow levels and the source and flow of nutrients and energy commencing in the upstream section and finishing in the downstream component (Thorp and Delong, 1994). Together these components determine the composition of the trophic (food web) structure in all areas of the river system as illustrated in Fig. 1.5. The lateral flow component refers to the variability of the river over time and space. In river systems such as the Amazon where river flow levels are relatively consistent on a year-on-year basis; the lateral flow component has a relatively low level of influence on trophic structures.

Ultimately, the health of a river system is measured by the health of its tertiary attributes, including the state of the natural ecosystem. Given that the state of the tertiary attributes is directly governed by the interaction between primary and secondary attributes, the key to understanding how river health is affected by human intervention is found in understanding the impact of development on flow regimes, land use and channel forms. It is these major secondary attributes that are most likely to be affected by resource development and management practices. Failure to recognize the links between the primary, secondary and tertiary attributes has been largely responsible for the damage that has occurred to many fluvial systems that have been developed for uses such as irrigation and waste disposal.

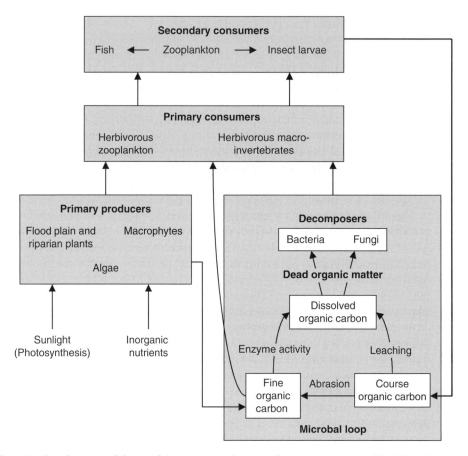

Fig. 1.5. The elements of the trophic structure of a typical river system. (Modified from Young et al., 2001, p. 40.)

River ecology

The previous discussion highlighted the links that occur between the three levels of river attributes. The following sections briefly examine aspects of river ecology. Freshwater ecosystems contain 0.009% of the global water supply, cover 0.8% of the earth's surface and are home to some 41% of the world's known fish species (Postel and Carpenter, 1997). Freshwater ecosystems include:

- riverbanks (riparian);
- lotic, rapidly moving water in streams and ponds;
- lentic, slow-moving water including lakes and ponds; and
- wetlands, areas where soils are saturated or inundated for some part of the year.

The structure of these major zones is determined by the gradient of the river and/or the velocity of the current. The *lotic* zone is characterized by turbulent water, which usually has greater concentrations of dissolved oxygen and as a result is able to support more complex ecosystems. In *lentic* zones, slower-moving waters often lack oxygen and are typified by less-biodiverse ecosystems. Each of these zones supports ecosystems where flora and fauna have developed adaptations to cope with the specific conditions present in its specific ecosystem.

Riverine areas combine aquatic and terrestrial flora and fauna to create a range of distinctive ecosystems that have aquatic and terrestrial elements. The character of the riverine ecosystem is to a large extent determined by flows of water, energy and materials (including nutrients and sediments), as well as atmospheric temperature. The relationships created through the interaction of these flows are complex and not well understood. Essentially, sediments, nutrients and water are collected commencing in the river catchment system, transported down the river and deposited on flood plains, which may occur in a restricted form in upland valleys and more commonly in lowland areas. Any remaining sediment is deposited at river mouths often creating large delta areas such as those found at the mouth of the Mississippi, Nile and Amazon rivers. Within any river system a range of ecosystems will emerge, the structure of which is determined by specific river flow characteristics and atmospheric temperature regimes. For example, the headwaters of the Mekong River are located at high altitudes where alpine vegetation dominates. Later, the river flows through areas of lower elevation that support rainforests, before finally flowing into the sea through extensive marshlands and mangrove forests.

Flooding is a key element in river ecosystem maintenance and facilitates the deposition of sediments and nutrients that support plant communities in river flood plains. Flooding may also replenish groundwater structures that support plant communities during the remainder of the year. Interruption of river flow regimes through human intervention may have significant impacts on the structure of the river ecosystem by reducing flows of water, sediment and nutrients. For example, withdrawing water for irrigation and human consumption by pumping will reduce the level of water available to support swamp and marsh communities. Withdrawing water by damming will reduce the flow of water as well as the flows of sediments and nutrients. The level of withdrawal will often have a direct correlation with the level of impact on downstream ecosystems, sometimes reducing the extent of these communities or in more extreme cases causing ecosystem modification through reduction in species diversity.

Water re-entering the river after it has been used for irrigation, industrial purposes or human use may also have significant impacts on river ecosystems. Water that has been used for irrigation may re-enter the river carrying increased sediment and nutrient loads, as well as chemicals that will affect downstream plant communities. Similarly, waste water that has been used in industrial practices may carry toxic substances that poison flora and fauna. From a human perspective, the introduction of toxic waste requires downstream users to incur additional cost for water purification and increases the risk of poor health.

Aside from toxic wastes, river ecosystems are increasingly being modified, or in some cases endangered, by the introduction of exotic flora and fauna. Where non-endemic species are introduced, modification of the ecosystem may occur on a scale that ranges from minor to radical. Where introduced species are more successful than endemic species, extinctions may occur. In the Murray Darling system in Australia, the introduction of carp, a popular species for anglers in Asia and Europe, has created an ecological disaster for native species such as the Murray Cod. Between 1964, when introduced carp escaped from ponded fish farms at Boolarra into the Murray River, and 1999, the population of carp has spread from one isolated location to cover the entire Murray Darling Basin. Carp are benthic feeders, which suck in silt and mud to extract food. As a consequence of this feeding process, they excavate shallow depressions on the bottom of the river, uprooting aquatic plants and resuspending bottom sediments and increasing turbidity.

The various components of the riverine environment include the river itself (instream), the banks of the river (riparian) and the flood plains. Flood plains are also subject to other non-river bodies of water including aquifers (underground water) and aspects of groundwater hydrology. The linkages between the primary, secondary and tertiary attributes are significant. Development of parts of the river for agriculture or other uses such as irrigation will have a direct effect on secondary variables such as flow regime, channel forms and land use.

River Management

The previous discussion has referred to the various forms of human intervention in river systems to reduce flooding, capture water for irrigation and human use, construction of canals or the use of rivers for effluent discharge in urban areas and factories. Six main forms of human intervention can be identified:

- Canals – Canals are constructed to connect water bodies such as lakes and rivers for transport purposes; they are used extensively in Europe, China and the north-eastern USA.
- Dams – Dams are built for a number of reasons including water storage for the production of hydroelectricity, to control flows during flooding, for irrigation, for human drinking water and for industrial purposes.
- Flood control – Apart from dam construction (of the type illustrated in Fig. 1.6), floods may be controlled via the construction of levees.
- Transportation – To improve navigation, rivers may be dredged or otherwise modified.
- Drainage – In some areas, marshes and swamps connected to river systems have been drained and reclaimed for farming and settlement.
- Disposal of waste – Rivers are also used for human and industrial waste disposal.

Because human use of rivers has often had unanticipated consequences, river management, as illustrated in Fig. 1.2, is essential for planning, allocation of water and monitoring of river and associated ecosystem health. Unfortunately,

Fig. 1.6. Glen Canyon dam, Arizona, forms Lake Powell on the Colorado River. (Photograph courtesy of Jim Davis.)

management is often shared between several jurisdictions, some of which may have conflicting interests. In these circumstances, effective and overall river-system management may be difficult. In these cases conflict may occur, creating further potential for river degradation. Examples include the Ganges River (Chapter 2, this volume) where extensive deforestation in river catchments in Nepal and India has resulted in an annual cycle of extensive flooding in Bangladesh, and the Mekong (Chapter 4, this volume) and its tributaries where extensive dam construction upriver in China and Thailand has caused problems downstream in Cambodia and Vietnam.

Figure 1.7 illustrates the relationship between the regional economy, ecosystem health, environmental health and management of river hydrology. As in any system, a change in one part will cause change in other parts of the system. Not all changes can be predicted, and unanticipated consequences may occur as was demonstrated in the unanticipated escape of carp into the Murray Darling system discussed previously. In the past, the key concern of policy makers has been to enhance human welfare through intervention in river systems via processes such as damming to ensure water security for farming and urban populations. Damming may, however, have unanticipated consequences on the health of the river ecosystem, which in turn have an impact on its ability to sustain ecosystem services. River managers have often failed to take a systems perspective, leading to the problems seen in many parts of the world (Chapter 14, this volume). Where there is a tourism use of a river, the ability of the tourism industry to make its specific needs apparent with river management authorities will become crucial, particularly in circumstances where there are conflicting demands.

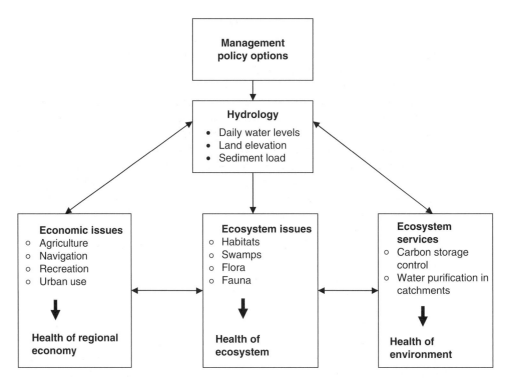

Fig. 1.7. Relationship matrix of riverine hydrology, economy, ecosystem, ecosystems services and the policy environment. (Modified from Sparks *et al.*, 2000.)

Tourism Perspectives

Rivers are a major tourism resource providing spectacular settings, recreational opportunities, waterfront landscapes in many centres of tourism interest, a means of transport and an essential source of water for human consumption. The world's great rivers have long intrigued travellers and even in ancient times provided the backdrop for travel. Herodotus, describing a journey to Egypt in 450 BC, writes that when the Nile overflows 'the whole of Egypt becomes a sea, and only the towns stick out above the surface of the water. When this happens, people use boats right in the middle of the land and not just along the course of the river. Anyone going from Naucratis to Memphis sails right by the pyramids' (Carson, 1994, p. 22).

Hulme and Youngs (2002) remind us that writing and travel have always been intimately connected. The traveller's tale is a form of fiction that is as old as travel itself. Rivers have taken their place beside sea voyages and overland travel as the setting for travel in ancient times. From a tourism perspective, travel writing has been the mechanism that fired the imagination of readers in the eras that preceded mass public transport and visual media. Armchair travellers created an enormous market for tales of fact and fiction that fired the imagination of readers. Many of the themes associated with travel writing in the modern era can be found in the writings of John Mandeville and Marco Polo (Hulme and Youngs, 2002). Their writings fascinated readers in the Middle Ages offering a different form of travel narrative to the pilgrimages and stories of warfare that had dominated writing during the Middle Ages.

Several centuries later, Columbus was deeply influenced by Marco Polo and Mandeville and echoes of their words appear in his descriptions of the islands of the Caribbean (Hulme and Youngs, 2002). Later, Thomas More's *Utopia* became an inspiration for new generations of travel writers. Marco Polo, Mandeville, More and other writers of the time ushered in a new era of the craft of writing, with claims on the authority shifting from recourse to the ancients to the discovery of truth based on observation and personal experience. In contemporary times, other media have replaced the written word as the major outlet for recounting travel stories. It is not that the written word has been superseded; rather it has been supplemented, and as the flow of new offerings in book shops attests, interest in travel writing continues to guarantee sales.

The great rivers of the word have long provided the backdrop for travel writing. As Prideaux and Lohmann (Chapter 9, this volume) point out, the travel writings of Francisco de Orellana, the first European traveller to follow the Amazon from the Andes to its mouth between 1541 and 1542, stimulated interest in further travel and discovery of the Amazon. Of the first accounts of Orellana's journey along the Amazon published by Gaspar de Carvajal, Whitehead (2002) observed that they were to become one of the most important accounts of exploration in the New World and a lasting description of Amazonian society. The Amazon, perhaps because of its vast size and relatively unexplored landscapes, has continued to fascinate travel writers in the centuries after Orellana's first epic river voyage. Tales of lost cities, the story of El Dorado – the lost city of gold – fierce tribes of warriors and wild animals have stirred the interest of generations of adventurers and their readers. In a modern story of adventure in the Amazon, Reuss (1954, p. 10) writes:

> *My story is of an expedition through the almost impenetrable forests and jungles of Brazilian-Amazonia which I made in 1902 in search of gold. It tells of the discovery of great treasure in an unknown, lost city of great age, so deeply hidden in the primeval forest that it escaped discovery by Pizarro at the time of his conquest of Peru in 1531. The narrative relates the perils and hardships endured by members of the expedition…[a]ttacks by wild Indians, and the revolting rites practices by the priests of the Sun God.*

In 1991, Popescu's (1991) account of Loren McIntyre's expedition to find the source of the Amazon added a further adventure to the impressive list of books on the Amazon that included one written by Theodore Roosevelt, the 26th President of the USA. Describing one of McIntyre's many encounters with the indigenous tribes of the forest, Popescu (1991, p. 210) writes:

> *Half an hour later. I'm living in a state of mild hallucination…here it is still morning, a morning loaded with events as yet unhappened. One of those events might be out death. I plunge ahead into a future that may never occur, travel to the green escarpment of the Andes, then climb to the source of the river.*

Billing himself as a professional tourist, Borthwick (2002) recounts a more restrained journey on the Amazon, of the type more likely to be encountered by the average tourist rather than the exploits of writers of the past. Taking a tour out of Manaus, Borthwick (2002, p. 217) writes of the experience:

> The air is littered with birds: crimson tanagers and caciques, kingfishers and yellow-headed caracaras. Each zodiac driver is an expert naturalist: ours, Guillermo, seems to know everything about each bird except its birthday.

In Asia, the Yangtze River has proved as equally fascinating for travel writers at least since the time Li Bai who lived during the 8th century, Tang Dynasty; (Winchester, 1996) penned the following poem:

> Looking at the old river
> From the opposite banks
> Of a yellow ribbon
> Like reading an ancient scroll-
> Pictographs of man's flailing
> Against the eddies
> Of oft told histories...

Of the Yangtze and its role in China, Winchester (p. 52) observed:

> To those who knew its geography and its importance, the Yangtze was the principal gateway into the mysterious heart of the Middle Kingdom, the choicest place for the West's wholesale penetration of China.

Later in the same book, Winchester (p. 349) wrote of more recent adventures on the river:

> Mao Zedong had swum across the Yangtze down at Wuhan, and so had conquered it, in a manner of speaking. Other men, and at later dates, had tried to voyage their way down the entire length of the river, paddling it in specially strengthened boats.

Winchester is not alone in modern commentaries of travel along the Yangtze (see also Chapter 7, this volume). Hessler's 2001 account of his 2-year sojourn travelling the Yangtze is set against the backdrop of events that continue to shape modern China, including the death of Deng Xiaoping and the return of Hong Kong to Chinese rule. He describes travel along the river as a mixture of excitement and tedium (p. 128):

> Soon they (the boat and its crew) will be bound for the city of Jiangyin in Jiangsu province, a thousand miles down the Yangtze. They will float under the cliffs of the Three Gorges, past the lowlands and lakes of central China, and on to the country's far east. The journey will take seven days.

Through the eyes of a Chinese boat captain, Hessler (p. 129) writes of the river journey:

> The Three Gorges aren't too risky if you understand the river, though. Of course, if you don't know the river, its difficult, but we've been through there many times. And after all those trips it's not so interesting anymore. The scenery is beautiful, of course, but I've seen it many, many times.

Other writings on the Yangtze are more businesslike. Shaw's (2007) travel guide of the river from Chongqing to Wuhan is written not to evoke the spirit of adventure and recount personal adventure, but as a 'how to do it' guide to creating a personal adventure.

In the modern era, the Nile Valley (Chapter 5, this volume) remains an important tourism resource for Egypt, while to a lesser extent cruises along the Amazon, Danube and Mississippi (respectively Chapters 3, 6 and 9, this volume) support large day and overnight cruise industries. Waterfalls, including Victoria Falls and Niagara Falls, also support large tourism industries. In addition, tourism icons created by fluvial geomorphological processes best typified by the Grand Canyon have become major national and international attractions. The myriad of smaller rivers that dot the face of the earth host recreation possibilities ranging from fishing to canoeing, and draw visitors from nearby or far localities. Surprisingly, little research has been undertaken into the patterns of use that have emerged from the extensive role of rivers in the tourism industry. The following discussion seeks to develop a typology of river tourism as a means of classifying and comparing these patterns.

The need for a typology of this nature is evident through the increasing use of rivers as tourism resources either as an attraction, a transport corridor or a source of water. In a study of tourism in the Yunnan Great Rivers National Park in China, Cater (2000) observed that the natural and cultural assets of this area, which includes the Salween, Mekong and Yangtze Rivers, are under threat from a variety of practices including unsustainable logging, agriculture, hunting and tourism activities. In that study, a zoning scheme that divides the park into Preservation, Economic, Scenic/Recreation and Cultural zones is proposed, and a range of factors that can affect the tourism potential of the river park are discussed. Factors that degrade rivers are evident in numerous river systems throughout the world. In the USA, the Colorado River is utilized for many purposes that include recreation, agriculture and importantly dammed water to supply the water needs of the rapidly growing populations of Nevada, Arizona and California. In these states, tourism is an important economic sector and further expansion of tourism in both Las Vegas and Phoenix is inextricably bound up in the ability of the Colorado River to supply a dependable volume of water for domestic, commercial and industrial use. The golf course belt of Scottsdale/Phoenix (Arizona) is just one example of the dependence of the region's tourism industry on sustainable water supplies.

Sustainability of river systems that support tourism is therefore important but has until now been a neglected area of tourism research (Chapters 12 and 13, this volume). As already noted, rivers fulfil a number of significant direct and indirect roles in tourism. Direct roles include:

- location for activities and places of tourist interest, including built and natural environments;
- transport, including cargo barges and river cruising;
- providing recreational activities (including water sports and fishing);
- supply of potable drinking water.

Indirect roles include:

- food source, either directly through the supply of fish and other food sources or indirectly through the agriculture that the river supports;
- transport zone;
- support for manufacturing activities;
- disposal of human and industrial waste;
- provision of hydroelectricity.

It is apparent that the unsustainable use of rivers for any individual or combination of the direct and indirect uses outlined above will degrade their ability to support all forms of human activity, including tourism. In Australia, this is apparent from the extensive harvesting of water from the Murray Darling system to support irrigation that has led to increasing salinity and if not reversed will have severe implications for major downstream urban areas as typified by Adelaide in South Australia, which relies almost entirely on the river system for its water needs.

Rapid population growth in many countries, increasing use of water for industrial and human purposes, increasing affluence and the growth in recreation have combined to place enormous pressure on river systems throughout the world. Most of the world's great cities are built around or near rivers and depend on these systems for potable water, yet the same rivers or adjacent oceans are often used for the disposal of human effluent and industrial waste. These factors have placed great stress on river systems and even in remote regions such as Yunnan, China, rivers are being subject to increasing use for tourism and other purposes. Sustainability is therefore a major issue and the need for tourism to compete with other river users will increasingly determine the extent to which rivers will continue to support tourism activities.

Towards a rivers and tourism typology

The typology developed in this chapter is based on an extensive literature review of factors that may exert some influence on rivers, as well as the authors' observations of rivers undertaken over a long period of time. Table 1.1 illustrates a large number of factors that impact rivers, some of which appear to overlap or have little relevance to tourism. These are represented diagrammatically in Fig. 1.8. The value of Table 1.1 and Fig.1.8 for description and comparison is demonstrated for several of the rivers discussed later in this book. River systems support extensive tourism industries but also exhibit considerable differences in many of the factors outlined in Table 1.1. In this discussion, rivers are analysed from a systems perspective because of the interconnectedness of many of the factors outlined in Table 1.1. From the perspective of riverine tourism, factors that impact on one sector of a river may have significant though unanticipated consequences elsewhere along the river. For example, clearing of forests in river catchments for agriculture may cause downstream flooding imperiling an archaeological site or other area of tourist interest. Similarly, damming a river for hydroelectricity may lead to the

Table 1.1. Factors that affect tourist use of river systems.

Spatial	Change in species composition
Length	Fishing impacts
Width	Trophic structures
Seasonality	
Location	*Industrial use of the river*
Navigability	Irrigation
Reserves (including forests and human)	Manufacturing/cooling
	Sewerage disposal
Political factors including borders	Human consumption
Local	Hydro electricity
State	
National	*Recreational use*
Legislative	Swimming
Riparian conflict	Boating
	Diving
Management	Fishing
Political power sharing	
Planning	*Transportation use*
Catchment	Industrial (for heavy tonnage shipping)
Resource allocation, i.e. irrigation	Passenger
	Pleasure cruises
Land use adjacent to river	
Agriculture	*Environmental concerns*
Urban	Toxicity
Wilderness	Invasive species
Recreation	Salinity
Biological factors	
Endemic species	
Number of species	

drowning of significant areas of scenic beauty as will occur when the Three Gorges Dam on the Yangtze River in China is completed and its hydroelectric plant is operational in 2011.

Conclusion

Since the beginning of humankind, rivers have played a critical role in human survival, modernization and, more recently, economic development. In ancient times, rivers facilitated long- and short-distance travel, trade and hunting. They were also instrumental in the Industrial Revolution and in many transportation innovations still utilized throughout the world today. Rivers and their manipulation by humans allow deserts to bloom with agricultural produce and recreational opportunities to be corrected.

Several direct relationships between tourism and rivers have been identified in this introductory chapter. First, rivers provide a wealth of attractions

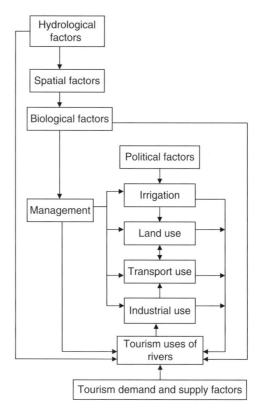

Fig. 1.8. The river tourism typology simplified flow diagram illustrates the range of factors that affect the ability of the tourism industry to use rivers for touristic purposes.

and aesthetic appeal for tourists and a unique venue in which tourism can take place. In some parts of the world, the physical morphology created by fluvial systems results in amazing natural landscapes that draw visitors from all parts of the globe. Perhaps less impressive, but no less important, most rivers provide solitude, beauty and interesting history that appeal to local recreationists and tourists from further away. The second relationship is rivers as transportation corridors. Navigable rivers are a valuable asset to any region or country for the transportation of raw materials and manufactured products. However, in a post-Fordist economy, where services are becoming more important than primary resource extraction and manufacturing, as is the case in most of the developed world, rivers are taking on an additional element of commerce and trade – that of transporting tourists on sightseeing cruises. Third, rivers are an important resource for tourist destinations in three ways: to provide drinking and domestic water, to facilitate the development of intense tourism-oriented environments such as landscaping and golf courses and to fill swimming pools. These are especially important considerations in arid regions (e.g. Las Vegas and the greater Phoenix/Scottsdale urban area), where local residents are often required to sacrifice their own water use for the broader benefit of tourism. Finally, river water is necessary to grow many of the agricultural products and generate electricity needed to sustain tourism in all regions of the world.

In summary, river systems are complex ecosystems that are noticeably influenced by many human activities, including tourism and recreation. The continued tourism use of the world's rivers must be monitored and well managed to be able to conserve the natural and cultural wealth of these unique ecosystems for present and future generations.

References

Adams, C.E. (1993) Environmentally sensitive predictors of boat traffic loading on inland waterways. *Leisure Studies* 12(1), 71–79.

Bayley, P.B. (1995) Understanding large river-floodplain ecosystems. *BioScience* 45(3), 153–158.

Borthwick, J. (2002) *Chasing Gauguin's Ghost: Tales of a Professional Tourist*. Lothian Books, South Melbourne, Australia.

Bricker, K.S. and Kerstetter, D.L. (2000) Level of specialization and place attachment: an exploratory study of whitewater recreationists. *Leisure Sciences* 22(4), 233–257.

Carson, L. (1994) *Travel in the Ancient World*. John Hopkins University Press, Baltimore, Maryland.

Cater, E.A. (2000) Tourism in the Yunnan great rivers national parks system project: prospects for sustainability. *Tourism Geographies* 12(4), 472–489.

Coulthard, T.J. and Macklin, M.G. (2001) How sensitive are river systems to climate and land-use changes? A model-based evaluation. *Journal of Quaternary Science* 16(4), 347–351.

Dowling, R.K. (ed.) (2006) *Cruise Ship Tourism*. CAB International, Wallingford, UK.

Garcia, S. and Thomas, A. (2001) The structure of municipal water supply costs: an application to a panel of French local communities. *Journal of Productivity Analysis* 16(1), 5–29.

Gustafson, A., Fleischer, S. and Joelsson, A. (2000) A catchment-oriented and cost-effective policy for water protection. *Ecological Engineering* 14(4), 419–427.

Herrick, T.A. and McDonald, C.D. (1992) Factors affecting overall satisfaction with a river recreation experience. *Environmental Management* 16(2), 243–247.

Hessler, P. (2001) *River Town Two Years on the Yangtze*. John Murray, Great Britain.

Hofer, T. (1993) Himalayan deforestation, changing river discharge, and increasing floods: myth or reality? *Mountain Research and Development* 13(3), 213–233.

Howell, D., Alexandra, J. and Eyre, D. (1993) Water: the Science. In: Johnson, M. and Rix, S. (eds) *Water in Australia, Managing Economic, Environmental and Community Reform*. Pluto Press, Sydney, Australia.

Hulme, P. and Youngs, T. (2002) Introduction. In: Hulme, P. and Youngs, T. (eds) *The Cambridge to Travel Writing*. Cambridge University Press, Cambridge, pp. 1–16.

Martín-Vide, J.P. (2001) Restoration of an urban river in Barcelona, Spain. *Environmental Engineering and Policy* 2(3), 113–119.

McKean, J.R., Johnson, D., Taylor, R.G. and Johnson, R.L. (2005) Willingness to pay for non angler recreation at the lower Snake River reservoirs. *Journal of Leisure Research* 37(2), 178–194.

Popescu, P. (1991) *Amazon Beaming*. MacDonald, London and Sydney, Australia.

Postel, S. and Carpenter, S. (1997) Freshwater ecosystem services. In: Daily, G.C. (ed.) *Nature's Services: Societal Dependence on Natural Ecosystems*. Island Press, Washington, DC, pp. 195–214.

Reuss, P. (1954) *The Amazon Trail*. The Batchworth Press, London.

Shaw, R. (2007) *Three Gorges of the Yangtze River Chongqing to Wuhan*. Odyssey Books, Hong Kong.

Siebentritt, M.A., Ganf, G.G. and Walker, K.F. (2004) Effects of an enhanced flood in riparian plants of the River Murray, South Australia. *River Research and Applications* 20(7), 765–774.

Sparks, R., Braden, J., Demissie, M., Mitra, P. and Schneider, D. (2000) Technical support of public decisions to restore floodplain ecosystems: a status report of the Illinois river project, USA. In: Smits, A., Nienhuis, P. and Leuven, R. (eds) *New Approaches to River Management*. Backhuys Publishers, Leiden, The Netherlands.

Thorp, J. and Delong, M. (1994) *The river productivity model: an heuristic view of carbon sources and organic processing in large river systems*. OIKOS 70; 305–8.

Whitehead, B. (2002) South America/ Amazonia: the forests of Marvels. In: Hulme, P. and Youngs, T. (eds) *The Cambridge to Travel Writing*. Cambridge University Press, Cambridge, pp. 122–138.

Winchester, S. (2004) *The River at the Centre of the World: A Journey up the Yangtze, and Back in Chinese time*. Picador, New York.

Winpenny, J. (1994) *Managing Water as an Economic Resource*. Routledge, London.

Xie, L.Q., Xie, P. and Tang, H.J. (2003) Enhancement of dissolved phosphorus release from sediment to lake water by Microcystis blooms – an enclosure experiment in a hyper-eutrophic, subtropical Chinese lake. *Environmental Pollution* 122(3), 391–399.

Young, W., Schiller, C., Roberts, J. and Hillman, T. (2001) The rivers of the basin and how they work. In: Young, W. (ed.) *Rivers as Ecological Systems: The Murray Darling Basin*. Murray Darling Basin Commission, Canberra.

Zhang, Z., Huang, J., Yu, G. and Hong, H. (2004) Occurrence of PAHs, PCBs and organochlorine pesticides in the Tonghui River of Beijing, China. *Environmental Pollution* 130(2), 249–261.

2 River Tourism in the South Asian Subcontinent

M. COOPER

Ritsumeikan Asia Pacific University, Beppu, Japan

Introduction

The South Asian subcontinent (Fig. 2.1) is home to around 1.5 billion people, with 1.1 billion in India alone (2006 estimates; http://www.infoplease.com/). The inclusion of neighbouring Pakistan (165.8 million), Nepal (28.3 million) and Bangladesh (147.4 million) adds another 341.5 million. Inclusion of the remaining nations of South Asia, Afghanistan (31.8 million), Bhutan (2.1 million), the Maldives (0.3 million) and Sri Lanka (20.9 million) adds to this total. This enormous population exerts extreme pressures upon the environment and will continue to do so with the current and projected high population growth rates in the region. In the headwaters areas of the region's major rivers, encroachment upon forests and other (previously) sparsely populated areas has led to Himalayan climate change and increased desertification in the lowlands, an alarming decrease in the wildlife population and soil erosion that has irreparably damaged ecosystems. Coupled with the widespread pollution from developing industries and mushrooming population densities in urban centres, as well as from river and other forms of tourism, environmental pressures have become of critical importance to the major river systems in the subcontinent.

Physically and environmentally among the most distinctive features of the Indian subcontinent, its major rivers are also of high religious importance to its peoples. The rivers in India, for example, cover a geographical area of 329 million hectares, and carry a wide importance in cultural, economical, geographical and religious terms. To the Hindu people rivers in India are considered as Gods and Goddesses and are worshiped as such by many (Alter, 2001); for the international tourist they thus provide the possibility for insights into the historical, cultural and traditional aspects of India, Pakistan and Bangladesh/Assam. In this sense, some of the most prominent rivers include the Indus, Ganga, Brahmaputra, Yamuna (Uttaranchal), Krishna

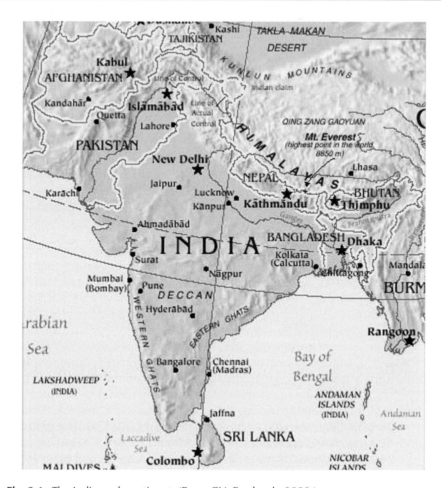

Fig. 2.1. The Indian subcontinent. (From CIA Factbook, 2008.)

(Maharashtra/Andhra Pradesh), Godavari (Maharashtra/Andra Pradesh), Tapi (Madhya Pradesh/Gujarat/Maharashtra), Narmada (Madhya Pradesh/Gujarat/Maharashtra) and Kaveri (Karnataka/Tamil Nadu; see Fig. 2.2). This chapter will mainly concentrate on the first three of these as they are the iconic rivers associated with the Indian subcontinent and its human history, and are therefore of great interest to any analysis of river tourism in this region. The role in river tourism of the other major rivers will however be discussed where appropriate.

Apart from being the environment for river tourism, the major rivers of the subcontinent fulfil other extremely important roles. One of the most important environmental issues in this region is in fact the *scarcity* of water and the need to share freshwater resources between India, Bangladesh and Pakistan. Large rivers such as the Indus, Ganges and the Brahmaputra are born in the Himalayas and are now harnessed for hydroelectric power, tourism and local water supplies even before they flow into the plains of the Deccan and on to either the

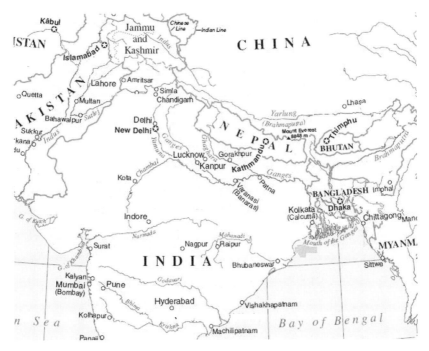

Fig. 2.2. Major rivers of the South Asian subcontinent. (Modified from United Nations, Department of Peacekeeping Operations, 2004.)

Arabian Sea to the west or the Bay of Bengal to the east. The problem of water resource allocation and sharing, initially primarily for irrigation purposes but now increasingly for urban settlements and religious and other forms of lowland tourism, has affected relations between the countries of the subcontinent, and has led to a situation where environmental issues are entwined with national security issues (Samanta Roy, 1997).

This chapter outlines the geography, history and tourism usage of the major rivers, concentrating on the Indus, Ganges and the Brahmaputra river systems but mentioning the other systems where significant differences may be observed in their tourism-use patterns. It does not cover the minor rivers or those in Afghanistan, Bhutan or Sri Lanka. Significant tourism resources are revealed, but it is apparent that apart from domestic religious tourism these are scarcely tapped. The reasons for this pattern are outlined and discussed.

The Geography of the River Systems

The common Himalayan origin for the Indus, Ganges, Brahmaputra and their tributaries, and from similar mountainous areas for the other rivers (e.g. Western Ghats for the Krishna and the Maikal Range for the Narmada Rivers) mentioned in this chapter (Fig. 2.2), means similar topographical, environmental and hydrological regimes for all, at least in their areas of origin.

Physical and environmental characteristics of the rivers

Figure 2.2 shows that the Indus River is formed in western Tibet by the confluence of glacial streams from the Himalayas, flows from Tibet north-west across the state of Jammu and Kashmir, India, and passes between the western extremity of the Himalaya and the northern extremity of the Hindu Kush mountain range into Pakistan. It then flows generally south through Pakistan to the Arabian Sea, covering a total distance of about 2736 km. With a basin coverage area of over 900,000 km², the Indus has a flow volume twice that of the Nile, and three times that of the Tigris–Euphrates river system (Wescoat, 1991). The major tributaries of the Indus are the Sutlej, Ravi and Chenab. The Indus enters the Punjab 1304 km from its source, and, at a point 77 km farther on, it becomes navigable as a result of its junction with the Kabul River from Afghanistan. It borders the North-west Frontier Province of Pakistan, and then flows through the Punjab and Sindh Provinces before branching into the generally infertile delta that covers an area of about 7770 km² and extends for about 201 km along the Arabian Sea.

The Ganges also originates in the Himalayas, taking in five headstreams – Bhagirathi, Mandakini, Alaknanda, Dhauliganga and Pindar – on the way from its source in the Gangotri glacier at an elevation of 7756 m (Jayaraman, 1996). After travelling 200 km through the Himalayas, the Ganges emerges at the pilgrimage town of Haridwar in the Shiwalik Hills and begins to flow in a south-eastern direction through the plains of northern India. From Haridwar, the river follows an 800 km winding course passing through the city of Kanpur (Fig. 2.2) before being joined by the Yamuna from the south-west at Allahabad. This point, known as the Sangam, is a sacred place in Hinduism (Chakraborti, 2001). Further to the east is the holy city of Varanasi (Benaras), centre of Hindu usage of the river for religious tourism, but unfortunately also a place where over 200 million litres of untreated sewage is added to the river's flow (Hamner et al., 2006).

The Ganges is joined by numerous other rivers out of the Himalayas such as the Kosi and Ghaghra in the stretch beyond Allahabad. At Bhagalpur, the river changes course southwards to meet the Brahmaputra and spins off a distributary, the Hooghly. In environmental and geological terms, the Lower Ganges Basin contains both an active delta at the mouth of the Meghna branch, and an inactive delta containing the Sundarbans and several oxbow lakes (Rashid and Kabir, 1998), both of which are affected by flood flows, tidal pressures and occasional severe cyclonic storms capable of disrupting environmental systems. The balance of environmental factors is extremely delicate and complicated as a result, so small changes in one factor affect all the others. The major environmental issues which are associated with this river include:

- increasing demands on natural resources from development activities, including tourism;
- the inward penetration of higher salinity levels;
- the spread of waterborne diseases due to the extensive embankment of former spread-out bodies of water;
- water and soil pollution;

- decline in fisheries due to human intervention; and
- the excessive felling of the Sunderbans deltaic forest.

After entering Bangladesh, the main branch of the Ganges is known as the Padma River until it is joined by the Jamuna River, the largest distributary of the Brahmaputra. Further downstream, the Ganges is fed by the Meghna River, the second largest distributary of the Brahmaputra and takes on its name before entering the Meghna estuary and out into the Bay of Bengal. Only two rivers, the Amazon and Congo, have a higher discharge than the combined flow of the Ganges, the Brahmaputra and the Surma–Meghna river systems (Faisal, 2002).

The Brahmaputra (Tsangpo in Tibetan) itself originates in the Jima Yangzong glacier in the northern Himalayas. It then flows east for about 1700 km, at an average altitude of 4000 m and is thus the highest major river in the world. At its easternmost point inside China, it enters the deepest canyon in the world, before emerging at an elevation of 300 m into the Indian states of Arunachal Pradesh and Assam (Fig. 2.2) and becomes the Brahmaputra proper. It then turns westward and southward until it enters Bangladesh and joins the Ganges to flow out to the Bay of Bengal. During the monsoon season (June–October) floods are a common occurrence. Deforestation in the river's watershed has resulted in increased siltation levels, flash floods and soil erosion in critical downstream habitats, as well as affecting salinity levels in the delta (Sarma, 2005).

The south-eastern coastline of Bangladesh and India is vulnerable to cyclones during the monsoon season. Storm surges can cause dramatic increases in the water level of up to 4 m above tide and seasonal levels. While the southwest coastline is protected to some extent by the dampening effects of the Sunderbans, storm surges do progress up the major rivers as a consequence of the flat topography. Tidal propagation into the delta system carries saline water inland, which mixes with the fresh water to create different levels of salinity in the river system, depending on the upland freshwater discharges. In addition, the western half of the Ganges delta contains the Sunderbans, the largest single block of natural mangrove forest in the world and an increasingly attractive place for river tourists. Inscribed on the World Heritage List in 1997, it covers 6017 km², and contains a continuing, dynamic and changing mosaic of plant and animal communities, including the only habitat of the Bengal Tiger, an endangered species. At present, the Sunderbans is under considerable threat, which may be attributed to the reduction in the freshwater flushing action caused by upstream extraction at the Farakka Barrage, increasing shrimp cultivation, over-exploitation of wood resources, increased agriculture and increased silt deposits (Iftekhar and Islam, 2004). While ecotourism is encouraged, tourists are only allowed to view the world heritage site from the waterways that cross it.

Water quality

While the Indus system is relatively lightly polluted (the Indus River freshwater Dolphin survives despite human modification of the riverine environment over the past 4000 years), the Ganges and its tributaries collect massive amounts of human pollutants as they flow through the densely populated North Indian plain. The Ganges River Basin is the most populous river basin in the world; within its 750,000 km^2 area live more than 400 million people. These populous areas and Bangladeshi communities downstream are then exposed to potentially hazardous accumulations of human and industrial waste (Alley, 2002). While proposals have been made for remediating this condition so far no great progress has been achieved. The major polluting industries on the Ganges are the leather industries, especially near Kanpur (Fig. 2.2), which use large amounts of chromium and other chemicals: much of it finds its way into the Ganges. However, industry is not the only source of pollution. The sheer volume of human waste – estimated at nearly 1 billion litres per day, mostly untreated raw sewage – is a significant factor. Also, inadequate cremation procedures contribute to a large number of partially burnt or unburnt corpses floating down the Ganga after religious ceremonies, in addition to livestock corpses.

Some 20 years ago the Indian Government approved the Ganga Action Plan (GAP) for the immediate reduction of pollution load on the Ganges (April 1985) as a 100% centrally sponsored scheme. This plan aimed to build a number of waste management facilities with international assistance and in collaboration with a number of voluntary organizations. Although some 250+ wastewater treatment plants have been completed under the scheme, sewage continues to flow virtually unabated into the Ganges and its tributaries. Faulty engineering, intermittent electricity supplies and maintenance problems severely affect those plants that do exist, such that *The Hindu* newspaper of New Delhi, Saturday 28 August 2004, carried the headline *Ganga Action Plan Bears No Fruit*. This situation severely limits the opportunities for river tourism throughout the Ganges–Brahmaputra–Surma–Meghna river system and rest of the Indian subcontinent (Alley, 2002; UNITAR, 2004).

There are many other rivers in India and its neighbours, and while none are as large as the three that form the major context for this discussion, many have similar types of river tourism to the Indus, Ganges and Brahmaputra. Common types of river tourism are those related to religious tourism, to cultural tourism, to adventure tourism, to nature-based tourism and to river cruises. Where appropriate, other major rivers will be mentioned in the discussion of the various types of river tourism in later sections of this chapter.

Human History and the Rivers of the Indian Subcontinent

In the Hindu religion and society the river Ganges is sacred. It is worshipped and personified as a goddess, Ganga, who holds an important place in the Hindu religion. The Ganga is mentioned in the *Rig Veda*, the earliest of the Hindu scriptures (from 1500 BC; Flood, 2003), but during the early Indo-Aryan ages the epics refer to the Indus and the Sarasvati (the former in Pakistan and the latter now extinct) as the major rivers on the subcontinent in terms of human use, not the Ganges. By the time of the *Mahabharata*, this had changed and in fact Ganga is a major character in the *Mahabharata* (Alter, 2001; Chakraborti, 2001).

Hindu belief holds that bathing in the river on certain occasions causes the forgiveness of sins and helps to attain salvation (Darian, 1978; Eck, 1999), but many Hindus believe that this will come from bathing in the Ganges at any time. People also travel to cremate and immerse the ashes of their kin in the waters of the Ganges; this immersion also is believed to send the ashes to heaven. Also, several specific places sacred to the Hindu religion lie along the banks of the river, including Haridwar and Varanasi, and as a result some of the most important Hindu festivals and religious congregations are celebrated using the river as an essential adjunct to the ceremonies. The hundreds of temples along the major rivers also act as loci for religious festivals of all types. The next Maha Kumbh Mela will be held at Haridwar in the foothills of the Himalayas in 2010. The hundreds of temples along the banks of the Ganges and the other major rivers are also locations for festivals of all types and sizes. These may also act as cremation grounds.

The Indus Valley civilization

Four millennia ago the Indus River basin was one of the cradles of human civilization, based on the cities of Harappa and Mohenjodaro. Irrigation agriculture was the main activity and the Indus River Valley was a very fertile and well-watered region (Wheeler, 1976; Wescoat, 1991). Excavations in central Pakistan have revealed farming settlements dating back to the early Neolithic period (3300–2800 BC) in the Indus Valley (Jarridge and Meadow, 1980). Following these formative stages (Mughal, 1981), the development of one of the world's first great civilizations occurred, based on the Pre-Iron-Age sites of Harappa and Mohenjodaro lasting from 2300 BC to 1700 BC. Some 800 sites are known, from the Ganges basin to the peripheral region of Rajasthan and the Yamuna River, but are mainly concentrated in the upper Indus Valley. As with Copper/Bronze-Age communities only the semi-arid Indus Valley could be occupied densely by the Harappans; it was not until the Iron Age around 800 BC that the heavier forests of the Ganges basin could be colonized in a systematic way.

Among the general characteristics of the Indus Valley civilization were the gridiron (planned) pattern of the cities, the burnt brick fortifications, a distinctive script, sculptures and pottery, the elaborate drainage systems and their sophisticated water management, and above all extensive international trade routes connecting them to Mesopotamia, Egypt and China. Bitumen was also used in the Great Bath of Mohenjodaro to make it water tight. Sophisticated architecture and city planning are the most striking features of this civilization. Excavations and reconstruction of the sites reveal a continuity of styles. Cities were planned at two distinct levels: the citadel and the lower town. All streets were cut at right angles running north to south and east to west to facilitate the passage of breezes thus keeping the city cool (Jarridge and Meadow, 1980).

Various theories have been advanced for the decline of the Indus Valley civilization after 1700 BC. Wars, invasions by Indo-Aryans, disruption of trade routes, climate change, all have been canvassed and all probably had some influence. Politically, the region morphed into successor states like Gandhara (650 BC–AD 1100 with a Persian influence from the 5th century) and the Mauryan Empire (Ashoka, 250 BC); environmentally, the populations began to colonize the Ganges and other river basins. In the Indus River Valley, continuity of settlement is found in the smaller sites as the Bronze Age gave way to the iron. Mohenjodaro, though, was affected by climate change involving the drying up of one of its lifelines (the Ghaggar) and the shifting of the bed of the Indus to the east and largely abandoned.

The Mauryan Empire of 321–185 BC was one such successor state (Buddhist), but one which by this time covered much of the northern and central areas of the subcontinent. This was followed by a short-lived Indo-Greek kingdom (185–80 BC), then Hindu (Gupta AD 320–550, Chola 250 BC–AD 1070) and Islamic empires such as that of the Mughals (1526–1858) and the British Raj (1858–1947; Hussain, 1983). The British Raj included areas directly administered by the UK and the Princely States ruled by individual rulers under the British Crown. The resulting political union was officially designated the Indian Empire, but commonly called India in contemporary usage. The Indian Empire issued its own passports, and was a founding member of the League of Nations. Post 1947, the British Indian Empire was partitioned into the Union of India and the Dominion of Pakistan, the former to become the Republic of India and the latter to be further divided into the Islamic Republic of Pakistan and the People's Republic of Bangladesh. Since that time each country has exercised sovereign power over its territory.

Transboundary disputes

The British, during their occupation of the Indian subcontinent, actively encouraged the revitalization of agriculture in the region of the Punjab (translated as 'the land of five rivers') that today straddles the border between present day India and Pakistan (Gilmartin, 2003). In 1947, the area was partitioned between India and Pakistan, and an agreement was signed between the two newly formed countries to maintain water supplies at the pre-independence level. However, disputes over water allocation soon arose and in 1948 India cut off the water in canals flowing to Pakistan. After many years of discussions, the Indus Water Treaty was signed in 1960 (Biswas, 1993), in which it was agreed that the amount of water available from the Indus would be increased by various engineering works funded by the World Bank, and the six primary rivers of the Indus basin would be split evenly between India and Pakistan (three to each party). The Indus Water Treaty remains in effect today, and is largely intact because the amount of water available was able to be increased to both parties by the construction of various works that were funded by other countries.

The situation, with regard to relations between Bangladesh and India over the other major river systems formed when the Ganges and Brahmaputra meet, is not so promising, however. Close to the border with Bangladesh, the

Farakka Barrage, which was built by India in 1974 to control the flow of the Ganges, diverts some of the water into a feeder canal linking with the Hooghly to keep that river relatively silt free as it passes through Kolkata Port on its way to rejoin the Ganges/Brahmaputra in the delta. The net effect of full diversion of water is however that Bangladesh agricultural, transport and tourism industries suffer from water shortages and the environmental flows in the main river are insufficient to maintain the historical hydrological balance of the area (Crow, 1995; Singh, 1997). As a result, the Ganges Treaty of 1996 was signed to ensure that Bangladesh gained sufficient flows in dry season months (January–May) and salinity levels in the delta are kept under control (Nishat and Pasha, 2001).

Despite this treaty the Ganges River dispute between India and Bangladesh has continued to fester (Samanta Roy, 1997; Faisal, 2002). In this conflict, one party (India) completely dominates the other and it is only through other channels, such as the pressures of illegal immigration caused by environmental disaster that the conflict has truly manifested itself. As a result, due to the lack of a comprehensive solution that treats the Ganges basin as a system independent of artificial national boundaries, as well as the complexity of the secondary repercussions, water allocation issues associated with the Ganges river system continue to pose problems for international relations in the Indian subcontinent.

River Tourism

Basic demographic and summary tourism data for the countries with major river tourism on the Indian subcontinent are given in Tables 2.1 and 2.2. Afghanistan and Sri Lanka are omitted as their tourism trade is basically non-existent at the time of writing due to war, and Bhutan and the Maldives contribute little to this form of tourism. However, Bhutan, Afghanistan and Sri Lanka support some river tourism, mainly white-water rafting when conditions permit; the comments made below in the sections on this form of adventure tourism apply to them also. Also, the data of Tables 2.1 and 2.2 are indications only as consistent estimates are difficult to obtain, data are missing and/or controlled by sources who charge considerable sums for data of unknown quality, and most are continuously and retrospectively modified as new information come to light. The available data do however show that the Indian subcontinent's attractiveness for international tourism (percentage of international visitor numbers) is very low compared with its proportion of the world's total population (0.1% and 22.7%, respectively); compared with China at 3% and 19.7%, or France with 8.3% and 1.1%. Nevertheless, employment in the industry is important at 15.5 million, and there are significant flows of both domestic and international tourists based on river and cultural tourism to particular sites in the region. International visitors are mainly from the Asia-Pacific region (Table 2.2) or are intraregional to South Asia, although significant flows originate in Europe, mainly from countries like Germany and the UK. Domestic tourism is very large in India and Pakistan, made up primarily of religious pilgrims, and

Table 2.1. Basic demographic and tourism characteristics of selected subcontinent countries. (From United Nations World Tourism Organization, 2008; World Bank, 2007; CIA Factbook, 2008; WTTC TSA for each country, 2008.)

Country	Population 2008 (est)	GDP per capita 2008 (US$)	Visitor numbers 2006 (other)	Tourism revenue (US$)	GDP (%)	Domestic tourism (year)	Direct employment 2008
India	1.15 billion	947	4,459,554	28.0 billion	2.3	430,000,000 (2006)	13,127,000
Pakistan	167.8 million	633	898,400	3.78 billion	2.3	44,500,000 (2007)	1,056,000
Bangladesh	153 million	460	277,129 (2005)	1.18 billion	1.6	NA	801,000
Nepal	29.5 million	326	550,000 (2007)	153 million	3.5	NA	371,000
Total South Asia	1.5 billion	–	9,000,000	34.8 billion	2.3	NA	15,448,000
World (%)	22.7	–	0.1	1.7	3.4	NA	19.3

NA = not available.

Table 2.2. International tourist markets (2006). (From United Nations World Tourism Organization, 2008; World Bank, 2007; CIA Factbook, 2008; WTTC TSA for each country, 2008.)

Country	Tourist arrivals India	Tourist arrivals Nepal	Tourist arrivals Pakistan	Tourist arrivals Bangladesh
Americas	518,474	26,400	160,615	18,673
Europe	903,218	155,650	383,751	48,961
Africa	93,353	NA	15,840	1,730
Asia-Pacific[a]	2,530,116	118,250	130,438	38,839
Afghanistan	NAS	NAS	80,459	NAS
India	–	181,000	48,242	NA
Nepal	42,771	–	1,655	NA
Pakistan	10,364	2,397	–	NA
Bangladesh	454,611	20,217	6,352	–
Total South Asia	507,687	206,800	148,856	99,459
Total	4,459,554	550,000	839,500	207,662

NAS = not available separately; NA = not available.
[a]Excluding India, Nepal, Pakistan, Bangladesh (in South Asia total).

this latter pattern may also be the case with Bangladesh but figures were not available at time of writing.

It is also not possible to separate the forms of river tourism with reliable statistics from the Indian subcontinent, except to say that religious tourism is by far the largest and that this is basically domestic in nature. International river tourism is concentrated in the upper, less-polluted regions of the rivers or is cultural tourism on their banks.

Religious tourism

The river Ganges and associated rivers are intimately bound up with the chief religion of India, Hinduism. The ancient Vedic scriptures that form the core of Hinduism were written on the banks of this river as people started migrating from the Indus Valley to the Ganges plains at the end of the Indus Valley civilization period (Darian, 1978; Chakraborti, 2001). The river is central to the pure Hindu way of life, as it is believed that the soul is not freed from this world after death until the ashes of the deceased are immersed in the holy waters of the Ganges (Alter, 2001; Alley, 2002; Flood, 2003). There are many holy sites along the river, ranging from Haridwar and Rishikesh to Varanasi. The latter is the most revered city among the Hindus; it is here that the Hindu population of India and the other countries of the subcontinent hope to attain salvation after death by bathing in the river Ganges and drinking from its water. In fact, water from the holy river is essential for most Hindu rites. The river is also worshipped as a female deity and appears in the Mahabharata as one of the characters of that saga (Alter, 2001). Besides Hinduism, the river is also important for other religions which have branched out of or have roots in Hinduism like Buddhism, Jainism and Sikhism (Darian, 1978).

Varanasi (also known as Benaras) is among the most important pilgrimage sites in India and is famous for the approximately 100 distinctive 'ghats' or bathing steps that have been built over the years along the river. Varanasi is visited by millions of Hindu pilgrims and tourists from India and abroad every year, and most Ganges tours include Varanasi in their itinerary. The ghats are crowded from dawn until the end of the evening prayers every day of the year with 'Sadhus' (holy men) and locals taking a dip in the river and chanting ancient Vedic mantras, giving a spiritual feel to the entire atmosphere (Alter, 2001). The most famous ghats of Varanasi are Dasashwamedh Ghat, where at evening prayers the priests stand with ornate lamps and move in synchronized patterns to the constant chanting of mantras, Manikarnika Ghat (associated with Shiva) and Harishchandra Ghat, also favoured as a site for cremation. The temples and narrow streets of Varanasi are another of its characteristic features. The streets are lined by shops selling sweets, other food and religious items. Many of the sweet shops have become famous over the years and are mentioned in tour itineraries. Kashi Vishwanath temple in Varanasi is one of the 12 shrines of the god Shiva, collectively called the Jyotirlingas, and is visited by millions of pilgrims every year. Varanasi is also home to Benaras Hindu University, one of the major centres of religious learning in India, and Sarnath, one of the most important Buddhist pilgrimage centres in India.

Religious tourism or pilgrimage is in fact important throughout the Ganges river system, from its origins in the Himalayas to its confluence with the Brahmaputra. Centres and locations such as Haridwar, or the 'door to god' (Alter, 2001), Yamunotri at the confluence with the Yamuna River (also has hot springs) and Gangotri (its origins on the Gangotri glacier) are particularly attractive to pilgrims and have become the sites of mass river tourism. One of the greatest of these mass movements is the Khumb Mela Festival (*great festival of the pot of nectar of immortality*), held every 3 years in each of four different locations, returning to each of these every 12 years. An Ardh (half) Mela takes place 6 years after the Kumbh Mela in each location. This sacred Hindu pilgrimage and bathing festival that takes place at the following four locations in India: Allahabad (Prayag), Haridwar, Ujjain (Shipra River) and Nasik (Godavari River). Some 50 million visitors (10 million on the first day) are attracted to this festival, which makes it the largest religious festival held anywhere in the world.

River cruising

River cruising on the other hand is not well developed in the Indian subconti- nent. It is however set to materialize fairly soon in a small way based out of Kolkata and is available as short river cruises elsewhere. The Kolkata Port Trust (KoPT) has developed a plan to allow cruising on the waterways that connect Kolkata – 'the City of Joy' and the only river port in India – with many destina- tions along the Hooghly branch of the Ganges and coastal sites like the Andaman and Nicobar Islands, Puri in Orissa and the Sagar Islands of the Sundarbans. KoPT also has plans to introduce luxury boats for tourists from Kolkata to the West Bengal towns of Murshidabad, Malda and Nadia. All these sites are rich in historical importance and have emerged as tourism hot spots for people coming from different parts of the world (Hillary, 1980). In order to achieve this outcome, the state government of West Bengal has set up a com- mittee headed by the chairman of the KoPT and with representatives from the tourism departments of West Bengal, Orissa and the Andamans as members. Its brief is to encourage river tourism based on Kolkata, and it is looking for global partners such as the Viking Company to join in this venture in order that vessels of international standard will be made available (www.kolkataporttrust. com, accessed 4 May 2008).

Short-distance cruises on the Ganges from the Daswamedh Ghat in Varanasi allow tourists to see the cremation Ghats and witness the living tradi- tions of Hinduism, and there are other such river tours available at most reli- gious sites. Dry-season (winter) local cruises of the Brahmaputra system at Dhaka are available, which take in both city and rural sights. Further up this river in Assam, the cruises are more long distance and involve 12 cabin river boats (Fig. 2.3) from October to April each year on 4-, 7- and 10-day cycles. These cruises feature wildlife (Ganges Dolphin, Bengal tiger, birds) and wilder- ness and give access to a number of National Parks. Such tours are replicated along the Indus Valley, with the addition of houseboat hire for visitors such as fully independent travellers (FIT).

Cultural and historical tourism

Adjunct to, but distinct from, river tourism are the temples, forts and other historical cultural attractions of the subcontinent. Ranging from the remains of the Indus Valley civilization (Fig. 2.4), through the Red Fort at Agra, to the Taj

Fig. 2.3. Brahmaputra river cruises. (From Assam Bengal Navigation, Guwhati.)

Fig. 2.4. The great bath at Mohenjodaro. (From Images of Asia.com.)

Mahal and many other sites bound together in history and modern times by the major rivers, these cultural artefacts are also an important tourism resource. Their importance lies also in the fact that a high proportion of international tourism to India and the other countries of the subcontinent is concentrated at these sites and in urban areas associated with them, and does not take part in the river-based religious festivals unless particular visitors are expatriates returning home or converts to the religions in question. The central cultural practices related to domestic river tourism are described above in the section on religious tourism.

White-water rafting

All the major rivers of the subcontinent have white-water rafting at an international standard associated with them. Given this form of river tourism's inherent danger, all tour operators are experienced and well equipped even in the most inaccessible of places (Fig. 2.5). In terms of the resources available, the Indus for example is one of the most scenic white-water runs anywhere in the Himalayas and has the advantage of having cultural assets along its raftable length, with various monasteries or gompas along the river bank. The rapids are only of difficulty grades 1–3, however, and are therefore quite mild in comparison to those

Fig. 2.5. Example of white-water rafting. (P. Erfurt-Cooper.)

on the rivers entering the Ganges out of Nepal (see Chapter 11, this volume). Nevertheless, a white-water river rafting expedition along the 26 km stretch of the Indus from Fhey to Nimo is taken at the highest point where river rafting is possible in the world. Indeed, rafting is one of the best ways to explore the typical cross section of natural as well as ethnocultural heritage of the upper reaches and tributaries of the Indus, Ganges and Brahmaputra rivers. This is especially true of those stretches in Nepal where the Government has opened sections of ten rivers for commercial rafting. Of these the Karnali and Sun Kosi rivers (rapid grades 4–5) provide some of the most challenging rapids in the world. The associated sport of Canyoning into almost inaccessible stretches of the rivers, which is popular in Europe, is also now available in Nepal.

Trekking

The same mountainous regions that create the white-water rafting experiences offer other associated forms of adventure tourism. Mountaineering, rock climbing, trekking, skiing, mountain biking and wildlife safaris in National Parks are offered in conjunction with the river tourism pursuits.

Problems and Opportunities for River Tourism

In view of its importance as a major development option for all the countries of the subcontinent, tourism generally receives backing from national and state governments. Nevertheless, awareness also exists of the negative environmental impact that tourism can bring to fragile mountain, riverine and coastal ecosystems. There is already a serious problem of land degradation in many parts of the subcontinent. Ninety per cent of water in Pakistan for example originates from northern mountainous watersheds and the figures for Nepal and India are similar. With the construction of dams and reservoirs to generate hydropower for the growing cities on the plains and to supply water to the massive irrigation networks for agricultural production, watershed management in the mountains has become a national priority for these countries. Any loss of vegetation cover in the watershed areas resulting from increased tourist activity and infrastructure provision seriously impacts the hydrological cycle resulting in landslides and flash floods causing damage to infrastructure, settlements and loss of human and animal life. Equally, the massive water pollution arising from untreated urban wastes and overuse of water supplies in the major river systems seriously constrains downstream river tourism (Staff Reporter, *The Hindu*, Saturday, 28 August 2004).

Hope for the future of river and other forms of tourism in addressing these problems is contained within the growing strength of the South Asian Association for Regional Cooperation (SAARC). This regional organization was formally established in December 1985 with membership of Bangladesh, Bhutan, India, the Maldives, Nepal, Pakistan and Sri Lanka. SAARC's purpose is to promote the socio-economic interests and cultural development of the peoples of South Asia (Timothy, 2003), with the long-term vision of removing internal barriers and allowing free movement of goods, services, capital and people throughout the region. Trade, commerce and tourism are at the centre of this movement, which in addition to providing economic opportunities is viewed as a means of developing trust between nations in a region where distrust has dominated for many years (Hall and Page, 2000). Immediate benefits for river tourism, given the transboundary issues associated with many of the rivers of the subcontinent, lie in the reduction of the barriers between nations and therefore the potential to create larger origin and destination markets, increased joint promotion budgets and more sophisticated regional touring opportunities (Chawla, 1989).

Regional tourism policies

To date however, SAARC's efforts at regional promotion have been minimal so far and flow of people has been enhanced only for elite government and business leaders, as only they and their families are permitted to travel freely throughout the region (Timothy, 2003). Tourism policy remains internal to the nations of the subcontinent and little cross-border traffic occurs compared with the obvious potential (see Table 2.2). Visa requirements and border-crossing procedures remain a difficult area of concern for residents of these countries, as well as for international tourists. In this situation, cross-border river tourism cannot flourish. The SAARC Technical Committee on tourism has met many times and formulated plans for producing marketing materials and joint tourism policies to counter the negative images held by the rest of the world of the region (poverty, health problems, pollution and poor hygiene, crowded conditions, ethnic conflict and drought and floods), but its plans are yet to come to fruition (Hall and Page, 2000).

The failure to understand river systems in a comprehensive manner (see Chapter 14, this volume) on the Indian subcontinent has meant that engineering solutions to flooding and other problems have exacerbated these problems rather than fixed them (Bandyopadhyay, 1987; Bandyopadhyay and Gyawali, 1994). While it is not possible to explore this situation in detail in this chapter, it is necessary to point out that significant river tourism resources are in danger of being destroyed or made inaccessible by such actions and the political tensions that many of them have contributed to (Singh, 1997).

Summary and Conclusions

The management and sharing of water which crosses international borders is a matter of regional concern – because it is a transboundary environmental resource and does not recognize borders (Attanayake, 2001). Given the geography, demographics and politics of the subcontinent as outlined in this chapter, regional cooperation over the use and distribution of water will be decisive for the sustainable development of its river tourism (Butler and Mao, 1996).

The bases of cooperation have been outlined in this chapter and, even though the historical barriers of the past and the problems of the present stand as hurdles, it is important to accept that river tourism needs cooperation for its development. All that is needed for the emergence of significant river tourism in the subcontinent is a genuine dedication of its partner countries towards attaining this goal. As Richter (1999) pointed out, while travel consultants (and national tourism organizations) may have excellent specific advice on how to reach a particular market, or on how to develop a land-use proposal for tourism purposes or on how to negotiate a management contract with a multinational hotel chain, all that is wasted if the tourism sector is not considered in the context of the entire economy and existing geopolitical situation. All the physical and cultural attractions in the world cannot bring river tourists to the Indian subcontinent in a situation of political conflict over the very resource that it requires for its continuation.

References

Alley, K.D. (2002) *On the Banks of the Ganga: When Wastewater Meets a Sacred River*. University of Michigan Press, Michigan.

Alter, S. (2001) *Sacred Waters: A Pilgrimage Up the Ganges River to the Source of Hindu Culture*. Harcourt, London.

Attanayake, A. (2001) South-Asia: identity and ethnicity as state-borders and environment as common factor. Presented to the NASA Conference *Waters of Hope? The Role of Water in South-Asian Development*. September, Voss, Norway, pp. 20–22.

Bandyopadhyay, J. (1987) Political ecology of drought and water scarcity: need for an ecological water resources policy. *Economic and Political Weekly* 22(50), 2159–2169.

Bandyopadhyay, J. and Gyawali, D. (1994) Ecological and political aspects of Himalayan water resource management. *Water Nepal* 4(1), 7–24.

Biswas, A. (1993) Management of international waters: problems and perspective. *International Journal of Water Resources Development* 9(22), 167–188.

Butler, R.W. and Mao, B. (1996) Conceptual and theoretical implications of tourism between partitioned states. *Asia Pacific Journal of Tourism Research* 1(1), 25–34.

Chakraborti, D.H. (2001) The archaeology of Hinduism. In: Insoll, T. (ed.) *Archaeology and World Religion*. Routledge, London, pp. 33–60.

Chawla, K.L. (1989) Identifying potential areas of economic cooperation among the countries of the SAARC region. *South Asian Studies* 24(1), 51–77.

CIA Factbook (2008) World factbook: area and population of countries. Available at: https://www.cia.gov/library/publications/the-world-factbook/

Crow, B. (1995) *Sharing the Ganges*. Sage Publications, New Delhi, pp. 89–94.

Darian, S.G. (1978) *The Ganges in Myth and History*. The University Press of Hawaii, Honolulu.

Eck, D.L. (1999) *Banaras, City of Light*. Columbia University Press, New York.

Faisal, I.M. (2002) Managing common waters in the Ganges–Brahmaputra–Meghna region: looking ahead. *SAIS Review* 22(2), 309–327.

Flood, G. (ed.) (2003) *The Blackwell Companion to Hinduism*. Blackwell, Malden, Massachusetts.

Gilmartin, D. (2003) Water and waste: nature, productivity and colonialism in the Indus basin. *Economic and Political Weekly* 38, 5057–5065.

Hall, C.M. and Page, S. (2000) Developing tourism in South Asia: India, Pakistan, Bangladesh – SAARC and beyond. In: Hall, C.M. and Page, S. (eds) *Tourism in South*

East Asia: Issues and Cases. Butterworth-Heinemann, Oxford, pp. 198–224.

Hamner, S., Tripathi, A., Mishra, R., Bouskill, N., Broadaway, S., Pyle, B. and Ford, T. (2006) The role of water use patterns and sewage pollution in the incidence of waterborne/enteric diseases along the Ganges river in Varanasi, India. *International Journal of Environmental Health Research* 6(2), 113–132.

Hillary, E. (1980) *From the Ocean to the Sky: Jet Boating Up the Ganges.* Ulverscroft Large Print Books, Anstey, Leicestershire, UK.

Hussain, J. (1983) *An Illustrated History of Pakistan.* Oxford University Press, Oxford.

Iftekhar, M.S. and Islam, M.R. (2004) Degeneration of Bangladesh's Sundarbans mangroves: a management issue. *International Forestry Review* 6(2), 123–135.

Jarridge, J.-F. and Meadow, R. (1980) The antecedents of civilisation in the Indus Valley. *Scientific American* 243(2), 122–133.

Jayaraman, K.S. (1996) Ban tourists call to save glacier source of the Ganges. *Nature* 384(6610), 602.

Mughal, M.R. (1981) New archaeological evidence from Bahawalpur. In: Dani, A.H. (ed.) *Indus Valley: New Perspectives.* Quaid-i-Azam University, Islamabad, pp. 33–42.

Nishat, A. and Pasha, M.F.K. (2001) A review of the Ganges treaty of 1996. Presented to *The Globalization and Water Resources Management: The Changing Value of Water AWRA/IWLRI – University of Dundee International Specialty Conference.* University of Dundee, Dundee, Scotland.

Rashid, H.E. and Kabir, B. (1998) Bangladesh. In: De Sherbin, A. and Dompka, V. (eds) *Proceedings of the IUCN World Conservation Congress Water and Population Dynamics: Case Studies and Policy Implications.* Montreal, Canada.

Richter, L.K. (1999) After political turmoil: the lessons of rebuilding tourism in three Asian countries. *Journal of Travel Research* 38, 41–45.

Samanta Roy, R.I. (1997) India–Bangladesh water dispute, ICE Case 78. *The Mandala Projects: Trade and Environment Database.* American University, Washington, DC.

Sarma, J.N. (2005) Fluvial processes and morphology of the Brahmaputra river in Assam, India. *Geomorphology* 70(3–4), 226–256.

Singh, S. (1997) *Taming the Water: Political Economy of Large Dams.* Oxford University Press, New Delhi.

Staff Reporter (2004) Ganga action plan bears no fruit. *The Hindu,* Saturday 28 August.

Timothy, D.J. (2003) Supranationalist alliances and tourism: insights from ASEAN and SAARC. *Current Issues in Tourism* 6(3), 250–266.

UNITAR (2004) *Wetlands, Biodiversity and Water: New Tools for Ecosystem Management.* Series on Biodiversity Training Workshop, UNITAR: Hiroshima Office for Asia and the Pacific, Kushiro, Japan, 29 November–3 December.

United Nations, Department of Peacekeeping Operations (2004) *Map No. 4140 Rev. 3.* United Nations, Department of Peacekeeping Operations, Cartographic Section, New York.

United Nations World Tourism Organization (2008) *World Tourism Barometer 2008.* UNWTO, Madrid.

Wescoat, J. (1991) Managing the Indus river basin in light of climate change: four conceptual approaches. *Global Environmental Change* December, 381–395.

Wheeler, M. (1976) *The Indus Civilization,* 3rd edn. Book Club Associates, London.

World Bank (2007) *World Development Indicators Database.* April, World Bank, Washington, DC.

World Travel and Tourism Council (WTTC) (2008) Tourism Satellite Accounts (TSA). WTTC, London.

3   River-based Tourism in the USA: Tourism and Recreation on the Colorado and Mississippi Rivers

D.J. Timothy

Arizona State University, Phoenix, Arizona, USA

Introduction

Tourism has been an important socio-economic activity in the USA since Europeans began settling and expanding westward. The North American landmass extends over many different climatic and physiographic regions, providing many tourism and outdoor recreation opportunities based on a vast array of natural surroundings and resources. Foremost among these physiographic features are high mountains, rainforests, deserts, beaches and coastlines, volcanoes, swamps, canyons, lakes, oceans and many more too numerous to highlight here. These provide bountiful opportunities for outdoor recreation-based tourism, ranging from snow skiing and glacier climbing to desert safaris and rainforest treks. Most tourism in the USA is based on nature; nature-based activities and natural features are the most visited attractions in the country among domestic and foreign tourists.

Among the natural elements important for tourists, rivers are one of the most salient recreation resources in the USA. Rivers have been important for human survival in North America since the arrival of the ancestors of today's Native Americans thousands of years ago. Hunting, fishing, irrigation and transportation were rivers' earliest uses, while today they are critical for agriculture, energy generation and recreation, particularly as America's cities continue to grow in area and population, increasing demand for water consumption. This is of particular concern in the western states, where dry climatic conditions prevail and where life is more dependent on river water sources than in the eastern states.

Rivers have been developed in the past century beyond their natural courses to include dams for reservoirs, wildlife preserves, national parklands and regions of cultural heritage. Likewise, many river corridors have been developed throughout the USA as important tourism assets (Zube, 1995). The purpose of this chapter is to describe the current situation of tourism and recreation on the Mississippi and Colorado Rivers in the USA. It highlights the unique trends and problems associated with each and then examines how they are used in contemporary society and how they assist in forming regional tourism products.

The Mississippi River Experience

The Mississippi River, the second longest in the USA (a close second after its tributary, the Missouri River), extends over 2300 miles (3730 km) from its source in Minnesota to its outlet on the Gulf of Mexico near New Orleans. The Mississippi nearly bisects the country into half from north to south, beginning as a small stream and extending further south to widths of over 1 mile (1 mile = 1.609344 km) in some locations. Its primary tributaries are the Missouri, Arkansas and Ohio rivers although along its entire course it receives water from dozens of streams and rivers in 31 of the 50 American states. The collective Mississippi–Missouri River system is the third longest in the world (some observers claim it to be the fourth longest) after the Nile and Amazon systems and has a drainage basin/catchment of 3.1 million square kilometres (Walsh, 2003). Its cities include several of America's largest and most strategic locations, including New Orleans, Baton Rouge, Minneapolis/St Paul, Memphis and St Louis. More than 12 million people live along the Mississippi, and millions more rely indirectly on the river for their water supply. In addition, over 90 million tonnes of cargo is transported along the river each year, including grain, coal, iron and steel (Walsh, 2003).

Today, the Mississippi remains a vital transportation corridor and source of water for agriculture and human consumption. A series of locks and dams in the river's northern reaches facilitates commercial barge traffic and recreation (Becker, 1979; Gramann et al., 1985; Espeseth, 1992; Vogel et al., 1996), and the wider portions further south are highly navigable and used extensively for transportation and commerce. Many of the regions attached to the Mississippi are among the poorest areas in the USA. To improve local standards of living, several tourism and recreation corridors have been delimited and planned in recent years to increase riverine tourism along the Mississippi (Aamodt et al., 1992).

Cultural heritage

Native Americans relied on the Mississippi for much of their survival and were familiar with its courses and resources. With the arrival of Europeans, the mighty Mississippi played a crucial role in the settlement history of the USA and served for a long time as the 'frontier' between the settled east and the 'wild west'. Even today, in popular American lexicon, the river is spoken of as a figurative dividing line: 'east of the Mississippi' and 'west of the Mississippi'. It also played an important role in the slave trade as a transportation corridor between the slave-free north and the slave-holding south, as well as a pivotal function in the Civil War. Indeed, much of the history of the southern states is directly linked to the Mississippi as a transportation route, dividing line and water source.

This unique history with its nostalgic elements (e.g. plantations and steam-boats propelled by paddle wheels) creates an important heritage product that focuses on the white and African-American historic settlement and socio-economic activities of the past. The writings of American author Mark Twain, particularly his *Life on the Mississippi*, *The Adventures of Tom Sawyer* and *Huckleberry Finn*, romanticized the river steamboat and embedded within the American psyche the vitality and romance associated with the Mississippi River. Steamboats continue to ply the waters of the Mississippi, primarily south of Iowa where the waters are deeper and wider. Today, several cruise lines in several states travel the Mississippi. Tours run between cities with dinner 'cruises to nowhere' being a popular pastime among local residents and tourists (Fig. 3.1). Many riverboat cruise companies have made an effort to tap into feelings of nostalgia for Twain's old Mississippi and to cater to less-nostalgic family vaca-tioners as well (Truitt, 1996; Walsh, 2003).

Some of the most significant tourist attractions along the banks of the Mississippi River are historic towns and cities (Keating and Stanfield, 1971; Aamodt *et al.*, 1992; Anfinson *et al.*, 2003; Smith, 2007). St Louis, Missouri, for example, is a major urban area and important tourist destination with its developing waterfront (Judd, 2002). Nauvoo, a stronghold in the Mormon migration to the western USA in the 1840s, draws hundreds of thousands of Mormon and non-Mormon visitors each year to a historic community that is preserved and interpreted as a 'living museum' (Davis and Austin, 2002). New

Fig. 3.1. The Creole Queen on the Mississippi River. (Photograph courtesy of Jim Davis.)

Orleans, Louisiana, another important US destination, is bisected by the river, and much of that city's heritage appeal (e.g. Cajun culture and jazz music) focuses directly or indirectly on the Mississippi (Walsh, 2003; Gotham, 2007). Emblems of the slave heritage of the South (e.g. plantation houses, slave quarters and African-American history museums) are also commonly attached to the lower part of the river, especially in Mississippi and Louisiana where they lie on the banks of the river or on nearby farmland (Aamodt *et al*., 1992; Walsh, 2003).

Outdoor recreational activities

In addition to its human heritage, the Mississippi system is rich in natural heritage, particularly aquaculture, bird migrations and various natural landscapes. Owing to these characteristics, much of the Mississippi River along its course is protected in various public forms, such as municipal waterfront parks, nature preserves and US National Park Service properties, including the Mississippi National River and Recreation Area in the upper reaches of the river in Minnesota.

The northern dams create several lakes that are popular among boaters, particularly for water skiing. Nearly the entire length of the Mississippi is accessible for tourist traffic, and various nature trails and scenic drives have been established in the past 30 years along the watercourse. Bicycling, horseback riding, fishing, boating, hot air ballooning, canoeing, visiting arboreta, birdwatching and visits to scenic areas are among the fastest-growing outdoor activities in the area today (Aamodt *et al*., 1992; Walsh, 2003). Despite its value as a recreational resource, not all is rosy on the mighty Mississippi. Owing to the growing popularity of recreational activities on the upper Mississippi in conjunction with the already well-used transportation corridors, several negative impacts have begun to appear over the past quarter century, including environmental degradation (Becker, 1979; Welle and Baer, 1997; Brown *et al*., 2005; Delong, 2005;), with the most prevalent being overcrowding and the resultant decreased satisfaction of experience that accompanies it (Becker, 1981; Clements, 1993; Lee, 1993; Welle and Baer, 1997).

Uniquely Mississippi

Perhaps the most distinctive tourism-related trend today on the Mississippi River is riverboat gambling, which was popular, albeit illegal, on the Mississippi as early as the 1820s (Meyer-Arendt, 1998; Hsu, 1999). Since the 1980s, several related gaming trends have begun in the USA, namely Indian reservation casinos, brought on by the enactment of the federal Indian Gaming Regulatory Act of 1988, which allows Native American communities that fall directly under national jurisdiction to build and operate high-stakes casinos, even in states where casinos are not permitted. This trend supplements the 1931 beginnings of gambling in Nevada and the 1970s and 1980s permissiveness and legalization of casinos in Florida, New York, Colorado, Minnesota, Ohio, Pennsylvania, Massachusetts and South Dakota. As part of this growing trend towards tolerance of an activity long viewed as a negative vice and the growing popularity of Indian casinos, riverboat gambling was approved on the Mississippi River in Iowa in 1989 and initiated in 1991. Many riverfront communities operated paddle-wheel boats as a tourist attraction and touring vehicle. When the idea of utilizing them for casinos was born, politicians felt that their constituents could be more easily convinced about legalized casinos, if they were located on extant riverboats, owing to the nostalgic and romantic connotations of steamboats and the fact that casinos relegated to small, enclosed areas would be easier to control and monitor for illegal activities (Hsu, 1999, p. 64). Their convincing arguments worked. This river-based activity has accelerated to the point that the Mississippi and several of its largest tributaries (e.g. the Ohio and Missouri rivers) of the east have become crowded with floating casinos (Truitt, 1996; Dixon, 1998; Mosher and Wheeler, 1998; Eadington, 1999; Hsu, 1999).

As already noted, Iowa was the first state to enact legislation permitting the use of riverboats as casino venues. Soon after, with the promise of increased dollars in the Iowa economy, Illinois and other neighbouring states caught riverboat gaming fever and thus began Iowa's competition for gaming dollars (Hsu, 2000). Several other states – Mississippi, Missouri, Louisiana and Indiana – quickly joined in with their own riverboat casinos. Many of these states would have preferred not to legalize gambling, but they felt they had few other choices. Riverboat casinos were adopted by many states 'to keep residents and their money at home' (Truitt, 1996, p. 89). According to Truitt's (1996, p. 89) study, many legislators, even those morally opposed to gambling, felt that since riverboat casinos appeared to be inevitable, it would have been best to legalize them and reap at least some economic benefits before the market became saturated. By 1994, 57 riverboat casinos operated on the Mississippi River in five states, comprising the largest and fastest-growing sector of the casino industry in the USA (Madhusudhan, 1996).

Iowa and the other riverfront states targeted this style of gaming, much as non-river states pursued other forms of gambling, for its promised economic benefits in societies where Fordist industrialization began to give way to post-Fordist service economies. The early 1980s recession accompanied by the rapid decline in agriculture, mining and manufacturing in the upper Midwest states, Mississippi River-focused tourism seemed a viable economic alternative for much-needed jobs and tax revenue. Likewise, the state of Mississippi, traditionally the poorest in the country, saw tourism, especially gambling, as a means of growing its economy (McCormack, 1991; Turner, 1991; Arland-Fye and Pellin, 1992; Lee, 1993; Long, 1995; Hsu, 1999; Siegel and Anders, 1999; Stokowski, 1999a). On the southern flank of the river, the decline of the Gulf of Mexico oil industry in Louisiana and Mississippi had a profound economic effect in the already underdeveloped regions. As a result, in 1992 Louisiana passed legislation to allow 15 riverboat casinos to ply its

Mississippi waters, including five in New Orleans (Dimanche and Speyrer, 1996; Hsu, 1999).

Several studies have identified public perceptions of the effects of riverboat gaming on the Mississippi, with unsurprising mixed results. Many conservative residents dislike what they feel are the negative social repercussions of gaming, namely addiction, debt and fragmentation of families. Others, however, argue that the river-based casinos create jobs and tax dollars that can be used to improve the lives of residents, including counselling for addicted gamblers (Volberg, 1997; Stokowski, 1999b; Hsu, 2000). River cruises in general, but particularly those with a gaming slant, have been instrumental in rejuvenating the economies of several riverfront towns from Iowa to Louisiana, as well as inciting the growth of several waterfront development projects in river-based cities (Sieber, 1991; Truitt, 1996).

Variations on the riverboats themselves are quite interesting. For instance, in the state of Mississippi, the law requires that riverboat casinos remain permanently docked, and many do not resemble riverboats or even possess a crew or engine (Meyer-Arendt, 1998). From the air, in fact, many appear as warehouses surrounded by moats and are completely immobile (Rose, 1995, p. 28).

The Colorado River Experience

The 2300 km (1450 mile) Colorado River is one of western America's most important and influential bodies of water. It flows from humble beginnings in the Rocky Mountains in the state of Colorado to a salty, sparse and essentially unusable delta at the Gulf of California in Mexico. The Colorado River has a large drainage basin of approximately 243,000 square miles (630,000 km²) and flows through five American states (Colorado, Utah, Arizona, Nevada and California) and two states in Mexico (Sonora and Baja California).

The Colorado and its tributaries have long been a lifeline for indigenous Americans who relied on the system for drinking water, hunting, fishing and agriculture. It has also long been an important part of western American life as well and has found its place as a national icon, largely because of President Roosevelt's edict regarding the Grand Canyon that 'every American if he can travel at all should see' (quoted in Watkins, 1969, p. 227). Today, although the riverfront itself is largely non-urban, the river is a source or partial source of drinking water for large desert cities such as Phoenix, Las Vegas, Los Angeles, Tucson and San Diego, and supports a vast agricultural belt in an otherwise inhospitable arid region. A number of dams have been erected on the Colorado to divert and store water for agricultural and energy purposes. The Glen Canyon Dam, near the Arizona–Utah border, is one of the most important of these dams and creates Lake Powell – a popular recreation spot. Hoover Dam and Lake Mead, just outside of Las Vegas, were another major undertaking to enable human beings to live in an uncongenial desert environment. Further south, several other dams, aqueducts and canal systems have been developed to contain and divert Colorado waters for human use.

Due to the fact that the Colorado River forms the interstate Nevada–Arizona and California–Arizona borders, and because of the extraordinary value of its water resources in a highly arid region, many debates and interstate quarrels have ensued over the years regarding riparian rights along the Colorado. Many of these US domestic disputes are still ongoing (Terrell, 1965; Carothers and Brown, 1991; Fradkin, 1996; Wollebæk Toset *et al.*, 2000), in addition to international conflict between the USA and Mexico over Mexico's small and highly saline share of the trickle that is the Colorado River at its mouth (Bernal and Solis, 2000).

Outdoor recreational activities

Perhaps the most significant association with the Colorado River is the canyons and other geophysical landscapes it helped create, including the Grand Canyon, Canyonlands and Glen Canyon. The Grand Canyon (Arizona) is the second most visited National Park in the USA (*c*.4.4 million visitors in 2007) and draws people from around the globe to witness its spectacular scenery, much of which was created over millions of years by the Colorado River. Since the late 1800s, the Grand Canyon and the Colorado River at large have been a major attraction for hikers, rafter, trekkers, poets, artists, sightseers and nature 'pilgrims' (Zierer, 1952; Watkins, 1969). They were also a major impetus for the development of tourism in the American west before and after the beginnings of the interstate highway system in the 1950s (Gunn, 2004).

While almost all rivers in the USA are utilized for recreational and tourism purposes to some degree, the Colorado is among the most heavily used, largely because of the natural scenery it traverses. Although the human-created dams and lakes are impressive and create a unique tourist appeal, the natural features through which the river runs are the most impressive (Warzecha and Lime, 2001). Research suggests that recreationists' favourite characteristics about the Colorado and their favoured activities are its shaded beaches, observing plant and animal life, learning about the history of the canyons, camping, visiting archaeological sites, fishing, hiking and looking at waterfalls, alcoves and other spectacular scenery (Cole, 1989; Stewart *et al.*, 2003). The lakes created by several dams along the river have become important recreation and tourism resources in the south-west. Lake Mead and Lake Powell are perhaps the best known of these, and both are designated National Recreation Areas under the auspices of the US National Park Service. Lake Mead is located in Arizona and Nevada; Lake Powell is located in Arizona and Utah, and both draw visitors from around the USA and abroad for water-based recreation, primarily fishing, speed-boating, house-boating and skiing.

Cultural heritage and gambling

The Colorado River system has played an important part in western American history and settlement. It is home to several areas of Native American ruins and archaeological sites (Cole, 1989), historic ranches and pioneer settlements. Likewise, several dams have been erected in an effort to harness water for agriculture, drinking, energy generation and recreation. With the building of Parker Dam, the creation of Lake Havasu on the border of California and Arizona created one of the most prized recreation resources in the arid southwest. In addition to water sports, Lake Havasu is home to the London Bridge, which was built in London, England, in the 1830s but was later sold to a developer in Lake Havasu City, Arizona, where it was reassembled in 1968 (Stroud, 1995; Jewesbury, 2003). The London Bridge, which extends over a small channel of Lake Havasu, has become a major tourist attraction in this popular Colorado River resort community, and a small-scale English village was built beside it to add to the ambience.

Besides Lake Havasu City, many communities along the Colorado River in Nevada, Arizona and California are dependent on tourism for their economic well-being with water-based recreation and gambling being the most important drivers (Borden and Grumbles, 2006). Many scenic areas along the California–Arizona border have been designated as state parks and are open to camping and other recreational activities (Fig. 3.2). While physically, the Colorado River and the lands it traverses bear little resemblance to the Mississippi, economically and politically there are some important similarities. Perhaps most significant of these is the existence of gambling along the banks of the Colorado River on which the river's role as an interstate border has a major bearing. Between Laughlin, Nevada, and Bullhead City, Arizona, two neighbouring

Fig. 3.2. Recreation on the Colorado River, Arizona/California. (Photograph courtesy of Dallen Timothy.)

communities on the Colorado River, there is a distinct economic disparity. Casino gambling is permitted in Nevada, but not in Arizona. This has resulted in a rapid growth of casinos and riverfront resorts on the Nevada side of the boundary. Bullhead City, Arizona, on the other hand has not achieved the level of economic development seen by its neighbour Laughlin. This has led to some serious disputes, primarily on the part of the Arizona community, which believes it is being left out of economic development. However, what Bullhead City sometimes fails to realize is that it shares in the gaming wealth of Laughlin, with 75% of Laughlin's casino workers living on the Arizona side of the river paying property tax, sales tax and creating jobs (Borden and Grumbles, 2006).

Uniquely Colorado

What gambling is to the Mississippi, white-water rafting is to the Colorado. Rafting is probably the most unique aspect of recreation and tourism on the Colorado River. The unique Canyon landscapes that the river helped create are at the root of this appeal and set the Colorado apart from the Mississippi. The Grand Canyon portion of the Colorado River is the longest stretch of rec-reational water within a national park and provides some of the world's best white water, attracting people from all over the world (Brickler *et al.*, 1983; Hjerpe and Kim, 2007).

Based on the water and energy needs of cities in the region, releases of water from Glen Canyon Dam significantly affect rafting and other recreational activities in the Colorado River south of the dam, especially in the Grand Canyon (Schulze *et al.*, 1981; Cole, 1989). Borkan and Underhill (1989, p. 347) identified several ways in which these human-induced flow changes affect white-water rafting in the Canyon. First is the fluctuation of the river level. Second is the velocity of river flow, which varies depending on the volume of water released. Third, rapids become unsafe because of changes in velocity and flow. Fourth, when water levels are low, large rocks are exposed and rafts might be grounded. Finally, in high waters there is an added danger of water turbulence and large waves. Research by Stewart *et al.* (2003) concluded that the release flows have decreased the number and quality of beaches and camp-sites in the Grand Canyon and on other parts of the river.

While the dam (completed in 1966) affects boating and rafting in the Grand Canyon in these ways, it has allowed the water to be regulated better and thereby improved rafting conditions in the parks and lakes below it (Underhill *et al.*, 1986). None the less, water level and stream flow have been found to influence the physical characteristics of the river and thus recreationists' per-ceptions of their experiences, in particular related to raft operators having to require passengers to walk around shallow rapids and using the motor to com-pensate for low current speeds (Borkan and Underhill, 1989; Shelby *et al.*, 1992; Stewart *et al.*, 2003).

Like the Mississippi, the Colorado River faces several significant impacts from heavy recreational use and tourism. One primary concern among bio-logists and conservationists is the introduction of non-native plant and animal species by the means of recreational vehicles, most notably boats and rafts (Dahm *et al.*, 2005). Perhaps the most important negative impact of recreational use of the Colorado is the decreased aesthetic value associated with too many users. Overcrowding has created a shortage of river space, and a lack of safety, as well as a 'shortage of solitude' in the area (McCool, 1978; Groff, 1998, p. 130). Groff suggests that the creation of Lake Powell has also resulted in widespread graffiti, vandalism, litter, crime, noise, congestion and trampled vegetation with the growth of the lake in areas that were previously inaccessible, but are now accessible by boat. In response to some of these concerns, in the 1970s, the National Park Service began capping the number of people who could raft on the Colorado as a way of controlling overuse and reducing the potential negative implications (Underhill *et al.*, 1986). This permit system allows commercial and non-commercial users to utilize the river, although the waiting list can be as long as 10 years (Groff, 1998). Another concern commonly noted by Lake Powell users is the decline in aesthetic appeal of the region because of the large power plants near Glen Canyon Dam (Schulze *et al.*, 1981).

White-water rafting has contributed significantly to the economic development of northern Arizona near the Grand Canyon. Regional expenditures on rafting are estimated to be approximately US$21 million (Hjerpe and Kim, 2007) on items such as raft fees, gas and oil, car rentals, groceries, restaurants, hiking and rafting gear, lodging, fishing licences and guide fees (Douglas and Harpman, 1995). These expenditures have generated hundreds of jobs directly and indirectly in that part of the state (Douglas and Harpman, 1995).

Conclusion

It is clear that rivers are among America's most significant outdoor assets for tourism and recreation. Like all water bodies, they have become important venues for sports and other water-related activities for which many people travel long distances to experience. However, the rivers of the USA, as noted in the two cases described here, are unique and many of their characteristics differ somewhat from rivers in many other parts of the world.

The great rivers of the USA often help define what it means to be American. Their role in the settlement of the south, the Midwest and the western states no doubt is an important component of this. This settlement role, as well as the rivers' role as national frontiers and state boundaries, plants them within the American national ethos and renders them sacrosanct to some degree. Also, rivers have been important in the writings of several prominent literary heroes. These writings about rivers have further romanticized America's rivers in all parts of the country and built a somewhat nostalgic yearning for a more innocent and rural Americana that still plays a part in the American nationalist psyche.

Another interesting pattern is that many rivers of the USA are ostensibly associated with gambling. This can be viewed from two perspectives. First, sometimes because of their role as state borders, gaming is allowed on rivers where it would not be permitted on shore or in 'state territory' (Timothy, 2001). Thus, rivers have in some cases become sub-national 'neutral zones' where an activity not fit for land, because of its negative social implications or simply legal ramifications, is seen as suitable for neutral spaces that are neither Illinois or Iowa, or Louisiana or Mississippi. The second border implication regards where gaming is allowed on one side of a river but not the other, as was illustrated by the Colorado River. This is common on state borders in the USA and national borders throughout the world. However, in the USA, on a domestic scale, one state's economy is permitted to benefit directly from gaming, while neighbouring communities in a neighbouring state languish economically, despite their sharing a common water boundary that is used on both sides as a recreation attraction.

Finally, the rivers of America are both a cultural and natural resource for recreation and tourism. Rivers flowing through some of the country's most spectacular natural scenery concomitantly flow through some of the most interesting cultural areas that epitomize the cultural and ethnic diversity that is also so much a part of the US tourism industry.

References

Aamodt, P.D., Alvarez-Requejo, S., Apostolos, C., Becnel, K.D., Davis, P.G., Flurry, R., Frey, J.T., LaCour, A., McLaughlin, S.E., Savin, S.M., Sporl, C.F. and Yang, C.C. (1992) *Recreation and Tourism in the Mississippi River Corridor: Natchez to Baton Rouge*. School of Landscape Architecture, Louisiana State University, Baton Rouge, Louisiana.

Anfinson, J.O., Madigan, T., Forsberg, D.M. and Nunnally, P. (2003) *River of History: A Historic Resources Study of the Mississippi National River and Recreation Area*. US Army Corps of Engineers, St Paul, Minnesota.

Arland-Fye, B. and Pellin, R. (1992) Riverboat gambling: recreational revenue? *Parks and Recreation* 27(11), 64–66.

Becker, R.H. (1979) Travel compatibility on the upper Mississippi River. *Journal of Travel Research* 18(1), 33–36.

Becker, R.H. (1981) Displacement of recreational users between the Lower St Croix and Upper Mississippi Rivers. *Journal of Environmental Management* 13(3), 259–267.

Bernal, J.M. and Solis, A.H. (2000) Conflict and cooperation on international rivers: the case of the Colorado River on the US–Mexico border. *International Journal of Water Resources* 16(4), 651–660.

Borden, B. and Grumbles, R. (2006) *Economic Impact of Tourism on Colorado River Communities Including Laughlin, Bullhead City, Fort Mohave, Mohave Valley, Golden Valley*. Nevada Cooperative Extension, Reno, Nevada.

Borkan, R.E. and Underhill, A.H. (1989) Simulating the effects of Grand Canyon dam releases on Grand Canyon river trips. *Environmental Management* 13(3), 347–354.

Brickler, S., Tunnicliff, B. and Utter, J. (1983) Use and quality of wildland water: the case of the Colorado River corridor in the Grand Canyon. *Western Wildlands* 9(2), 20–25.

Brown, A.V., Brown, K.B., Jackson, D.C. and Pierson, W.K. (2005) Lower Mississippi River and its tributaries. In: Benke, A.C. and Cushing, C.E. (eds) *Rivers of North America*. Elsevier, Amsterdam, pp. 231–281.

Carothers, S.W. and Brown, B.T. (1991) *The Colorado River Through Grand Canyon: Natural History and Human Change.* University of Arizona Press, Tucson, Arizona.

Clements, C.J. (1993) The perceived impacts of tourism on the Mississippi National River and Recreation Area. Doctoral Dissertation, University of Minnesota, Minnesota.

Cole, D.N. (1989) The Grand Canyon of the Colorado: a challenge to float, a challenge to manage. *Western Wildlands* 15(3), 2–7.

Dahm, C.N., Edwards, R.J. and Gelwick, F.P. (2005) Gulf Coast rivers of the southwestern United States. In: Benke, A.C. and Cushing, C.E. (eds) *Rivers of North America*, Elsevier, Amsterdam, pp. 181–228.

Davis, J.A. and Austin, K. (2002) Nauvoo, Illinois: a different kind of heritage tourism site. *Tourism Recreation Research* 27(2), 35–40.

Delong, M.D. (2005) The Upper Mississippi River Basin. In: Benke, A.C. and Cushing, C. (eds) *Rivers of North America*. Academic Press, New York, pp. 327–374.

Dimanche, F. and Speyrer, J.F. (1996) Report on a comprehensive five-year gambling impact research plan in New Orleans. *Journal of Travel Research* 34(3), 97–100.

Dixon, D.P. (1998) The only game in town: the cultural politics of riverboat gambling in Cape Girardeau and Scott City, MO. In: Meyer-Arendt, K.J. and Hartmann, R. (eds) *Casino Gambling in America: Origins, Trends and Impacts*. Cognizant, New York, pp. 168–179.

Douglas, A.J. and Harpmann, D.A. (1995) Estimating recreation employment effects with IMPLAN for the Glen Canyon Dam region. *Journal of Environmental Management* 44(3), 233–247.

Eadington, W.R. (1999) The economics of casino gambling. *The Journal of Economic Perspectives* 13(3), 173–192.

Espeseth, R.D. (1992) Parks and open space along the Upper Mississippi River. *Téoros* 11(3), 13–14.

Fradkin, P.L. (1996) *A River No More: The Colorado River and the West.* University of California Press, Berkeley, California.

Gotham, K.F. (2007) Destination New Orleans: commodification, rationalization, and the rise of urban tourism. *Journal of Consumer Culture* 7(3), 305–334.

Gramann, J.H., McAvoy, L., Absher, J.D. and Burdge, R.J. (1985) Barge traffic impacts on recreational lock use: the case of the Upper Mississippi River. In: Anderson, L.M. (ed.) *Proceedings of the Southeastern Recreation Research Conference*. USDA Forest Service, Asheville, North Carolina, pp. 15–22.

Groff, C. (1998) Demarketing in park and recreation management. *Managing Leisure* 3(3), 128–135.

Gunn, C. (2004) *Western Tourism: Can Paradise Be Reclaimed?* Cognizant, New York.

Hjerpe, E.E. and Kim, Y.S. (2007) Regional economic impacts of Grand Canyon river runners. *Journal of Environmental Management* 85(1), 137–149.

Hsu, C.H.C. (1999) History, development, and legislation of riverboat and land-based non-Native American casino gaming. In: Hsu, C.H.C. (ed.) *Legalized Casino Gaming in the United States: The Economic and Social Impact*. Haworth, New York, pp. 63–90.

Hsu, C.H.C. (2000) Residents' support for legalized gaming and perceived impacts of riverboat casinos: changes in five years. *Journal of Travel Research* 38(4), 390–395.

Jewesbury, D. (2003) Tourist: pioneer: hybrid: London Bridge, the mirage in the Arizona desert. In: Crouch, D. and Lübbren, N. (eds) *Visual Culture and Tourism*. Berg, Oxford, pp. 223–240.

Judd, D.R. (2002) Promoting tourism in US cities. In: Fainstein, S.S. and Campbell, S. (eds) *Readings in Urban Theory*. Blackwell, Oxford, pp. 278–301.

Keating, B. and Stanfield, J.L. (1971) *The Mighty Mississippi*. National Geographic Society, Washington, DC.

Lee, A. (1993) Mississippi stakes all on riverboat gambling. *Planning* 59, 8–13.

Long, P.T. (1995) Casino gaming in the United States: 1994 status and implications. *Tourism Management* 16(3), 189–197.

Madhusudhan, R.G. (1996) Betting on casino revenues: lessons from state experiences. *National Tax Journal* 49(3), 401–412.

McCool, S.F. (1978) Recreation use limits: issues for the tourism industry. *Journal of Travel Research* 17(2), 2–7.

McCormack, P.J. (1991) *Riverboat Gambling.* Minnesota Senate, St Paul, Minnesota.

Meyer-Arendt, K.J. (1998) From the river to the sea: casino gambling in Mississippi. In: Meyer-Arendt, K.J. and Hartmann, R. (eds) *Casino Gambling in America: Origins, Trends and Impacts.* Cognizant, New York, pp. 151–167.

Mosher, A.E. and Wheeler, M.M. (1998) Riverboat gambling as urban revitalization Lagniappe: the case of Baton Rouge, LA. In: Meyer-Arendt, K.J. and Hartmann, R. (eds) *Casino Gambling in America: Origins, Trends and Impacts.* Cognizant, New York, pp. 180–202.

Rose, I.N. (1995) Gambling and the law: endless fields of dreams. *Journal of Gambling Studies* 11(1), 15–33.

Schulze, W.D., Brookshire, D., Ben-David, S. and Rosenbaum, D. (1981) Recreation in the Lake Powell area: alternatives for preservation and development. *Southwestern Review of Management and Economics* 1(1), 1–18.

Shelby, B., Brown, T.C. and Baumgartner, R. (1992) Effects of streamflows on river trips on the Colorado River in Grand Canyon, Arizona. *Rivers* 3(3), 191–201.

Sieber, R.T. (1991) Waterfront revitalization in postindustrial port cities of North America. *City and Society* 5(2), 120–136.

Siegal, D. and Anders, G. (1999) Public policy and the displacement effects of casinos: a case study of riverboat gambling in Missouri. *Journal of Gambling Studies* 15(2), 105–121.

Smith, T.R. (2007) *River of Dreams: Imagining the Mississippi Before Mark Twain.* Louisiana State University Press, Baton Rouge, Louisiana.

Stewart, W., Larkin, K., Orland, B. and Anderson, D. (2003) Boater preferences for beach characteristics downstream from Glen Canyon Dam, Arizona. *Journal of Environmental Management* 69(2), 201–211.

Stokowski, P.A. (1999a) Economic impacts of riverboat and land-based non-native American casino gaming. In: Hsu, C.H.C. (ed.) *Legalized Casino Gaming in the United States: The Economic and Social Impact.* Haworth, New York, pp. 155–174.

Stokowski, P.A. (1999b) Social impacts of riverboat and land-based non-native American casino gaming. In: Hsu, C.H.C. (ed.) *Legalized Casino Gaming in the United States: The Economic and Social Impact.* Haworth, New York, pp. 233–251.

Stroud, H.B. (1995) *The Promise of Paradise: Recreational and Retirement Communities in the United States Since 1950.* Johns Hopkins University Press, Baltimore, Maryland.

Terrell, J.U. (1965) *War for the Colorado River.* A.H. Clark, Glendale, California.

Truitt, L.J. (1996) Casino gambling in Illinois: riverboats, revenues, and economic development. *Journal of Travel Research* 34(3), 89–96.

Turner, W.B. (1991) *New Life on the Mississippi – and Elsewhere: The Promising Potential of Modern Riverboat Gaming.* Raymond James and Associates, St Petersburg, Florida.

Underhill, A.H., Xaba, A.B. and Borkan, R.E. (1986) The wilderness use simulation model applied to Colorado River boating in Grand Canyon National Park, USA. *Environmental Management* 10(3), 367–374.

Vogel, J.J., Titre, J.P. and Chilman, K.C. (1996) *A Study of Water-Based Recreation on the Upper Mississippi River.* Army Engineer Waterways Experiment Station, Vicksburg, Mississippi.

Volberg, R.A. (1997) *Gambling and Problem Gambling in Mississippi.* Social Science Research Center, Mississippi State University, Starkville, Mississippi.

Walsh, K. (2003) *The Mississippi.* World Almanac, Milwaukee, Mississippi.

Warzecha, C.A. and Lime, D.W. (2001) Place attachment in Canyonlands National Park: visitors' assessment of setting attributes on the Colorado and Green Rivers. *Journal of*

Park and Recreation Administration 19(1), 59–78.

Watkins, T.H. (1969) *The Grand Colorado: The Story of a River and Its Canyons.* American West, Palo Alto, California.

Welle, P.G. and Baer, N.W. (1997) Uses, attitudes and values of recreation participants on the Mississippi headwaters. *Journal of Applied Recreation Research* 22(2), 123–156.

Wollebæk Toset, H.P., Gleditsch, N.P. and Hegre, H. (2000) Shared rivers and interstate conflict. *Political Geography* 19(8), 971–996.

Zierer, C.M. (1952) Tourism and recreation in the west. *Geographical Review* 42(3), 462–481.

Zube, E.H. (1995) Greenways and the US National Park system. *Landscape and Urban Planning* 33(1), 17–25.

4 The Mekong: Developing a New Tourism Region

E. Laws[1] and P. Semone[2]

[1]James Cook University, Cairns, Australia; [2]Grandville House Unit, Bangkok, Thailand

Introduction

The Mekong River rises on the high Tibetan plateau, and then flows through Yunnan province, Myanmar, Laos PDR, Thailand, Cambodia and Viet Nam where it reaches the South China Sea. This vast area is known as the 'Greater Mekong Subregion' (GMS). It has a complex history which has left a legacy of temples and palaces, many of which are now World Heritage sites under the protection of UNESCO. The tourism potential of the GMS is further enhanced by a great diversity of cultural groups, and its ecology is rich and varied. However, much of the region is lacking in modern infrastructure and has suffered great political and military turmoil in recent decades. Many of the countries are ranked in the lowest social and economic categories. The Asian Development Bank (ADB) is actively encouraging their development, with tourism identified as a lead sector. This chapter provides readers with an introduction to the Mekong region, sets regional tourism policy in the broader context of regional social and economic development initiatives, and summarizes the recent emergence of a cohesive regional approach to Pro-Poor Tourism development (PPT).

A Brief Geography and History of the Greater Mekong Subregion

The Mekong is one of the world's longest rivers (Fig. 4.1), flowing 4909 km through very challenging terrain (Liu *et al.*, 2007). It was only in 1994 that the Japanese photographer and explorer Masayuki Kitamura identified its source in eastern Tibet at an altitude of 5224 m (Kitamura, 2001). In Tibet, the Mekong is known as the River of Rock (Dza Chu River). It then flows through the Chinese province of Yunnan (where it is called the 'Lacang'). Tibet, Yunnan and Laos PDR are estimated to have 80% of the river's hydroelectric generation potential (Hirsch and Cheong, 2006) because of the more than 4800m drop in altitude. In its final 2400km after flowing past Luang Prabang in Laos PDR, the river falls less than 400m before reaching its estuary in the Mekong Delta region of Viet Nam.

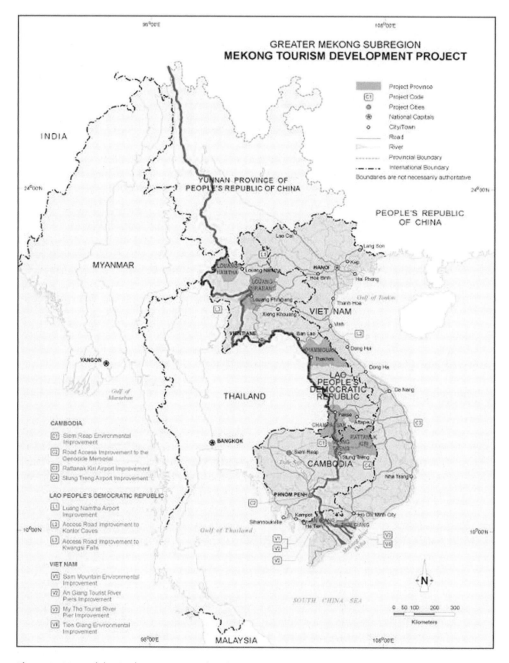

Fig. 4.1. Map of the Mekong tourism development project. (From ADB, 2004.)

European missionaries and traders began exploration of its lower reaches in 1555 but the 19th century was the great era of river exploration throughout Asia, Africa, Australia and America, memorably described as the 'geography of power' by Malay (2006, p. 22). In the case of the Mekong, the epic French de Lagree-Garnier expedition of 1866–1868 encountered increasingly difficult conditions on their voyage upstream from Phnom Penh during their search for a trading route into the southern Chinese provinces (Gomane, 1994). The depth of the river fluctuated greatly, with rapids and waterfalls barring the lower 3000 km at several points. They eventually abandoned the Mekong near Jinghong in Southern Yunnan and then travelled overland to the Yangtze which was already well known to European traders. Efforts to develop reliable transport along the Mekong continued in the 20th century, but with limited success (see Keay, 2005; Osborne, 2006 for accounts of the exploration of the Mekong and detailed bibliographies).

As part of its rapid industrialization at the end of the 20th century, China initiated a programme of hydroelectric dam building and riverbed clearance on many of its major rivers, including extensive works on the Mekong. Further development along the lower Mekong and many of its tributaries is also exploiting its hydroelectric potential, estimated at 30,000 MW, more than enough to meet the expected demand in the coming decade (Hirsch and Cheong, 2006). Osborne (2006) notes that these projects have the stated aim of reducing annual flooding but warns, as have others, of detrimental consequences for fishing and agriculture in Cambodia and Viet Nam. He also cautions that development may cause problems for the emergent adventure tourism operators using Mekong resources for activities such as white-water rafting.

Theoretical Contexts of GMS Tourism Development

A strategic approach to regional development

Governments have increasingly recognized the economic significance of tourism and its role as a tool for regional development. One consequence of this has been the active development and promotion of towns, regions and countries, as if they were tourism place-products (Kotler *et al.*, 1993). However, most of the GMS is remote from established economic areas, and so may be considered 'peripheral'. Distinguishing between core and peripheral tourism areas is common in the tourism literature (Christaller, 1963; Keller, 1987; Weaver, 1998). Peripheries are separated from the more developed and more densely populated cores both in terms of physical distance and the time required to travel to and from them. Yet in many countries peripheral areas are being developed for tourism. The purpose of developing remoter areas for tourism is twofold: to provide a sustainable economic activity for populations in those areas, and to reduce pressure of tourist visitation on established destinations (Middleton and Hawkins, 1998).

Recent attention has focused on the issue of whether states that share a given resource can cooperate effectively in its use and management

(Stallings, 1997). Makim (2002, p. 5), discussing the Mekong region, notes: 'There is now considerable evidence to suggest that, in matters of trans-boundary resource use, states are often able to establish and sustain collect-ive action.' The range of development programmes discussed in this chapter confirms Makim's finding that there is willingness and ability among the countries bordering the Mekong to cooperate in mutually beneficial projects, despite the political and historical tensions among them. This chapter con-centrates on tourism development but in evaluating this, it is important to recognize the wider contexts of trade and power cooperation as well as the underlying commitment to pro-poor development approaches being pioneered by the ADB.

A strategic approach has become increasingly common where decisions are taken in terms of the direction of the product offering and the markets to target. Strategic market planning provides an effective framework for the consideration of these issues, while also providing clear advantages. 'The process of goal setting provides a common sense of ownership and direction for the many stakeholders in the resort, whilst at the same time sharpening the guiding objectives. The coherence provided by the approach provides a framework for joint initiatives between the commercial and public sectors and demands the clear identification of roles and responsibilities' (Laws and Cooper, 1998, p. 341). Wilkinson (1997, p. 13) states that 'little attention has been paid in the tourism literature to the analysis of tourism policy and its subsequent implementation'. Hall (1994) has also highlighted the need for more research into the political and administrative dimensions of tour-ism. Other studies of regional development have noted the complexity of tourist destination areas and the need for leadership both to identify appro-priate ways forward and to ensure cohesive approaches among the many stakeholders.

Tourism development is an amalgam of the two concepts of tourism and development and can be defined in different ways and viewed from different perspectives. Pearce (1989, p. 15) describes it simply as 'the provision or enhancement of facilities and services to meet the needs of tourists'. Additionally, tourism may also be seen as a means of development in a much broader sense, the path to achieving some end state or condition (Murphy, 1985; Inskeep, 1991). In this chapter, marketing of the Mekong region is given less prominence than the suite of programmes being implemented to develop the infrastructure and provide the skills needed for a sustainable destination region.

The ADB is actively investing in selected tourism projects throughout the GMS as a key action in the promotion of economic and social benefits in a 'pro-poor' way, and to give cohesion to the region. Cohesion is partly being achieved by developing infrastructure for tourism corridors and trans-border tourism, promoted under the general banner of the Mekong River. Discussing tourist routes, Murray and Graham (1997, p. 514) noted that a tourist route 'functions as a regional definition, a theme that transcends geo-graphical diversity and distance to provide a spatially expansive but integrated marketable theme'.

Pro-poor tourism

The tourism sector's potential to promote pro-poor development increasingly features in policy and as the subject of academic research (Ashley and Roe, 2002; Dann, 2002). Murphy (1985) has criticized the short-term objectives of much tourism development, and particularly the lack of consideration of developing a viable tourism product, and the sociocultural and environmental consequences of the development. 'PPT interventions aim to increase the net benefits for the poor from tourism, and ensure that tourism growth contributes to poverty reduction....PPT strategies aim to unlock opportunities for the poor – whether for economic gain, other livelihood benefits, or participation in decision-making.' (Ashley *et al.*, 2001, p. viii). Pearce and Butler (1999) have also noted that individual entrepreneurs and/or national and regional authorities often set the objectives for tourism development with little regard for potential impacts on others. Similarly, 'Tourism First' approaches have been distinguished by Burns (1999) from PPT. This chapter emphasizes the prominence given to the pro-poor aspects of river tourism development in the GMS region.

Kakwani and Pernia (2000) define pro-poor growth as growth that 'enables the poor to actively participate in and significantly benefit from economic activity'. Klasen (2003) suggests that there are two possible ways to achieve pro-poor growth. The direct way implies that growth is pro-poor if it immediately raises the incomes of the poor. This is most likely to occur in sectors or regions where the poor are employed and using the factors of production they own. In agriculture, non-farm rural and informal sector activities, pro-poor projects are labour-intensive and land-intensive, and concentrated in areas with high poverty rates. The second, indirect way of pro-poor growth occurs if the gains from overall economic growth are redistributed to the poor via progressive taxation and targeted government spending, either by direct financial transfers or investment in the assets of the poor, usually by providing basic social services.

Scheyvens (2002) argues that participation and empowerment of host communities are essential objectives in any tourism initiative that seeks to address issues of poverty. Similarly, Ashley *et al.* (2001) consider that pro-poor projects might benefit from inclusion in the decision making of the target beneficiaries. But Johnson (2001) finds little evidence that either democracy or decentralization is necessary for poverty reduction in rural or urban areas. He reports that projects were successful where three conditions were met: an appropriate balance between autonomy and accountability; a constructive support from external actors; and a commitment to democratic deepening. 'It is worth building on these conditions because democratic activity is not merely an instrumental good; it also has intrinsic benefits for the rural poor' Johnson (2001, p. 522).

The former President of the ADB, Tadao Chino, declared that 'poverty is the deprivation of essential assets and opportunities to which every human being is entitled' and that 'poverty reduction is now the overarching goal of ADB' (Chino, 2002, p. 45). Pro-poor growth is cited as one of the three pillars of the Bank's Poverty Reduction Strategy, and occurs when it is (ADB, 1999a, p. 6):

1. labour-absorbing;
2. accompanied by policies and programmes that mitigate inequalities;
3. facilitative to income and employment generation for the poor, particularly women and other traditionally excluded groups.

Warr (2005, p. 2) points out that this describes some characteristics that pro-poor growth might reasonably possess, but it falls short of a definition. He advocates more research to distinguish between growth that is pro-poor and growth that is not, and queries whether policy can be effectively directed towards achieving an undefined target. However, Kappel *et al.* (2005, p. 28) note that 'yet, understanding pro-poor growth does not only depend on a proper definition of the concept, but also on its adequate practical operationalisation'.

Tourism and Economic Development in the GMS

The Lower Mekong River Basin (Cambodia, Laos PDR, Thailand and Viet Nam) is home to approximately 60 million people. Over 100 different ethnic groups live within the basin's boundaries, making it one of the most culturally diverse regions of the world. Their economic conditions are among the poorest in the world (see Kaosa-ard, 2003 for an analysis), and it is a priority of the ADB to assist in their modernization in line with the 1999a ADB Poverty Reduction Strategy (ADB, 1999a) and the GMS Tourism Sector Strategy 2005–2015 (ADB, 2005).

As most of the GMS is an area of extreme poverty it might appear that tourism, with its privileged overtones of hedonism and its reliance on both general and specialized infrastructure, is not an appropriate investment priority. However, by including tourism as one of the 11 flagship programmes of its GMS Economic Cooperation Programme, the ADB sees tourism as a key development sector, and one of the few from which benefits can rapidly trickle down to the village level. At the national level, tourism is not always seen as a priority for the six GMS governments as, compared to mining, industrialized agricultural projects and other capital-intensive industries, tourism has limited ability to stimulate inward capital investment. Nevertheless, the impetus created by the initiatives described in this chapter, combined with the growth of intraregional demand for tourism, has facilitated the exponential growth of tourism activity in the GMS region, as shown in Table 4.1.

In the lead up to the development of the Greater Mekong Subregion Tourism Sector Strategy the ADB stated:

> The GMS countries possess a wide range of highly attractive and relatively undeveloped natural, cultural, and historical heritage tourism resources. In 2003, GMS tourism resources attracted about 17 million international tourists and around $10 billion in receipts. Estimates based on the WTO 2020 Vision forecasts indicate that if a subregional approach to develop and promote the tourism sector is adopted, the GMS countries could attract about 29.2 million international tourists by 2010 and about 61.3 million by 2020. If the forecast is realized, by 2010 there could be an additional $7.56 billion expenditure; an additional 194,000 hotel

Table 4.1. GMS tourism activity.

| Destination | International visitor arrivals to Mekong nations | | | | | |
	2001	2002	2003	2004	2005	2006
Cambodia	604,919	786,524	701,014	987,359	1,333,000	1,591,350
Guangxi (China)	1,267,228	1,363,383	650,192	1,175,835	1,477,099	1,707,729
Yunnan (China)	1,131,303	1,303,550	1,000,101	1,100,994	1,502,787	1,810,017
Laos PDR	673,823	735,662	636,361	894,806	1,095,315	1,215,106
Myanmar	204,862	217,212	205,610	241,938	232,218	263,514
Thailand	10,061,950	10,799,067	10,004,453	11,650,703	11,516,936	13,821,802
Viet Nam	2,330,050	2,627,988	2,428,735	2,927,876	3,467,757	3,583,486
GMS total (as of March 23, 2007)	16,274,135	17,833,386	15,626,466	18,979,511	20,625,112	23,993,004

rooms and related services and facilities with investment requirements of about $14.5 billion; a substantial increase in the demand for and supply of transportation equipment and services; and about 194,000 new jobs in the hotel sector. The contribution to household incomes can be significant, especially in the rural areas with tourism potential and among disadvantaged groups such as the youth, women, and ethnic minorities, who will be able to get better paying jobs, or new jobs, or create their own small business. The volume of taxes accruing to national and local governments in the GMS will also increase and boost local economies and overall trade activity. However, these benefits will not occur, or may not be equitably distributed unless a subregional Tourism Sector Strategy is adopted.

(ADB, 2004, p. 2)

Tourism resources of the GMS

The key elements in marketing tourism to the subregion are its cultural, historical and natural resources. The cultural and natural resources of the GMS countries include prehistoric archaeological sites such as Ban Chiang (Thailand), spectacular historical monuments and temples such as Angkor (Cambodia), Vat Phou (Laos PDR) and Sukhothai (Thailand), and historical towns such as Lijiang (Yunnan), Hoi An (Viet Nam) and Luang Prabang (Laos PDR). The GMS has more than 300 protected areas, wildlife sanctuaries and reserves containing a wealth of biodiversity of plants and animals, many found nowhere else in the world, and some at risk of extinction.

An early GMS programme (ADB, 1999) was aimed to promote the GMS by means of 'The Thirty Subregional Tourism Jewels'. The intention was to create international awareness of the wider region and to complement existing marketing initiatives by the various National Tourism Organizations promoting their own

Table 4.2. Mekong tourism development zones. (From ADB, 2004.)

1. **Cambodia** – Stung Treng and Rattankirri provinces. A nature-based destination with good tourism potential, situated in the GMS Green Triangle Zone
2. **Laos PDR** – Phongsaly, Houaphan and Xienghuang provinces. Important ecological Karst landscapes excellent tourism potential, and the birthplace of modern Laos PDR
3. **Myanmar** – Mount Popa. National Park includes a heavily forested old volcano with significant cultural values
4. **Thailand** – Ubon Ratchathani and Sisaket provinces. This rural border area is the poorest region in Thailand and is situated on a high plateau that butts into the Mekong River and is in the GMS Emerald Triangle
5. **Viet Nam** – Son La and Dien Bien provinces. This highland, forested, ethnically diverse area and site of important battles from the Indo-China wars shares a common border with Laos' PPT priority tourism priority area (2 above)
6. **Yunnan** – Xishuanbanna area of the GMS Golden Quadrangle. Rich in wildlife resources including China's main tropical rainforest; very diverse ethnically, with about a third being Dai

resources. The programme capitalized on more general regional development initiatives, including improvements to the road system and attempts to ease tourists' passage across the borders of the Mekong countries. More recently, six zones have been identified for tourism development as noted in Table 4.2.

GMS Framework for Tourism Development

Economic cooperation

In 1992, the countries of the GMS embarked on a programme of economic cooperation to promote development through closer economic linkages. The GMS Programme, supported by the ADB and other donors, through grants, loans and co-financing schemes focuses on high priority subregional projects in transport, energy, telecommunications, environment, human resource development, tourism, trade, private sector investment and agriculture. As indicated in Fig. 4.2, these are strategically linked. By 2006, priority infrastructure projects worth over US$6 billion had either been completed or were being implemented. Among these are the upgrading of the Phnom Penh (Cambodia)–Ho Chi Minh City (Viet Nam) highway and the East–West Economic Corridor that will eventually extend from the Andaman Sea to Da Nang.

The Mekong River Commission

The Mekong River Commission (MRC) is a country-driven river basin organization that provides the institutional framework to promote regional cooperation. It was formed in April 1995 when the governments of Cambodia, Laos PDR, Thailand and Viet Nam signed the agreement on the Cooperation for the Sustainable Development of the Mekong River Basin, which provides a frame-

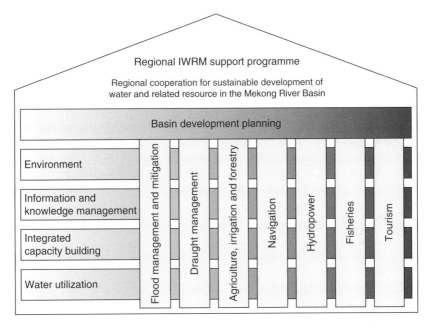

Fig. 4.2. Cascade of Mekong development programmes. (From Cogels, 2005.)

work for joint management of their shared water resources and development of the economic potential of the river (see Browder, 2000 for an analysis of water resource management in the Mekong). The MRC serves its member states by supporting decisions and promoting action on sustainable development and poverty alleviation as a contribution to the UN Millennium Development Goals. According to Cogels (2005) the four goals for 2006–2010 are to promote and support coordinated, sustainable and pro-poor development, to enhance effective regional cooperation, to strengthen basin-wide environmental monitoring and impact assessment and to strengthen the Integrated Water Resources Management capacity and knowledge base of the MRC bodies, National Mekong Committees, Line Agencies and other stakeholders.

The Mekong Programme is complementary to the Greater Mekong Subregion Economic Cooperation Programme, promoted by the ADB. The Mekong Programme also engages with other regional initiatives such as the Association of South-east Asian Nations (ASEAN) Mekong Basin Development Cooperation and the United Nations Economic and Social Commission for Asia and the Pacific (UNESCAP).

Evolving tourism administration for the Mekong subregion

Both bilateral and subregional tourism cooperation initiatives between the region's governments have taken place in recent decades. Each government in the GMS has its own tourism policy and tourism marketing organization, and for many of them GMS cooperation is a low-priority activity. It should be noted that Thailand is by far the most developed tourism destination in the region, and as such, the Thai government, Thai Airways International and Bangkok Airways have regularly taken leading roles in regional initiatives to market and develop GMS tourism. 'Strengthening cooperation with the neighbouring countries of the Greater Mekong subregion has been an integral part of Thai travel and tourism marketing plans for more than a decade' (TAT, 2007, p. 1; see Tirasatayapitak and Laws (2003) for a discussion of the significance to Thailand of tourism development for the GMS).

The Tourism Authority of Thailand (TAT) set up an Agency for the Coordination of Mekong Tourism Activities (AMTA) in 1997 in cooperation with the Pacific Asia Travel Association (PATA) and the World Tourism Organization (WTO). AMTA subsequently became the main forum for tourism marketing and development in the subregion, with participation by all governments and financial and technical sponsorship from the ADB, UNESCAP and PATA. In 2006, in accordance with a 2005 decision of the GMS Tourism Working Group, AMTA was replaced by the Mekong Tourism Coordination Office (MTCO). The mission of the MTCO is twofold: (i) to develop and promote the GMS as a single tourism destination, offering a diversity of good-quality and high-yielding subregional products that help to distribute the benefits of tourism more widely; and (ii) to support and coordinate each GMS member country, at the subregional level, in the implementation of projects identified and committed to under the GMS Tourism Sector Strategy. The Strategy states that the MTCO is tasked with the marketing and promotion of tourism in one of the World's most dynamic and alluring tourism destinations – the six nation GMS – and fostering its development as a single destination under the 'Mekong Tourism' brand (ADB, 2004).

In order to provide continuity to cooperative dialogue, an annual Mekong Tourism Forum (MTF) was organized and co-financed by the ADB, PATA and UNESCAP. In 2006, the MTF was replaced by Mekong Tourism Investment Summit (MTIS) which was held in Luang Prabang, Laos PDR. This event was hosted by the Laos National Tourism Administration (LNTA), Bangkok Airways and other private sector organizations. The MTIS succeeded in its objective of providing an arena for governments and development organizations to communicate progress to Mekong Tourism's stakeholders and to mobilize support for key initiatives from top GMS and regional travel executives, multinational investors and government. In April 2007, through the support of the ADB and the Viet Nam National Administration of Tourism (VNAT), a GMS Tourism Investment Forum was held in Ho Chi Minh City, Viet Nam. The event attracted over 100 tourism practitioners, investors and academics. Future events in 2008 and beyond are currently being discussed and will probably be organized through the MTCO.

Theoretical perspective on GMS tourism administration

The foregoing discussion accords with the trend noted by Laws and Cooper (1998) among successful destination authorities that they tend to take proactive decisions about their product and market position. Ohm's (1999) guidelines for tourism cooperation focus on the need for countries to cooperate in the development of packaged products, transport links, tourism facilities and resort complexes, to establish a joint tourism policy council to prepare a strategic tourism cooperation plan and to adopt a common tourism promotion policy. Tourism planning and development at international and cross-border sub-national scales has recently been recognized as a means of developing tourism and is often viewed as a way of improving economic benefits and political relations between neighbouring countries (Reed, 1997; Dore, 2003; Tirasatayapitak and Laws, 2003). This chapter now provides an account of how tourism development in the GMS is organized and supported on a regional basis with economic and social development as key policy objectives.

The Mekong Tourism Development Project

In early 2000, the ADB began the development of a loan project known as the Mekong Tourism Development Project (MTDP) for the lower Mekong River Basin countries of Laos PDR (US$10.9 million), Cambodia (US$15.6 million) and Viet Nam (US$8.5 million), with very low interest rates and a 32-year repayment period (ADB, 2002, p. v). The MTDP is comprised of four distinct components: (i) tourism-related infrastructure improvements; (ii) pro-poor community-based tourism development; (iii) subregional cooperation for sustainable tourism; and (iv) implementation assistance and institutional strengthening. As described in the ADB-MTDP Report and Recommendations of the President to the ADB Board of Directors:

> [T]he project will promote the development of the tourism sector in the lower Mekong River basin. It will improve tourism-related infrastructure in Cambodia, Lao PDR and Viet Nam (Greater Mekong Subregion)GMS participating countries [GMSPC]), support pro-poor community based tourism projects in the rural areas of these countries, facilitate private sector participation in tourism marketing and promotion, establish mechanisms to increase sub-regional cooperation, and facilitate the movement of tourists across borders.
>
> (ADB, 2002, p. iii)

At the time of writing (November 2007), negotiations were under way for the GMS Sustainable Tourism Development Project (STDP) which is anticipated to commence in late 2008. The STDP will focus on four priority areas, including: (i) sustainable tourism development in natural, cultural and urban tourism sites; (ii) PPT subprojects; (iii) cross-border and Economic Corridor tourism facilitation subprojects; and (iv) human resource development subprojects. In addition, initiatives for tourism sector small and medium enterprises (SME) development and investment promotion are being prepared in parallel with the design of the subprojects (Interim Report GMS Sustainable Tourism Development Project: 2). Both the MTDP and STDP represent important GMS tourism development projects supported by ADB loans. These projects focus on loans to Laos PDR, Cambodia and Viet Nam. Albeit Thailand and China have foregone any interest in ADB tourism development loans, and Myanmar is not qualified because of international sanctions, these three countries continue to play an active role in subregional cooperation as outlined in the GMS Tourism Strategy.

GMS Tourism Strategy

The GMS Tourism Strategy is founded on seven core strategic programmes which are summarized in Table 4.3. The core strategies outlined in Table 4.3 will be implemented through 16 major thematic projects and 13 major spatial projects for implementation in the period 2006–2010. Each of the GMS member countries, along with the Mekong Tourism Office (MTO), is responsible for taking the lead in specific projects as indicated in Table 4.4. According to the ADB, the GMS Tourism Strategy has the potential to lift 1.2 million people out of poverty. It would also create a more equitable distribution of tourism benefits between the countries of the subregion. Other positive impacts include improved conservation of the subregion's natural and cultural heritage, minimizing adverse social impacts and providing increased opportunities for participation by women and ethnic communities. Table 4.5 then indicates the anticipated scale of the potential benefits to be derived from these actions.

In addition to a range of tourism initiatives for each of the Mekong countries summarized in Table 4.4, the ADB has developed 16 thematic projects within the context of the GMS Tourism Strategy to enhance regional tourism management capacity and to further its aims of poverty reduction in the GMS. This section provides a synopsis of three current projects to indicate the range and nature of ADB involvement in GMS tourism development.

Tourism initiatives to alleviate poverty
While many projects contribute to poverty alleviation through employment creation, human resource development (HRD) and infrastructure development, the pro-poor projects outlined below target the poor directly. To date, much of the focus of pro-poor tourism development has been based upon preparing single village communities to host either day trips or overnight visitors. The ADB identified several key issues confronting PPT development in the subregion:

- Poverty alleviation is still not mainstreamed in many tourism policies, plans and programmes of the GMS countries.
- The need to move away from the current rather narrow approach towards a wider and more inclusive conception of PPT for poverty alleviation (in other words focus needs to be given to mainstreaming opportunities to allow the poor and disadvantaged greater access to the tourism economy).
- The currently low levels of tourism's contributions to poverty reduction and the benefits of this approach; effective PPT development principles and practices including ensuring that all the stakeholders are engaged in the product development process to maximize buy-in and commitment are not being applied.
- The failure to act and adopt (and where necessary adapt) sustainable development principles and practices at the natural and cultural resource management and community levels is threatening overall progress (based on ADB, 2004).

Table 4.3. Seven core strategies of the GMS tourism strategy. (From ADB, 2004.)

Programme	Description
Promote the Subregion as a Single Destination	The subregion will be branded as 'the Mekong' and marketed as a single destination based on culture, nature and adventure tourism. AMTA will be strengthened and renamed the MTO, which will position and promote the subregion in primary source markets using the Internet as well as Mekong-branded promotional materials.
Enhance Product Development and Quality	Thirteen priority tourism zones and circuits, with the Mekong River as the core, have been identified. These contain most of the subregion's major culture-, nature- and adventure-based tourism resources and around 12.5 million people living in poverty – the target beneficiaries. Within the zones, access roads leading to tourism sites and related communities will be improved; pollution control infrastructure strengthened at in key sites; protection infrastructure at heritage sites upgraded; and visitor information services developed. Higher standards in food and beverage preparation, accommodations, and protection and presentation of cultural and natural heritage sites will be encouraged
Develop Human Resources	Over 2.14 million additional qualified workers will be required by 2015. This will require upgrading of training at the subregion's tourism training institutions. It will be necessary to create a culture of human resources development within national tourism organizations (NTOs) and train NTOs and related agencies, vocational training institutions and academic institutions with tourism programmes. The capacity training will be gender-sensitive
Manage Heritage Conservation and Social Impacts	To protect the important heritage sites of the subregion, the technical capacities of heritage site managers to manage tourism will be improved, and the interpretative skills of heritage tour guides upgraded. Cross-border ecological corridors of protected areas will be created and managed in a spirit of cooperation. Through coordination with existing subregional programmes, the adverse social impacts of tourism including trafficking, sex work, exploitation of children and HIV/AIDS will be addressed. This will require support at both the highest levels of government and in the grass roots communities where the impact is most immediately felt
Promote Pro-poor and Equitable Tourism Development	Pro-poor pilot projects will be undertaken in seven clusters of villages and towns with high poverty incidence. These will distribute the benefits of tourism to a larger number of people by providing more opportunities for the local population to engage in tourism businesses and employment, both directly and indirectly
Promote Private Sector Partnership and Investment	The vision, technology, entrepreneurial skills and financial capacity of the private sector will be harnessed by strengthening private sector tourism institutions; encouraging micro-, small- and medium-enterprise development in the lodging; travel and tourism-related businesses; and through public-private partnership mechanisms such as tourism marketing and promotion boards
Streamline Cross-border Tourism	To facilitate the movement of tourists to and within the subregion; border checkpoints will be upgraded, visa-on-arrival and one-stop inspection and processing extended to more sites, visa extensions made easier, and the smooth operation of international air, sea and land transportation services across borders encouraged. Finally, a single GMS-wide visa will be developed

Table 4.4. Strategic subregional projects 2006–2010. (From ADB, 2004.)

Project name	Lead country
1. Marketing and Product Development	MTCO
2. Human Resource Development and Capacity Building in the GMS (Target: Middle-level public officials)	Cambodia
3. Human Resource Development and Capacity Building in the GMS (Target: Hospitality skills trainers in vocational schools)	Cambodia
4. Preparing and Implementing an HRD Plan for NTOs (Target: Top and senior levels and technical personnel in the NTOs)	Cambodia
5. Human Resource Development and Capacity Building in the GMS (Target: Deans and professors/lecturers in institutions with tourism and hospitality management degree programmes)	PRC (Guangxi)
6. Training of Guides at Heritage Sites	Laos PDR
7. Saving Cultures, Saving Lives: Confronting the Reality of Negative Social Impacts of Tourism Development on the People of the GMS	Cambodia
8. Preserving the Soul of the Ancestors: Protection of Traditional Living Cultures in the Framework of Tourism Development in the GMS	PRC (Guangxi)
9. Capacity Building for Heritage Managers to Protect and Manage Priority Sites for Tourism	Thailand
10. Creating Biodiversity Conservation Corridors: Setting Up Transborder Complementarity to Strengthen Tourism Management in and Around Protected Areas	Laos PDR
11. In the Steps of Shiva and the Lord Buddha: Linking the Ancient Monumental Heritage of the GMS	Cambodia
12. GMS Tourism Initiatives to Reduce Poverty	All countries
13. Project to Promote Small and Medium-sized Enterprise Development and Investment in Tourism-related Facilities and Infrastructure in the GMS	Cambodia
14. GMS-wide Visa Scheme	ACMECS
15. Tourism Facility and Processing Improvements at Key Border Checkpoints in the GMS	MTCO
16. Information Databank and Monitoring of Progress on Travel Facilitation Initiatives	MTCO
17. The Mekong World Tourism River Corridor – An Endless Stream of Tourism Cooperation	Thailand
18. Development of the Tourism Potential of the North-south Economic Corridor – The Golden Quadrangle Area	PRC (Yunnan)
19. East-West Economic Corridor Tourism Development Study	Laos PDR
20. Tourism Development Plan with Infrastructure Support for the Implementation of the Emerald Triangle Area Tourism Zone	Thailand
21. Tourism and Infrastructure Feasibility Study and Development Along Coastal Route of the Southern Economic Corridor	Cambodia
22. Tourism Sector Development in the Cambodia – Laos PDR – Viet Nam Green Development Triangle Area	Viet Nam
23. Infrastructure, Conservation and Development Support for the Development of the Heritage Necklace Circuit	Thailand
24. Laos PDR–Viet Nam Cross-border Community-based Tourism Zone	Laos PDR
25. Andaman Coast Tourism Zone	Thailand
26. Red River Valley Tourism Zone	Vietnam
27. Shangri-la–Tengchong–Myitkyina Tourism Development Zone	PRC (Yunnan)
28. Guangxi–North-east Viet Nam Borderlands Tourism Zone	PRC (Guangxi)
29. GMS Coastal and River Cruise Lines	PRC (Guangxi)

ACMECS = Ayeyarwady–Chao Phraya–Mekong Economic Cooperation Strategy.
MTCO = Mekong Tourism Coordinating Office.

Table 4.5. Potential benefits of GMS tourism strategy. (From ADB, 2004.)

Impact indicator	2004	2010	2015
International tourist arrivals	18.9 million	31.9 million	52.0 million
Receipts from international tourism	US$14.75 billion	$29.45 billion	$52.40 billion
Number of new jobs created		1.73 million	2.14 million
Number of people taken out of poverty		Up to 158,000	Up to 1.2 million

ADB cultural site management programme

Interviews conducted by ADB with GMS heritage experts and managers identified the need for better resources and improved capacity and training for heritage managers at priority sites. The training and certification of heritage guides has also been identified as one of the key priorities at heritage sites throughout Asia, particularly at World Heritage sites.

In response, the ADB set up a project aimed at training and strengthening the management capacity at heritage sites for tourism. A specialized training course and curriculum will be designed by experts to upgrade the skills and build the capacity of a core group of 100 middle-level heritage managers and national tourism organizations (NTO) professionals who specialize in cultural and nature tourism. Successful trainees will receive certificates enabling them to serve as primary trainers in their own countries The curriculum, in addition to traditional protection and conservation issues, will concentrate on tourism-related topics such as: management and coordination of visitors to natural and cultural sites; designing and implementing good conservation and visitor management plans; carrying capacity and how good management can increase carrying capacity at a site; and risk preparedness and management. Three sets of training programmes are being developed for: (i) cultural heritage management; (ii) natural heritage management; and (iii) heritage guides. They will be translated into six languages, customized for each country and delivered over a period of 4 years (ADB, 2004).

The Mekong world tourism river corridor

Although six tourism zones have been identified for development in the GMS region (see Table 4.2), there is also a need to facilitate the movement of tourists between the main tourism zones. The opportunities to reduce poverty, promote economic development and expand investment and SMEs can be maximized in a sustainable manner under this 'corridor' project. The benefits are intended for four target groups: (i) the poor living within the catchment area would be provided with better infrastructure, leading to better health, higher incomes and generating employment; (ii) international and domestic tourists would also gain through better infrastructure; (iii) the private travel sector would gain from better and increased business; and (iv) the governments would gain from increased revenue.

The corridor links the six proposed priority tourism zones along the Mekong into a single product concept by:

- developing secondary and feeder roads between the major tourism zones;
- developing river-based infrastructure such as riverbank development, passenger jetties, river training, navigation and safety;
- small-scale infrastructure water supply, electricity, sanitation, markets, landscape beautification, waste management, etc. in cities, towns, villages;
- provision of efficient and modern border facilities in areas outside the six priority tourism zones;
- basic visitor infrastructure including rest areas and toilets, signage and interpretation, information facilities, health and safety facilities; and
- human resource development, marketing and capacity-building studies and implementation activities.

An estimated budget of US$47 million over 5 years has been proposed for the Mekong River Corridor project (ADB, 2004).

Further Research Needs

The GMS tourism projects are at an early stage of development: evolution and change is inevitable. Careful monitoring of the various elements of these programmes and the development of ways of measuring their effectiveness against the objectives outlined in this chapter are contributions which academic as well as field experts should pay attention to. Najam (1999) discusses the significant roles of non-governmental organizations (NGOs) in such processes (see also Fisher, 1998). Administratively, the forms of cooperation between sovereign governments, supranational organizations, NGOs and commercial interests will also attract the further attention of researchers (McGovern, 1996). The lessons drawn from future research may inform development schemes in other regions of the world where social and economic development is an urgent need, and where tourism offers one of the most rapid ways forward.

Conclusion

The Mekong is one of the great rivers of the world, in terms of its length, and the rugged and varied terrain it passes through on its course from the highlands of Tibet to the South China Sea. The rich cultural heritage and ecological resources of the region provide great potential for tourism development, and this is being actively encouraged by the region's governments with the expertise and support of the tourism industry, the ADB and UNESCO, among many other organizations. It is therefore fitting that a study of this region is included in the first book to concentrate attention on river tourism.

This chapter has summarized some of the main tourism development initiatives under way, and it has drawn attention to the broader regional issues of economic development, poverty alleviation and regional cooperation within which tourism developments in the GMS should be understood and evaluated. As the ADB (2002, p. iv) has pointed out

> Tourism in the GMS has become increasingly multi-country. In a highly competitive world tourism market, the GMS can survive and grow only if it promotes a 'one holiday, several destinations' type of tourism. Individual tourism sectors in the GMS countries can only prosper when they are strongly linked to others.

But tourism development does not necessarily contribute to poverty alleviation or cooperation between neighbouring governments; the achievement of these and other aims depends on effective management at a regional scale.

References

Ashley, C. and Roe, D. (2002) Making tourism work for the poor: strategies and challenges in Southern Africa. *Development Southern Africa* 19, 61–82.

Ashley, C., Roe, D. and Goodwin, H. (2001) *Pro-poor Tourism Strategies: Making Tourism Work for the Poor.* Overseas Development Institute, London.

Asian Development Bank (ADB) (1999a) *Fighting Poverty in Asia and the Pacific, the Poverty Reduction Strategy.* Asia Development Bank, Manila.

Asian Development Bank (ADB) (1999b) *Report of the Tenth Meeting of the Greater Mekong Subregion (GMS) Tourism Sector.* Vientiane, Laos PDR.

Asian Development Bank (ADB) (1999c) *Policy on Indigenous Peoples.* Asian Development Bank, Manila.

Asian Development Bank (ADB) (2002) *Mekong Tourism Development Project Report.* Asian Development Bank, Manila.

Asian Development Bank (ADB) (2004) *Technical Assistance for the Greater Mekong Subregion Tourism Sector Strategy.* Asian Development Bank, Manila.

Asian Development Bank (ADB) (2005) *The Greater Mekong Subregion Tourism Sector Strategy.* Asian Development Bank, Manila.

Browder, G. (2000) The evolution of an international water resources management regime in the Mekong river basin. *Natural Resources Journal* 40(3), 499–531.

Burns, P. (1999) Paradoxes in planning tourism: elitism or brutalism. *Annals of Tourism Research* 26(2), 329–348.

Chino, T. (2002) Inaugural address. In: Edmonds, C. and Medina, S. (eds) *Defining an Agenda for Poverty Reduction*, vol. 1. Asian Development Bank, Manila, pp. 45–48.

Christaller, W. (1963) Greater Mekong Subregion Sustainable Tourism Development Project, Interim Report, Manila 2006. Some Considerations of Tourism Location in Europe: The Peripheral Regions in Underdeveloped Countries' Recreation Areas. *Regional Science Association: Papers XII*, Lund Congress, pp. 95–105.

Cogels, O. (2005) *Regional Cooperation Programme for Sustainable Development of Water and Related Resources in the Mekong Basin.* Mekong River Commission, Vientiane, Laos PDR.

Dann, G. (2002) Tourism and development. In: Desai, V. and Potter, R.B. (eds) *The Companion to Development Studies.* Arnold, London, pp. 236–240.

Dore, J. (2003) The governance of increasing Mekong regionalism. In: Kaosa-ard, M. and Dore, J. (eds) *Social Challenges for the Mekong Region*, 2nd edn. White Lotus, Bangkok, pp. 406–435.

Fisher, J. (1998) *Non-governments: NGOs and the Political Development of the Third World.* Kumarian Press, West Hartford, Connecticut.

Gomane, J.-P. (1994) *L'Exploration du Mekong: La Mission Ernest Doudart de Lagree-Francis Garnier.* L'Harmattan, collectionnes Recherches Asiatiques, Paris.

Hall, C. (1994) *Tourism and Politics, Policy, Power and Place.* Wiley, Chichester, UK.

Hirsch, P. and Cheong, G. (2006) *Natural Resource Management in the Mekong Basin: Perspectives for Australian Development Cooperation*. Final Report to Ausaid, University of Sydney, Sydney, Australia.

Inskeep, E. (1991) *Tourism Planning. An Integrated and Sustainable Development Approach*. Van Nostrand Reinhold, New York.

Johnson, C. (2001) Local democracy, democratic decentralization and rural development: theories, challenges and options for policy development. *Policy Review* 19(4), 521–532.

Kakwani, N. and Pernia, E.M. (2000) What is pro-poor growth? *Asian Development Review* 18(1), 1–16.

Kappel, R., Lay, J. and Steiner, S. (2005) Uganda: no more pro-poor growth? *Development Policy Review* 23(1), 27–53.

Kaosa-ard, M. (2003) Poverty and globalization. In: Kaosa-ard, M. and Dore, J. (eds) *Social Challenges for the Mekong Region*, 2nd edn. White Lotus, Bangkok, pp. 81–108.

Keay, J. (2005) *Mad About the Mekong, Exploration and Empire in South-East Asia*. Harper Perennial, London.

Keller, C.P. (1987) Stages of peripheral tourism development – Canada's North West territories. *Tourism Management* 8, 20–32.

Kitamura, M. October (2001) The source of the Mekong river. *Japanese Alpine News* 1(1), 1–12.

Klasen, S. (2003) In search of the holy grail. How to achieve pro-poor growth? In: Tungodden, B. and Stern, N. (eds) *Towards Pro-poor Policies*. World Bank, Washington, DC.

Kotler, P., Haider, D. and Rein, I. (1993) *Marketing Places*. Free Press, New York.

Laws, E. and Cooper, C. (1998) Inclusive tours and commodification: the marketing constraints for mass market resorts. *Journal of Vacation Marketing* 4(4), 337–352.

Liu, S., Lu, P., Liu, D. and Jin, P. (2007) Pinpointing source of Mekong and measuring its length through analysis of satellite imagery and field investigations. *Geo-spatial Information Science* 10(1), 51–56.

Makim, A. (2002) Resources for security and stability? The politics of regional cooperation on the Mekong, 1957–2001. *The Journal of Environment Development* 11, 5.

Malay, A. Jr. (2006) Configuring IndoChina: the 19th century exploration of the Mekong. In: Diokina, M. and Chinh, N. (eds) *The Mekong Arranged and Rearranged*. Mekong Press, Chiang Mai, Thailand, pp. 19–41.

McGovern, I. (1996) Regional development in the Mekong basin. In: Stensholt, B. (ed.) *Development Dilemmas in the Mekong Subregion*. Monash University, Melbourne, Australia, pp. 86–96.

Middleton, V. and Hawkins, R. (1998) *Sustainable Tourism, A Marketing Perspective*. Butterworth Heinemann, Oxford.

Murphy, P. (1985) *Tourism a Community Approach*. Methuen, London.

Murray, M. and Graham, B. (1997) Exploring the dialectics of route-based tourism: the Camino de Santiago. *Tourism Management* 18(8), 513–524.

Najam, A. (1999) Non-governments: NGOs and the political development of the third world. *Nonprofit and Voluntary Sector Quarterly* 28(3), 364–367.

Ohm, Y.-S. (1999) Promoting tourism cooperation and exchange in East Asia. *Proceedings of the Asia Pacific Tourism Association Fifth Annual Conference*. Hong Kong SAR, China, pp. 45–49.

Osborne, M. (2006) *Mekong*. Allen and Unwin, Crow's Nest, Australia.

Pearce, D. (1989) *Tourist Development*. Longman Scientific, Harlow, UK.

Pearce, D.G. and Butler, R.W. (eds) (1999) *Contemporary Issues in Tourism Development*. Routledge, London.

Reed, M. (1997) Power relationships and community-based tourism planning. *Annals of Tourism Research* 21(3), 566–591.

Scheyvens, R. (2002) *Tourism for Development: Empowering Communities*. Prentice-Hall, Harlow, UK.

Stallings, B. (ed.) (1997) *Global Change, Regional Response: The New Inter-*

national Context of Development. Cambridge University Press, Cambridge.

TAT Newsroom (2007) Tourism Authority of Thailand. 2 July 2007.

Tirasatayapitak, A. and Laws, E. (2003) Developing a new multi-nation tourism region, Thai perspectives on the Mekong initiatives. *Asia Pacific Journal of Tourism Research* 8(1), 48–57.

Warr, P. (2005) Pro-poor growth. *Asian-Pacific Economic Literature* 19(2), 1–17.

Weaver, D. (1998) Peripheries of the periphery tourism in Tobago and Barbuda. *Annals of Tourism Research* 25, 292–313.

Wilkinson, P. (1997) *Tourism Policy and Planning: Case Studies from the Commonwealth and Caribbean.* Cognizant Communications, Elmsford, New York.

5 River Tourism: Sailing the Nile

M. COOPER

Ritsumeikan Asia Pacific University, Beppu, Japan

Introduction

'Egypt is the gift of the River Nile', wrote Herodotus in The Geography of Egypt (Logos 2.1–34) of his *Histories* (Lloyd, 2002). The person popularly known as the first historian (and a keen geographer/traveller/researcher), Herodotus of Halicarnassus (modern Bodrum in South-western Turkey), who lived and wrote in the 5th century BC (*c*.480–*c*.429), was the first to write about river tourism within his description of the expansion of the Achaemenid Empire of Persia. After the death of Cyrus the Great in 530 BC, his son Cambyses became the new ruler of Persia. This monarch's efforts to conquer Egypt and Nubia (526–523 BC) gave Herodotus the opportunity to dedicate three books to the ancient kingdoms on the banks of the Nile. In the first logos of Book Two, he gives a description of the country. He starts with a discussion of the Egyptian language as one of the oldest in the world, then discusses the Egyptian calendar and explains that Egypt consists of alluvial deposits of the Nile (the origin of the phrase 'a gift of the Nile'). He continues with a description of the size of the country and describes the inundation of the Nile, tries to explain its rising, tells several stories about the sources of the river and describes his voyages along it (Lloyd, 2002).

As a researcher and topographer, Herodotus had no equal for centuries; he was the first to understand the relative size and situation of Europe, Africa and Asia. He was aware of the fact that the Caspian Sea was surrounded on all sides by land, and knew of reports about the circumnavigation of Africa. And he was aware that the Nile was a very long river with its source in a mountainous country very far from the mouth. His having placed that source in the Atlas Mountains of North Africa (Fig. 5.1) is no real impediment to the accuracy of his tourism geography of Egypt and Nubia that was created from first-hand experience and careful interviews with contemporaries on site along the Nile.

'If you ever visit Egypt and drink water from its Nile, you will sure come back to it once again' is a more modern proverb quoted by travel and real

©CAB International 2009. *River Tourism* (eds B. Prideaux and M. Cooper)

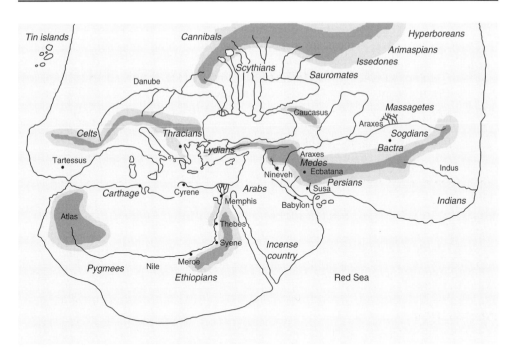

Fig. 5.1. The sources of the Nile and the Danube according to Herodotus. (From www.livius.org by permission.)

estate agents alike (e.g. www.2travel2egypt.com; www.egyptresidential.com) to explain the modern world's desire to visit Egypt and to a lesser extent Nubia in northern Sudan – a desire that is perhaps not dissimilar to that of Herodotus and the many writers, travellers, conquerors (including those as far apart as Cambyses, Napoleon and the Nubian Kings of the 25th Dynasty), and other visitors to Egypt, Nubia and Ethiopia over the centuries. The reason for this is that the Nile is both the longest river on earth – 6695 km or 4160 miles in length and flowing across or intercepting tributary waters from many countries in Africa, including Burundi, the Democratic Republic of Congo, Ethiopia, Eritrea, Kenya, Rwanda, Sudan, Tanzania, Uganda and Egypt – and one of the cradles of human civilization. It has two main branches and therefore two sources: the Blue Nile rises in Ethiopia and the White Nile in Uganda. The White Nile flows through Uganda, Sudan and Egypt and the Blue Nile starts in Ethiopia. Rwanda, Congo, Tanzania, Kenya and Burundi all have tributaries which flow into the White Nile. Each has a range of tourism attractions and markets, but the main focus of river tourism in the Nile's case lies in the cultural heritage of the lower reaches, forming as it did the lifeline of Ancient Egypt and Nubia, one of the oldest civilized areas in the world (Cerveny and Cerveny, 2006).

In this chapter, readers will find much that they already know something of perhaps, given that the history of ancient Egypt and Nubia (Sudan) occupies a central place in the history of mankind and of modern-day tourism, and many may even have already visited the river's lower reaches in search of their own version of that history. Fewer may understand that the river Nile is important in tourism terms for many countries besides Egypt and Sudan, and that the range of tourism attractions and activities throughout the length of the river is much wider than that of viewing ancient civilizations or of river cruising. This chapter thus provides readers with an introduction to this wider picture, sets the policy framework relating to river tourism in the context of the differing social, environmental and economic conditions of the countries bordering the river and summarizes the recent emergence of the Nile Basin Initiative (NBI) and its likely impact on the use of the river for tourism in the future. The chapter also mentions the associated water bodies (lakes, waterfalls) and oases that are intimately connected to the river in tourism terms.

Geography (Physical, Social and Environmental)

About 90% of the total flow of more than 300 million cubic metres of water per day in the Nile comes from Lake Tana, 1800m above sea level in the Ethiopian mountains (Fig. 5.2; Marshall *et al.*, 2006). Lake Tana floods every

Fig. 5.2. Origins and course of the Blue and White Nile Rivers. (From GNU image, Wikipedia Commons, 2008.)

summer, providing for the flood that supported the rise of Pharonic civilization, but today is tamed by barrages and dams in Sudan and Egypt. This Ethiopian branch is known as the Blue Nile (Abbay) and flows for over 800 km until it joins the White Nile in Sudan at Khartoum to form the Nile proper. The second main source is the White Nile that originates in Uganda and Burundi (Fig. 5.2). This branch contributes only 16% of the total flow, but that flow is steady all year-round (Barron, 2006; Fig. 5.3). Without it, the Nile would run dry in May in years of low rainfall. The third main contributor is the Atbara River, also from the Ethiopian highlands, which joins the main course of the Nile 300 km north of Khartoum but only contributes around 1% of total flow, and often runs dry during the summer (Figs 5.2 and 5.3).

As there are many other smaller contributors to the Nile, the question of where the Nile really starts remains open. The longest definition of the Nile incorporates the stream emerging from the Nyungwe Forest in Rwanda, via the Rukarara, Mwogo, Nyabarongo and Kagera rivers, before flowing into Lake Victoria in Tanzania near the town of Bukoba. This stream goes through the Rift Valley Lakes including Lake Victoria, where it is named the Victoria Nile until it enters Lake Albert, after which it is known as the Albert Nile until it crosses the Sudan border when it becomes the Mountain Nile (Bahr al Jabal). The Bahr al Jabal then winds through rapids before entering the Sudan plain and the vast swamp of the Sudd. It eventually makes its way to Lake No, where it merges with the Bahr el Ghazal and passes through Juba, the capital of southern Sudan as the Bahr al Abyad, or White Nile (Fig. 5.2 – the southernmost

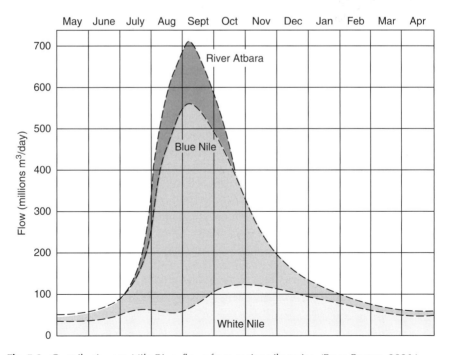

Fig. 5.3. Contributions to Nile River flows from major tributaries. (From Barron, 2006.)

navigable point on the Nile River System), before merging with the larger Blue
Nile at Khartoum to form the Nile.

Physical and environmental characteristics of the river

Lake Tana, Ethiopia, source of the Blue Nile, is one of a string of Great Rift
Valley Lakes, many within national parks, and is home to a wealth of bird and
animal life. The Simien Mountains in the north and the Bale Mountains in the
south are also home to some unique wild life, and are ideal for trekking, while
the river itself is becoming famous for white-water rafting. The Blue Nile flows
generally south from Lake Tana and then west across Ethiopia and north-west
into Sudan. Within 30 km of its source at Lake Tana, the river enters a canyon
about 400 km long. This gorge is a tremendous obstacle for travel and communication from the north half of Ethiopia to the southern half, but is now slowly
being opened up for white-water rafting tourism. For the tourist, the attraction
and power of the Blue Nile is seen at Tisissat Falls (translated as 'a smoking
fire'), which is 45 m high and is located about 40 km downstream of Lake Tana,
although a recently built hydropower station has reduced its flow considerably
(http://www.13suns.com/). The flow of the Blue Nile reaches maximum volume in the rainy season (from June to September), when it supplies about two-
thirds of the water of the Nile proper (Barron, 2006). This branch, along with
that of the Atbara River to the north which also flows out of the Ethiopian
highlands, is responsible for the annual Nile floods that contributed to the fertility of the Nile Valley (and 96% of transported sediment). It is also an important
resource for Sudan; the Roseires and Sennar dams produce 80% of the country's power and there are significant agricultural areas dependent on it.

Sensu stricto, the term White Nile refers to the river formed at Lake No
at the confluence of the Bahr al Jabal and Bahr el Ghazal rivers north of the
area known as the Sudd (Petersen *et al.*, 2007). In the wider sense, it refers to
the approximately 3700 km (2300 miles) of rivers draining into and from Lake
Victoria into the White Nile proper. The 19th-century search by Europeans for
the source of the Nile was mainly focused on this branch, which disappeared
into the depths of what was then known as Darkest Africa (Stanley, 1890). The
discovery of the source of the White Nile thus came to symbolize European
penetration of the unknown.

The topography of the upper White Nile River Basin is mountainous and
isolated although it is becoming important in adventure tourism terms. As a
result, the falls and lakes on this branch of the river are particularly important
both environmentally and for tourism. From Rusumo (Rwanda/Tanzania)
through Lake Victoria to Lake Kyoga in the centre of Uganda and then out
through the Karuma Falls to Lake Albert through the Murchison Falls National
Park, where the river is compressed into a passage some 7 m in width at
Murchison Falls (Fig. 5.4), the river is fast becoming an adventure tourism
attraction (The Monitor, 2008). Exiting Lake Albert, the river continues north
to Sudan and becomes known as the Bahr al Jabal. The river then winds
through rapids before entering the Sudan plain and the Sudd, one of the world's

Fig. 5.4. Murchison Falls, White Nile, Uganda. (From GNU image, Wikipedia Commons, accessed 22 April 2008.)

largest wetland areas (Shahin, 2002). This shallow and very flat inland delta covers an area which averages 30,000 km² and may during the wet season be over 130,000 km² in size. An important hydrological influence on the environmental flow of the river system as a whole and on the water needs of the communities that depend upon it downstream is that within the Sudd area over half the inflowing water is lost through *evapotranspiration* (Petersen *et al.*, 2007). In 1978, this situation had led to an agreement to construct a 360 km long diversion channel (since halted by civil war), the Jonglei diversion canal, planned to bypass the Sudd to avoid evaporation losses and increase the amount of water discharged at its outlet. However, pastoralists use the Sudd and the surrounding areas extensively as valuable grazing lands and the swamps and flood plains support a rich biota, including over 400 bird species and 100 mammal species (Hickley and Bailey, 1987; Denny, 1991; Kingdon, 1997); therefore, any further construction and operation of the diversion canal should be subject to strict environmental controls (UNEP, 2001).

After the Sudd, which is incidentally an almost impenetrable barrier to river-borne tourism, the northern section of the Nile River flows almost entirely through desert from Sudan into Egypt. These are countries whose human populations have as a result of their environment depended on the river since ancient times (Stanley *et al.*, 2003). Most of the population of Egypt and Sudan and virtually all of their cities, with the exception of those near the Mediterranean coast, lie along the Nile Valley; and nearly all the cultural and historical sites of Ancient Egypt and Nubia (Sudan) are found along the banks of the river. At its end, the Nile ends in a large delta that empties into the Mediterranean Sea. Environmentally, the northern Nile River Valley is a hot and dry region which receives very little rain at any time of the year. Because of this environment, settlement is very closely tied to the river itself and the resulting tourism assumes a distinctly river-based nature.

Associated water bodies and oases

The Nile Valley does, however, have associated water bodies including canals, lakes and oases, which are important urban, agricultural and now tourist resources. While not directly associated with river tourism, except with respect to the lakes of Uganda and Ethiopia, they are nevertheless often included in organized tours. The large depressions in the Western Desert where the water table is close to the ground surface contain the five major oases of Siwa, Bahariya, Farafra, Dakhla, Kharga plus the Fayum, which is the closest to the Nile Valley proper (Fig. 5.5). Geophysically and environmentally these oases are important for human settlement and tourism; perhaps less consequently they are also currently the focus of an ambitious project of land reclamation and interconnection (Rossi, 2007). The Suez Canal and the canals of the Nile Delta also feature strongly in the tourism of the Nile River Valley.

Social environments: the Nile and the 21st century

In the 21st century attention has shifted to the question of how to best use the $80\,km^3$ of water that the Nile annually transports from Equatorial Africa across the Sahara to the Mediterranean Sea (Nile Basin Initiative, 2008). The answer to this question will most affect Egypt, with its rapidly growing population of 65 million people almost totally dependent on the Nile. Population growth in Egypt is expected to outstrip the available water resources of the Nile early in the 21st century. This problem will be greatly complicated by population and economic growth in the upstream nations of Sudan, Ethiopia and Uganda (for current demographics see Table 5.1), though perhaps not by absolute tourism numbers as Table 5.1 points out.

The NBI, which began in February 1999, is a partnership initiated and led by the riparian states of the Nile River through the Council of Ministers of Water Affairs of the Nile Basin States (Nile Council of Ministers, or Nile-COM) in order to provide a framework of research and policy to allow the effective addressing of this basin-wide problem. The NBI seeks to develop the river in a cooperative manner, share substantial socio-economic benefits and promote regional peace and security. The NBI started with a participatory process of dialogue among the riparian countries that resulted in their agreeing on a shared vision: to 'achieve sustainable socioeconomic development through the equitable utilization of, and benefit from, the common Nile Basin water resources', and a Strategic Action Programme to translate this vision into concrete activities and projects (http://www.nilebasin.org/). The Nile Transboundary Environmental

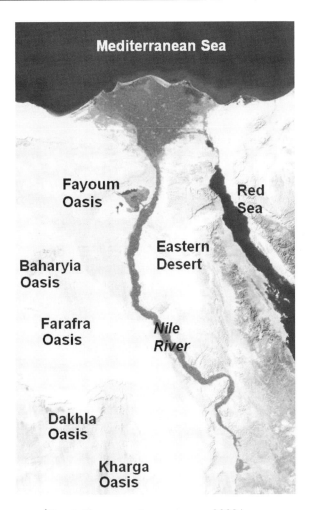

Fig. 5.5. The oases of Egypt. (From egyptvoyager.com, 2008.)

Action Project is the largest of eight basin-wide projects in the Shared Vision Programme (SVP) of the NBI, and together with the Water Resource Planning and Management (WRPM) Project provides a strategic framework for environmentally sustainable development of the Nile River Basin. These projects support basin-wide environmental action linked to transboundary issues in the context of the NBI Strategic Action Programme. As yet though, there is very little attention being paid to tourism in any of the eight projects.

With only 5% of Egypt's land area currently habitable and little or no other sources of water, the NBI response to the largest country in the region's water needs will likely be one of the more difficult problems to be faced by the Council of Ministers in the future as Egypt's population is expected to double by 2050. In addition, the Egyptian government has begun to encourage its people to move into the desert south of Cairo by pressing ahead with an estimated US$70 billion investment to reclaim 3.4 million acres (1 acre = 0.4047 ha)

Table 5.1. Basic demographic and tourism characteristics of the Nile River countries. (From CIA World FactBook, 2008; UNdata, 2008; World Tourism Organization, 2007.)

Country	Population (2008 estimates)	GDP/capita (2007 esti-mates; US$)	Visitor numbers 2007 (other)	Visitor nights	Revenue from tourism (US$)
Egypt	81,713,517	5,400	8,963,302	89,560,960	8,890,000,000
Sudan	40,218,455	2,500	61,000 (2004)	–	126,000,000
Ethiopia	78,254,090	700	210,000 (2004)	–	77,098,000
Uganda	31,367,972	1,100	512,000 (2004)	–	270,000,000
Rwanda	10,186,063	1,000	113,000 (2001)	–	35,900,000
Burundi	8,691,000	800	36,000 (2001)	–	5,000,000
The Democratic Republic of Congo	66,514,506	300	35,000 (2003)	–	–
Kenya	37,953,838	1,600	1,536,000 (2005)	–	688,000,000
Tanzania	40,213,162	1,100	566,000 (2004)	–	9,300,000[a]

[a]This figure is the revenue gained from hunting tourism, not total tourism (www.iipt.org/conference/africanconference2003/).

over the next 10 years. Known as the 'Toshka' plan, this initiative would expand Egypt's farmland by about 40% by 2017, but only by using an extra 5 billion cubic metres of water a year from the Nile (Rasmussen, 2007). These reclamations will add to regional tension over Nile water sharing arrangements as in order to green its deserts Egypt may need to take more than its share of Nile water as determined by international treaties. Under a 1959 treaty between Egypt and Sudan, Egypt secured rights to 55.5 billion cubic metres per year, more than half of the Nile's total flow, and the river has little extra left to give as other upstream countries like Ethiopia, where the Blue Nile begins, receive no formal allocation of Nile water, but are heavily dependent on the water it carries for their own agricultural and river-based tourism development. In summary, Egypt's water needs as the largest country, and specifically the Toshka and similar projects, will complicate the challenge of achieving a more equitable allocation of the Nile River with Ethiopia and the other Nile Basin countries. River tourism could well be affected also, if environmental flows are not enough to maintain river depth for cruise ships when extra allocations are taken for greening the desert.

The river and its associated tourism have also been subject to increasing tensions within the local communities in the Sudan and Egypt over endemic poverty as well as lack of environmental resources. These tensions culminated in attacks on tourists during the 1990s, largely resulting from disparities between the beneficiaries of tourism development and the sociocultural and economic situation of the rest of the community (Aziz, 1995). Sustainable tourism, which can deliver benefits to all groups, is the key to solving the problem of violence towards tourists, which actually originated in attacks by disaffected soldiers on tourist establishments not as popularly portrayed in the western media through religious extremism. Protests over the very apparent disparity between tourist luxury and local poverty remain ever possible given the way tourism is promoted along the Nile as a series of luxury ghettos (including river crises). The cultural violence overlay so popular in the western media is not the root cause of these problems, although it may contribute in certain circumstances and places.

Human History and the Nile

The tourism resources of the riparian countries along the Nile largely stem from the river's long association with human settlement. The river has been providing Egypt, Sudan, Uganda, Ethiopia and the other nations along its route with water for millennia and this led to the growth of human settlement along it. Deserving of its reputation as the world's largest open-air museum, the Nile River Valley contains thousands of monuments at various sites in all countries. For this reason, it is more common for tourists to visit actual locations where history occurred in this area than it is to spend time in modern museums detailing that history; and adventure and other forms of environmentally based tourism remain much less important overall than cultural tourism throughout much of the river's route north of Khartoum.

Egypt and Nubia (Kush)

The generally accepted view of the development of human settlement around the Nile River Valley has proto-Egyptians and Nubians migrating into the valley as the surrounding areas became progressively more desiccated from climate change and perhaps overgrazing (c.8000 BC, Stanley *et al.*, 2003). The Nile made the land surrounding it extremely fertile when it flooded annually; the Egyptians for example were able to cultivate crops and domesticate cattle, while the water attracted game and was useful for transportation. Stable and quite large populations (up to 3 million by the time of the Egyptian New Kingdom, c.1800 BC; Rice, 1999) developed in the valley north of Khartoum to the Mediterranean from about 3000 BC, infusing the Nile River with spiritual and cultural as well as economic and social values. The abundant flow of water each summer had to be systematically and regularly conducted over the fields. It was necessary to construct dams and dykes and to provide canals and sluices. Swamps had to be drained and converted into meadows. Such operations, however, could not possibly be accomplished by villages working individually; the inhabitants of the land were obliged to organize themselves into large communities under a leader whose guiding hand assisted them to centralize their efforts in the direction of the common interest (Steindorff and Seele, 1957).

Thus, the Nile awakened to a need for an adequate law code and an ordered society in the populations settled along its banks. For the sake of reckoning when the rise and retreat of the Nile flood would occur, determining the season for cultivating the fields and/or measuring plots of land after an unusually high

Nile inundation had obliterated them, it was imperative to observe such phenomena and record the change of the seasons and the new surveys in an official registry. So it was the behaviour of the Nile again which encouraged the development of writing, reckoning time by a systematic calendar and the study of astronomy (Steindorff and Seele, 1957). When later in the historical period pyramids, temples and other monuments were constructed in both countries, or statues and obelisks were set up in honour of the gods and the kings, it was the Nile once more which facilitated the transport of heavy building materials to create the monuments that are now the objects of cultural tourism.

Contact between Nubia and Egypt proper was also facilitated by the river, and both countries took turns at political domination of the lower valley populations; the Egyptians between 1950 and 1100 BC and the Nubians from about 750–660 BC, while each ruled over its own area at other times in their 3000-year joint history (Grzymski, 1993; Rice, 1999). After the Pharonic period (including Hyksos, Persian, Assyrian, Greek and Roman domination) came the Christian period from about AD 550–1400 (in Nubia, earlier in Egypt), followed by Islam up to the present day but also including a brief period of colonization by European powers in the 19th century. River-borne tourism has been a feature of these contacts and control, from the inscriptions of Pharoah Pepy II (approximately 2278–2184 BC; von Beckerath, 1997) to the writings of Napoleon (Cole, 2007) and subsequent observers.

Ethiopia, Uganda and the other countries of the Nile River System

The people of the lower Nile Valley also had strong connections with those of the upper valley (Ofcansky and Berry, 1993; Shackley, 1999). East African hunters following the herds of wild cattle formed a distinct ancestral group to the Egyptians and Nubians, and the upper Nile a major migration route from the south. The first-recorded kingdom in Ethiopia grew around Axum after 500 BC and became economically important to Ptolemaic Egypt during the 3rd century BC. Axum was an offshoot of the Semitic Kingdoms of southern Arabia, became a great ivory market and eventually conquered the Nubian Kingdom of Meroe in the 4th century AD. At this time, the country was Christian and it has remained so to the present day despite severe pressure from the Islamic Red Sea area and Turkey. Occupation by Italy and periods of civil war characterized its 19th- and 20th-century history (Ofcansky and Berry, 1993).

The creation and fortunes of Uganda and the other Nile States of sub-Saharan Africa were a different matter (Cohen, 1986). Formed from migrations of cattle owners and small-scale agriculturalists, they did not develop an urban-based literate civilization to the same extent as did Egypt and Nubia. Rwanda, for example, developed from migrations of Hutu and Tutsi cattle breeders, at the apex of which by the 19th century was the 'Mwami' or King as head of a tribal confederation. Shortly thereafter, the 1885 Conference of Berlin declared that the area that later became Rwanda and Burundi would be under German colonial influence and control irrespective of local wishes (Chamberlain, 1999). But it was not until 9 years after this conference that the first European travelled into Rwanda, the German Count Adolf von Götzen, who later became the Governor of German East Africa (1901–1906).

The areas that later became Rwanda and Burundi were in fact located at the juncture of three competing European 19th-century colonial empires and became the object of a diplomatic fight for possession that mirrored the colonial power's wider conflicts (Colville, 1895; Louis, 1963). The Belgians, the Germans and the British all originally wanted possession of these territories. However, by 1910 all had agreed to hand control of Rwanda and Burundi to the Germans. Shortly after this during World War I, the Belgians gained control of the two countries and after the war, on 23 August 1923, the League of Nations mandated Rwanda and Burundi under Belgian supervision. On 27 June 1962, the UN General Assembly voted to terminate this Belgian Trusteeship Agreement, and both attained independence (Lemarchand, 1970).

The earliest human inhabitants of Uganda and the other countries at the headwaters of the Nile were hunter-gatherers. Remnants of these people are today to be found among the pygmies in western Uganda. Between 1500 and 2000 years ago, Bantu-speaking populations from central and western Africa occupied most of the southern parts of the region. These migrants brought with them agriculture, ironworking skills and new ideas of social and political organization that by the 15th or 16th century had resulted in the development of centralized kingdoms, including Buganda, Bunyoro-Kitara and Ankole. Nilotic people, including the Luo and the Ateker, also entered the area from the north from about AD 100. They were also cattle herders and subsistence farmers who settled mainly in the northern and eastern parts of the region (Atkinson, 1994).

When Arab traders moved inland from the Indian Ocean coast of East Africa and reached the area of Uganda in the 1830s, they found several kingdoms with well-developed political institutions. These traders were followed in the 1860s by British explorers searching for the source of the Nile River ('discovered' by John Hanning Speke in 1859). Protestant missionaries entered the country in 1877, followed by Catholic missionaries in 1879. In 1888, control of the emerging British *sphere of interest* in East Africa was assigned by royal charter to the 'Imperial British East Africa Company', an arrangement strengthened in 1890 by an Anglo-German agreement confirming British dominance over Kenya and Uganda (http://open-site.org/Regional/Africa/Uganda/Society_and_Culture). The high cost of occupying the territory caused the company to withdraw in 1893, and its administrative functions were taken over by a British commissioner. In 1894, the Kingdom of Uganda was placed under a formal British protectorate. Britain granted internal self-government to Uganda in 1962, and in succeeding years, supporters of a centralized state vied with those in favour of a loose federation and a strong role for tribally based local kingdoms. This process climaxed in February 1966, when then Prime Minister Obote suspended the constitution and became President. In September 1967, a new constitution proclaimed Uganda a Republic, gave the President greater powers and abolished the traditional kingdoms. Since that time, Uganda has alternately been closed to foreign tourists while in the throes of civil wars, or open as it is at the time of writing, with a growing attractiveness for tourists.

Current Tourism Resources and Their Use

The Blue Nile

Lake Tana, the largest lake in Ethiopia, is the source of the Blue Nile. The 37 islands in the lake support churches and monasteries, some of which have histories dating back to the 13th century AD, bird habitats and wetlands and the castles and palaces of the former Ethiopian Emperors (Beckham and Huntingford, 1954), and the lake also supports sailing and a wide variety of other environmental experiences. The variety of habitats, from rocky crags to riparian forests and important wetlands, ensures that the region is potentially extremely attractive for ecotourism.

The Ethiopian Rift Valley, which is part of the East African Rift Valley, contains the Blue Nile Gorge, a chain of seven lakes and a variety of wildlife. Each of these lakes (including Lake Tana described above) has distinctive habitats for the variety of flora and fauna that make the region an attractive destination for tourists. Most of the lakes are also suitable and safe for swimming and other water sports, but most are not fully exploited for tourist purposes except Lake Langano where tourist class hotels are built. The Rift Valley is also a site of numerous natural hot and mineral springs which are highly valued for their therapeutic purposes. As a result of these attractions, the valley is considered to be an important area for the development of international tourism in Ethiopia (Ofcansky and Berry, 1993). In terms of access, the Blue Nile falls at Tisissat and the scenic beauty of the Blue Nile Gorge, 225 km from Addis Ababa, can be enjoyed as part of an excursion from the capital. Ethiopia received approximately US$77 million per year from around 210,000 tourists in 2002 (see Table 5.1).

The White Nile

In early 2007, an agreement was announced between the Mayor of Jinja in Uganda and Malaysian investors to develop a multi-billion resort at the 'Source of the Nile' (Mukyala, 2007). The resort site is 75 km away from the capital Kampala and 4 km from Jinja town. Entebbe International Airport is 105 km away and the actual source of the Nile in Lake Victoria is only 4 km from the resort. While the new resort is being built the existing Jinja Nile Resort Hotel remains the core of the tourism industry locally and will maintain continuity for rafting, mountain trekking and the other forms of adventure tourism (including game fishing) that have developed in this area based on the river (Tourism Uganda, 2007, http://www.visituganda.com). Uganda earned approximately US$270 million from tourism in 2007 (see Table 5.1).

In the areas of Rwanda, Kenya, Tanzania and Burundi that the river traverses are found the same wildlife safari, mountain trekking (Kilimanjaro, Nyiragongo volcanoes) and Gorilla tours as in Uganda. Some dark tourism (the Kigali Genocide Memorial to Tutsi and Hutu victims of the 1990s civil war) and rafting are also presented to the visitor. The efforts of Rwanda especially to develop new tourism products, including the highly popular *kwita izina* (gorilla naming) ceremonies, can be seen in the statistics: in 2007, tourist arrivals to Rwanda were up by 19% compared to 2006, revenues by 36% to US$35.9 million (The Monitor, 22 March 2008). Burundi earned US$5 million from 36,000 visitors in 2007 (see Table 5.1), while Kenya and Tanzania earned US$688 million and more than US$9.3 million from 1.5 million and 0.5 million visitors, respectively (Table 5.1), although their tourism is not very strongly bound up with the Nile itself.

Along the sections of the river further towards and past Khartoum in the Sudan, cruise boats as well as white-water rafting, kayaking and nature trekking (jungle and savannah tours) can be found. For example, a boat cruise along the Nile at Murchison Falls gives a visitor the opportunity to see a variety of game, hippopotamus and crocodiles as well as the falls themselves. Sudan, however, has been affected by civil war between North and South for 40 years, culminating in the Dafur war. Tourism cannot develop and prosper in this situation; the latest statistics put the number of foreign tourists at 61,000, centred mainly on Khartoum, domestic numbers are unknown (http://data.un.org/CountryProfile.aspx?crName=Sudan).

The Nile in Sudan and Egypt

The confluence of the Blue and White Nile rivers near Khartoum marks the beginning of major river cruise tourism and the cultural sites of antiquity traditionally associated with the river. The Sudanese sites at Gebel Barkal, 400 km north of Khartoum and stretching over more than 60 km in the Nile Valley, are relics of the Napatan (900 to 270 BC) and Meroitic (270 BC to AD 350) cultures, each part of the second kingdom of Kush. Earlier the Pharaoh Thutmosis III of the New Kingdom extended Egyptian control over Nubia to this point in 1450 BC (Lipińska, 2001). The temple ruins, pyramids and palaces together with the hill of Gebel Barkal itself were given World Heritage Listing in 2003 (http://whc.unesco.org/). Other attractions in and near Khartoum include the site of the battle of Omdurman (1898) and the Sudan National Museum, for Dark and Cultural tourism, respectively.

North of the Egyptian border, the volume and nature of river tourism change. The range of experiences, services and methods of access is considerably greater than in Sudan, Ethiopia or sub-Saharan Africa, allowing for many different forms of tourism and attracting nearly 9 million tourists a year (see Table 5.1). The classical (Egyptian antiquities) experience predominates as would be expected, but the Egyptian Tourist Authority actually distinguishes some 15 categories of tourism in the country (Table 5.2). The recent reopening of the Library of Alexandria in 2000 (Sami, 2005), after a delay of some 2000 years, the growth of travel to the 21 nature reserves that have been established since the 1980s – several of which are situated close to Lake Nasser (Aswan High Dam) – and Islamic and Christian monuments along the river are evidence of this diversity.

Table 5.2. Tourism attractions and types of tourism in Egypt. (Modified from Egyptian Tourist Authority, 2008.)

Pharaonic Egypt	Beaches	Diving
Graeco-Roman Egypt	Residential tourism	Safari
Coptic Egypt	Nile cruises	Nature and wildlife
Islamic Egypt	Leisure, fun and shopping (including meeting, incentive, convention and exhibition (MICE) tourism and casinos)	Golf and other sports
Modern Egypt (the art of living)	Wellness tourism	Sea activities

Of these types of tourism, historically the Nile cruise was the only way to visit the temples and tombs of the Pharonic and Graeco-Roman eras located along much of the river, and remains a popular means of visiting upper Egypt, with many advantages over other means of travel. Typical Nile cruises are either three, four or seven nights; the shorter tours usually operate between Luxor and Aswan, while the longer cruises travel further north to Dendera, often offering day tours overland to more remote locations (Egyptian Tourist Authority, 2008). A fairly typical 14-day tour of Egypt might include several days around Cairo (pyramids, museums and other antiquities), a short flight to Abu Simbel in the very southern part of Egypt or train to Luxor, culminating in a 7-day Nile cruise on a floating hotel back to Cairo and/or Alexandria (currently over 225 boats operate on the Nile with a capacity of 12,300 rooms).

A more adventurous style of Nile cruise, very different from the floating hotels, can be taken aboard a 'felucca', Egypt's traditional Nile sailboat. Most of these trips are short, but multi-day felucca cruises can be arranged aboard larger vessels travelling between Aswan and Luxor. The optimum time for a Nile cruise is between October and mid-April, when the weather is fairly cool, and the river-level regulating locks are all open. However, most cruise boats operate all year. If the locks are closed, cruise operators will arrange boats on either side of the locks, and a transfer must be made between boats.

Although river tourism in Egypt and Nubia dates back at least to Herodotus and probably much further, and includes both the Greeks and Romans and Napoleon among its recorded visitors, since about 1980, its growth has progressed at an unprecedented rate. Egypt now accounts for around 25% of the Middle East and North African tourism market, and 33% of North African tourism and travel demand (Business Monitor International (BMI) 2008). Despite some setbacks in 1997 from terror attacks on tourists in Cairo and Luxor, the subsequent Afghanistan and Iraqi conflicts and the bombings in Taba and Sharm el-Sheikh in 2005, the tourism product in Egypt has shown itself to be very resilient, and is predicted to grow even more strongly by 2012 (Table 5.3).

Table 5.3 shows constantly rising capital investment, receipts from tourism and employment since the terrorist incidents in 2005, with visitor numbers also

Table 5.3. Egyptian travel industry 2005–2012. (From Business Management International, WTTC, etc.)

Indicator	2005	2006	2007	2008	2009	2010	2011	2012
Arrivals (million)	8.61	9.01	8.96	10.30	10.79	11.27	11.72	12.19
Capital investment (US$ billion)	2.75	3.16	3.54	3.89	4.21	4.52	4.81	5.13
Receipts (US$ million)	7,210	8,110	8,890	9,423	9,942	10,439	10,910	11,400
Employment ('000)	1,390	1,437	1,505	1,543	1,573	1,598	1,622	1,646

generally increasing. The prediction is that these patterns will continue, resulting in a 40–50% increase in tourism activity from 2005 to 2012. As noted above, virtually 100% of this activity will occur in and around the Nile. Land-based river tourism in Egypt is typically illustrated by the City of Luxor in southern Egypt and the gateway to the Valley of the Kings. The history of Luxor in many ways is also the history of international tourism in Egypt: as the tourist market expanded, so did Luxor. What was once a village has now become a city whose very existence is primarily dependent upon the continued growth in mass tourism (Fig. 5.6).

Luxor is one of Egypt's wealthiest cities; however, it is unlike the rest of Egypt in that there is almost no other industry in the city other than tourism and a large proportion of the population works either directly or indirectly in the local tourism industry. Accommodation and other facilities are mainly situated on the East Bank of the Nile and in an ever-increasing fleet of cruise boats, while the cultural heritage lies on both banks. The most important sites in or near the city are the Karnak Temple complex and the Valley of the Kings (see case study below; Weeks and Hetherington, 2008).

Fig. 5.6. The changing face of Luxor. (From Weeks and Hetherington, 2008, p. 71.)

Case Study: Valley of the Kings, Luxor

Situated on the West Bank of the Nile across from the modern city of Luxor and the ancient city of Karnak (Thebes), the Valley of the Kings is by far the most visited site in the Luxor area. Precise data is not available but it would be reasonable to say that of the tourists visiting cultural heritage attractions in the city, nearly 100% of them visit the Valley of the Kings. It appears on almost all tourist itineraries in Egypt, for both groups and free independent travellers (FIT). The valley attracts approximately 2 million visitors per year, an average of more than 5000 per day. Figure 5.7 shows how these numbers have forced modification of the entrance to the narrow valley; the impact on the tombs is greater and has forced some closures due to visitor-induced humidity and similar effects.

Fig. 5.7. The changing face of tourism in the Valley of the Kings, Egypt, 1910 and 1996.

The Economic, Social and Cultural Impacts of River Tourism

A very sizeable investment in river tourism characterized Egypt's response to the growth of mass tourism in the 20th and 21st centuries. This has been true of both public and private sectors, and millions of dollars are spent annually to encourage and promote tourism. However, until very recently, growth in tourism was thought achievable without imposing any negative effects on Egypt's cultural heritage resource. Tourism was considered a non-consumable industry and was accepted as an essential component of the country's development strategy. In fact, it was regarded as essential to the success of Egypt's economy. However, the country is now aware that this comfortable scenario of little or no impact has turned out not to be true; tourism *does* consume resources of the host nation, not just natural and human-made resources but cultural ones also (Weeks and Hetherington, 2008). Cultural resources are finite and have to be managed like any other scarce resource, and this new reality is one with which the Egyptian authorities are now having to deal. While the goal of previous

Table 5.4. The benefits and costs of tourism. (After ICOMOS, 2000.)

Benefits	Costs	Remedy
Economic value	Degradation of cultural heritage, adverse social changes	Diversify tourism, protect and conserve culture
Sustainable development can be achieved	Neo-colonial nature of tourism reduces this	Facilitate *local* ownership and environmental protection
Cultural heritage protection can be achieved through revenue raising from tourists	Access to sites needs to be controlled	Sell Egypt's cultural importance, not Egypt
Social benefits and cohesion rises as wealth rises	Security situation can worsen if this does not happen	More income at local level is vital
Restoration and conservation can be financed in the same way through revenue raising	Mass tourism impacts on environment	Restrict mass tourism wherever possible in favour of higher income segments
Worldwide profile	Disneyfication	Defend own culture strongly
Employment and skill-up potential	Reliance on tourism not sustainable?	Diversify tourism and other industries to counter any shortfall

administrations with respect to cultural heritage was to maximize revenue by a dual approach of opening more sites to visitors and promoting visits through advertising and high-profile overseas tours of antiquities, this approach has begun to change (see Table 5.4).

Policy changes

The cultural heritage organization, ICOMOS (2000), provides a policy framework that shows the way forward in this situation:

- Comprehensive tourist development plans are essential as the precondition for developing any tourist potential.
- It should be a fundamental principle of any tourist development plan that both conservation in its widest sense and tourism benefit from it. This principle should be part of the constitutional purpose of all national tourist agencies in the Nile region, and of local authority tourism and recreational departments.
- A significant proportion of revenue earned from tourism should be applied for the benefit of conservation, both nationally and regionally.
- The best long-term interests of the people living and working in any host community should be the primary determining factor in selecting options for tourist development.
- Educational programmes should assist and invite tourists to respect and understand the way of life, culture, history and religion of host communities. Tourism policy should take these factors into account.

- The design of new buildings, sites and transport systems should minimize the potentially harmful visual effects of tourism. Pollution controls should be built into all forms of infrastructure. Where sites of great natural beauty are concerned, the intrusion of human-made structures should be avoided if possible.
- Good management should define the level of acceptable tourism development and provide controls to maintain that level.

Social and cultural protection

The reason such a policy direction is needed is that monuments, historic ensembles and cultural landscapes in Egypt are critically endangered. This applies to the sites on UNESCO's World Heritage List such as the Sphinx as well as to the great number of other monuments from Prehistoric, Pharaonic, Christian and Islamic times. Due to an expansion of cities and tourism into the desert and to large-scale irrigation projects, the many witnesses of early history – which very often have been neither documented nor studied – are at risk of being destroyed through water and other encroachments from residential building (ICOMOS, 2000). As noted earlier, the Nile River and its associated tourism have also been subject to increasing tensions within local communities in the Sudan and Egypt over endemic poverty as well as the lack of environmental resources. Sustainable tourism, which can deliver benefits to all groups, is the key to solving the problem of violence towards tourists and protests over the very apparent disparity between tourist luxury and local poverty.

Summary and Conclusions

With a length of 6695 km and a river basin population of some 89 million people distributed across ten countries, the Nile is always going to be significant in the global context. When the facts of its topography, hydrology and human settlement patterns are added into this equation it becomes a world heritage tourism icon. Having been home to one of the earliest major civilizations in history in such a narrow valley has meant also that cultural tourism predominates in its lower reaches, but in the context of river-based tourism almost exclusively. While not of course unique on a global basis, this situation is certainly important for the nature of tourism in the countries affected.

Several iconic forms of tourism can be attributed to the Nile. These range from river cruising to cultural tourism based on antiquities, which happen to be accessible from this major waterway, and are also its greatest legacy apart from the water itself in such a dry environment. In many respects, the other modern tourism attractions and resources have also received a major boost in popularity through association with this river (rafting, trekking and fishing). But, as with most major water sources in these days of climate-change concerns, the Nile is also in danger of becoming a victim of international conflict over the scarcity of water. The potential for conflict over water in this case is undeniable. For example, some 95% of the Egyptian and Sudanese populations are packed on to the fertile ribbon of land along the banks of the Nile and its delta, along with the majority of the approximately 12,000,000 tourists who visit the valley every year, which are their only source of water. In addition, the Blue Nile has long been eyed as a possible source for irrigation, hydroelectricity and general economic growth in Ethiopia, a country whose population is set to boom.

Until very recently, only one agreement had been signed by Egypt and its neighbours – the Nile Waters Agreement of 1959 between Sudan and Egypt, itself based on a deal made by the region's then colonial powers in 1929. Ethiopia and the other riparian states were not even mentioned in this accord, and the case for some more equitable distribution of the river waters has become pressing. In July 2007, after 5 years of preliminary talks, the ten states of the Nile basin signed the NBI to explore how the river's waters can best be shared. It is to be hoped that the needs of river tourism will also be taken into account in any protocols that result.

References

Atkinson, R.R. (1994) *The Roots of Ethnicity: The Origins of the Acholi of Uganda Before 1800*. University of Pennsylvania Press, Philadelphia, Pennsylvania.

Aziz, H. (1995) Understanding attacks on tourists in Egypt. *Tourism Management* 16(2), 91–95.

Barron, M. (2006) *A Fact File About the Nile River*. Available at: http://www.mbarron.net/Nile/

Beckham, C.F. and Huntingford, G.W.B. (1954) *Some Records of Ethiopia, 1593–1646* Series 2, No. 107, Hakluyt Society, London, p. 35 and note.

Business Monitor International (BMI) (2008) *The Egyptian Tourism Report 2008*. BMI, London.

Cerveny, R. and Cerveny, N. (2006) Egypt and water: lifeline of a civilisation. *Weatherwise* 59(6), 20–26.

Chamberlain, M.E. (1999) *The Scramble for Africa*, 2nd edn. Longman, London.

CIA World FactBook (2008) Available at: https://www.cia.gov/library/publications/the-world-factbook/geos/ke.html.

Cohen, D.W. (ed.) (1986) *Towards a Reconstructed Past: Historical Texts from Busoga Uganda*. Oxford University Press, Oxford.

Cole, J. (2007) *Napoleon's Egypt: Invading the Middle East*. Palgrave Macmillan, New York.

Colville, H.E. (1895) *The Land of the Nile Springs, Being Chiefly an Account of How We Fought Kabarega*. Arnold, London.

Denny, P. (1991) Africa. In: Finlayson, M. and Moser, M. (eds) *Wetlands, Facts on File*. International Waterfowl and Wetlands Research Bureau, Oxford, pp. 115–148.

Egyptian Tourist Authority (2008) Tourism attractions and types of tourism in Egypt. Available at: http://www.egypt.travel/

Grzymski, K. (1993) Nubia: rediscovering African kingdoms. *American Visions* 20(6) 42–48.

Hickley, P. and Bailey, R.G. (1987) Food and feeding relationships of fish in the Sudd swamps. *Journal of Fish Biology* 30, 147–160.

ICOMOS (2000) *Restoration, Preservation and Conservation of Egyptian Cultural Heritage*. ICOMOS, Cairo, pp. 99–108.

Kingdon, J. (1997) *The Kingdon Field Guide to African Mammals*. Academic Press, London.

Lemarchand, R. (1970) *Rwanda and Burundi*. Pall Mall Press, London.

Lipińska, J. (2001) Thutmose III. In: Redford, D. (ed.) *The Oxford Encyclopedia of Ancient*

Egypt. Oxford University Press, Oxford, pp. 401–403.

Lloyd, A.B. (2002) Egypt. In: Bakker, E., de Jong, I. and van Wees, H. (eds) *Brill's Companion to Herodotus*, Leiden, The Netherlands, pp. 415–436.

Louis, W.R. (1963) *Ruanda-Urundi 1884–1919*. Clarendon Press, Oxford.

Marshall, M.H., Lambla, H.F., Bates, C.R., Coombes, P.V.C., Davies, S.J., Umer, M. and Dejen, E. (2006) *Late Pleistocene and Holocene Environmental and Climatic Change from Lake Tana, Source of the Blue Nile*, Institute of Geography and Earth Sciences, University of Wales Aberystwyth, Aberystwyth, UK.

Mukyala, E. (2007) Uganda: source of Nile to get mega hotel. Available at: http://allafrica.com/stories/200708100070.htm

Nile Basin Initiative (2008) Available at: http://www.nilebasin.org/.

Ofcansky, T.P. and Berry, L. (eds) (1993) *Ethiopia: A Country Study*. Federal Research Division, Library of Congress, Washington, DC.

Petersen, G., Abya, J.A. and Fohrer, N. (2007) Spatio-temporal water body and vegetation changes in the Nile swamps of Southern Sudan. *Advanced Geoscience* 11, 113–116.

Rasmussen, W. (2007) *Egypt Plan to Green Sahara Stirs Controversy*, PlanetArk, Reuters, Cairo.

Rice, M. (1999) *Who's Who in Ancient Egypt*. Routledge, London.

Rossi, C. (2007) Oases: explorers and travelers. Available at: www.egyptvoyager.com

Sami, N. (2005) The antiquities museum in the Alexandrine library. Available at: http://touregypt.net/featurestories/alexmuseum.htm

Shackley, M. (1999) Tourism development and environmental protection in Southern Sinai, *Tourism Management* 20, 543–548.

Shahin, M. (2002) *Hydrology and Water Resources of Africa*. Springer, New York.

Stanley, J-D., Krom, M.D., Cliff, R.A. and Woodward, J.C. (2003) Short contribution: Nile flow failure at the end of the Old Kingdom, Egypt: Strontium Isotopic and Petrologic evidence. *Geoarchaeology* 18(3), 395–402.

Stanley, H.M. (1890) *In Darkest Africa* (Vols 1 & 2). Narrative Press, New York.

Steindorff, G. and Seele, K. (1957) *When Egypt Ruled the East,* 2nd edn. University of Chicago, Chicago, Illinois.

The Monitor (2008) *Uganda: Confused, As Rwanda Shines Again* Opinion Piece, 22 March, The Monitor, Kampala, uploaded 24 March.

Tourism Uganda (2007) Latest news. Available at: http://www.visituganda.com

UNdata (2008) Available at: http://data.un.org/CountryProfile.aspx?

UNEP (2001) Biodiversity and climate change: ecosystems. Available at: http://www.unep-wcmc.org/climate/impacts.htm

von Beckerath, J. (1997) Munchen: Chronologie des Pharaonischen Agypten, Verlag Philipp von Zabern.

Weeks, K. and Hetherington, N. (2008) The Valley of the Kings site management masterplan, *Theban Mapping Project* (TMP). Available at: http://www.thebanmappingproject.com/

World Tourism Organization (2007) UNWTO World Tourism Barometer. UNWTO, Madrid.

Additional Internet Resources available at:

www.2travel2egypt.com

www.egyptresidential.com

http://www.13suns.com/bnile.htm

http://data.un.org/CountryProfile.aspx?crName=Sudan

http://open-site.org/Regional/Africa/Uganda/Society_and_Culture

http://whc.unesco.org/en/list/1073

www.iipt.org/conference/africanconference2003/

6 European Waterways as a Source of Leisure and Recreation

P. Erfurt-Cooper

James Cook University, Cairns, Australia and Ritsumeikan Asia Pacific University, Beppu, Japan

Introduction

Recent interest in travel along European waterways has revived a form of passenger transport that predates the Roman occupation of much of Europe almost two millennia ago (Steinbach, 1995; Baranowski and Furlough, 2001). Europe's waterways have a long history of having been utilized to transport freight and travellers from one settlement or country to another (Davies, 1998). Europe's geography provides an extensive network of natural waterways which, over time, have been connected by numerous canals. A number of European countries including France built many short canals to connect rivers while other countries including Germany focused on large canal developments to connect their waterways. These extensive canal networks now support growing river tourism activity throughout Europe, particularly in the long-distance segment (Roberts and Simpson, 1999). Currently, the main focus of river tourism development is on cruises of the major river systems with an emphasis on central Europe (Ely, 2003). Elsewhere in Europe cruising can be found in most areas where there are suitable waterways and development in these areas includes cruises on rivers, canals and lakes. River tourism can be land-based as well as water-based. This chapter will use examples from a variety of European waterways and their immediate surrounds to present an overview of activities that are both water- and land-based and which collectively constitute Europe's river tourism sector.

In many European cities, river banks are a preferred location for hotels and restaurants primarily because river settings attract customers by providing them with an interesting view and creating a relaxing setting for dining, accommodation and other activities. Recreational parks and golf courses also make use of local streams where these are available to increase their attractiveness and profitability. Over the last few decades, waterways have become more prominent as sites for recreation and leisure activities. This in turn has resulted in an increased interest in taking time to explore rivers and their surrounding areas, even if it is only for a short activity such as a sunset sailing, dinner cruise or walking along the banks. In many areas, parks and open spaces beside the waterfront are being redeveloped to encourage heritage, nature-based and eco-tourism activity. There has also been a renewed interest in encouraging water-front festivals, markets and water-based recreation as activities that are able to generate extra income for local communities. However, despite the apparently beneficial economic effects of river tourism in terms of job creation, infrastruc-ture provision and stimulation of local businesses, there continues to be a lack of statistical data than can be used to estimate the net economic contribution of river tourism activity. Because of this gap in data the current estimates of the contribution of river tourism are vague and fail to provide a reliable data set that can be used for comparison and analysis.

European Rivers in History

European history is closely linked to the rivers that include the Rhine, the Danube, the Loire, the Thames, the Volga and many others (Fig. 6.1; Jones, 2003). Settlements were established on or near waterways to transport goods and people and to maintain contact with other communities. Rivers were also important transport routes for troops in times of war, a recurrent theme in European history. The Romans for example used the Rhine and the Danube to move troops and supplies allowing them to maintain dominance over the terri-tories they controlled. They also built military bases along river banks and at river junctions (*Encyclopaedia Britannica* – Danube, 2008) as a strategy for dominating hinterland regions.

The Rhine is a classical example of the range of influences that rivers exert on the areas through which they flow; it has provided a gateway for the spread of cultural influence and commerce as well as providing a political boundary (*Encyclopaedia Britannica* – Rhine, 2008) within Europe. In a forerunner to river tourism, the 'Grand Tour' or 'Tour d'Europe' that became an educational rite of passage for the sons of the British and later European elites included sailing on the Rhine and French and Italian rivers (Kernohan, 2006). Rivers such as the Rhine with its panorama of numerous castles and impressive medi-aeval architecture, and a vista that according to Marx (2004) is inspirational as well as educational, have also inspired generations of artists and writers.

The most popular region along the Rhine according to the German National Tourist Board is the Middle Rhine and the Rhine Valley between Mainz and Bonn. The Upper Middle Rhine Valley is a UNESCO World Heritage Site that has many magnificent castles and is regarded as one of the most beautiful destinations in Europe. The famous composer Richard Wagner was inspired by the melodramatic panorama and the Emperor Wilhelm built a number of archi-tectural monuments along the river. The region, which includes the Rhine, Moselle, Lahn and Nahe rivers, is also well known for its mythology and leg-ends which inspired the *Rhine Legends Route*; a themed tourist route that is 586 km in length (German National Tourist Board, 2008). Centuries of warfare for control of the Rhine and bordering countries culminated in mass destruction

Fig. 6.1. Overview of the major rivers of the European continent. (From European Rivers, n.d.)

during World War II, when bombed bridges, trains and ships caused extensive flooding as their remnants blocked the river. In the decades following World War II, the ages old struggle for possession of the Rhine had been superseded by a drive for economic and even political union of the rival countries (Rhine River, 2008).

The river Danube has a similar history of being used for trade, transport and as a political boundary. Forming the northern boundary of the Roman Empire, the Roman fleet patrolled the river and its associated waterways from strategic riverside military bases ensuring dominance of the immediate hinterland regions (*Encyclopaedia Britannica* – Danube, 2008). The Danube has maintained a position of economic importance as a waterway throughout history. As was the case with the Rhine, control of the Danube and its hinterland had strategic value and this area has changed hands a number of times after the region was abandoned by the Romans (Danube River Cruising, n.d.).

In Poland, the river Vistula played an important role in north European history with the region's economic development commencing in the early Stone Age when the river served as a trade route. Since those times, it has maintained its role as a conduit for trade, and supported the movement of peoples and cultures, including the Romans, within the regions through which it flows (*Encyclopaedia Britannica* – Vistula, 2008). In Russia, the Volga River has played a central part in the development of Russian social, economic, political and cultural life from early times. The Volga system is extensive, draining an area of about 1.35 million square kilometres and has many tributaries, the most important of which are the Kama, Oka, Vetluga and Sura. The river system supports extensive rural areas and the basin is the most heavily populated part of Russia. The river provides access to many of Russia's most unique architectural and cultural heritage sites which collectively reflect the history of the nation's political, economic and cultural development. Both Moscow and St Petersburg are built adjacent to the river. In addition, the many river-located sites connected with the 'Golden Ring', one of Russia's oldest trade routes, provide cruise passengers with opportunities to visit a large number of heritage sites. Many of the overnight cruises along the river include educational programmes that feature lectures by on-board experts about history, culture and economy (Travel Signposts, 2006).

River Cruises on the Saône and Rhône rivers in France take their travellers past some of the most beautiful vineyards and landscapes in the French countryside. The famous wine region of Burgundy and the lavender fields of the Provence have inspired artists of the stature of Van Gogh and Cézanne. For the French, this area is perhaps the leading culinary region of the country and the river provides access to Roman amphitheatres, Gallo-Roman ruins, famous bridges and palaces, shopping and gastronomic experiences (Travel Signposts, 2006).

Dutch and Belgian rivers and canals also have a long history of connecting communities, as well as transporting goods and services between their countries. Today, the rivers and canals are used as a network for cruise boat holidays and barging with the most popular time being spring when the world renowned tulip fields come into flower along the rivers and canals. Cruising companies promote Dutch and Flemish history including the scenes painted by van Gogh and Rembrandt as well as museums, medieval townships, windmills and the scenic backdrop of the countryside (Travel Signposts, 2006).

The environmental problem

A rather dark part of European river history centres around the abuse of rivers by factories, agriculture and urban areas (UNEP, 2000). In the past, rivers have been used as a giant waste water disposal facility, where chemical factories pumped toxic waste into waterways, pesticide and herbicide residues washed off adjoining plantations and fields, and municipalities pumped their untreated sewerage. The most harmful freshwater pollutants include nitrate, pesticides, heavy metals and hydrocarbons. Consequences of this form of pollution include eutrophication of surface waters and harmful effects on human health. In some areas, overuse of river water has resulted in the lowering of the water table causing salt water intrusion into groundwater, particularly in coastal regions

(Szabolcs, 1991; UNEP/ISRIC, 1991). In a number of areas environmental pollution finally reached the point when people realized that rivers were dying as demonstrated in the following case study based on the author's personal experiences.

Case Study

In the early 1970s, a sign on the banks of the river Elbe near Hitzacker in Germany warned that contact with river water could cause skin irritation (personal observation). This sign was posted on a sandy beach adjacent to where people were water skiing and children were wading in the shallow water. At the time, advice had already been given that recreational fishing could lead to health problems. Other activities such as week-end boating, sailing and swimming were however not actively discouraged. The reason for the deterioration of this waterway originated upstream, where heavy industry was not required to introduce environmental best practice management and allowed to pump untreated waste directly into the river (Erfurt-Cooper, 1973, personal observation). For many years, most European rivers suffered a similar fate with the rivers Rhine, Main and Wupper described as open sewers that even changed in colour (Walgate, 1986). Water wells along the river Rhine had to be shut down because of high pollution levels. The only tourist activity undertaken on the Rhine at that time was wine and dinner cruises. Eventually, growing public concern forced the German Government to develop a series of strategies designed to clean up the nation's river systems (Francesch, 2002).

Other countries faced similar problems with their waterways. The river Thames in England is a classic example of a heavily polluted waterway that was restored through vigorous government action and is now acknowledged as being one of the cleanest metropolitan rivers in the world. The success of the clean-up process can be measured by the fact that salmon fishing is again possible (Andrews, 1984). In Europe, some of the worst affected rivers were those flowing through more than one country. However, the level of public concern has been such that intergovernmental strategies have become possible and have resulted in remediation efforts that in the last two decades have produced positive improvements in water quality of many European rivers (see, e.g. International Commission for the Protection of the Rhine (ICPR), 2008). The success of these strategies has had a positive impact on river tourism reflected in the increasing numbers of visitors who now participate in a range of activities in fluvial settings including visiting wetlands and other river-related ecosystems as well as visiting land-based attractions. Another significant benefit of the recovery of Europe's rivers has been an upsurge in interest in boating and fishing.

River Tourism: What Is the Attraction?

The main feature of river tourism is water, one of the most popular natural settings for rest and recreation. Even short periods near water are claimed to have a beneficial soothing effect on most people (Frazier, 2000). This observation explains why tourist destinations promote water features in various forms including rivers, lakes, waterfalls, hot springs and beaches. If water is not available in a natural state, manmade landscaping includes fountains, ponds, swimming pools and artificial waterfalls are created to appeal to the tourist. The potential attractiveness of rivers is even greater, a consequence of changing scenery and the potential for natural and urban settings along their riverbanks (see Fig. 6.2).

Safety on the water away from the activity of large cities is another drawcard of river and canal cruises. A view from the river is often preferred to finding one's way through unfamiliar streets by car or on foot. A further benefit is the general absence of seasickness because of the sedate nature of the flow of most rivers and canals. For many river tourists, this is an important factor particularity if they are affected by wave motion.

River cruises offer a range of unique experiences while travelling in a relaxing manner that is different from other forms of travel. River cruises offer opportunities for passengers to view exceptional scenery, experience local culture and visit a range of heritage sites that in Europe often include historic monuments, old castles and quaint little villages. In addition, most cruises offer opportunities for passengers to undertake shore excursions which facilitate engagement with the communities, shopping, sightseeing and experience local cuisine. According to Köln Tourismus GmbH (2008), a cruise on the river Rhine is a must for every visitor to the region. Rhine cruises have an iconic status and are included in the itineraries of most tours operated by coach tour operators in the region and beyond.

Local wine and cuisine offer excellent opportunities for interacting with local communities as well as with fellow passengers and contribute to a greater understanding and appreciation of other cultures. Many cruise operators offer a range of themes on their cruises including gastronomy, heritage, nature,

Fig. 6.2. Cruise ship on the Danube on its way to the Black Sea taking in the sights of Budapest. (Photograph courtesy of P.J. Erfurt-Cooper.)

wilderness and adventure. Most cruise tours involve both land- and water-based programmes. For many cruise participants the ability to participate in a wide range of activities is a major selling point. Exploring waterways and adjacent nature corridors also offers a wide range of water-based outdoor activities and recreation. For many urban residents this may represent the closest thing to a 'wilderness' experience they may have the opportunity to participate in (Robertson and Burge, 1993). River tourism is a lucrative trade with the potential of making a major contribution to the local economies through employment on cruise ships, pleasure boats, and parks and recreational facilities along the riverbanks (Shakiry, 2007) and in the numerous services that support the industry.

River Tourism Activities

River-oriented tourism activities are based on waterways as well as on the tourism opportunities offered by the surrounding landscape including built and natural features. In recent years, as interest in river cruising has grown, significant investment has been made in boats and onshore infrastructure resulting in a suite of experiences that are attractive to a range of market sectors including younger generations and families (Steinbach, 1995). With the growing interest in this form of tourism has come recognition that additional policies are required to protect remaining natural and built heritage sites and on a broader scale the landscapes in which they are located. In a number of regions, ecotourism activities have been incorporated into river cruise programmes. Ecotourism experience defined by Newsome *et al.* (2002, p. 15) as being activities 'based on the natural environment with a focus on its biological, physical and cultural features' have facilitated further interest in preservation of remaining natural areas. Previous research into the tourism use of fluvial landforms focused primarily on large European rivers including the Danube and the Rhine with specific consideration of their ecotourism aspects as well as social carrying capacity (Steinbach, 1995; Roberts and Simpson, 1999; Baranowski and Furlough, 2001). However, current research has recognized that river tourism now embraces a wider scope of activities and settings and includes any waterway that is accessible and includes both the river and the adjacent shore's natural and cultural environments.

Leisure and recreation by the riverside

Bike tourism on designated bike paths along rivers is very popular in Germany, as well as in other parts of Europe. The slow pace of travel, matched only by the slow pace of the ships on the rivers and canals, offers participants a relaxing view often within a natural setting and importantly, away from heavy vehicle traffic. Safe for children who accompany their parents, this form of river tourism activity offers a combination of water and land experiences with the benefits of both available through boat tours that allow passengers to take their bikes on board. There are many examples of bike-hiking ('radwandern') or river-biking areas throughout Germany. One example, the Flussradroute which extends for 195 km along the Fulda River, follows the river from its source in the Rhön Mountains to Hannoversch-Münden where the rivers Werra and Fulda join to create the river Weser. A further long-distance (450–500 km) river-biking trail has been established along the banks of the Weser (Allgemeiner Deutscher Fahrrad-Club, 1996). Along the Fulda, built and natural attractions have been used to create a thematic touring route that includes a range of land-scapes ranging from river valleys to mountains.

The region in the vicinity of the former border between East and West Germany including the river Elbe is being rehabilitated with an emphasis placed on leisure and recreation activities, a striking contrast to the political division and industrial pollution that previously predominated. River-biking has become a popular method of visiting old country towns and participating in local cultural and culinary offerings. The region's industrial history has also been developed as a tourist attraction and a number of canal locks have built museums (e.g. Schiffshebewerk Scharnebeck) and viewing platforms (Fig. 6.3). In some areas, reunification celebrations are held on the riverbank and have become significant tourism attractions (Hummel, 1999).

Fig. 6.3. The big ship lock at Scharnebeck offers visitors a maritime museum which contains models of a range of ship locks, displays recounting the history of region and viewing platforms to observe the raising and lowering of barges the 38 m between the Elbe and Seiten rivers. (Photographs courtesy of P.J. Erfurt-Cooper.)

River-based ecology is also of special interest for ecotourists and geotourists. Seasonally flooded wetlands along many rivers dominate the landscape and offer rare flora and fauna, and many have been designated as protected natural areas (Tiefenbach, 1998). One site of particular importance is the wetlands of the Danube Delta located near the mouth of the river on the Black Sea. This area contains one of Europe's last remaining wetlands that have been spared from intensive development (Danube Watch, 2007; Romanian Tourist Office, 2008).

River cruises

In recent years, there has been growing interest in river cruising in Europe. Between 1996 and 2003, the numbers of river cruise passengers in Germany increased by 168% according to figures from the German Travel Association (Deutscher Reiseverband, 2006; Table 6.1). By 2007, passenger numbers had grown to 334,000 per annum, growth that has been attributed to investment in new cruise boats, the success of marketing strategies and a possible substitution factor where there has been a transport mode substitution effect from trains, airlines and the private car to cruising.

One of the reasons for the growth of river cruise fans according to Reiter (2004) is that river cruising allows participants to 'halve the speed and double your perception and awareness'. This awareness is increasing and is reflected in rising passenger numbers, a growing number of whom are summer visitors from the USA. Most European countries offer river cruises in various forms (Table 6.2). Combined, Europe's major river systems offer nearly 16,000 km of waterways as illustrated in Table 6.3.

Large cruise companies offer individually themed cruises that include the different seasons (the main cruising season extends from the end of March until end of October), and cultural or educational themes such as UNESCO World Heritage Sites (Elbe, 2008). To take full advantage of the smaller waterways, barges and cruise boats have been downsized and while offering fewer cabins

Table 6.1. Growth patterns in the German river cruise market between 2002 and 2007. (From Deutscher Reiseverband, 2006.)

Germany	Numbers of passengers	Passenger increase to previous year (%)	Revenue (million €)	Increase of revenue to previous year (%)	Travel time
2002	221,000	2.2	–	–	–
2003	274,792	19.5	313.9	24.0	–
2004	306,516	11.5	355.6	13.3	8.08 days
2005	325,634	6.2	370.4	4.1	8.06 days
2006	310,655	4.6 (down)	364.4	1.6 (down)	7.64 days
2007	334,280	7.6	394.5	8.3	7.76 days

Table 6.2. List of countries that actively participate in river tourism activities.

European countries with river tourism activities			
Austria	France	Italy	Russia
Belgium	Germany	Liechtenstein	Scotland
Croatia	Holland	Norway	Serbia
Czech Republic	Hungary	Poland	Spain
England	Iceland	Portugal	Sweden
Finland	Ireland	Romania	Switzerland

Table 6.3. Major European rivers in order of length.

River	Length (km)	Country
Volga	3700	Russia
Danube	2888	Nineteen countries share the Danube River Basin
Rhine	1319	Germany
Elbe	1165	Germany
Vistula	1086	Poland
Loire	1020	France
Tagus	1007	Spain
Oder	912	Germany
Rhone	813	France
Seine	776	France
Po	652	Italy
Thames	338	England
Laxá	58	Iceland

and having a less impressive appearance compared to the larger cruise ships, are able to offer more rustic charm and comfort, even if the on-board entertainment is less flamboyant (Reiserat, n.d.).

River and canal barging

Barges are flat-bottomed vessels designed to navigate shallow rivers and canals and have historically been used for the transportation of cargo. Over the last few decades many have been renovated and refurbished to convert them into floating accommodation. Many barges, some of which may be up to 100 years old, now feature air conditioning, modern cabins, tasteful décor, fine dining including regional specialities, and are able to offer guests a luxurious haven and a quiet and slow-moving form of travelling. According to Levin (2007) barges glide along Europe's waterways offering picture-book landscapes dotted with castles in the distance, quaint historic villages and awe-inspiring natural scenery.

Barging holidays are attracting increasing interest in many parts of Europe including France, which has a reputation as one of the best places in the world to cruise on canals and rivers. Most barges also carry bicycles on board and offer guests the option of shore excursions to explore the surrounding towns and villages. In England, Barge tours offer many quiet areas of countryside where it is possible to ride bikes, walk along the towpath and assist the lock keeper. Most barges have a library and some offer a sauna or a hot tub for extra comfort and entertainment.

Tour companies have been offering barge cruises for several decades and their barges can be found from the Caledonian Canal in Scotland to the south of France, as well as in Italy, Germany, Ireland, England, Holland, Belgium and the Czech Republic. More countries are being added due to demand. Research (Levin, 2007) indicates that barge passengers are generally well-educated, well-travelled and primarily over 50 years of age. Approximately 80% of passengers on European canal boat tours are from the USA with the remaining 20% from the UK and Europe (Levin, 2007).

Combination of river and land activities

River cruises can offer a style of luxury similar to that found on large ocean cruise ships including swimming pools, saunas, fitness centres, spas, hair and beauty salons, library and media rooms. Larger river cruise ships may also offer seminars and presentations as well as cultural entertainment. Some cruise operators offer a combination where passengers can use bicycles or canoes for part of the trip. The German term 'bootwandern' refers to sharing the mode of travel between a boat and hiking or cycling, allowing the passenger to stay on board during the night. The same principle works for bicycles and canoes (see Fig. 6.4).

Fig. 6.4. Canoeing and kayaking is an integrated part of the Bootwandern. (Photograph courtesy of Bootwandern, n.d.)

River tourism including interaction of the land–water interface can also extend to smaller streams or tributaries. This type of travelling is also popular in conjunction with house boats on quiet river sections where traffic volumes are lower. Although the main aspect of river tourism is related to the aquatic environment, other forms of tourism including events may be incorporated into programmes to increase appeal. Conference visits and cultural festivals at the destination or functions such as seminars and presentations on board are examples of the extended range of activities available to river cruise tourists. Aspects of wellness tourism are also offered by the larger cruise companies in the form of first-class facilities and qualified staff.

Many European countries have recognized the importance of waterways and have invested in a range of facilities including providing various forms of entertainment and activity on the river banks (Shakiry, 2007). Adventure tourism, cultural tourism and geotourism can be both land- and water-based and incorporated in the river cruise programme. They may be in the form of visits to national parks and geoparks or to interesting cultural and historical locations. Activities such as mountain climbing and white-water rafting may also be offered as optional activities.

River exploration

There are many ways visitors can utilize a waterway and its land interface. One of the main attractions is having access to landscapes that are otherwise not accessible. Viewing the natural environment from a slow-moving cruise boat and observing wildlife may create a sense of discovery. Observing otherwise inaccessible parts of the fluvial environment can be both exciting and educational. Tour guides are able to provide interpretation of landscape features, wildlife and vegetation, usually in several languages. River cruises vary greatly in length, and can last from a few hours, an afternoon, a whole day or many days. River cruises are often combined with other modes of transport to optimize the travel experience. For example, a day trip to the Alto Douro Wine Region in Portugal leaves the city of Porto in the morning by train, reaching the inland destination (e.g. Regua) after several hours. Waiting cruise boats then take visitors down the river Douro (see Fig. 6.5) taking them back to Porto by the late afternoon. This river cruise includes passing through several ship locks, as well as offering an insight into the rural architecture, the changing landscapes and finally a view of Porto from the river Douro. Since the 18th century the main product of the Porto region has been port wine, which is world famous for its quality (UNESCO World Heritage Centre, 2008). The fact that both the city of Porto and the Alto Douro Wine Region are World Heritage listed creates additional interest for river tourists.

Many European cities feature short river or canal cruises because they present a genuine experience of the destination and offer exploration at a slow speed. Examples for short cruises or boat tours on rivers and canals are found in Trondheim in Norway (see Fig. 6.6) and Malmo in Sweden. Both cities have a river or canal running through parts of the main urban area and offer tourists a few hours of cruising through areas otherwise not readily accessible.

Fig. 6.5. The Alto Douro wine region from a cruise boat on the river Douro. The traffic runs at a leisurely pace and most of the time no other boats or ships are in view. (Photograph courtesy of P.J. Erfurt-Cooper.)

Fig. 6.6. Boat cruises on Trondheim's waterways include the Nidelva river, harbour channels and the Trondheim Fjord. The boat tours depend on the tidal waterlevel to fit underneath the many narrow bridges. (Photograph courtesy of P.J. Erfurt-Cooper.)

Trondheim is also fortunate in having access to the Trondheim Fjord, an interesting addition to a boat cruise which includes a visit to the island Munkeholmen, tide and weather permitting.

Norway is rich in unusual waterways and although fjords are technically not rivers they are mentioned here as an example for a unique aquatic environment for water-based tourism. Fjords are deep channels carved by glaciers over time and are surrounded by high mountain ranges and many feature spectacular waterfalls. Their pristine beauty has been a drawcard for travellers ever since the first modern tourists arrived in Norway over 200 years ago. The fjords of Norway were UNESCO World Heritage listed in the year 2004 and were named by the National Geographic Traveller Magazine as 'the best unspoiled travel destination in the world' (Fjord Norway, 2007). Fjord waters are generally calm and allow for a wide range of water-based activities such as sailing, canoeing, kayaking and swimming with the added benefit of staying mostly ice-free during winter, which makes them popular cruise ship destinations in Scandinavia. In the south-east of Norway, canals and rivers link four large lakes and offer cultural history combined with opportunities for exploring the waterways. The 105 km long Telemark canal (Telemarkskanalen) with a total of 28 lock chambers has been a tourist attraction since it was built in the year 1892 and can be toured with nostalgic canal boats just as the first tourists did over hundred years ago (Kumpch, 2007; Skien Norway Directory, 2008).

While Icelandic rivers are generally too unpredictable for river cruising, salmon (lax) and trout fishing are popular although expensive. The Laxá river flows from Lake Myvatn in three channels through the Laxárdalur valley and the Adaldalur valley, with quiet pools alternating with fast currents cascading over rocks. Apart from salmon and trout fishing, which is strictly controlled, the river is home to many varieties of ducks and is the most fertile stream in Iceland due to algae (which provide the basis of the food chain) carried from lake Myvatn. The fishing season is very short, beginning on 1 June and ending on 31 August, with fly-fishing allowed only where tour guides are available. The area surrounding the rivers Laxa and Myvatnsveit are protected and is popular with birdwatchers, many of whom are international visitors (Umhverfisstofnun, 2002; Iceland Complete, 2005).

River development examples

Since 2005, the river Limmat in Zürich (Switzerland) has been involved in a staged process of being made more accessible as a landscape experience for leisure and recreation, including opportunities for walking, biking, swimming and relaxing in the park. Sport facilities, gardens and playgrounds will be connected to a network of walking trails and bike paths and linked to tourist accommodation (Stadt Zürich, n.d.). Commercial activites include restaurants and special events. The quality of the recreational areas along the Limmat is further improved by strategies to reduce the noise level from the nearby motorway (Leisi, 2000).

France has a long history of August summer vacations and many Parisians leave for holidays in the country or at coastal resorts. To entice tourists to visit the city, the local government has constructed river beaches on the banks of the Seine. Other European cities have undertaken similar projects (Shakiry, 2007).

Canal Tourism in Europe

Canals are described in the German Maritime Dictionary (Maritimes Lexikon, 2008) as an artificial, navigable waterway, which connects oceans, rivers and

lakes. To build a canal is an ambitious project and involves considerable planning and development, although this did not stop canal development in the
past. The first canals were built in Mesopotamia (now Iraq) and in Egypt as
drainage channels for agricultural purposes. Approximately 3500 years ago, a
bold project was initiated: the connection of the Mediterranean Sea to the Red
Sea to reduce the long travel time around the Horn of Africa. In China, the
Emperor or Grand Canal is said to have taken 1775 years to build (between
485 BC and AD 1290, but more correctly it took this long to join pre-existing
sections into one canal). While continuing to be used for moving cargo, this
canal has recently become a significant tourism attraction.

In Germany, King Ludwig I of Bavaria used his patriotic enthusiasm to
plan a canal that was to unite all the smaller German States (Heidenreich,
2007; Österreich-Lexikon, n.d.). The first section (173 km long) was built
between 1836 and 1845 (Maritimes Lexikon, 2008) and was the forerunner
of the Rhine–Main–Danube Canal. In 1992, the river Rhine and Danube were
finally connected, providing unrestricted travel on a transcontinental route for
boats and ships from the North Sea to the Black Sea near Odessa in the
Ukraine (Rhine River, 2008).

About 100 years ago, the unique French network of waterways measured
over 12,000 km in length and was acclaimed internationaly as an example of
effective canal development. Competition from rail and road reduced the
demand for canals and much of the network fell into disrepair. Presently, there
are about 8,500 km of navigable waterways (canals and rivers combined)
remaining in France (Mc Knight, 1999). In recent times, however, there has
been a revival in interest in waterways, spured by their appeal as a tourism
resource (Simon, 2006).

France is not the only country with an extensive canal network that is now
being used for cruising and other river based recreation. In Holland, the network of drainage channels ('grachten') which were originally constructed to
control water levels and for defence purposes, as well as to transport goods and
people (see Fig. 6.7), have become popular sites for cruising. Amsterdam is
reputed to have been built on drained wetlands (Dam in een watering gebied)
which the Dutch then renamed as Aeme Stelle Redamme (Amsterdam Info,
2008). From a marshy fishing village at the end of the Amstel River, Amsterdam
developed a distinct character through deliberate planning and development of
land below sea level (Boucher, 2007). More canals were added while the city
was growing and the grachten now constitutes about a quarter of the city's
area. Over time the city's extensive network of canals increased to about
100 km in length and is spanned by more than 400 bridges. Amsterdam is
sometimes called the Venice of the North with a historic centre that has retained
its character and is a unique tourist attraction.

In Amsterdam alone approximately 15,000 pleasure craft are registered,
and during summer, boats and yachts from Holland and Germany use the
grachten as a holiday destination. Waterfront tourism includes large events such
as Koninginnedag (Day of the Queen) and parades, with over 3 million passengers per year cruising through the grachten in one of the 200 strong fleet of
'rondvaartboten' (cruise boats). Cruise themes include romantic dinners by can-
dlelight with five-star service on antique saloon boats, theatre cruises, disco

Fig. 6.7. A small canal in Leiden in Holland which attracts people to sit in the cafés alongside the water under the trees. (Photograph courtesy of P.J. Erfurt-Cooper.)

cruises, live music and party cruises. Tourists who want to explore the grachten on their own have the option of hiring a hydro-bike ('waterfiets'), which looks like a boat-mounted bicycle and is an ideal way to explore the canal network.

During the industrial revolution more than two centuries ago, Britain developed an inland waterway network to link industrial areas with markets and deepwater ports. Large parts of this canal network remain and about 3540 km of the network is now owned and maintained by 'British Waterways', a publicly owned organization that has been given the responsibility of providing a waterway network able to offer a wide range of recreational activities that increase social, economic, environmental and heritage opportunities for the community (Fig. 6.8; British Waterways, n.d.).

Waterway associations and canal recovery groups have campaigned successfully for the restoration and the upkeep of the British canal system due in part to their attractiveness as a tourism attraction. To encourage use of the system waterway guides have been devloped that assist in the selection of canal sections based on a range of qualities that include: scenery, peaceful or hustle and bustle, number of locks, historic cities, interesting villages, canal features, industrial history, pubs and literary connections (Inland Waterways Association (IWA), 2006). The list of points of interest is extensive and includes:

- 2555 heritage listed buildings and structures;
- 69 scheduled monuments;
- 4763 bridges;
- 397 aqueducts;
- 1549 locks;
- 1036 lock cottages and dwellings; and
- 60 tunnels.

Fig. 6.8. The Caledonian Canal at the ship lock at Fort Augustus. The canal is nearly 100 km long and connects the Beauly Firth on the Scottish east coast with Loch Linhe on the west coast. Along the canal the lock gates draw a crowd watching the slow process of the raising and lowering of the boats. (Photograph courtesy of P.J. Erfurt-Cooper.)

Every country in Europe has produced guide books on canal travel and navigation. Most guidebooks for inland boating and cruising contain descriptions of particular canals as leisure and recreational zones as well as providing essential nautical facts, maps, technical data including measurements of the canal, height and size of the ship locks, height and clearance of bridges, harbour and mooring information, and other basic services that are necessary for safe boat travel (Frenzl, 2006).

Potential Threats to River and Canal Tourism

As a natural environment, a river can be subjected to a range of negative impacts caused by human actions including overdevelopment, overcrowding, pollution, lack of regulation and disturbance of natural wildlife (Newsome *et al.*, 2002). The sustainability of river and canal tourism in part depends on preventing mass tourism or 'recreational overcrowding', as development of this nature may lead to congestion in a setting where participants are seeking to escape from the crowds. From this perspective, the issue is not one of 'carrying capacity' of a river or canal, but more of what current users are able to tolerate.

Pressure on the health of a river can arise from natural processes and human activities that include increased storm runoff from cleared catchments. Runoff of this nature causes erosion of sediments of the river banks and deposition of these sediments in the stream bed, with the potential to create siltation and the eventual choking of a river channel. This erosive stress is greatly accelerated through settlement (Ziebell, 1999) when riparian vegetation is cleared for unrestricted river access and water views for new urban developments. However, a new appreciation of the natural environment is accommodating conservation of recreational areas for the benefit of tourists who want to 'see and experience' the natural environment during their holidays. For example, the Rhine delta with its wild habitats makes a particular contribution to diversity and is a wetland of international significance (Vorarlberg Austria, n.d.). This area holds a special appeal for tourists interested in natural wetlands and their wildlife, particularly birds that use the wetlands as a resting place in winter. For endangered plant species, the wetlands also offer a sanctuary. However, tourism of the Rhine delta wetlands may become more restricted if boating access is reduced further (Tiefenbach, 1998).

Rivers can also be subjected to natural forces that are not always able to be controlled. This can include flooding caused by melting snow in spring and by intense rainfall events. On the other hand, lack of sufficient water flow and depth of the river channel may occur during periods of extended drought or from excessive sedimentation of the river bed. Wave action generated by storms can also contribute to erosion of the channel and lead to a reduction of traffic. These events can be detrimental to the tourism industry making it difficult for river- and cruise-related businesses to plan ahead. As with most environmental problems of this nature, it usually takes both the river *and* the tourism industry to recover.

Additional problems for canals include maintenance of the water channel, especially in areas where they are no longer used on a commercial basis. If the maintenance costs of canals cannot be justified, they may deteriorate to the point that they become unnavigable for vessels. Failing lock gates and bank collapses can also contribute to a decline in the use of canals for tourism activities. Channel banks of both rivers and canals also suffer damages through human activities such as boat wash-generating wave action; particularly in shallow waters where it can cause bank erosion (Gadd, 1995; Mosisch and Arthington, 2004). Although boat wash is mainly caused by fast-moving boats, the damage affects all users of a water channel through bank erosion.

Economic considerations by inland cruise companies are also likely to affect river or canal tourism. If tour operators are unprofitable, departures as well as service standards may be reduced. In these circumstances, land-based service industry and the attractions sector will also suffer. However, despite some potentially negative effects on the sustainability of river tourism, the future outlook is promising at this stage.

Conclusion

The sustainability of river and canal tourism depends on a balanced approach of responsible planning and management of the natural tourism resource (Newsome *et al.*, 2002), in order to prevent overcrowding and other detrimental effects through mass tourism. On the other hand, tourism is often an initiating force to bring about the conservation of endangered natural resources. For canal tourism, it is mainly a question of financial viability, especially in the case of smaller outdated waterways that could impact on cruise tourism as well as waterfront tourism. In a 'problem statement' relating to the development of public parks along scenic and historic river corridors published over 10 years ago, Robertson and Burge (1993) were already emphasizing the importance of achieving the right balance between economic growth and the protection of recreation and scenic values. To maintain long-term economic and ecological sustainability, it is apparent that the river cruise sector needs to find this balance. One factor that has to date impeded the achievement of this balance is the lack of data on the size and economic impact of the cruise industry. The volume of river- and canal-related tourism in Europe makes this task difficult, but not impossible. While there is a growing volume of literature available in the form of guide books, there remains a lack of published research that examines the value of scenery, the impact of cruising on local economies and potential ecological problems.

References

Allgemeiner Deutscher Fahrrad-Club (1996) Weserradtour entlang des Weserradweges von Hannoversch Münden bis Bremerhaven. Available at: http://www.tu-chemnitz.de/chemnitz/vereine/adfc/routen/wand_weser.htm

Amsterdam Info (2008) De Amsterdamse grachten. Available at: http://www.amsterdam.info/nl/grachten/

Andrews, M.J. (1984) Thames estuary: pollution and recovery. In: Sheehan, P.J., Miller, D.R., Butler, G.C., Bourdeau, P. and Ridgeway, J.M. (eds) *Effects of Pollution at the Ecosystem Level*. Wiley, Chichester, UK.

Baranowski, S. and Furlough, E. (eds) (2001) *Being Elsewhere: Tourism, Consumer Culture and Identity in Modern Europe and North America*. University of Michigan Press, Ann Arbor, Michigan.

Bootwandern (n.d.) Auf dem langsamsten Fluß Bayerns…das Altmühltal aktiv aber gemächlich genießen. Available at: http://www.eichstaett.info/freizeit/bootwandern.htm

Boucher, J. (2007) Amsterdam urban history. Available at: http://courses.umass.edu/latour/2007/boucher/index.html

British Waterways (n.d.) Creating sustainable waterways for the future. Available at: http://www.britishwaterways.co.uk/home/index.html

Danube River Cruising (n.d.) Danube cruising information. Available at: http://www.danubecruising.com/

Danube Watch (2007) The Danube delta – Landscape of the year – 2007–2009. Available at: http://icpdr01.danubeday.org/icpdr-pages/dw0701_p_03.htm

Davies, N. (1998) *Europe: A History*. Harper Perennial, London.

Deutscher Reiseverband (DRV) (2006) Kreuzfahrten sind hoch im Kurs, DRV-Exklusiv-Studie: 2005 neues Spitzenjahr. Available at: http://www.drv.de/drv/fachbereiche/verkehrstraeger/schiff/detail.html?L=0&tx_ttnews%5Btt_news%5D=456&tx_ttnews%5BbackPid%5D=132&cHash=3c98c4b3d6

Elbe (2008) *Oster- und Vortragsreisen auf der Elbe*. Viking Flusskreuzfahrten. Themen- Und Sonderreisen. Available at: http://www.vikingrivercruises.de/offers_de/PDF2008/vik_11_elbe_themenreisen.pdf

Ely, C. (2003) The origins of Russian scenery: Volga river tourism and Russian landscape aesthetics. *Slavic Review* 62(4), 666–682.

Encyclopaedia Britannica – Danube (2008) Danube river history. Available at: http://www.britannica.com/eb/article-34471/Danube-River

Encyclopaedia Britannica – Rhine (2008) Rhine river history. Available at: http://www.britannica.com/eb/article-34453/Rhine-River

Encyclopaedia Britannica – Vistula (2008) Vistula river history. Available at: http://www.britannica.com/eb/article-34491/Vistula-River

Erfurt-Cooper, P. (1973) Hitzacker, Germany.

European Rivers (n.d.) Major rivers – map. Available at: http://www.worldatlas.com/ webimage/countrys/euriv.htm

Fjord Norway (2007) UNESCO includes Norwegian fjords on World Heritage List. Available at: http://www.fjordnorway.no/ CustomModules/ReadNews.aspx?ModuleI D=401&ItemID=9&tabID=1206 &subtabID=0&subsubtabid=0

Francesch, M. (2002) Europe's Rhine river delta and China's Pearl river delta: issues and lessons for integrated water resources management. *Asian Journal of Public Administration* 24(1), 23–56.

Frazier, D. (2000) *Colorado's Hot Springs*, 2nd edn. Pruett Publishing Company, Boulder, Colorado.

Frenzl, M. (2006) *Vom Rhein zur Nord- und Ostsee – Mit Flüssen und Kanälen zwischen Ems und Elbe*. Edition Maritim GmbH.

Gadd, G.E. (1995) Boat wash at channel banks. *Journal of the Institution of Water and Environmental Management* 9(1), 49–54.

German National Tourist Board (2008) *Destination Germany – The Legendary Rhine-Romantic-Route, Tales and Legends to the Left and Right of the Rhine*. Official Tourism Web site of Germany. Available at: http://www.germany-tourism.de/ENG/ destination_germany/master_tlfstrasse- id43.htm?cc_lang=

Heidenreich, B. (2007) *Kanäle – Künstliche Wasserwege*. Planet Wissen. Available at: http://www.planet-wissen.de/pw/Artikel ,,,,,,,38B0D928F720172DE0440003BA 5E08BC,,,,,,,,,,,,,,.html

Hummel, G. (1999) Radwandertour Unterelbe. Available at: http://www.tu-chemnitz.de/ chemnitz/vereine/adfc/routen/wand_ unterelbe.htm

Iceland Complete (2005) River Laxá is fed by Lake Mývatn. Available at: http://www.ice landcomplete.is/default2.asp?active_ page_id=104

Inland Waterways Association (2006). Available at: http://www.waterways.org.uk/Home

International Commission for the Protection of the Rhine (ICPR) (2008) Nine states one river basin. Available at: http://www.iksr. org/

Jones, E.L. (2003) *The European Miracle: Environments, Economies and Geopolitics in the History of Europe and Asia*. Cambridge University Press, Cambridge.

Kernohan, R.D. (2006) Cruising down the rivers of the world. *Contemporary Review* Autumn, 367–372.

Köln Tourismus GmbH (2008) Cologne from A to Z, Rhine cruises. Available at: http:// www.koeln.de/tourismus/koelntourismus/ cms/artikel.php/29/289/artikel.html

Kumpch, J.U. (2007) *Insight Compact Guide Norway*. Discovery Channel. APA Publications, London.

Leisi, C. (2000) *Limmatraum Stadt Zürich – Landschaftsentwicklungskonzept (LEK)*. Grün Stadt Zürich.

Levin, M. (2007) About Go Barging, Cruise critic – Cruise reviews and news. Available at: http://www.cruisecritic.com/reviews/ cruiseline.cfm?CruiseLineID=102

Maritimes Lexikon (2008) Maritime Begriffe – Kanal. Available at: http://www.modelskip per.de/Archive/Maritimes/Dokumente/ maritime_Begriffe_Abschnitt_ka_kb/Kanal. htm

Marx, K. (2004) Rheinreise und Rheintourismus vor dem Eisenbahnbau, in *Wettereauer Zeitung*, 27.01.2004. Available at: http:// www.friedberger-geschichtsverein.de/ 6presse/2004/03marxvortrag150104. html

Mc Knight, H. (1999) *Cruising French Waterways*, 3rd edn. Sheridan House, New York.

Mosisch, T.D. and Arthington, A.H. (2004) Impacts of recreational power-boating on freshwater ecosystems. In: Buckley, R. (ed.) *Environmental Impacts of Ecotourism*. CAB International, Wallingford, UK, pp. 125–154.

Newsome, D., Moore, S.A. and Dowling, R.K. (2002) *Natural Area Tourism: Ecology, Impacts and Management*. Channel View Books, Clevedon, UK.

Österreich-Lexikon (n.d.) Rhein-Main-Donau- Kanal. Available at: http://aeiou.iicm.

tugraz.at/aeiou.encyclop.r/r576124. htm#ggviewer-offsite-nav-9056264

Reiserat (n.d.) Auf den Kanälen, Fluss-Kreuzfahrten Deutschland, Viele nasse Kombinationen. Available at: http://www.reiserat.de/schiffsreisen/kanaele.htm

Reiter, A. (2004) The hybrid consumer of leisure squeezed between fun maximisation, chill out, and the radical search for inner values. In: Weiermair, K. and Mathies, C. (eds) *The Tourism and Leisure Industry: Shaping the Future*. The Haworth Hospitality Press, New York, pp. 173–180.

Rhine River (2008) Rhine river – introductory facts. Available at: http://www.rollintl.com/roll/rhine.htm

Roberts, L. and Simpson, F. (1999) Developing partnership approaches to tourism in Central and Eastern Europe. *Journal of Sustainable Tourism* 7 (Part 3 & 4), 314–330.

Robertson, R.A. and Burge, R.J. (1993) The interface between commercial and industrial development and recreational use in an urban river corridor. *Journal of Leisure Research* 25, 53–77.

Romanian Tourist Office (2008) Danube river cruises. Available at: http://www.romaniatourism.com/danube.html

Shakiry, A.S. (2007) *River Tourism: Can Iraq Benefit from Europe's experience?* Islamic Tourism Prospects, Islamic Tourism, Issue 8. Available at: http://www.islamictourism.com/Articles/articles.php?issue=8

Simon, M.P. (2006) *Die Kanäle Frankreichs*, 2nd edn. Heel Verlag GmbH. ISBN: 3898804852.

Skien Norway Directory (2008) The Telemark canal – historical/cultural sites. Available at: http://www.norway.com/directories/d_company.asp?id=3634

Stadt Zürich (n.d.) Grün Stadt Zürich – Erholung. Available at: http://www.stadt-zuerich.ch/internet/gsz/home/planung/planung/konzepte_leitbilder/landschaft/lek_limmat/erholung.html

Steinbach, J. (1995) River related tourism in Europe – an overview. *GeoJournal* 35(4/April), 443–458. Available at: http://www.

springerlink.com/content/h557g 77104144j87/

Szabolcs, I. (1991) Salinisation potential of European soils. In: Brower, F.M., Thomas, A. and Chadwick, M.J. (eds) *Land Use Changes in Europe: A Process of Change, Environmental Transformation and Future Patterns*. Kluwer Academic Publishers, Dordrecht, The Netherlands.

Tiefenbach, M. (1998) *Naturschutz in Österreich*. Bundesministerium für Umwelt, Jugend und Familie. Umweltbundesamt (Federal Environment Agency). Wien, Austria. Available at: http://www.umweltbundesamt.at/fileadmin/site/publikationen/M091.pdf

Travel Signposts (2006a) Russia: Volga – European river cruise routes, Moscow and St Petersburg tourist sights covered. Available at: http://www.travelsignposts.com/travelinfo/rivercruiseVolga.php

Travel Signposts (2006b) France: Burgundy and Provence – European river cruise routes, river cruises on the Saône and Rhône rivers in France. Available at: http://www.travelsignposts.com/travelinfo/rivercruiseSaRh.php

Travel Signposts (2006c) Holland and Belgium – European river cruise routes, Holland (The Netherlands) and Belgium (Rivers – Ijssel, Schelde and Waal). Available at: http://www.travelsignposts.com/travelinfo/rivercruiseHollandBelgium.php

Travel Signposts (2006d) The Elbe (Berlin to Prague) – European river cruise routes. Available at: http://www.travelsignposts.com/travelinfo/rivercruiseElbe.php

Umhverfisstofnun (2002) Lake Mývatn and the River Laxá, flora and fauna at Myvatn Lake and Laxá River. Available at: http://english.ust.is/National-Parks/Protected areas/MyvatnandLaxa/

UNEP (2000) Freshwater. In: *Geo-2000*, Chapter 2, 8.

UNEP/ISRIC (1991) In: Oldeman, L.R., Hakkeling, R.T. and Sombroek, W.G. (eds) *World Map of the Status of Human-induced Soil Degradation (GLASOD): An*

Explanatory Note, 2nd edn. UNEP, Wageningen, ISRIC, Nairobi.

UNESCO World Heritage Centre (2008) Alto Douro wine region. Available at: http://whc.unesco.org/en/list/1046

Vorarlberg Austria (n.d.) Rhine delta nature conservation zone: Environment and future – nature and environmental protection. Available at: http://www.vorarlberg.at/ english/vorarlberg-english/environment_ future/natureandenvironmentalpro/ rhinedeltanatureconservat.htm

Walgate, R. (1986) Rhine pollution: death of Europe's sewer? *Nature* 324(6094), 201.

Ziebell, D. (1999) *Stream bank erosion.* Landcare Notes. November 1999. LC0096. ISSN 1329-833X.

7 The Yangzi River Tourism Zone

W.G. Arlt[1] and G. Feng[2]

[1]FH Westkueste/West Coast University of Applied Sciences, Heide, Germany; [2]Ningbo University, China

Introduction: Does a Yangzi River Tourism Region Exist?

This chapter discusses tourism activity along the Yangzi River and examines the need for a 'Yangzi River Tourism Region'. Currently the river has no unified approach to market and as discussed in this chapter, the lack of a regional approach has created a number of difficulties. The Yangzi flows through 11 provinces before entering into the East China Sea at Shanghai. Each province through which the river flows has its own independent tourism administration and marketing organization. As a consequence, a regional superstructure or common brand has yet to emerge. There are a number of factors that have contributed to this situation including the traditional view of the river as the border between northern and southern China. From this perspective, the river is seen as having quite separate upper and lower reaches. A further distinction that can be made is the organization of tourism activity between tourism *on* the river and tourism *along* the river. Along the river, there are many important tourism destinations including Shanghai, Nanjing, Wuhan and Yichang on the Yangzi plain and Chongqing in the upper reaches. Between these cities, there are more than a dozen '4A-List' tourism attractions, the highest level according to the Chinese national tourism classification system. These places do not however use the concept of a 'Yangzi River Tourism Region' in their self-definition or marketing. Along the river, the most famous tourism attractions are concentrated in the lower reaches, whereas on the river attractions are mainly concentrated in the upper reaches, where tourism products including 'Yangzi cruises' operate and the Yangzi itself is the main attraction.

Due to its geographical and hydraulic differences and the decentralized nature of the administrative structure that is engaged in promotion, the perception of the Yangzi River as one tourism region has more resonance with international tourists than with domestic tourists. From an academic perspective, however, the river may be classified as a river zone for a number of reasons:

- It is a major location for activities and places of tourist interest, including the built and natural environments.
- As the biggest river in China, it has always been used for transport and was for a long time the only access route to the Sichuan basin.
- It provides some recreational opportunities, especially fishing.
- It is an important source of drinking water.
- Its indirect roles include supply of fish and of irrigation water for agriculture, support of manufacturing activities and use as a disposal site for a range of waste products.
- With the completion of the Three Gorges Dam, it will become one of the main sources of hydroelectric power in China.

This chapter concentrates on the tourist activities on the river, along the river and the river's main attraction, the 'Three Gorges'.

Rivers in China's History and the Yangzi in China's History

To most Chinese the Yangzi River is known by its modern name as 'Chang Jiang' (长江), the Long River. The names Yangtze or Yangtse River and Yangtze Kiang are derived from Yangzi Jiang (扬子江), which since the 6th century AD has been the Chinese name for the stretch of the river between Yangzhou and Zhenjiang in its lower reaches. The first Western visitors to China mistakenly applied this name in English to the entire river. In Chinese, Yangzi Jiang is considered a poetic name for the river.

The river's 6300 km length makes it the world's third longest, after the Nile and the Amazon. The river flows from west to east more or less following the northern latitude of $30°$, with a total drainage area of $1.8 \times 10^6 \text{km}^2$ and a yearly water volume of $976 \times 10^9 \text{m}^3$ (Fig. 7.1). It originates on the eastern part of the Tibetan plateau, dropping in elevation from more than 5000 m to less than 1000 m while running through Qinghai, along the border between Sichuan and Tibet and into Yunnan. These parts of the river are called 'Dangqu', 'Tuotuo', 'Tongtian' and 'Jinsha', respectively. The river takes the name of Yangzi when it enters the basin of Sichuan, where it collects significant amounts of waters from several tributaries, increasing its water volume significantly. It then cuts through Mount Wushan to create the famous Three Gorges (Qutang, Wu and Xilang) which are flooded as the Three Gorges Dam is built. Another passage flows through the Leaping Tiger Gorge which was first opened to tourists in 1993. On its long journey eastward the Yangzi collects more water from four of China's five main freshwater lakes and further tributaries including the 'Han' River, becoming broader and slower along the way.

In the upper reaches, the tourism activities connected to the Yangzi River are characterized by the mountainous morphology, the multifarious climatology, and the ancient cultures and diverse minorities living along its banks, including the Tibetans. With its narrow and rapid torrent, many tributaries and big rapids, this part is still awaiting the development of rafting adventure tourism

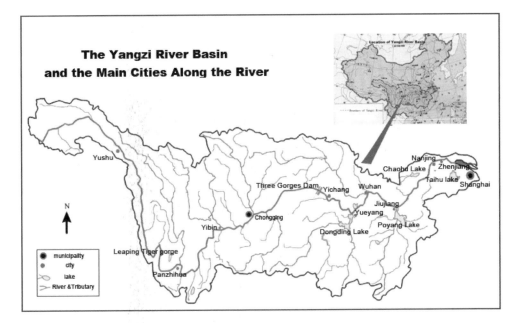

Fig. 7.1. The Yangzi river zone.

and ecotourism. The middle and lower Yangzi River Area is one of the four clusters of World Heritage Sites that include the Classical Gardens of Suzhou, the Huangshan and Wuyi Mountains, the Ancient Villages of Southern Anhui, the Lushan National Park, the Ancient Buildings on Mount Wudang and the Wulingyuan Scenic Area (Li *et al.*, 2008).

The river is of national significance in terms of its geographical scale, its volume and its significant economic role as well as its freak temperaments. The dragon shape of the river makes it a symbol for Chinese civilization and it is often named the 'mother river' by the Chinese. Its watershed divides the country into north and south and with an area of 1.8 million square kilometres and encompasses a fifth of China's total land area. The Yangzi River irrigates China's 'land of fish and rice', the great central valley where close to half the nation's food is grown, and carries three-quarters of China's internal water-borne commerce. The river has a strong symbolic aspect and has been central to much of China's history and myths. Yet at the same time, the river has repeatedly also brought misery. Devastating floods have again and again inundated thousands of square kilometres and claimed more than 300,000 lives in the last century alone.

In addition to playing an essential role in traditional transportation, Chinese history and the development of its civilization, the river has often posed a threat beyond the control of the people. The Chinese character for 'law' *fa* (法) consists of the parts 'water' and 'movement'. Control of the movement of water, building flood levees and organizing the irrigation systems used for rice production, has been for many centuries the *raison d'être* of a centralized government in China. The central role of the river in the life of China was recognized by Karl August Wittfogel and expressed through his concept of a 'hydraulic society' (Wittfogel, 1957).

Development of Tourism and Yangzi River Tourism in China

'In Chinese culture, travelling is a way of learning' (Chen, 1998). During the more than 2000 years of history of Imperial China, mobility inside China was cherished by scholars, monks and pilgrims as well as by traders and administrators and was helped by major infrastructure works such as the Grand Canal. Travel was seen first of all as a way to broaden one's mind, an intellectual undertaking, as expressed in the saying 'He who travels far knows much'. Educated persons were even advised 'to seek ultimate truth from the landscape' (Petersen, 1995). The classical Confucian writings are based on experiences collected during travels through China, and the opening paragraph of the *Analects* includes the oft-quoted sentence 'Is it not a joy to have friends come from afar?' (Lau, 1989). Under the imperial administrative system, administrators ('Mandarins') had to move throughout their career being normally employed in a different province every few years. This presented a lot of opportunities for long-distance travel, including trips on the Yangzi River or its tributaries.

Some emperors travelled on 'inspection tours' or hunting trips or pilgrimages to Mount Tai or to summer retreats. However, the main obligation of the emperor was to remain in his Forbidden City and to carry out the prescribed rituals at the right time. Roaming the country was left to poets such as Li Bai or Su Dongpu and scientists such as Xu Xiake, whose works influenced the perception of later generations of travellers (Wang, 1998; Guo et al., 2002). Monks wandered throughout the country, visiting the four holy mountains of Buddhism and the five holy mountains of Daoism. Guest houses for travelling officials and for commoners existed throughout China 2000 years ago (Shu, 1995). But for the agrarian population, the only form of travel usually undertaken was to visit towns and cities in the vicinity to participate in festivals and fairs. These journeys often included an economic element as well as leisure and pilgrimage. Normally their journey tended to be short in duration and spatial reach. This was helped by the proliferation of temples and monasteries in the country. 'The sites multiplied over the centuries and as Buddhism became established; even more sacred sites were added' (Sofield and Li, 1998a).

The People's Republic of China during the rule of Mao Zedong regarded travelling for leisure within China as a wasteful behaviour, as a sign of bourgeois lifestyle 'which one should always guard against' (Zhang, 1989) and as a potential source of unrest. As in other socialist countries, domestic leisure tourism was organized by large companies and institutions before the Cultural Revolution. Travelling in China was confined to the privileged few or organized for political reasons especially during the Cultural Revolution, when 'the Red Guards...combined sightseeing with the arduous work of building a socialist China' (Graburn, 2001, p. 80).

The systems of household registration ('hukou') and ration coupons made it almost impossible to travel outside the normal place of residence for Chinese citizens before the 1980s. All travel had to be approved by the 'danwei', the work unit every Chinese citizen had to belong to, otherwise a train or bus ticket could not be obtained legally. Ration coupons were necessary to buy food and other items and were only valid locally, so travellers had to apply at the Public Security Office for special coupons with nationwide validity. The traditional visits to local fairs and temples were stopped when free peasant markets were abolished and attacks against religion and the *four old* (old ideas, customs, culture and habits – and all the local customs connected to it) were common (Sofield and Li, 1998b). Pilgrimages, which still could be practised more or less openly in the 1950s, ceased during the Cultural Revolution. After the beginning of the reform and opening policy in 1978, domestic tourism 'often took the form of organized package tours, such as round trips for employees and "travel meetings"....Hence it came to be viewed by some as a legitimate excuse for squandering public funds' (Wen and Tisdell, 2001, p. 131).

With more disposable income and available leisure time, domestic tourism developed quickly into a billion-Yuan business with millions of participants. By the mid-1980s, the growth of the domestic travel demand could no longer be ignored. The size and pace of the emerging tourism industry grew rapidly and in some areas demand began to outstrip supply. Local authorities in some areas supported the mobilization of resources to cater for domestic tourism because of the obvious positive effects on income and regional development. The 'First National Conference on Domestic Tourism' held in Tianjin in 1987 acknowledged the growing importance for the first time and emphasized its possible positive role as a regional development factor. 'Domestic tourism policy was discussed and formulated at a time when much development had already taken place in many parts of the country' (Xu, 1999, p. 75), and travel restrictions disappeared step by step with the abolishment of food and textile rationing in the early 1980s and the easing of the 'hukou' system in the 1990s. With a 'floating' population of more than 100 million migrant workers, there remains little ability to control the movement of people within the country. The construction of highways, railways and airports and the provision of convenient transport services developed quickly from a small base during the 1990s.

To cement the 'travel bug' (Yatsko and Tasker, 1998) in Chinese society, however, more was needed than just an increase of discretionary time and money, however necessary these are. The move away from agrarian and Maoist frugality was supported by the redefinition of collective identity to embrace globalized consumerism and enhanced nationalism. In the 1990s, attempts by the government to restrict growing demand for domestic recreational tourism weakened further. Domestic tourism started to be actively supported with hasty but hefty investment at local and provincial levels. The introduction of a 5-day working week in 1995 and three collective week-long holidays in 2000 by the central government also underpinned this development. Today, China has the largest domestic tourism market in the world (Arlt, 2006). In 2008, the week-long May holidays were transformed into several shorter holidays during traditional Chinese festivals like the Dragon Boat Racing day to ease the strains on the infrastructure during the 'Golden Weeks'.

Inbound tourism has, except for a brief period during the Cultural Revolution, always been welcomed by the People's Republic of China. Inbound tourism was favoured especially after 1978 as a supposedly easy way to earn hard currencies needed for the modernization of the country. Before 1978, the few visitors passing the 'bamboo curtain' were used to earn international political support for the regime. However, from the very beginning of the existence of the People's Republic, inbound tourism was also used to strengthen the bonds with ethnic Chinese living in Hong Kong, Macao, Taiwan and overseas (Arlt, 2006; Nyiri, 2006). Today, China is the No. 4 destination in international tourism and expected to become No. 1 within the next decade (UNWTO, 2008).

River tourism

Rivers have always formed a major transportation route during the long history of China, even though the main rivers flow west to east, whereas the main transport routes run south to north. For leisure travel, taking a boat is often mentioned in novels and poems as a favoured way to feast on good food, wine and sometimes amorous company. Poets drifting along a river in a small craft, composing couplets under a full moon are part and parcel of Chinese literary tradition. The Yangzi River, however, with its rapids, dangerous swift currents and its huge size was not always suitable for leisure activities. The 'West Lake' in Hangzhou and the 'Li' River near Guilin are much more likely backdrops, if not the Water Towns south of the Yangzi like Zhujiajiao or Luzhi (Bei *et al.*, 2007; Fan *et al.*, 2008).

The river started to become an instrument of leisure consumption with the advent of steamships in China. The British were forerunners in the process. The first part of the journey commenced at Shanghai where steamships took passengers to Hankou, Yichang and further to the west or even to Burma by other means of transportation. In 1898, Chongqing was opened to foreign steamers (Bird, 1985; Wang, 2003). In modern China, the fleets of Yangzi boats called Dong Fang Hong ('The East is Red') are mainly engaged in regional transport tasks but also carry increasing number of domestic tourists. Luxury river cruise ships were first introduced for Western tourists and Chinese dignitaries in the 1980s, concentrating on the passage through the wonders of the Three Gorges. In the 1990s, the increase in demand led to the introduction of ships such as the *Yangzi* and *Changjiang* that were designed for domestic visitors travelling between Chongqing and Wuhan. After the official announcement by the Chinese National Congress in 1992 that the Three Gorges Dam was to be built after the first interception of the river a large number of 'Farewell to the Three Gorges' tours were promoted. Before the dam was built, most cruises ran the entire course from Chongqing to Shanghai in about 10 days. In recent years, there has been a shift to shortened cruises from Chongqing to Wuhan or Chongqing to Yichang or even short cruises in the stretches of the river within the Three Gorges area. Beside these tours, package tours which include about 20 scenic spots have now become increasingly popular. The increased interest in river cruising has generated some rather irrational investments in cruise ships and hotels, resulting in overcapacity and poor service quality. This oversupply has damaged regional tourism development in terms of management, infrastructure, local administration, poor personal service and safety incidents.

In the early 1980s, the number of cruise ships and tourists was very limited. By 1988, ten cruise ships were operating with 25,000 tourists taking part in cruises. By 1993, the number had increased to about 50 cruise ships with 430,000 tourists, and in 1998 there were 60 ships with 580,000 tourists aboard. In recent years, the number of cruise tourists has increased very rapidly, especially tourists from Europe and America. There are currently more than 100 cruise ships operating river tours, and almost half of them rated as three-star and above. Five-star ships run by companies including the Chinese-owned China Regal Cruises and the American-owned Victoria line operate vessels with names that include *Princess*, *Goddess* or *Monkey King*. During the cruise, passengers are entertained with fashion shows and acrobatics, offered calligraphy and taijiquan courses and are able to participate in a range of other activities. It is expected that the 2008 Olympics, the completion of the Three Gorges Dam in 2009 and Expo 2010 in Shanghai will boost tourism development in this region. The river will be easier to navigate for cruise ships after the Three Gorges Dam is completed and the range of tourist attractions along the river will be more comprehensive (Wang, 2006). Figure 7.2 illustrates a cruise boat in the Three Gorges area.

The industrial development of China has resulted in major pollution problems including river pollution. Swimming in the Yangzi River is not advisable. Visitors coming for wildlife experiences are certainly too late: of the two major animals indigenous to the river, the Chinese or Yangzi Alligator (揚子鱷, *Alligator sinensis*) is down to about 200 animals and features on the list of highly endangered species. With this status, it is still luckier than the Yangzi

Fig. 7.2. Cruising in the Three Gorges.

River Dolphin (白鱀豚, *Lipotes vexillifer*), which was last sighted in 2004 and declared as 'functionally extinct' in 2007. The *L. vexillifer* was the only remaining member of the Lipotidae, an ancient mammal family that is understood to have separated from other marine mammals, including whales, dolphins and porpoises, about 40–20 million years ago (Baiji.org., 2008).

The Perception of Nature in China

> When Western tourists look at the Yangtze, they see a river; the Chinese see a poem replete with philosophical ideals. Part of the 'common knowledge' of Chineseness is to recognize representations of the picturesque hills of Guilin, the sea of clouds of Wu-shan (Mount Wu), the Three Gorges of the Yangtze River, and the Yellow Crane Terrace pagoda. These images bring spiritual unity even if the people have never visited them; but when they do visit the importance of these images is reinforced.
>
> (Sofield and Li, 1998a, p. 367)

The Chinese developed an appreciation for nature as a philosophical and artistic inspiration very early. They produced a great number not only of nature-related paintings as well as travel books in the form of poems, diaries, essays, travelogues written by great travellers including Xu Xiake and others. Most of the travel accounts are descriptions about geographical elements, local products and customs, mysteries and even personal feelings touched by nature.

Even today Chinese tourists demonstrate a strong preference for familiar landscapes through various images created through poets and artists. It is very difficult to distinguish whether it is the landscape which brings the people or the famous poem which attracts people to the place. The attractions of the mountains and scenic places are not evaluated according to the natural beauty per se but according to the tangible and intangible cultural heritage embodied, especially to its connections with these famous people and famous poets. It can be said that while Chinese have a systematic view towards nature and human, the interests and concerns for most of the people are still dominated by the cultural perspective. This forms the cultural background of nature apprehension which to a western person like the American author Peter Hessler appears curious, but is important in understanding the different evaluation of the modern development in the Yangzi River area:

> The guide showed us the rock formations we had paid to see-the Pig God Praising Buddha, the Dragon's Head, the Horse's Ass, the Lying Beauty – and the (...) tourists, all of whom were Chinese, squealed in delight as they tried to recognize the shapes in the broken cliffs. This was ritual at every Chinese nature site; there seemed to be no value in the natural world unless it was linked to man-some shape that a mountain recalled, or a poem that had been written about it, or an ancient legend that brought the rocks to life.
>
> (Hessler, 2001, p. 121)

There is an obvious behaviour gap between what Chinese and foreigners appreciate on the Yangzi River. Most Chinese tourists regard the cruise tours as a kind of social experience and communication on its own. They are often organized as group tours and are more interested in various social entertainment, showing their conspicuous wealth, spending time chatting and playing in the cruise rooms and taking part in sightseeing activities during excursions. On the other hand, foreign tourists often stay on the decks to appreciate the landscape vistas. Once the cruise approaches the Three Gorges Dam, Chinese tourists become excited about the famous new building and take photos of themselves in front of the dam as a souvenir. Western tourists are more likely to complain about the intervention by man into nature.

The Three Gorges and the Three Gorges Dam

When talking about Yangzi River tourism, the image is often fragmented into several stretches, with the main focus often concentrated in the Three Gorges (Sanxia, 三峡), an approximately 120 km long stretch located between Yichang in Hubei Province and Chongqing City; since 1997, one of the four provincial-level municipalities of China. The 'Wu Gorge' rises from the estuary of the Daning River in Wushan County (Chongqing municipality), and ends in Guandukou, Badong County (Hubei Province), meandering over 45 km. The Wu Gorge features beautiful hills and cliffs and is known for its deepness, serenity and beauty. The 'Xiling Gorge' starts from Xiangxikou, Zigui County (Hubei Province), and ends in Nanjinguan, Yichang City, and is over 76 km long. There are reefs and surging swirls in the Gorge which had a reputation for rapids and dangerous shoals before the construction of the Three Gorges Dam. Finally, the 'Qutang Gorge' is the shortest of the three with a length of only 8 km, stretching from Baidi City to Daxi town. The steep and towering hills in this Gorge are connected to the saying 'Controlling thousands of ravines in the west, overwhelming rolling hills while adjoining Hubei and Hunan provinces in the east'.

Before the 1950s, the Three Gorges made Sichuan a nearly impenetrable redoubt. This was especially true for the Kingdom of Shu during China's Three Kingdoms era 1800 years ago – and so again for the Nationalist government during the Japanese occupation of large parts of China after 1937. With pinnacles soaring up to more than 1000 m from the river, the gorges have inspired China's landscape artists and poets for thousands of years (Table 7.1). For the Chinese, the Three Gorges are first of all connected to the poem by China's most celebrated poet Li Bai (pp. 701–762):

> *Through the Yangzi Gorges*
> *From the walls of Baidi high in the colored dawn*
> *To Jiangling by night-fall is three hundred miles.*
> *Yet monkeys are still calling on both banks behind me*
> *To my boat these ten thousand mountains away.*
> (Li, 1996)

This layer of cultural significance has however been partly superseded by the construction of the Three Gorges Dam as a symbol of triumph of man over nature, or in the view of many environmentalists, a symbol of triumph of brinkmanship over economic and ecologic reason. According to the recent master plan 'Regional Tourism Development Planning in the Sanxia Area', it is

Table 7.1. The most important tourism attractions in the Three Gorges area. (From State Development and Reform Commission: masterplan for regional tourism development planning in the Sanxia Area.)

Type	No.	Chongqing Municipality	Hubei Province
World heritage	3	Dazu stone sculpture	Dragon boat
National 4A tourism area	15	Three Gorges, Mini Three Gorges, etc.	Shennongjia Reserve
National tourism spots	6	Three Gorges Corridor	
National forest park	17	Wushan Mountain and the surrounding mountains	Da Lao Ling, Longmen River and Xisai
National nature reserve	5		Shennong Reserve
National seismic relic	1	1856 relic	
Important cultural relics	22	Stone sculptures, temples	
Patriotic education	8	Old houses of generals and other celebrities	Gezhou Dam Construction
Excellent tourism cities	3	Chongqing	Yichang
Historical cultural cities	2	Chongqing	

expected that the number of domestic tourists to the Three Gorges will reach more than 30 million per year while the number of foreign tourists are hoped to exceed 1 million per year after the completion of the Three Gorges Dam. Table 7.1 summarizes the major attractions of the river. Between 1978 and 2007, the Three Gorges area has attracted more than 5 million foreign tourists, mainly from Europe and North America (Table 7.2).

Because of the remoteness of the region and the difficult land conditions for agriculture and industry, local governments regard tourism as an important engine of regional development. Over the last two decades, tourism development has undergone a series of fluctuations because of limited infrastructure and poor access to this region. Though the tourism infrastructure is mainly concentrated in the core cities of Chongqing and Yichang, the overall supply of hotels, tour buses, luxurious ships and professionals has not been satisfactory in this region. According to the master plan designed by the State Development and Reform Commission, an estimated investment of 26 billion RMB (€2.3 billion in 2008) will be used to boost tourism development in the

Table 7.2. Tourism development in the Three Gorges area, 1997–2007. (From Chinagate, 2007.)

Component	Chongqing			Yichang		
	1997	2002	2007	1997	2002	2007
Tourists (million)	n.d.	46.65	68.47	n.d.	8.03	10.00
Domestic tourists (million)	n.d.	46.19	67.87	n.d.	7.61	9.66
Foreign tourists (million)	0.16	0.46	0.60	n.d.	0.42	0.34
Domestic income (billion RMB)	n.d.	20.15	31.83	n.d.	4.36	6.75
Foreign income ($ million)	71	218	309	n.d.	84	63
Total income (billion RMB)	n.d.	21.89	34.62	n.d.	5.06	7.23

period from 2007 to 2020. A considerable amount of the funds will be used to support key attractions and to fund infrastructure development. The aim of the plan is to promote tourism as the backbone industry in the region and provide alternative employment for immigrants who were moved because of the building of the Three Gorges Dam.

There are however a number of problems which hamper tourism development and are hotly discussed among Chinese experts (Wan and Liu, 2006):

- Administrative divisions and regions lead to mismanagement, especially since the two cities of Chongqing and Yichang are competing with each other to hold the 'International tourism festival of the Yangzi', and each city is trying to promote its own local tourism resources at the cost of the other, resulting in chaotic competition.
- There is no regional tourism association which regulates prices and controls management structures and operations in different destinations.
- The distribution of brochures and online information about the tourism products on offer in the region are not well organized, potentially causing a reduction in visitor numbers.
- Most tourism companies are rather small. Price competition among the small agencies is ferocious, often leading to low-quality service and even to cheating of customers.
- There is a clear lack of coordination between different tourism administrative sectors and authorities. For the tourists, the image of the products is fragmented and blurred. As a result, there is no integrated tourism structure to promote development. Moreover the region as a whole lacks positive image building.
- The 'Farewell to Three Gorges' campaigns in the end of 1990s created the impression that the Three Gorges would completely disappear after the dam building, making it harder to sell them today, particularly to international visitors.
- The tourism development for the Three Gorges is based on the resource and hardware development, other issues such as marketing, cultural prospects and software are often neglected.
- Too few training programmes for staff working in the tourism industry are offered.
- Marketing strategies are not differentiated for various segments, for instance for different age groups.
- Tourism products are rather monotonous with the Three Gorges and the Dam as major products. Although other various tourism products are put forward in the master plan, including adventure, cultural, ecological and ethnic tourism, they have not been developed. In addition, artificial landscapes and destructive constructions are replacing the traditional original scenic spots. Since a great number of ancient temples and relics were submerged with the rising water level, the temples are displaced and the architecture styles are imitated.
- The river is choked with a great deal of waste from tourists and residents who live beside the river. Eyewitnesses report that sometimes the surface

of the water is covered with a thick layer of garbage, as there is no garbage collection system on the river.

The construction of the Three Gorges Dam had been the subject of discussion for some time. Sun Yatsen, the first president of the Republic of China, conceived a vision of the dam as a national project (Sun, 1922). This dream was remembered by Mao Zedong in his 1956 poem *Swimming*:

> *Great plans are afoot:*
> *A bridge will fly to span the north and south,*
> *Turning a deep chasm into a thoroughfare;*
> *Walls of stone will stand upstream to the west*
> *To hold back Wushan's clouds and rain*
> *Till a smooth lake rises in the narrow gorges.*
> *The mountain goddess if she is still there*
> *Will marvel at a world so changed.*
> (Mao, 1998)

The mobilization of the whole nation to tame the wild, to regulate rivers and terrace mountains was a typical feature of Maoist policies after the foundation of the People's Republic of China in 1949. Big engineering achievements like the Yangzi River Bridge in Nanjing, which was completed without international assistance in 1968, are still presented as big victories of the Chinese nation.

The decision to build the Three Gorges Dam, named as the biggest engineering achievement since the construction of the Great Wall, was approved in 1992 despite national and international scepticism about the economic value and the ecological consequences of the construction. For the tourism industry, the dam with its 2 km long main wall is expected to become an artificial miracle destination for Chinese tourists, satisfying their search for superlatives as well as celebrating the ingenuity of the Chinese people – and of course their leaders. Construction is supposed to be finished in 2011, but already the raising of the water level upstream of the dam has led to the displacement of at least 2 million people and the loss of many sites along the river and an incalculable number of relics in unexplored archaeological sites have been lost forever.

As with all dams of such dimensions, the question of the speed of sedimentation in front of the dam has been discussed with different scenarios put forward. The fact that the Three Gorges Dam lies on a seismic fault was brought back to attention during the big earthquake which struck adjacent Sichuan province in May 2008. An additional unexpected environmental change in the river's condition since the construction of the dam is that the number of foggy days has increased significantly, not only endangering sightseers, but also possibly threatening navigation.

The construction of the dam transforms the main tourism resource on the Yangzi River, with man-made sights such as the reservoir and its landscape and the dam itself becoming the major attractions. Unlike the Three Gorges and their unique historical and cultural associations, such artificial landscape lack uniqueness. Another effect is the opening up of Chongqing and Yichang harbours for ocean-going ships, adding to the industrialized look of the river.

Conclusion

The Yangzi River has been of major importance to China for many centuries, as a source of identity as well as a source for irrigation and transportation of goods and passengers. It is however not perceived in any way as a unified tourism region. The river itself, like most other Chinese tourism attractions, is endangered by overuse, pollution and a lack of efficient environmental regulation and long-term planning. However, tourism connected to the Three Gorges area, including the Three Gorges Dam, is supposed to develop strongly in the coming years. The Chinese government has given priority to developing tourism as the regional backbone industry, helping the development of all of Western China.

International tourism along and on the Yangzi River is of limited importance in terms of numbers or turnover, but seen by the central and local governments as important for increasing the prestige of tourism. Again as in many other parts of China, the gigantic amounts of concrete used for the construction of city centres, theme parks and dams alike, will further reduce the Country's attractiveness for non-Chinese foreigners by putting ecological as well as artistic pollution in the way of the sought-after romantic experience of the traditional Chinese culture. Dams are not very high on the must-see agenda of western visitors to China, although it could be argued that the hype surrounding the Three Gorges Dam will make it so for a time.

Domestic tourism can be expected to be much more resilient, as the Yangzi cultural experience based on poems and stories is still available even when reality changes. As long as no obvious major technical and environmental problems smear the image of the dam as a technological marvel, it will add an extra dimension of nationalistic pride to the visit.

It is obvious that the Yangzi is a significant tourism zone with unique vistas of scenery and cultural attractions. Currently, the concept of a tourism zone exists as a geographic space but not as an administrative reality. The establishment of a tourism region offers a number of advantages from planning and marketing perspectives but given the current scale of competition between the regions along the river this may take some time to occur.

References

Arlt, W. (2006) *China's Outbound Tourism.* Routledge, Oxon, UK.

Baiji.org (2008) Rare river dolphin 'now extinct'. Available at: www.Baiji.org. 2007

Bei, H., Helene, Y., Wall, G. and Mitchell, C. (2007) Creative destruction. Zhu Jia Jiao, China. *Annals of Tourism Research* 34, 1033–1055.

Bird, I. (1985) *The Yangtze Valley and Beyond*. Virago, London.

Chen, C. (1998) Rising Overseas Travel Market and Potential for the United States. In: proceedings of 3rd Annual Graduate Education and Graduate Students Research Conference in Hospitality and Tourism, Houston. Available at: www.hotelonline.com Trends Advances Inhospitality Research.

Chinagate (2007) The three gorges. Available at: http://cn.chinagate.com.cn/reports/2007-03/02/content_2368315.htm

Fan, C., Wall, G. and Mitchell, C. (2008) Creative destruction and the water town of Luzhi, China. *Tourism Management* 29, 648–660.

Graburn, N. (2001) Tourism and anthropology in East Asia today: some comparisons. In: Tan, C., Cheung, S. and Yang, H. (eds) *Tourism, Anthropology and China.* (Studies in Asian Tourism No. 1), White Lotus, Bangkok, pp. 71–92.

Guo, W., Turner, L. and King, B. (2002) The emerging golden age of Chinese tourism and its historical antecedents: a thematic investigation. *Tourism, Culture and Communication* 3: 131–146.

Guo, W., Turner, L. and King, B. (2003) The emerging golden age of Chinese tourism and its historical antecedents: a thematic investigation. *Tourism, Culture and Communication* 3, 131–146.

Hessler, P. (2001) *River Town: Two Years on the Yangtze.* Harper, New York.

Lau, D.C. (1989) *Confucius: The Analects.* Penguin Classics, London.

Li, M., Wu, B. and Cai, L. (2008) Tourism development of world heritage sites in China: a geographic perspective. *Tourism Management* 29, 308–319.

Li, P. (1996) *The Selected Poems of Li Po.* New Directions, New York.

Mao, Z. (Du, X. transl.) (1998) *Poems.* Foreign Languages Press, Beijing.

Nyiri, P. (2006) *Scenic Spots. Chinese Tourism, the State, and Cultural Authority.* University of Washington Press, Seattle, Washington.

Petersen, Y. (1995) The chinese landscape as a tourist attraction: image and reality. In: Lew, A. and Yu, L. (eds) *Tourism in China: Geographical, Political and Economic Perspectives.* Westview, Boulder, Colorado, pp. 141–154.

Shu, T. (1995) The Establishment and Development of Tourism in China. In: Umesao, T., Befu, H. and Ishimori, S. (eds) *Japanese Civilization in the Modern World.* IX Tourism. (Senri Ethnological Studies No 38). Osaka (National Museum of Ethnology) pp. 155–167.

Sofield, T. and Li, F. (1998a) Tourism development and cultural politics in China. *Annals of Tourism Research* 25(2), 362–392.

Sofield, T. and Li, F. (1998b) Historical methodology and sustainability: an 800-year-old festival from China. *Journal of Sustainable Tourism* 6, 267–292.

Sun, Y. (1922) *The International Development of China.* New York.

UNWTO (2008) Facts and figures. Available at: www.unwto.org 2008

Wan, X., and Liu, Y. (2006) Study on the current situation and countermeasures of the tourism industry competitiveness in Sanxia area. *Economic Geography* 26(3), 516–520.

Wang, N. (2006) Yangzi river gorges cruise tour and the periodic characteristics of its development. *Tourism Tribune*, 21(10), 55–58, 10.

Wang, S. (1998) *History of China's Tourism.* Tourism Educational Publishing House, Beijing (in Chinese).

Wang, X. (2003) China in the eyes of western travelers, 1860–1990. In: Lew, A., Yu, L., Ap, J. and Guangrui, Z. (eds) *Tourism in China.* Hayworth, New York, pp. 35–50.

Wen, J. and Tisdell, C. (2001) *Tourism and China's Development. Policies, Regional Economic Growth and Ecotourism.* World Scientific Publishing, Singapore.

Wittfogel, K. (1957) *Oriental Despotism. A Comparative Study of Total Power.* Yale University Press, New Haven, Connecticut.

Xu, G. (1999) *Tourism and Local Economic Development in China. Case Studies of Guilin, Suzhou and Beidaihe.* Curzon Press, Richmond, UK.

Yatsko, P. and Tasker, R. (1998) Outward bound: just in time, ordinary Chinese catch the travel bug. *Far Eastern Economic Review*, 26 March.

Zhang, G. (1989) Ten years of Chinese tourism: profile and assessment. *Tourism Management* 10, 51–62.

8 Fishing the 'Big Rivers' in Australia's Northern Territory: Market Diversification for the Daly River

D. CARSON[1] AND D. SCHMALLEGGER[2]

[1]*Tourism Research Fellow, Charles Darwin University, Darwin, Australia;*
[2]*James Cook University, Cairns, Australia*

Introduction

The destination marketing organization of Australia's Northern territory (Tourism NT) has made a strategic decision to increase the diversity of its product mix and to focus its attention more on the development of niche or special interest tourism (SIT) markets (AEC Group, 2007). Recent research into tourism in the Northern Territory indicates a decline in value received from more general interest markets such as backpackers (Carson *et al.*, 2007) and increase in value from SIT markets focusing on nature, culture and soft adventure (McKercher and Chan, 2005), including four-wheel drive tourism (Carson and Taylor, 2007), heritage tourism (Carson *et al.*, 2006b) and bird-watching tourism (Carson and Harwood, 2007). Other potentially valuable special interest markets may be fossicking, trekking or fishing (Carson *et al.*, 2006a). This chapter is interested in innovation in the fishing tourism marketplace, which is largely centred on the 'big rivers' in the Top End of the Northern Territory.

The need for innovation has been recognized as central to sustainable tourism development and to maintaining destination competitiveness (Carson and Jacobsen, 2005). Having the capacity to innovate allows the destination as a system (Lawrence, 2005) to adapt quickly to changing circumstances, take advantage of new opportunities and optimize the outcome from product or process delivery. Systemic innovation is generally described as a continuous process of generating and applying new ideas to the creation and upgrading of products, processes and services (Lee *et al.*, 2000). In tourism, innovation involves finding multiple ways of using existing resources while looking to develop new ones (Macbeth and Carson, 2005). In this sense, diversity in the marketplace (both in terms of demand and supply) can indicate the extent to which innovation is taking, or has taken, place (Patel and Pavitt, 1994).

Jacobsen (2005) identified a range of characteristics which are likely to be necessary in innovative tourism destination systems:

- a sense of leadership to take risks necessary for change and the skills to identify and acquire necessary resources;
- a propensity to form effective collaborations and partnerships with other stakeholders in the system;
- an ability to obtain and share knowledge about the market;
- effective interactions between the public and private sector;
- a sufficient amount of resources, including financial resources, infrastructure and know-how, to test new ideas and to allow for failures; and
- points of focus including natural and cultural assets which inspire alternative views about their use and lead to multiple options for development.

While these inputs to innovation are well described in the literature, it is less clear how to identify where (long-term) innovative processes occur (Lanjouw and Schankerman, 2004). Tourism destinations which attract high numbers of visitors are not necessarily innovative (see e.g. Faulkner, 2003). Rather, the evidence of innovation is likely to include emergence of new products and markets, and multiple strategies for exploiting the destination's assets. Faulkner and Vikulov (2001) found this to be particularly salient in destinations facing market shocks.

In this chapter, we are concerned with the fishing assets (including rivers, estuaries, lakes and billabongs) of the Northern Territory and how their use might reflect on innovation in the tourism destination system. Specifically, the purpose of this chapter is to examine the level of diversity in the fishing tourism marketplace in the Northern Territory. The research considers two aspects: the first is the diversity of trips taken to the Northern Territory which feature fishing as an activity (trip patterns); and the second is the industry response to the market in terms of the structure of the product mix and marketing strategies (industrial organization) of one of the big-river fishing destinations in the Territory's Top End. Data from the Northern Territory Travel Monitor (2000–2004) are used to describe trip patterns and a case study of the Daly River is used to analyse industrial organization.

International Research on Fishing Tourism

Recreational fishing appears to be a popular pastime in many countries in the developed world. Estimates are that 25% of New Zealand adults, 20% of US adult citizens, 12% of Canadians and up to one-third of Australian adults go fishing at least once per year (Bauer and Herr, 2004; Davie and Kopf, 2006). Ditton *et al.* (2002) estimated that fishing tourism accounted for about 10% of all recreational fishing trips in the USA. Factors contributing to market growth include an ageing population looking for 'soft adventure' activities, an increase in ownership of holiday homes near beaches, lakes and rivers and a trend towards 'return to nature' activities particularly for urban dwellers (Sipponen and Muotka, 1996).

A body of literature has emerged about recreational fishing in the USA on the back of regular regional and national consumer surveys conducted by the

National Marine Fisheries Service (e.g. Ditton *et al.*, 2002). Similar surveys have been conducted in Canada by Fisheries and Oceans Canada (2000) and in Australia by the Australian Bureau of Statistics (2000) and the Australian Government Department of Agriculture, Fisheries and Forestry (Henry and Lyle, 2003); however, there has been less reporting of these in the academic literature. Zwirn *et al.* (2005) looked at the potential for a fishing-based ecotourism sector in the Kamchatka region of Russia, Alban and Boncoeur (1999) did the same for the Iroise Sea region in France, Shrestha *et al.* (2002) for the Brazilian Pantanal, Shelby and Vaske (1991) for New Zealand, and Sipponen and Muotka (1996) for the Lake District of Finland. The major themes across these various studies included economic valuation, market segmentation, substitutability of the activity and destinations, and managing environmental impacts.

Research from the USA has identified a proportional increase in fishing tourism and a decrease in local or resident recreation fishing. There may also be a trend towards specialization of the market, with overcrowding of popular fishing spots near urban centres dissuading the more casual end of the market (Ditton and Sutton, 2004). There is a theme in the literature that rural and remote regions may be well situated to benefit from fishing tourism because increasing urbanization and exploitation of fish stocks near urban centres requires anglers to travel greater distances to engage in their activities (Bauer and Herr, 2004; Hunt *et al.*, 2005). Remote areas may be particularly attractive to highly specialized or 'insider' anglers (Ditton and Sutton, 2004) who may pay a premium to fish in particular environments or for specific species (Shrestha *et al.*, 2002).

Chi (2006) incorporated some notions of specialization in segmenting fishing tourist markets in the state of Louisiana in the USA. Chi proposed three market segments differentiated according to the relative importance assigned to motivations for challenge, experience, skills and relaxation. Leisure anglers were more motivated by relaxation and the experience, sports anglers by skills and competitive anglers by challenge and skills. Sports and leisure anglers were each about 40% of the sample recruited by Chi, with competitive anglers about 20% of the market. All three markets were dominated by males aged over 40 years, an observation repeated throughout most of the studies reviewed.

While there appears to be some diversity in the motivations, settings and experiences of recreational anglers, generally, there is a lack of literature specifically describing tourist fishing trips to provide confirmation. Shrestha *et al.* (2002) observed a lack of diversity in trip structures, with the standard trip being 1 week. Hunt *et al.* (2005), on the other hand, associated different trip structures (length of stay, but also type of accommodation, use of guiding services and so on) with different forms of access to the fishing site. More regulated access (charter planes etc.) resulted in more similar trip structures than when sites could be accessed independently (e.g. by car or train).

Fishing tourism in the northern territory

A major national survey of recreational anglers was conducted under the auspices of the Australian Government Department of Agriculture, Fisheries and

Forestry in 2000 and 2001 (Henry and Lyle, 2003). While the results used a mix of definitions for tourism, and often failed to distinguish between local and tourist activities, there were indicators that the nature of fishing tourism in the Northern Territory was somewhat different to that in Australia's other states and territories. While just 10% of all recreational fishing activities in Australia was by people fishing in states or territories other than those in which they lived, interstate visitors were about 40% of the market in the Northern Territory. Charter or hire boats were used by just 7% of recreational anglers nationally, but by 17% in the Northern Territory. Fishing in rivers and estuaries accounted for less than half of all activities nationally (the majority being coasts and lakes), but for more than 70% of activity in the Northern Territory.

The Northern Territory fishing reputation appears to be built on the opportunity to catch barramundi, and to fish in the big rivers (Northern Territory Department of Primary Industry, Fisheries and Mines, 2004). Barramundi is the most popular sport and recreational fishing target in the Northern Territory's rivers and estuaries. The big rivers are those which receive substantial seasonal flood flows, and include the Daly, Mary, Adelaide, South Alligator and East Alligator Rivers (Fig. 8.1). The major fishing season is from March to May ('the runoff'), when wet-season flood waters recede, attracting large barramundi to river mouths and estuaries. About half of all recreational fishing activity occurred at this time of the year (Campbell and Murphy, 2005), with the dry season (June–September) accounting for a further 32%. The Northern Territory Department of Primary Industry, Fisheries and Mines (2004) noted that tourists had gone from less than one-quarter of all recreational anglers in the Northern Territory to about 40% between 1995 and 2004. The comparatively organized and touristic nature of the recreational fishing sector in the Northern Territory was noted by Gartside (2001), and the focus on rivers and barra-

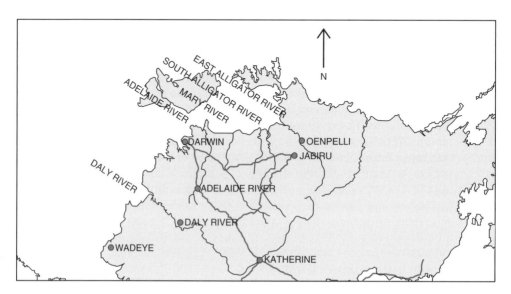

Fig. 8.1. The Northern Territory 'big rivers'. (From Anglers' Choice Fishing Safaris, 2007.)

mundi has been emphasized in destination marketing (Northern Territory Tourist Commission, *c*.2004).

It is estimated that tourists spent over AUS$10 million directly on fishing tourism in the Northern Territory in 2000/01 (Campbell and Murphy, 2005). Touristic expenditure items such as accommodation, airfares, and boat and equipment hire were a substantially larger proportion of visitor expenditure in the Northern Territory than in other states and territories. Gartside (2001) estimated around 250 fishing charter boats based in the Northern Territory (about one-quarter of the Australian fleet) with 120 of these being active at any one time. Tourism NT listed 77 charter or guiding operations and further 14 boat hire companies in its 'Fishing the Territory' guide book (Northern Territory Tourist Commission, *c*.2004).

The Daly River Case Study Destination

The Daly River begins at the intersection of the Katherine and Flora rivers and flows across the north-western parts of the Northern Territory to the Timor Sea. It encompasses the Daly River and the Douglas Daly regions, which are located almost halfway between the capital city Darwin and Katherine, one of the major tourist destinations in the Top End (Fig. 8.1). The population of the Daly River community and surroundings is estimated to be around 600 residents (Northern Territory Police, 2007), and the Daly River has been repeatedly promoted as one of the most popular waterways for recreational fishing and boating in the Northern Territory. The area also hosts two major annual fishing competitions – the 'Barra Classic' and the 'Barra Nationals'. Aside from recreational fishing, the region is promoted as a destination for bushwalking, birdwatching and crocodile-spotting. Additional attractions in the surroundings include the Douglas hot springs, gorges and Aboriginal art galleries in the surrounding Aboriginal communities (Katherine Region Tourist Association, 2007). The Tourism NT visitor web site (www.travelnt.com) listed six accommodation businesses near the Daly River in April 2008. It is difficult to estimate total capacity because all six establishments include powered and unpowered caravan and camping sites which can expand or contract depending on demand. Five of the establishments also had motel room or similar accommodation, but only a total of 12 such rooms were available. In order to stimulate growth in the fishing tourism market for the Daly River, the Northern Territory government has announced considerable investments in infrastructure including road upgrades and essential services (Northern Territory Government, 2007).

Methods

Trip patterns
Tourism NT conducted a rolling survey of visitors staying at commercial accommodation establishments between 1997 and 2004 (the Northern Territory Travel Monitor). A 5-year cohort (2000–2004) of international and interstate

leisure visitors was used for this research. About 3200 such visitors were sur-
veyed each year, with 15,457 in the cohort. Information relating to around 60
variables was collected, including whether fishing was an activity engaged in
during the trip, and also whether fishing was a reason for taking the trip to the
Northern Territory. Other variables referenced in this research were:

- destinations visited;
- composition and type of travel party;
- age and sex of visitors;
- length of stay in each destination visited;
- accommodation type in each destination visited;
- transport used within the Northern Territory;
- whether went on a fishing tour;
- activities engaged in during the trip;
- reasons for visiting the Northern Territory;
- whether had visited the Northern Territory previously.

Data were analysed using the Statistical Package for the Social Sciences (SPSS),
a statistical software package. Analysis of frequencies and distributions was
conducted, with chi-square tests and independent sample t-tests used to determine significant differences between groups. Key group comparisons were
between tourists who went fishing and those who did not, and between fishing
tourists who had fishing as a reason for visiting the Northern Territory and fishing tourists who did not. Data were generally analysed for all visitors to the
Northern Territory, but some observations are made about visitors to the Daly
River region, although the data set does not indicate whether visitors went fishing in that region or elsewhere.

Industrial organization

A 'destination audit' of the Daly River region was conducted using Internet-
mediated research (IMR). The IMR approach has been described by Taylor
(2005) and Cartan and Carson (forthcoming). The Google search engine (www.
google.com) was used to identify relevant business web sites. These were
sourced through a number of relatively broad search terms including 'Daly
River + fishing', 'Daly River + tours' and 'Northern Territory + fishing'. The
returned web sites were then scanned and manually filtered to exclude irrelevant URLs. In addition to the main Google search results, a snowballing technique identified further web sites of interest. This sampling procedure was
continued until significant repetition of returns indicated a satisfactory coverage
of the target population and it appeared that no new relevant URLs were forthcoming. A total sample of 31 web sites was achieved. These sites covered 36
businesses, given that some of the smaller businesses did not have their own
web sites. The final sample included tour operators (12), accommodation businesses (eight), intermediaries such as online travel guides or Internet booking
platforms (11), state and regional tourism offices (two), Aboriginal art galleries
(two) and a boat hire company (one). A content analysis was performed on
each web site to identify:

- the name and the type of the business or organization (e.g. accommodation, tour operator, online travel guides or destination marketing organization);
- the type of products offered or promoted (e.g. accommodation, guided tours, hire boats, etc.);
- the prominence of fishing as a tourism activity in the web site content (whether fishing is the core activity or just a side activity, how fishing is incorporated in the description of the product or destination or to what extent businesses appear to be targeting fishing tourists);
- the target group that the business is apparently aiming at (e.g. fishing tourists, independent travellers, tour groups);
- the suggested itineraries or trip characteristics (e.g. length of stay, stopovers, group size, etc.);
- the links to other businesses or business partners operating in the region; and
- the specific keywords which are used to differentiate the business from others (e.g. promotional slogans or words that are repeatedly used to promote the product or destination on the web site).

Results

Trip patterns
Nearly one-quarter (23%) of all leisure tourists to the Northern Territory between 2000 and 2004 included fishing as an activity during their trip. Smaller, river-based destinations such as Victoria (46%), Arnhem (44%), Gulf (41%) and Daly (38%) had a higher proportion of visitors who went fishing at some point during their Northern Territory trip. However, destinations that were unlikely to host fishing tourism such as Devil's Marbles (37%) were also popular among fishing tourists. Overall, destinations in the south of the territory (arid climate) were less likely to be visited by fishing tourists (15% of tourists there went fishing during their visit to the Northern Territory) than destinations in the wet tropics to the north (29%).

Fishing was cited as a reason for visiting the Northern Territory by 10% of leisure tourists between 2000 and 2004. The pattern of destinations visited by these tourists was similar to that by those who went fishing (even if fishing was not a reason for choosing the Northern Territory), with the river-based destinations of Gulf (25%), Arnhem (23%), Victoria (21%) and Daly (18%) being the more prominent. Southern destinations were visited by about 6% of tourists citing fishing as a reason to visit the Northern Territory, and northern destinations by about 12%. Overall, then, 13% of tourists who went fishing did not cite fishing as a reason for visiting the Northern Territory. This represented more than half the total number of fishing tourists. The gap is consistent for each destination, with 38% of visitors to the Daly region, for example, being fishing tourists, while only 18% cited fishing as a reason for visiting the Northern Territory.

Fishing tourists (defined now as those who went fishing, whether it was a reason for visiting or not) were statistically more likely to be aged 45–54 years (21% versus 15%; $p > 0.01$) and 55–64 years (27% versus 19%) than leisure visitors, generally. They were less likely to be aged under 35 (26% versus 40%; $p > 0.01$). Fishing tourists visiting the Daly region were similar in age profile to all fishing tourists. Fishing tourists were more likely to be male (60% versus 52%; $p > 0.01$) when compared to all leisure tourists and 56% of fishing tourists visiting the Daly region were male. Travel party size was around two people for all groups (leisure tourists, fishing tourists, Daly region fishing tourists). However, fishing tourists were more likely to be travelling in an 'adult couple' group (58% versus 47%) and less likely to be travelling unaccompanied (10% versus 21%), a pattern even more pronounced for fishing tourists visiting the Daly region (66% in adult couples and 5% unaccompanied).

While half of all leisure visitors were international visitors (with 39% from European countries), only 18% of fishing tourists were international visitors. Interstate markets were dominant, with one-quarter of fishing tourists from New South Wales and a further quarter from Victoria. The pattern was similar for fishing tourists who visited the Daly region. However, 'Fishing' was a reason for visiting the Northern Territory for less than half of the fishing tourists. The main reasons cited included 'to see the outback' (50%), 'to go somewhere different' (43%) and 'the weather and warmth' (40%). Reasons cited significantly more frequently by fishing tourists than leisure tourists generally were 'previous NT experience' (27% versus 20%) and 'the weather and warmth' (40% versus 30%). Otherwise, reasons for visiting the Northern Territory were very similar. Leisure tourists generally cited between four and five reasons for visiting, as did fishing tourists.

Other activities engaged in by fishing tourists included swimming (68% of fishing tourists), bushwalking (65%), wildlife viewing (48% plus 38% who went birdwatching) and consuming Aboriginal culture (46%). Fishing tourists listed between six and seven activities as part of their trip to the Northern Territory, while the overall mean was five activities. Wildlife viewing (especially bird-watching) and four-wheel driving were significantly more popular activities with fishing tourists who visited the Daly region (55% and 48%) than with fishing tourists (48% and 39%) and leisure visitors, generally (47% and 27%). Likewise, use of a four-wheel drive vehicle as the main form of transport around the Northern Territory was significantly more likely among fishing tourists (64% of those who visited Daly and 49% of all fishing tourists) than leisure visitors (26%). Private self-drive transport was more widely used by fishing tourists, while rental cars (7% compared with 14%) and tour coaches (5% compared with 22%) were less popular.

Less than 40% of fishing tourists went on a commercial fishing tour. The rate was similar for fishing tourists who visited the Daly region. Other commercial implications aside from transport and tours include use of accommodation. Fishing tourists were more likely to use caravan (69% versus 53%) and camping (17% versus 8%) styles of accommodation than leisure visitors generally, but less likely to use hotels (19% versus 34%) and backpacker accommodation (14% versus 31%). Fishing tourists who visited the Daly region had even higher rates of use of caravan (83%) and camping (22%) accommodation.

Fishing tourists spent significantly more nights in the Northern Territory than leisure visitors generally (19 nights versus 13 nights), and mean length of stay was even longer for fishing tourists who visited the Daly region (24 nights). The standard deviations were also greater, at around 2 weeks. While fishing tourists generally visited the same number of destinations as all leisure visitors to the Northern Territory (five or six destinations), fishing tourists who visited the Daly region visited an average of eight Northern Territory destinations. More fishing tourists (47%) than leisure tourists generally (32%) were repeat visitors to the Northern Territory.

Industrial organization

The sample of businesses identified through web sites was dominated by tour operators (12 businesses identified). Only two of these were based in the Daly region, with the other nine based in Darwin. Likewise, only two businesses provided tours exclusively to the Daly River, with the other nine businesses also offering tours to several Top End destinations including the Mary River, Shady Camp or the South and East Alligator River. Tour products were entirely based on fishing, with a particular focus on barramundi fishing. There was very little advertising of activities other than fishing by tour operators.

Five of the six accommodation businesses were physically located in the Daly region, with the sixth located in Darwin, but offering tours to the Daly River. Accommodation web sites emphasized fishing as the core activity for visitors (*The place to catch barramundi, Catch the experience!* or *Best guided fishing in the area*). Features that were highlighted included boat ramps, access to specific fishing sites, fish-cleaning facilities, and boat and tackle hire. The web sites included photographs of customers catching fish even more frequently than they included photographs of the accommodation facilities. Some sites (such as www.krol.com.au) even had live webcams covering the river, and provided regular updates on fishing conditions.

Apart from fishing, most accommodation businesses promoted bushwalking, four-wheel driving, birdwatching, heritage walks or Aboriginal culture as popular activities in the region. Most businesses provided basic accommodation facilities, including powered and unpowered camping sites, cabins, self-contained units or homestead accommodation. Only two businesses operated a restaurant and a licensed bar. All properties provided a swimming pool and a few emphasized television and mobile phone coverage (Next G) as special features.

Many of the tour operators explicitly recommended tour group sizes of two to four anglers, while others promoted opportunities for slightly larger groups (6–12). There was limited specific targeting of group types (family groups, friend groups, etc.), but there were two web sites who promoted their tours as *ideal for corporate groups, families and fishing clubs*. There appears to be a stronger focus on male fishing tourists as most photos on the web sites showed single men or a group of men catching fish (Fig. 8.2). All accommodation businesses seem to target mainly independent travellers arriving in their own vehicles. Maps or descriptions on how to get there are mostly included on the web sites but there are no references to either tours departing from Darwin

Fig. 8.2. Shows what may be a 'typical' Daly river fishing party – relatively small number of males fishing together from small craft commonly referred to as 'tinnies'. (Photograph courtesy of Tourism NT.)

or pick-up services. Some web sites mention explicitly that they are also catering to families with children.

Tour businesses often presented images and recommendations for travel during the 'runoff' fishing season, which occurs at the end of the wet (summer) season normally around March or April. Advertised tour packages had durations of up to 1 week. The most common trip lengths suggested were either 3- to 5-day or 2- to 7-day charters. Day tours appeared to be less popular and were only offered on three web sites. Longer charters (of up to 14 days) were occasionally promoted but featured the Daly River as just one of several fishing locations in the Top End. Extended tours in the Daly River were very similar across all web sites and typically included transfer to and from Darwin, lodge or camp accommodation at the Daly River, all meals and light refreshments, fishing tackle and a qualified and experienced guide. Only one operator offered tours to the Daly River on a 'mothership', where accommodation was provided on board.

Travel guide businesses which featured sections of their online guide books dedicated to the Daly region appeared to aim at independent travellers, including campers and caravanners. Although fishing was always presented as the main activity in the area, the guides did not exclusively target fishing tourists. Other activities that were regularly promoted included Aboriginal art, bushwalking and wildlife watching. These businesses typically contained directories (with links where available) of tour operator, accommodation, service (roadhouses etc.) and attraction businesses in the region.

Most tour operators linked directly to web sites for the accommodation businesses they included in their packages. However, only two tour operator web sites linked to other attractions or businesses in the Daly region. Guided fishing tours could be arranged upon request through almost all accommodation businesses but there was no further information provided on their web sites about specific tours, itineraries or operators. Only one business offered a direct link to a local fishing charter. Other businesses, such as Aboriginal art galleries and roadside inns, were sometimes mentioned on web sites but there were no links to the additional web sites for these businesses. There were some direct links to businesses outside the Daly region, including transport companies (car and camper-van hire) and fishing clubs mainly based in Darwin.

There were several travel intermediary sites referencing the Daly River. While they all offered fishing tour packages (including transport, accommodation, fishing guides and equipment), they did not name the tour operators who would supply the product. Tour descriptions, however, were identical to those described above. Marketing of tourism businesses with an interest in the Daly River was focused on fishing, and specifically on barramundi fishing. For example, five of the 11 tour operators included 'barramundi' or 'barra' in their business names. Other common promotional keywords and slogans focused on the close location to Darwin (*the perfect location for a weekend getaway for visitors staying in Darwin*) and customized service (*most experienced guiding team in the NT, We specialize in small groups and individual guidance*). Another common phrase for tour operators was *safari*.

There are two government auspiced destination marketing organizations which cover the Daly region. Content is similar for both web sites. The region is generally described as famous for its fishing but the fishing aspect was one of a number of promoted activities. There is substantial focus on Aboriginal cultural attractions and the natural environment (including hot springs, gorges, wildlife, etc.). The region is presented as a destination for independent travellers, including campers, caravanners and four-wheel drivers and there is a particular emphasis on rustic and basic outback-style accommodation and services. There are no direct links to businesses provided through the Tourism NT web site; however, information about service providers (including general descriptions and contact details) can be retrieved through the web site's search function. The Katherine Region tourism web site offers direct links to their association members.

Discussion and Conclusions

This trip patterns research suggests that there is a diversity, or potential for diversity, within the fishing tourism market to the Northern Territory. That only about half of all visitors who did fishing nominated fishing as a reason for coming to the Northern Territory may reflect on the degree of specialization in the marketplace. The 'casual' fishers (those whose visit to the Northern Territory was not directly fishing-related) constitute an important market segment that the analysis of industrial organization suggests may be overlooked by local businesses. Business promotion appears to assume that fishing is at the core of the reason for visiting the Daly River. Understanding the 'casual versus committed' dimension of the fishing tourism market is important in promoting fishing as a tourism activity, but also in destination marketing more generally. There may be a greater need to persuade the casual fishing group about the merits of the activity, and the market may be enlarged by linking fishing to other attractive activities. In the Daly River example, it did not appear that the potential diversity of the marketplace in terms of bundling of activities had been recognized by commercial operators.

Less than 40% of fishing tourists take fishing tours, which may reflect some product gap related to the destinations where tours operated, or their structure (length, composition of travel parties, types of accommodation and so on). However, the trip patterns of the independent fishing tourists (those who did not take a fishing tour) who visited the Daly region were similar to the itineraries offered by tour companies. Caravan and camping styles of accommodation were most popular, visitors travelled largely in couples, and they were in the Northern Territory for sufficient time to engage in multiple day fishing excursions. The gap may more likely lie therefore in the images that the fishing tour companies present. They may appear less attractive to mixed sex couples, for example. The lack of integration of other activities in fishing tours (particularly the popular activities among this tourist group of bushwalking, birdwatching and wildlife viewing) may also limit their appeal. The attractiveness of these other activities is recognized in the intermediary and destination marketing web sites, but less so in the accommodation and particularly the tour operator web sites.

Another factor related to the popularity of tours is the high use of private transport among fishing tourists and the consequent low use of hire or organized transport. Packages which appeal to self-drive tourists will be more dependent on in-destination product suppliers (fishing guides, for example), but the industrial analysis revealed that most guides were located outside of the destination, and so transport to the destination became a defining (but irrelevant) element of many of the products on offer.

The Daly River is closely linked to the other big-river fishing destinations in the Northern Territory through tour operators who include the Daly as one option among many. The dispersal of fishing tourists, and particularly the high concentration of those tourists in big-river destinations such as Arnhem, Gulf and Elsey, also indicates links between the key fishing destinations. The small scale of individual sites such as the Daly River can be compensated by the critical mass provided by a series of destinations offering similar experiences. While the critical mass issue makes maintaining links between destinations important, the Daly River can create its own niche through its advantages (for some markets) of close location to Darwin and the main road routes. These markets might have a preference for different styles of accommodation, and may combine fishing with other activities. The apparent lack of diversity in tour and accommodation options in the region suggests that such options have not been actively explored by the industry.

Seasonality was clearly important from an industrial perspective, with marketing focused on 'the runoff' and dry-season fishing in particular. Fishing tourists also nominated the 'weather and warmth' (assuming that this is a comment on the relatively cold winter weather in the south of Australia where more than half of fishing tourists originated) as a key attractor. There was not an obvious cohort of 'sports' fishers who might be attracted specifically to engage in the annual fishing competitions. Almost all of the competitions have been held in the runoff and dry seasons, so it is difficult to assess the extent to which they might add to a market that would be present even in the absence of competitions.

The product mix for fishing tourism was dominated by accommodation and tours. Food and beverage was notably absent, with most accommodation options involving self-catering. There was evidence of a range of transport services (fuel, mechanical repairs, etc.), but these sat to the side of the promotional material, rather than being constituted as important attractions and amenities in their own right. Again, the implication is a need to prepare specifically for a fishing trip (food and transport supplies, even provision of own bed linen in some cases) that might not appeal, or be possible, for the casual fishing market.

Fishing was an activity engaged in on trips that were longer in length, and particularly on repeat visits to the Northern Territory. This pattern may suggest that fishing is one of a number of 'special interest' activities (like birdwatching, wildlife viewing and bushwalking) which become more attractive once generalist activities (such as general sightseeing) have been completed. The special interest activities therefore become additional ways of exploring the destination and can encourage repeat visits and longer lengths of stay. There may also be a link between fishing tourist trip patterns and the relatively small number of international fishing tourists. International visitors to the Northern Territory tend to spend less time there than domestic visitors, and they are less likely to be repeat visitors. Additionally, there was no evidence of specific strategies to appeal to international markets.

Overall, the research found some strong and weak links between the behaviour of the market and the structure of the industry for fishing tourism in the Daly River. It could not reveal, however, whether the stronger links (accommodation used and destinations visited, for example) were a construct of limited choice or coinciding preferences. There was very little product differentiation, which manifested in much of the destination-oriented promotional material neglecting to identify specific products or even product types (such as specific accommodation establishments included in tour packages or even styles of accommodation that might be available). Likewise, there was little differentiation between tours, perhaps limiting the competitive advantages that might be gained by more skilled, experienced or charismatic guides.

The research suggests both some opportunities to explore innovation, particularly in relation to the casual and independent fishing markets, and a lack of diversity in industrial organization which may suggest a limited capacity to engage in innovation at a destination level. Few enterprises include offerings that are in any real way distinguishable from their competitors, and collaborative products (tour packages and the like) are also very similar to one another. Growing the fishing tourism market for the Daly River may require thinking beyond 'fishing' and consideration of the range of market segments with an interest in this activity but who may be better served by different forms of accommodation, more personalized and locally based tour options, attention to the potential international market/s, and integration of regional cuisine and greater gastronomic choices. The small size of the destination (number of businesses and number of visitors) suggests that innovation of this nature would need to operate across the Northern Territory more generally, but the Daly River can use its geographic location as competitive advantage within the wider network of destinations.

Fishing is a popular activity for some tourism markets in the Northern Territory, and is regularly featured in promotional images. There may be potential for fishing tourism to contribute to Tourism NT's ambitions to increase the diversity of its product mix and to foster SIT. What is evident from the case study of the Daly River, however, is a lack of diversity in fishing tourism product offerings, and a consequent lack of diversity in the profile of consumers. The Daly River region faces a number of challenges in achieving the characteristics Jacobsen (2005) claimed as necessary for systemic innovation. The small scale of tourism development and the remoteness of the location mean it is difficult to achieve critical mass, networks and collaborations are hard to maintain and resources are limited. There is increased emphasis therefore on entrepreneurship and knowledge management. This research has highlighted the need for more research into how remote regions can emerge as tourism systems of innovation.

References

AEC Group (2007) NT Tourism Industry Strategic Plan (2008–2012). Available at: http://www.aecgroupltd.com/files/images/AEC%20Report%20Draft%20Final.pdf

Alban, F. and Boncoeur, J. (1999) Commercial fishing, recreational fishing and tourism: investigating the potential for developing a pluri-activity. The case of the Iroise Sea, Western Brittany, France. *The XIth Annual Conference of the European Association of Fisheries Economists*. Dublin, Ireland.

Anglers' Choice Fishing Safaris (2007) Anglers' choice fishing locations. Available at: www.anglerschoice.com.au/map.html

Australian Bureau of Statistics (2000) *Participation in Sport and Physical Activities*. Australian Bureau of Statistics, Canberra.

Bauer, J. and Herr, A. (2004) Hunting and fishing tourism. In: Higginbottom, K. (ed.) *Wildlife Tourism: Impacts, Management and Planning*. Common Ground, Melbourne, Australia, pp. 57–77.

Campbell, D. and Murphy, J.J. (2005) *The 2000–1 National Recreational Fishing Survey: Economic Report*. Australian Government Department of Agriculture, Fisheries and Forestry, Canberra.

Carson, D. and Harwood, S. (2007) Authenticity as competitive advantage for remote tourism destinations. In: McDonnell, I., Grabowski, S. and March, R. (eds) *Proceedings of the 17th Annual CAUTHE Conference, Sydney, 11–14 Feb 2007*. University of Technology, Sydney, Australia.

Carson, D. and Jacobsen, D. (2005) Knowledge matters: harnessing innovation for regional tourism development. In: Carson, D. and Macbeth, J. (eds) *Regional Tourism Cases: Innovation in Regional Tourism*. Common Ground, Melbourne, Australia, pp. 7–27.

Carson, D. and Taylor, A. (2007) Economic development for remote communities: can 4WD tourism help? *3rd International Conference on Tourism*, Athens.

Carson, D., Middleton, S. and Jacobsen, D. (2006a) *Tourism Innovation in the Northern Territory: Product Gaps and Investment Strategies*. Charles Darwin University Tourism Research Group, Darwin, Northern Territory, Australia.

Carson, D., Richards, F., Lee, S. and McGrath, M. (2006b) The economic value of heritage tourism: the case of Australia's Alice springs. *International Symposium on Cultural Heritage Protection and Tourism Development*, Nanjing, China.

Carson, D., Boyle, A. and Hoedlmaier, A. (2007) Plan or no plan? The flexibility of backpacker travel in Australia. In: McDonnell, I., Grabowski, S. and March, R. (eds) *Proceedings of the 17th Annual CAUTHE Conference, Sydney, 11–14 February 2007*. University of Technology, Sydney, Australia.

Cartan, G. and Carson, D. (forthcoming) Local engagement in economic development and industrial collaboration around Australia's Gunbarrel highway. *Tourism Geographies*.

Chi, Y.N. (2006) Segmenting fishing markets using motivations. *e-Review of Tourism Research* 4(3), 64–73.

Davie, P.S. and Kopf, R.K. (2006) Physiology, behaviour and welfare of fish during recreational fishing and after release. *New Zealand Veterinary Journal* 54(4), 161–172.

Ditton, R.B. and Sutton, S.G. (2004) Substitutability in recreational fishing. *Human Dimensions of Wildlife* 9, 87–102.

Ditton, R.B., Holland, S.M. and Anderson, D.K. (2002) Recreational fishing as tourism. *Fisheries* 27(3), 17–24.

Faulkner, H.W. (2003) Rejuvenating a maturing tourist destination: the case of the Gold Coast. In: Faulkner, H.W., Fredline, L., Jago, L. and Cooper, C.P. (eds) *Progressing Tourism Research – Bill Faulkner*. Channel View, London.

Faulkner, H.W. and Vikulov, S. (2001) Katherine, washed out one day, back on track the next: a post-mortem of a tourism disaster. *Tourism Management* 22(4), 331–344.

Fisheries and Oceans Canada (2000) 2000 Survey of recreational fishing in Canada. Available at: http://www.dfo-mpo.gc.ca/communic/statistics/recreational/canada/2000/index_e.htm

Gartside, D. (2001) *Fishing Tourism: Charter Boat Fishing*. Wildlife Tourism Report No 12. Sustainable Tourism Cooperative Research Centre, Gold Coast, Australia.

Henry, G.W. and Lyle, J.M. (2003) *The National Recreational and Indigenous Fishing Survey*. Australian Government Department of Agriculture, Fisheries and Forestry, Canberra.

Hunt, L.M., Boxall, P., Englin, J. and Haider, W. (2005) Forest harvesting, resource-based tourism, and remoteness: an analysis of northern Ontario's sport fishing tourism. *Canadian Journal of Forestry Research* 35, 401–409.

Jacobsen, D. (2005) Processes influencing innovation in the tourism system in Woodburn, New South Wales. In: Carson, D. and Macbeth, J. (eds) *Regional Tourism Cases: Innovation in Regional Tourism*. Common Ground, Melbourne, Australia, pp. 131–136.

Katherine Region Tourist Association (2007) Douglas and Daly river. Available at: www.krta.com.au/images/library/File/Douglas_Daly_River.pdf

Lanjouw, J.O. and Schankerman, M. (2004) Patent quality and research productivity: measuring innovation with multiple indicators. *The Economic Journal* 114(495), 441–465.

Lawrence, M. (2005) The system matters: systems thinking and the study of regional tourism destinations. In: Carson, D. and Macbeth, J. (eds) *Regional Tourism Cases: Innovation in Regional Tourism*. Common Ground, Melbourne, Australia, pp. 9–17.

Lee, C.M., Miller, W., Hancock, M.G. and Rowen, H. (2000) *Silicon Valley Edge: The Habitat for Innovation and Entrepreneurship*. Stanford University Press, Palo Alto, California.

Macbeth, J. and Carson, D. (2005) Regional tourism systems and the implications of innovative behaviour. In: Carson, D. and Macbeth, J. (eds) *Regional Tourism Cases: Innovation in Regional Tourism*. Common Ground, Melbourne, Australia, pp. 28–129.

McKercher, B. and Chan, A. (2005) How special is special interest tourism? *Journal of Travel Research* 44(August), 21–31.

Northern Territory Department of Primary Industry, Fisheries and Mines (2004) Fishery Status Reports 2004: Recreational fishing. Available at: http://www.nt.gov.au/dpifm/

Fisheries/Content/File/2004_FSR_
recreational.pdf

Northern Territory Government (2007) Daly
river road seal extended. Available at:
http://newsroom.nt.gov.au/index.cfm?
fuseaction = viewRelease&id = 2545&d = 5

Northern Territory Police (2007) Available at:
http://nt.gov.au/pfes/index.cfm?
fuseaction = page&p = 43&m = 22&sm =
48&crumb = 33

Northern Territory Tourist Commission
(c.2004) Fishing the Territory: Share Our
Story. Tourism NT, Darwin, Australia.

Patel, P. and Pavitt, K. (1994) The nature of
economic importance of national innovation systems. STI Review 14, 9–32.

Shelby, B. and Vaske, J.J. (1991) Resource
and activity substitutes for recreational
salmon fishing in New Zealand. Leisure
Sciences 13, 21–32.

Shrestha, R.K., Seidl, A.F. and Moraes, A.S.
(2002) Value of recreational fishing in the
Brazilian pantanal: a travel cost analysis
using count data models. Ecological
Economics 42, 289–299.

Sipponen, M. and Muotka, M. (1996) Factors
affecting the demand for recreational fishing opportunities in Finnish lakes during the
1980s. Fisheries Research 26, 309–323.

Taylor, A. (2005) A critical evaluation of
aspects of the tourism information commodity marketplace in Australia and some
implications for innovation in tourism.
MBus Dissertation, School of Tourism and
Hospitality, Southern Cross University,
Lismore, New South Wales, Australia.

Zwirn, M., Pinsky, M. and Rahr, G. (2005)
Angling ecotourism: issues, guidelines and
experience from Kamchatka. Journal of
Ecotourism 4(1), 16–31.

9 The Amazon: a River Tourism Frontier

B. PRIDEAUX[1] AND G. LOHMANN[2]

[1]James Cook University, Cairns, Australia; [2]School of Travel Industry Management, Hawaii, USA

Introduction

The statistics of the Amazon region are impressive. The volume of water carried by the river is more than that of the next eight largest rivers combined while the Amazonian rainforest is the largest in area in the world and contains an extraordinary diversity of flora and fauna. The Amazon basin, which is approximately 6.9 million square kilometres in size, contains approximately 13% of the world's biota and sustains about 40% of the earth's remaining tropical rainforest (Brandon *et al.*, 2005). Although scientific interest in Amazonia started soon after it was explored by Francisco de Orellana, who travelled along the river from the Andes to the mouth of the river between 1541 and 1542, the region receives relatively few tourists even from Brazil or other Latin American countries.

Rather than a region of high tourist interest, the Amazon is better known as a place where rapid deforestation is occurring and where indigenous Indian tribes have been fighting for their rights. Given the popularity of nature-based tourism, and ecotourism in particular, it is surprising that the Amazon has not received more interest from the global tourism industry. The region's enormous biodiversity and the range of fauna that is present, in addition to the region's cultural and heritage resources, have the potential to become a major global nature tourism destination provided that demand can be stimulated and the infrastructure required to support tourism development is built. In the Amazon, sometimes referred to as Amazonia, the areas beyond the river are inextricably bound to the river to form a resource that has the potential to attract and sustain a tourism industry that with proper planning can be both sustainable and large scale. This chapter examines a number of issues relating to the use of the Amazon River and its tributaries as a tourism resource. After discussing significant ecological and geographical aspects of the Amazon region, the chapter examines development in the major tourism nodes of

Manaus and Belém. Unlike other chapters in this volume, the initial discussion involves a brief summary of issues (including deforestation) that have been associated with the Amazon and a more substantial discussion on economic issues related to development.

While there has been a major debate in the tourism literature, and others, about the role of tourism in conservation as well as its ability to promote sustainability (Leiper, 2006), this chapter restricts its focus to a number of development-related issues in the region. Based on the abundant evidence of the richness of the Amazon's natural heritage, this chapter assumes that there are significant opportunities for ecotourism development in the Amazon but does not engage in this debate. Apart from drawing on a range of secondary sources, the methodology used in the preparation of this chapter includes observations made by the authors during a field trip to the region and discussions held with a number of tourism and transportation industry leaders.

Landscapes

The Amazon rainforest spreads out over nine Latin American countries (Bolivia, Brazil, Colombia, Ecuador, French Guiana, Guyana, Peru, Suriname and Venezuela; Fig. 9.1) and covers an area of approximately 3.4 million square kilometres, down from 4.1 million square kilometres in 1970 (National

Fig. 9.1. The Amazon system. (From GNU Image Wikipedia Commons, 2008.)

Geographic, January 2006). Of this area, 62.4% is found in Brazil followed by 16.3% in Peru and 12% in Bolivia. The length of the Amazon has been a matter of contention for centuries with the latest claims (Roach, 2007) placing the river at 6800 km in length compared to the Nile's 6695 km length. From its reported source on the Nevado Mismi mountain in Peru (Smith, 2000), the river and its major tributaries including the Purus, Madeira, Yapura, Tocantins, Araguaia and Negro flow through a variety of landscapes ranging from high mountain ranges in the west to vast lowlands in the east. The length of the Amazon's major tributaries is impressive and is outlined in Table 9.1. In the west, the Amazon and its major tributaries have their source in the Andes Mountains. The mountain regions are characterized by vegetation types that range from alpine in the higher parts of the Andes to rainforests on the lower slopes. Later, the river flows through a savannah region known in Brazil as the *Cerrado*. This region, which covers about 25% of the Amazon basin, extends from Roraima in the central Amazon basin to the southern Mato Grosso in Brazil.

The rainforest regions form the largest ecological system in the Amazon basin. The remaining regions are flood plains and the coastal regions boarding the Atlantic Ocean. The flood plains cover up to 10% of the Amazon and are characterized by lakes, marches, wetlands and flooded forests (*igapó*). These areas are among the most biologically diverse in the Amazon but also are the most threatened because of encroachment by humans with some areas being converted to urban space, ranches and farmlands. The largest area of flood plain is found at the mouth of the Amazon where silt washed down by the river has formed numerous low-lying silt islands, the largest of which is Marajó. Also in the east, the Amazon region has a long coastline characterized by mangrove forests and river estuaries.

Unlike other major river systems the number of people living beside the river and its many tributaries is very small although in pre-Columbian times it is

Table 9.1. Length of major rivers in the Amazon system.

Name	Length (km)	Location
Amazon	6387	Peru, Brazil
Puurus	3379	Peru, Brazil
Madeira	3239	Bolivia, Brazil
Yapura	2820	Columbia, Brazil
Tocantins	2750	Brazil
Araguaia	2575	Brazil
Juruá	2410	Peru, Brazil
Negro	2250	Columbia, Brazil
Xingu	2100	Brazil
Tapajós	1900	Brazil
Guaporé	1749	Brazil, Bolivia
Icá (Putumayo)	1575	Columbia, Peru, Ecuador, Brazil
Marañón	1415	Peru
Iriri	1300	Brazil

Fig. 9.2. A typical example of the river craft that ply the Amazon connecting isolated settlements. (Photograph courtesy of Bruce Prideaux.)

apparent that some sections of the river supported an extensive sedentary population of indigenous people who practised intensive root-crop farming supplemented by hunting and fishing. The evidence of this civilization is today limited to the accounts of the early explorers and potsherds excavated by archaeologist. Because wood rather than stone was the primary building material our understanding of this society is very limited because of the shortage of evidence. One reason given for the decline of this civilization was the introduction of European diseases such as flu, smallpox and measles.

Today, the rivers of Amazonia constitute the primary transport corridor for people who live in the region. Where they exist, roads generally radiate inland from river ports rather than following the river and are subject to high and constant maintenance problems. Figure 9.2 illustrates the type of watercraft that ply the river connecting isolated communities with larger centres. Surprisingly, the river has attracted only a few cruise operators, including CVC, the largest tour operator in Brazil. Commercial passenger boats operate regular services in many areas and between the major cities, it is possible to join river tours operating half-day to multi-night luxury cruises as illustrated in Fig. 9.3.

Flora and fauna

The forests of Amazonia contain an extraordinary variety of flora and fauna creating excellent opportunities for ecotourism. In a recent estimate of the total number of species expected to occur in Brazil, Lewinsohn and Prado (2005)

Fig. 9.3. The *Atakan I*, one of a fleet of three luxury Amazon cruise boats based in Belém, operated by Atakan Amazon. (Photograph courtesy of Bruce Prideaux.)

found that Brazil contained between 1.4 million and 2.4 million species of larger taxa. Currently about 1500 new species are described each year. In other taxa, Brazil has high percentages of all known species. Of the 5023 mammalian species, Brazil has 541, while it has 633 of 8163 reptilians and 687 of 5504 amphibians (Lewinsohn and Prado, 2005). An interesting point made by these authors is that currently there is no way of establishing how much of the undescribed biodiversity exists outside of the regions that have been sampled by biologists.

Animals unique to the region include the Pink Dolphin (*Inia geoffrensis*), the grey dolphin (*Sotalia fluviatills*), numerous species of colourful birds including the Macaw (*Psittacidae*), the Jaguar (*Pantera onca*), Peccary (family *Tayassuidae*, a wild pig), Tamandua (a species of ant eater), Tapir (*Tapirus terrestris*), Giant Otter (*Pteronura brasiliensis*) and a large number of monkey species including the Squirrel Monkeys, Red Howlers, Brown Capuchins and Black Spider Monkeys, and the world's largest snake, the Anaconda (*Genus Eunectes*). The rivers of the region also contain a large variety of fish including the Arapima which may weigh up to 200 kg and the infamous Piranha (family Serrasalmidae). Of the 20 known species of Piranha, only four are known to have attacked humans. The forest has a large variety of trees and other plants, some of which have found their way into domestic gardens in many other countries. The rubber tree, a species endemic to the Amazon region, was the first of the region's flora to be commercialized and it underpinned substantial urban development primarily centred on Manaus and Belém.

National parks

The Brazilian Institute of Environment and Renewable Natural Resources (IBAMA) coordinates the process of establishing protected areas in Brazil. The tasks undertaken by IBAMA include the identification of suitable park areas, legal designation, management plan preparation, infrastructure development and staffing. IBAMA works in conjunction with state and municipal authorities and builds partnerships with local communities to ensure that park plans effectively integrate input from local residents. Currently, there are 68 official national parks in Brazil, mostly outside of the Amazon region.

Lack of funds and staff shortages have led to some critics commenting that Brazilian parks exist in name only. This is the case in the Amazon National Park, which straddles the border between the States of Pará and Amazonas. Comprising 994,000 ha of rainforest (an area the size of Jamaica), the Amazon National Park lies on the left bank of the river Tapajos. The park is the largest in Brazil, the only one in the State of Pará, and suffers from illegal logging. For many unique forest plant and animal species of Pará State, the Amazon National Park represents a last refuge. Other important Brazilian national parks located in the Amazon region are the Jaú National Park (2,272,000 ha), Pico da Neblina National Park (2,200,000 ha) and the Tumucumaque Mountains National Park (3,882,120 ha). In general, these parks do not provide tourism infrastructure, particularly in terms of access and accommodation.

Deforestation and Tourism

Collectively, Amazonia's landscapes, flora, fauna and indigenous cultures have enormous potential for tourism development ranging from ecotourism through to urban and mass coastal tourism on the Atlantic. However, the decades-long bad press that the Amazon has received because of deforestation and suppression of Indian rights has engendered a negativity that must be overcome if significant tourism development is to occur. Before looking in more detail at the type of river tourism that is occurring, it is useful to briefly review current developments in the level of deforestation occurring in the region.

Deforestation has been a major concern from a number of perspectives including loss of unique habitats and more recently from the contribution that deforestation has made to climate change. Most of the clearing has been to support the expansion of agriculture and pastoral activities and commenced on a large scale with the start of construction of the Trans-Amazon Highway system in 1970 (Fearnside, 2005). Settlement followed the roads and continued into the 1980s with large waves of poor farmers migrating into the region in search of land particularly in the Brazilian section of the region. According to the 2000 Brazilian national census (IBGE, 2002), the population of rural Amazonia is now stable. While this period of large-scale migration to the region has largely subsided new threats in the form of land clearing for biofuels, logging, ranching and construction of large hydroelectricity dams such as the one built at Balbina (north of Manaus) are currently posing dangers to the region's ecosystem.

It is apparent that deforestation is a consequence of government policy, perhaps not through direct strategies to develop the forest for other purposes but through the lack of coherent policy that directs development and conservation. For example, the Brazilian government's policy of promoting petroleum self-sufficiency based on ethanol production has been one factor behind the more recent clearing of the forest for agriculture. Another has been the growth in soybean production which is one of the principal export crops of Brazil. According to Williams (2006), Brazilians, and in a collective sense the Brazilian government, have long regarded the Amazon as a communal possession that is available for use and given that in strict monetary terms, cleared rainforest land is many times more valuable than forest, it is not surprising that deforestation has occurred. It is only recently that other measures of communal worth of natural areas such as rainforest have been recognized. Expanding the definition of economic worth to include ecosystem services such as carbon storage, oxygen generation, pest control provided by birds and water purification in water catchments led to a recent finding that the northern boreal forests were worth an estimated US$250 billion per year or about US$160 per hectare (Pearce, 2006). When the value of the forest is estimated on a basis that includes the value of ecosystem services, the true economic contribution of the Amazon to global economic services is enormous. In addition to ecosystem services, other uses such as tourism, the contribution of plants with medicinal properties and timber also add value to forest areas such as the Amazon. In an earlier study on the productive capacity of the Amazon at Mishana in Peru, Peters *et al.* (1989) estimated that 1 ha of the forest produces fruit worth about US$50 per year in addition to latex, also worth approximately US$50 per year (in 1989 prices). On an annualized basis, the value of sustainable rainforest production was estimated by these authors to be greater than conversion of the rainforest to grazing lands. The value of tourism as an alternative industry has not been assessed in any meaningful way although given the nature of the resource and its diversity, the potential value able to be derived from tourism is enormous.

Indigenous Culture

Indigenous in Latin America is most clearly defined as those ethnic groups who predated the European conquistadores. Despite the huge diversity of peoples and cultures, there seems to be some societal commonalities in Indigenous communities in the region: these are cultural (shared knowledge, identity and well-being strategies), political (self-determination, internal hierarchies, territorialism), spiritual (ideology, belief system, religion) and ecological (use of natural resources, ecological cycles, carrying capacity of ecosystems). Over 400 different Indigenous groups are estimated to live within the region – roughly 10% of the total population. Nevertheless, recent data suggest that Indigenous peoples remain some of the most marginalized in every country in the region (Montenegro and Stephens, 2006).

Besides its natural wealth, the State of Pará also is home to a valuable cultural treasure, about 40 indigenous groups, scattered through an area of over 23 million hectares. Of this area, more than 8 million hectares have been delimited by Funai (National Indigenous Foundation) as homelands for indigenous groups, ensuring security and preservation of that space. Among the biggest indigenous communities in Pará are the Andira Marau, Munduruku and the Kayapó.

Tourism Development

In stark contrast to the well-developed tourism industries that have emerged in other river systems, the Amazon has been largely ignored both by domestic tourists in the counties of the Amazon region and by the international tourism industry. In part, this can be attributed to isolation and distance. For example, from the major population centres of Brazil including São Paulo and Rio de Janeiro, a flight by schedule airline using Boeing 737 aircraft takes about 3.5 h. International tourists face even longer flights. Moreover, the focus of tourism development in Brazil and other nations in the Amazon region has been elsewhere. International tourism has focused on Rio de Janeiro and other centres to the south and to a lesser extent in the highlands of the west. In a similar manner, Peru's tourism industry has focused on Lima and the Inca sites in the Andes. In other South American countries, a similar pattern has emerged with tourism focused on major cities, coastal areas and in some cases on relatively accessible mountain regions. In reality, the Amazon has been viewed as occupying a peripheral location both by domestic and international tourists. While some areas have recently begun to actively promote Amazonian tourism, they continue to face problems of distance, lack of suitable infrastructure and products that can compete with other domestic and international destinations.

Given the size and diversity of the river system, it is surprising that a substantial river cruising industry has not emerged. Apart from CVC, the largest Brazilian tour operator, no major international cruise line has established regular routes in the Amazon River. Currently the main focus of tourism activity is Manaus, with Belém in the east beginning to develop a more competitive tourism sector that the local authorities hope will grow substantially in coming years. In addition to these well-known destinations, Santarém is beginning to emerge as a third tourism destination. Popularly called the 'Pearl of the Tapajós River', Santarém is the largest city in the western area of the State of Pará, and its second most important city. With origins that go back to the great indigenous nation of the Tapajós, the city is located on the margins of that river. It is surrounded by forests, 'igapós' (flooded wood areas), many ponds and 'igarapés' (small river lagoons formed by running, crystalline water), all located a few minutes away from downtown. In Vila de Alter-do-Chão, a small town located 30 km from Santarém, river beaches are formed during low water season (from August to December). One of the local attractions is the confluence of the Tapajós River and the Amazon, where the waters do not 'mix'. This spectacle can be seen from the city's port entrance where the greenish-blue waters of Tapajós River and the muddy waters of the great Amazon River flow side by side.

The following discussion focuses first on the structure of Amazonian river tourism that has emerged in Manus followed by an analysis of the emerging tourism sector in Belém, both cities being located in Brazil.

Manaus

Manaus, located about 1450 km up river from the Atlantic Ocean, has emerged as the best known Amazonian destination and has a developing reputation as a nature-based destination. Located on the Rio Negro (in English, 'Black River'), 18 km upstream from the point where the Rio Negro meets the Amazon River, the city first gained prominence as a centre for rubber collection. From 1892, visionary state governor Eduardo Ribeiro commenced a building programme that transformed the city from a jungle trading post into a European style city with Parisian style avenues and Italian piazzas and the world famous 700-seat teatro Amazona, an opera house inspired by Paris' Opera-Garnier. The city's elite built grand mansions. The wealth of the rubber trade also underwrote the construction of an electric tram system before London or Brussels and electric street lighting before London. Today the city is a major centre for the production of electronic goods including mobile phones. The city's electronics industry has underpinned the development of a number of major international standard hotels which is an asset for the city's tourism industry.

From a tourism perspective the city's major attractions are its heritage precincts, Parque Ecológico, a 9000 ha ecological park, river beaches, river cruises and further from the city, access to the Amazon's rainforest resources. Surprisingly, the rainforest lodge sector remains relatively small and most are located some distance from the city itself. On the river, a major attraction is the confluence of the beige coloured Solimões River and the black coloured (so coloured because of the high level of humus carried in suspension) Rio Negro. For some kilometres both rivers run side by side before converging. Cruising is also a major sector and the city has the largest river boat sector of any city in Amazonia. Cruises include day trips and overnight trips specifically tailored to the tourism industry as well as scheduled trips to other ports along the Amazon.

Belém

Although not as well known outside of South America as Manaus, Belém, the capital of the Brazilian State of Pará, is an emerging destination that has set itself some ambitious goals regarding future tourism development. Located on the Pará River, a major river which flows into the delta region at the mouth of the Amazon, the city and Pará State authorities have recently embarked on a strategy to develop the city as a major hub for Amazonian tourism. Belém is the largest city in Amazonia and has a European history that commenced in 1612 when Captain Francisco de Castelo Branco was dispatched by the

Portuguese colonial authorities to defend the region against attempts at colonization by the British, French and Dutch. Castelo Branco selected a suitable
river bank location in what is now the City of Belém to construct a fort to
defend Portuguese claims to the region. The fort now forms the southern
boundary of a significant waterfront heritage precinct that the city administration, in association with the State of Pará, has developed. Figure 9.4 illustrates
part of the heritage precinct.

Recognizing that tourism has the potential to provide significant economic benefits, the Pará State Government (one of a number of Brazilian
states in Amazonia) commissioned a report (THR International, 2001) into
the tourism potential of the state. The report was adopted and at the time of
writing provided the guiding strategies for development in the region. Based
on the report's recommendations six development poles have been identified
and are planned to collectively constitute the core of future tourism development in Pará State. The poles identified are centred on Belém and include
the Atlantic Coast, Marajó (a low-lying Amazon delta island normally reached
by light aircraft or boat from Belém), Tapajós (located on the Amazon about
1500 km west of Belém), the Araguaia and Tocantins rivers (the combined
basins of these rivers cover approximately 9.5% of Brazil's national territory)
and the Xingu river (a tributary of the Amazon River). In reality, most of the

Fig. 9.4. This photo shows the recently renovated Mercado Ver-o-Peso (Check the
Weight Market) in the foreground, with the dome and spire of the Cathedral of Sé in
the background. To the right of the markets is the Forte do Presépio (Presepio Fort).
Collectively this area forms the southern end of Belem's riverfront heritage precinct.
(Photograph courtesy of Bruce Prideaux.)

areas identified as growth poles currently have poor, if any, tourism infrastructure and will require substantial public investment in infrastructure before
the private sector will consider investing in tourism projects. The potential
growth poles identified in the report all have potential to complement tourism
development in Belém which would in effect serve as a hub of the other
development poles.

The Tourism and Hospitality Research (THR) report identified transport as
a major limitation that will need to be addressed if large-scale tourism development is to occur. Air is the obvious mode required to bring visitors to the region
while road and river transport are essential to distribute visitors to the attractions that should constitute the region's tourism product. While the city of
Belém has direct air services to a number of large Brazilian cities, the cost of
seats is relatively high and overseas visitors must hub through other airports
such as São Paulo and Brasília, the capital city. Flights from Belém to other
potential tourism growth poles within the state were limited and expensive. In
2001, there were 16,666 weekly seats available on flights into Belém from
other Brazilian cities but only 2767 seats for travel on flights to other cities
within the State of Pará. Although seats into the region are limited, the airport
at Belém is modern and capable of receiving a far higher numbers of arrivals
than is currently the case. It is obvious that additional road and river transport
links also need to be developed to connect the major urban centres along the
Amazon with areas of high tourism interest including forest regions and national
parks that are found beyond the intensively settled rural belts surrounding the
region's urban settlements. The limited road network often suffers extensive
damage during the rainy season while the river often contains natural obstacles,
thereby reducing the speed of water traffic.

Other deficiencies include lack of sanitation, the poor standard of maintenance of many of the heritage buildings that constitute the cities' older and
attractive heritage precincts, and a severe shortage of tourist standard accommodation. Suitable accommodation is also an important issue as illustrated in
Table 9.2 and will require substantial enhancement and expansion to support
tourism development. As of 2007, Belém had only four hotels suitable for
international tourism usage although even these do not offer the standards

Table 9.2. Distribution of accommodation in Pará's identified growth poles. (From
THR International, 2001.)

Tourist poles	Hotels	Rooms	Percentage of total rooms	Average number of rooms per hotel
Belém	50	2449	57.6	49.0
Tapajós	12	324	7.6	27.0
Araguaia/Tocantins	25	625	14.7	25.0
Marajó	14	269	6.3	19.2
Xingu	6	160	3.8	26.7
Atlantic Coast	21	432	10.0	20.1
Total	128	4250	100.0	33.2

normally found in more established tourism destinations. Other centres had even less suitable accommodation.

In addition to infrastructure deficiencies the city has a lack of organized tourist attractions. Currently the city's major attractions are its waterfront heritage zone, zoo, botanical gardens and a limited number of river tour operators. To develop a wider attractions base, new nature-based as well as cultural- and river-based attractions and experiences will be required.

Developing Amazonian Tourism

Further development of Belém and Manaus, as well as any other potential sites in Brazil and adjoining countries, will require investment from the public sector as well as entrepreneurs. Initiating the development process required to build the region's tourism industry is a complicated task. The process of growth is complex and may be ignited by a number of initiatives that may emanate from the public sector, the private sector or both (Inskeep, 1991). Typically, growth involves expansion of demand in the form of increased tourist numbers underpinned with an expansion in the supply of infrastructure. Growth may be either demand-led, where growing demand for tourism experiences creates the need for new investment in infrastructure such as airports and accommodation or supply-led, where investment in airports, hotels, etc. provides capacity to accept greater numbers of tourists. In the latter case, the destination will need to create awareness of the destination through targeted marketing strategies.

In a typical capitalist economic model, the public sector usually restricts involvement in economic development to legislative initiatives designed to assist the growth process usually aided by some form of public benefit including subsidies and investment in key infrastructure such as transport and education. Direct investment in commercial ventures is becoming rare because of the recognition that the profit-driven private sector is usually more efficient than the public sector. In the tourism sector, governments at all levels have increasingly adopted a position of guidance and investment in strategic infrastructure such as transport while leaving other investment such as attractions and accommodation to the private sector (Gunn, 1994). The one area where the public sector retains an ability to manage development is through controlling development by strategies that include zoning, licensing and environmental impact assessment (Oliveira, 2002). In Brazil, the public sector is beginning to realize there is a need to prime development through planning and in some cases investing in infrastructure including utilities, education and planning. However, as is the case in any free market economy, large-scale development will only occur when the private sector recognizes the potential of an area as an investment site.

It is also apparent at least in the case of infrastructure-poor peripheral regions such as the Amazon that there is an important role for government in supporting tourism in either building or underwriting the infrastructure that is required to underpin tourism development. Provision of transport is a key element as is the provision of communications, energy, water, public health and workforce training. These areas in particular form the key inputs required by the private sector if it is to invest in a region.

The private sector, driven by the profit motivate, will only invest in projects when opportunities for profit are available. As a consequence, development plans of the nature suggested for Pará are more effective at identifying supply-side deficiencies and opportunities for developing new market sectors than in identifying opportunities for profitable investment. As a consequence, the needs of the entrepreneur and the wider commercial sector including corporations and other investment bodies may differ from the strategies suggested by planners. Understanding this process is a key factor in initiating a successful growth strategy. Unfortunately the planning literature is largely silent on the role of investors and entrepreneurs in the development process.

Russell and Faulkner (1999) highlighted the role of leading entrepreneurs in their study of the expansion of the tourism industry on the Gold Coast Australia. According to these authors, constructs such as the Destination Life Cycle Model (Butler, 1980) overlook the role of entrepreneurs to whom they ascribe a more fundamental position in the processes of destination development. Development initiated by entrepreneurs is described as unpredictable, even chaotic. The behaviour of developers according to Russell and Faulkner (1999, p. 411) 'is a creative process where entrepreneurs play a primary role both as chaos-makers and as initiators of adaptive responses to chaos induced by external events'. While not specifically identifying the role of Russell and Faulkner's (1999) entrepreneurs, alternative models of development such as the *Resort Development Spectrum* suggested by Prideaux (2000) have a more evolutionary approach to development that in the case of the Amazon may offer some guidelines for the development process.

It is apparent that significant enhancement of the Amazon's tourism infrastructure particularly in the areas of transport, accommodation and ecotourism operations is required before a serious attempt can be made to build either a domestic and/or international tourism sector. The following discussion, based on the Destination Development Matrix (Prideaux, forthcoming), illustrates from a theoretical perspective the type of actions that are required in both the supply and demand sides for development to occur using a highly modified demand and supply model.

The destination development matrix

To understand the situation that destinations in Amazonia currently find themselves in relative to demand, supply, marketing and the public sector policy environment the Destination Development Matrix (Prideaux, forthcoming) may be used to demonstrate the various relationships and mechanisms that operate in destinations. By understanding these relationships, planners, investors and marketers will be better equipped to undertake the various tasks allocated to them. The mechanisms that underpin the development of the tourism industry can be found in the economic sectors of demand and supply (Prideaux, 2004). In a standard demand and supply curve model, the shape and points of intersection of the supply and demand lines reveal a range of relationships including the relationship between demand and supply at various combinations of demand and the price consumers are willing to pay. While a useful illustrative concept, the standard supply and demand curve model does not adequately identify other relationships that occur in the tourism market place. The tourism supply curve is in reality an aggregated measure of a range of tourism-related inputs such as accommodation, transport, attractions, food and beverage and a host of other factors. To more effectively illustrate the relationships that exist between demand and supply in a tourism context, the Destination Development Matrix (see Fig. 9.5) shows how destinations are able to grow over time in a context that recognizes that destinations have upper capacity limitations and must grow along a growth path where demand and supply expand in a parallel manner.

While acknowledging that growth is often seen as a desirable outcome for a number of reasons, including employment generation, growth should not be seen as an end in itself. Depending on the capacity of a region to sustain tourism in numbers that will not reduce long-term sustainability, growth may be seen as a desirable social and economic policy objective. Determining long-term sustainability is an issue that continues to be vigorously debated in the literature (Mowforth and Munt, 1998) and while acknowledged is not further debated in this chapter. Where it is apparent that the potential exists for growth that is sustainable, the benefits should ideally be shared by all sectors in the community. In the Amazonian context, Manaus and Belém both have substantial

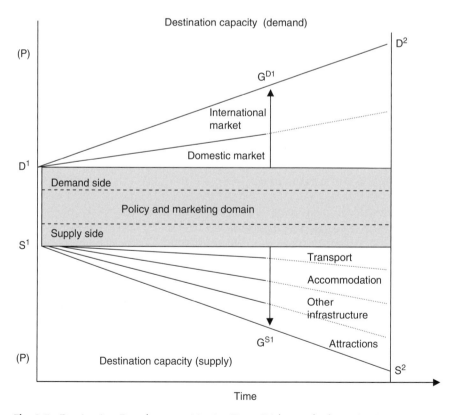

Fig. 9.5. Destination Development Matrix. (From Prideaux, forthcoming.)

capacity to expand their tourism sector without adversely affecting an already substantially modified local ecosystem. In addition, this process has the potential to share the benefits with socio-economic groups who currently live in improvised conditions. Tourism development also has the added benefit of assisting in employment creation and poverty alleviation.

Initiating the process of growth requires significant capacity building on the supply side in a partnership that will need to include the public and private sectors as well as the community (Prideaux, 2000). In parallel to the supply-side development required to underpin tourism development, strategies are also required to increase demand (Tribe, 1995). Figure 9.5 demonstrates the relationships that exist between a number of sectors in the destination using a time/volume of demand relationship based on destination capacity, growth, policy, marketing and the response of the demand and supply sides to growth. Economic growth occurs as the outcome of increased demand, provided it is underpinned by increased supply (Sinclair and Stabler, 1997). The growth path of this relationship can be traced through changes in demand and supply. Price (P) is also a key factor, as it will influence demand as well as the type and standards of tourism experiences that are offered.

Destination demand and supply relationships are usually illustrated using demand and supply curves with growth represented as a series of semi-equilibrium points along the demand curve. For the purposes of this discussion, the demand and supply relationship has been disaggregated in the form shown in Fig. 9.5 to allow the role of sectors such as transport and accommodation to be illustrated. Price is a significant factor and in a standard demand and supply diagram is the major determinant of the quantity of a service such as tourism demanded at various levels of demand and supply. In Fig. 9.5, price is shown as an implicit factor.

In Fig. 9.5 demand (D) and supply (S) are shown as mirror sectors where growth (G) in one sector is mirrored by growth in the other. D^1D^2 represents the theoretical demand curve of the destination that for the purposes of this illustration is able to expand to point D^2 after which further growth will cause a decline in long-term sustainability. In reality this point has yet to be determined for the study region. The destination's supply curve S^1S^2 must match the growth that occurs in the demand side at the rate indicated by the curve D^1D^2. It should be noted at this point that growth may be demand-led or if investors are confident that visitor numbers will increase in the future, growth may also be supply-led. At any point along the demand curve D^1D^2, demand should ideally match supply creating a temporary equilibrium point. For example, growth in demand to point G^{D1} must be mirrored by growth in supply to point G^{S1} on the destination supply curve S^1S^2. In the destination illustrated, growth is shown on the demand curve D^1D^2 and on the supply curve at S^1S^2. Thus, for the destination to grow to point G^{D1} on the demand line, supply expands along the supply line S^1S^2 to point G^{S1} where it will mirror demand and a new equilibrium point $G^{D1}G^{S1}$ is achieved. At this point the demand for domestic and international tourism is supported by the growth in supply of transport, accommodation, other infrastructure and attractions in the supply quadrant. If at this point bottlenecks occur in the supply side, expansion will be inhibited and infrastructure (for the purposes of this discussion infrastructure is illustrated here as transport, accommodation and attractions) will not be able to expand past capacity G^{S1}, preventing demand expanding beyond point G^{D1}. In Fig. 9.5, future growth in demand based on domestic and international tourism is illustrated by dotted lines beyond equilibrium point $G^{D1}G^{S1}$.

The Policy and Marketing Domain that lies between the demand and supply sector is the source of policy that determines the rate and form of growth and the marketing efforts that will be required to translate the desired level of growth into reality. Given the previous discussion on infrastructure, further growth will be dependent on improvements in the supply side supported by marketing to stimulate demand and a favourable policy environment that will favour projects that expand supply and generate demand.

Discussion

In the case of Belém, tourism development has followed a development pattern very similar to the one presented in the Destination Development Matrix (Fig. 9.5). Some parallel improvement has been undertaken by the public and private sectors in transport infrastructure, particularly at the airport, tourist attractions and accommodation. Since its official opening in 2001, Val de Cans Airport (Belém's international airport) has become the benchmark for airport development in other Brazilian cities. The new terminal incorporates a large shopping centre including banking, souvenirs, food and clothing. Both the state and local governments have funded new tourism-related initiatives including a redeveloped waterfront region where three old warehouses and one dock have been converted into a 32,000 m^2 air-conditioned space that contains restaurants, art galleries, a small beer distillery, artisanship stands, regional food kiosks, a space for fairs and events, a theatre for 400 spectators and a touristic harbour. Another example of support given by the public sector is the Mangal das Garças, a naturalistic park exhibiting numerous species of flora. In the private sector, new investment is occuring including a hotel to be built by the Accor group.

The major constraint for private sector investment has been the lack of a skilled and professional workforce although this is being addressed by new tourism and hospitality courses offered by local universities. Within the domestic market, Belém is still to be discovered. The Amazon region in general is considered a very expensive place to visit, particularly because it is located far away from the major tourist markets of São Paulo and Rio de Janeiro. Prior to airline deregulation in the 1990s, Brazilian domestic air travel was expensive and air travel between São Paulo or Rio de Janeiro to the Amazon region was more expensive than to Miami (USA), twice the distance from São Paulo to Belém or Manaus.

Domestically, the tourism market continues to focus on major coastal mass tourist destinations, such as Rio de Janeiro and most states located in the north-east of the country including Bahia, Ceará, Pernambuco e Rio Grande do Norte. As the domestic tourism market evolves and domestic tourists become more sophisticated, there will be opportunities for them to look for exotic destinations such as the Amazon region. Finally, even though Belém is the heart of the Amazon region, Manaus has successfully promoted itself as the 'real' Amazon. Aware of the need for tourism marketing improvements, the Pará State government has invested in new products as well as in promotion and marketing. Paratur, the tourism marketing department of the State of Pará, has been very active in organizing familiarization tours and inviting the national and international media to visit and write about the city of Belém and the rest of the state. In this respect, the public sector, in an example of public sector supply-led development, has taken the lead in investing in new infrastructure as well as providing marketing funds to assist the private sector to promote the region.

Conclusion

The Amazon region has enormous potential to develop river-orientated tourism; however, for a variety of reasons including the region's peripheral status and perceived high cost and isolation, tourism has remained a minor sector of the economies of the cities of Amazonia. It is likely that future development patterns will include land-based tourism adjacent to the river including ecoparks, ecolodges and urban tourism in the larger cities and more specific river-based tourism including cruising. This chapter has highlighted the opportunities that exist for developing tourism in the region including using the river for cruising and access to ecotourism locations. The chapter has also used the Destination Development Matrix to illustrate relationships that exist between the demand and supply sides and the central position occupied by the policy and marketing sectors in the development process. Using Belém as an example, it is apparent that the public sector will need to underwrite at least the first phase of development by providing essential infrastructure such as airports. Once essential infrastructure is in place, the private sector will have a significant opportunity to play its part in the development of tourism in the Amazonian region.

One question not addressed in this chapter is the sustainability of tourism in the Amazon. Given the size of the region, the sustainability of tourism in general does not appear to be a major problem; however, a prudent approach to development will be needed to avert future problems in the region. In specific areas and for specific forms of tourism, there may be issues that will need to be addressed. For example, in sensitive environmental areas, there may need to be specific visitor number levels established and in tourism involving the indigenous Indian population care will need to be exercised.

Acknowledgements

The authors would like to acknowledge the financial support provided by Paratur, the tourism marketing department of the State of Pará that underwrote the field work undertaken by the authors. The authors would also like to thank the owner of Atakan Amazon for his kind support in this project.

References

Brandon, K., Fonseca, G., Rylans, A. and Silva, J. (2005) Challenges and opportunities in Brazilian conservation. *Conservation Biology* 19, 595–600.

Butler, R. (1980) The concept of a tourist area cycle of evolution: implications for management of resources. *Canadian Geographer* 24(1), 5–12.

Fearnside, P. (2005) Deforestation in Brazilian Amazonia: history, rates and consequences. *Conservation Biology* 19(3), 680–688.

Gunn, C. (1994) *Tourism Planning: Basics, Cases and Concepts.* Taylor & Francis, London.

IBGE (2002) *Censo Demográfico 2000.* Instituto Brasileiro de Geografia e Estatística, Rio de Janeiro.

Inskeep, E. (1991) *Tourism Planning: An Integrated and Sustainable Development Approach.* Van Nostrand Reinhold, New York.

Lewinsohn, T. and Prado, P. (2005) How many species are there in Brazil. *Conservation Biology* 93, 619–624.

Montenegro, R.A. and Stephens, C. (2006) Indigenous health in Latin America and the Caribbean. *The Lancet* 367(9525), 1859–1869.

Mowforth, M. and Munt, I. (1998) *Tourism and Sustainability – New Tourism in the Third World.* Routledge, London.

Oliveira, J.A.P. (2002) Government responses to tourism development: three Brazilian case studies. *Tourism Management* 24, 97–110.

Pearce, F. (2006) One degree and we're done for. *New Scientist* 30 September, pp. 8–9.

Peters, C., Gentry, A. and Mendelsohn, R. (1989) Valuation of the Amazonian rainforest. *Nature* 339, 655–656.

Prideaux, B. (2000) The resort development spectrum. *Tourism Management* 21(3), 225–241.

Prideaux, B. (2004) The resort development spectrum: the case of the Gold Coast, Australia. *Tourism Geographies* 6(1), 26–59.

Prideaux, B. (forthcoming) *New Directions in the Study of Destinations.* Elsevier.

Roach, J. (2007) Amazon longer than the Nile River scientists say. *National Geographic News,* 18 June 2007. Available at: http//:news.nationalgeographic.com/news/2000

Russell, R. and Faulkner, B. (1999) Movers and shakers: chaos makers in tourism development. *Tourism Management* 20(4), 411–423.

Sinclair, T. and Stabler, M. (1997) *The Economics of Tourism.* Routledge, London.

Smith, D. (2000) Explorers pinpoint the source of the Amazon. *Geographic News,* 21 December 2000. Available at: http//:news.nationalgeographic.com/news on 8

THR International (2001) *Tourism Development Plan for the State of Pará,* Governo do Pará, Secretaria Especial de Produção.

Tribe, J. (1995) *The Economics of Leisure and Tourism: Environments, Markets and Impacts.* Butterworth-Heinemann, Oxford.

10 River Heritage: the Murray–Darling River

B. PRIDEAUX

James Cook University, Cairns, Australia

Introduction

The close association between rivers and civilization has left a rich heritage that in some areas has generated significant tourist interest. In its broadest sense river heritage includes both natural areas such as river banks, wetlands and the structure of the river itself, and a built element that includes buildings, places of special significance and even modified landscapes that bear witness to human activity that may stretch back in time for millennia. In the past and in some instances in the present, both the built and natural elements of river heritage have been subject to constant redevelopment where the value of the site, measured in terms of its ability to generate a net economic return, has been of foremost importance. Sites that failed this economic test were usually subject to redevelopment. The growing interest in tourism has introduced a new element into the estimation of economic worth where the wider contribution of specific sites, measured through its contribution of the regional tourism sector, has begun to be recognized.

While the idea of cultural heritage as a product for tourism consumption is relatively new in the literature (Ho and McKercher, 2008), the adaptive reuse of river heritage at least in the Australian context can be traced back to the 1960s when the river port town of Swan Hill first opened a 'Folk and Pioneers Settlement' museum on the banks of the Murray River in 1963 (Davidson and Spearritt, 2000). As a consequence, it is now easier to argue the case for the preservation of natural and built elements of river heritage than was the case in the past. Aside from their worth to the tourism industry, river heritage sites may also be viewed from a wider context including nostalgia, the contribution of natural sites to ecosystem services such as water supply and carbon absorption and their significance in personal, regional and national histories (Prideaux and Timothy, 2008). As McKercher (2001) noted, heritage is a powerful force for reintroducing people to their past and acts to rekindle their interest in history. In some cases, the contribution of a particular site may be measured on a global scale where some significant sites are given World Heritage status.

The growing recognition of the importance of river heritage as a resource that includes, but is wider than, the economic contribution of tourism has led to increased protection for many built and natural river heritage sites. This chapter examines aspects of river heritage and how the tourism industry has provided the impetus for the adaptive preservation of a significant heritage site on the Murray River, part of the larger Murray–Darling River System. The chapter commences with a brief overview of the Murray–Darling River System examining aspects that include its flow patterns and flora and fauna. The location and names of major rivers in the system are illustrated in Fig. 10.1. A short discussion on aspects of the history of human settlement of the river system follows. The development of the system's rural industries is briefly considered before the chapter examines the development of the river trade, which today has become a significant element of the tourism appeal of the river system. The chapter concludes with an examination of how elements of the river's built heritage based on the 19th-century river port of Echuca have been developed to support the region's tourism industry.

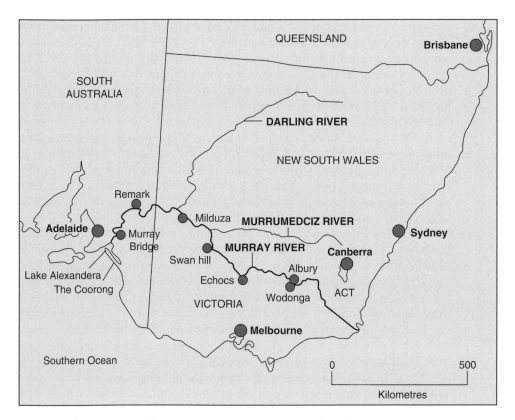

Fig. 10.1. The Murray–Darling system. (From GNU Image Wikipedia commons, 2008.)

The Murray–Darling River System

The Murray–Darling River System describes the entirety of Australia's largest river system that comprises the Murray River and its largest tributary the Darling River. The Murray is Australia's largest river flowing a total of 2575 km from its source in the Alpine region of Victoria to its mouth at Lake Alexandrina in the Coorong wetland region of South Australia. Major tributaries include the Murrumbidgee, Goulburn and Mitta Mitta Rivers. Flowing from east to west the river forms a significant part of the state border of New South Wales and Victoria. The Darling River is Australia's longest river measuring 2740 km at its confluence with the Murray at the western Victorian town of Wentworth. The Darling is fed by an extensive network of tributaries that join the river in its southern Queensland and northern New South Wales sections. In many sections of the Darling the river divides into numerous channels which flow only during periods of flood (Thoms *et al.*, 2004). Measuring 1061 million square kilometres in size, the Murray–Darling basin drains about one-seventh of Australia's land mass making it one of the world's largest river systems in area but not discharge volume.

The Murray–Darling supports a significant percentage of Australia's irrigated farmlands and, as is common with a number of the world's other great river systems, is closely associated with the history of inland settlement and the development of large-scale commercial farming. However, when compared to the major river systems in other continents the Murray–Darling has a very low discharge rate, a reflection of Australia's position as the world's driest continent where approximately 70% of the land mass receives less than 500 mm of rainfall per annum, and is classed as arid or desert (Geoscience Australia, 2006). As a comparison, the annual average flow of the Murray–Darling equals less than an average days flow from the Amazon (Gill, 1978) while in terms of water flow, each square kilometre of the river's catchments yield 75 times less water flow than the Amazon. In the Australian context, the Murray–Darling basin receives about 6% of Australia's total rainwater.

Rainfall is also highly variable on a year-to-year basis as well as on a regional basis (Thoms *et al.*, 2004), a result of the absence of high upland areas that are able to generate high levels of rainfall. River flows are therefore highly variable with alternating periods of floods and droughts (Young *et al.*, 2001). Rainfall in many areas is intermittent. Because of the variability of its flow, parts of the river system, particularly along the Darling, have dried up in extreme drought periods, although this is relatively rare. As a consequence of the development of large areas of the Murray–Darling basin for agriculture and pastoral industries, extensive irrigation systems have been built to service rural producers. The resulting modification of the river and importantly its flow characteristics has had significant adverse impacts on the river's ecosystems.

The topography of the river basin is characterized by upland sections which are found on the westward slopes of the Great Dividing Range. The Darling and its major tributaries have their source in the northern part of the Great Dividing Range and the Murray and its tributaries have their source in the southern section of the Great Dividing Range. The lowland sections of both rivers constitute the longest sections of both rivers and include extensive flood plains. The open flood plains found in the lowland sections of both rivers have a characteristic fan shape. A smaller number of confined flood plains are found in some upland sections of the rivers. After leaving the main catchments areas the river flows through large areas that do not contribute significant run-off. Two sections of the system, the Darling River and the Murray–Darling River west of the junction of the Murray and Darling rivers, are classed as 'exotic' rivers because the areas the rivers flow through do not contribute significant runoff and do not faction as catchments areas (Young *et al*., 2001). The Murray flows into the sea through a deltaic distributary system that has a weak connection through to the main river. This section of the river is not navigable by large boats.

The variability of the river systems' flow rate exercises a significant influence over the structure of the river system's aquatic and terrestrial ecosystems primarily because of the rate at which nutrients and energy is exchanged between the river and its flood plain. In the Murray–Darling the variability of flow rates has a significant impact on the exchanges of primary production to the higher-order organisms found on the flood plain and in wetlands in particular. The low predictability of river-level flows in the Murray–Darling System has resulted in specific adaptations in fresh water and terrestrial ecosystems.

In a typical time sequence, the river system will experience a large flood event causing the river to overflow its banks inundating its flood plains and depositing high levels of nutrients and energy on flood plains and recharging billabongs. Billabongs, formed when the river changed its course in the past and left a small oxbow lake, are recharged as are wetlands. In other areas, temporary wetlands are created and experience a rapid increase in food supplies that are able to sustain rapid population increases of species such as birds and some mammals. As the river flow decreases, billabongs again become isolated and begin drying out. Because the climatic cycle that governs river flows is not consistent, there may be periods of many years when there is no flooding followed by periods of repeated flooding on a year-on-year basis. This natural cycle has created a number of unique ecosystems along the Murray–Darling which have some potential to attract tourism interest.

Given the significance of the river system and the agricultural system it supports, the Murray–Darling Basin Commission was established as the executive arm of the Murray–Darling Basin Ministerial Council, an intergovernmental organization established by the State and Federal Governments and funded on a joint basis by member governments. The Commission is an autonomous organization and is responsible for managing the Murray River and the Menindee Lakes system on the lower Darling and advising the Ministerial Council on the use of the water, land and other environmental resources of the Murray–Darling System. By 2007, the combined effects of overuse of the basin's water resources for irrigation and a long period of drought had created a serious water shortage for both urban and rural populations as well as substantial damage to the rivers' ecosystems. The seriousness of this problem led to the announcement of a AUS$10 billion Federal Government takeover package designed to remove the basin from state government control and introduce a more equitable system of water allocation between the states through which the river flows and between competing water users.

Flora and fauna

The Murray–Darling basin has a rich flora and fauna consisting of dryland communities which comprise 90% of the basin's land area, a small Alpine community and up to 30,000 wetlands. From a biodiversity perspective, the wetlands, ten of which as are listed as Ramsar Wetlands of international significance (The Ramsar Convention (www.ramsar.org) was signed in Ramsar, Iran, in 1971 and is an intergovernmental treaty that provides a framework for international cooperation in the conservation of wetlands.), have a large number of species and are the basin's most complex communities. At the time when European settlement commenced the number of species in the basin (Murray–Darling Commission, www.mdbc.gov.au/about/basin_statistics) included 85 mammals, 365 birds, 151 reptiles, 24 frogs and 20 freshwater fish. Large-scale farming and pastoral activities have caused significant modifications to the basin's ecosystems leading to the extinction of 20 mammal species with a further 35 bird and 16 mammal species are now classed as endangered. Land clearing and damming of the river has also stressed many of the basins' wetlands (see Fig. 1.4 in Chapter 1, this volume). The introduction of 11 exotic species of fish, including carp (*Hypseleotis* ssp.) which were accidentally introduced in 1964 when a small number of individuals escaped from a fish farm, has created further stress on the system's freshwater ecosystems. In some reaches of the river, carp are reported to be the only species found. Extensive timber harvesting of the region's endemic River Red Gum (*Eucalyptus camaldulensis*) forests for building and firewood had greatly depleted these forests almost to the point of extinction in some areas (Coulson, 1995). In the region's fragile and arid rangeland areas overgrazing has encouraged the invasion of woody weeds further degrading these areas as well as leading to increasing salinity in other areas.

The river system has a number of fish species favoured by anglers including the Murray cod (*Maccullochella peelii*) and golden perch (*Macquaria ambigua*), but the sustainability of the fishery is strongly influenced by the river's lateral flow component and populations can fluctuate based on the cycle of flood and drought. For populations of wild fish to remain healthy, there needs to be barrier-free movement between the upper and lower reaches of the river. While this occurs naturally, even in periods of drought, the construction of barriers such as dams creates 'isolated' reaches where stock may decline and become genetically depauperate. Similarly, other species which live in billabongs and in temporary swamps depend on the recharging of nutrients and energy that occurs after flooding. Interruption of this cycle by dams has had an impact on the biological diversity and richness of the system's aquatic and terrestrial ecosystems.

Agriculture

European settlement of the basin is closely tied to the expansion of pastoralism based on both cattle and sheep in the 19th century followed later by agriculture after irrigation schemes were constructed to provide a secure source of water for farming. By the mid-1840s, a large number of sheep and cattle stations had been established on the rangelands in the Riverina region of south-west New South Wales and along the Darling and Murray rivers. By the beginning of the 21st century the total area of irrigated crops and pastures had grown to approximately 1.47 million hectares. The basin is recognized as Australia's most important agriculture region and uses about 70% of all water used for irrigation. The Murray–Darling basin collectively produces 41% of the nation's gross agricultural production by value.

River transport

Because the Murray lacks an estuary, shipping is unable to reach the river via the sea; however, the value of the river as a transport route that could connect coastal ports with the interior rangelands via a land transport corridor was recognized by the colonial authorities. After explorer Captain Charles Sturt had established that both the Murray and Murrumbidgee were navigable, the South Australian Colonial government offered £2000 in prize money to the owners of the first two commercial river boats that could successfully navigate the Murray between Goolwa near the mouth of the Murray River in South Australia and the Murray–Darling junction (Coulson, 1995). Two vessels (the *Mary Ann* and the *Lady Augusta*) entered the competition and both successfully navigated the river in 1853. Both vessels reached the confluence of the Murray and Darling rivers with *Mary Ann* continuing up to Moama on the river Murray demonstrating the feasibility of operating boats along the river. Prior to that time cargo had been transported by drays, a form of transport that was slow and expensive.

The discovery of gold near Bendigo in Victoria sparked a gold rush that together with the expansion of the wool and cattle industries created further demand for river transport. River steamers operated along the river transporting passengers and cargo between a series of river ports that emerged as transport hubs through which flowed supplies to pastoralists, and from the pastoralists, wool for export from Victoria. Figure 10.2 illustrates the typical layout of a river steamer; in this case, the PS *Pevensey* built in Echuca in 1911 and now operated as a tourism attraction at the Port of Echuca.

The number of river boats grew rapidly, encouraging further expansion of the wool and cattle industries, and by 1860, 12 paddle steamers were operating on the Murray. The volume of trade increased after the opening of the Melbourne to Echuca railway line in 1864. Given the speed with which the wool clip could be transported to the Port of Melbourne, the bulk of the wool produced in the Riverina region of New South Wales and along the Murray and Darling rivers was shipped through Echuca. By the 1870s, the volume and value of trade saw Echuca become Victoria's second port. The presence of 79 hotels operating in the town testifies the wealth that the river trade generated (Christopher, 2006). East of Echuca, smaller boats were

Fig. 10.2. The PS *Pevensey* built in 1911 and now operated as a tourist attraction at the Port of Echuca. In 1988, the steamer featured in a television mini series *All the Rivers Run*. (Photograph courtesy of Bruce Prideaux.)

used to transport goods and passengers to up-river ports such as Tocumwal and Albany. River steamers had a shallow draft, and cargo was carried on the deck and in barges that were towed behind the steamer. Passenger quarters were also constructed, usually on the aft section of the vessel. Between 1852 and 1899, a total of 159 river boats were built followed by a further 34 boats between 1900 and 1928. As of 2006, 26 river boats remain, with 21 being fully operational and the remaining five being used as static displays (Christopher, 2006).

Operating river boats on the Murray and Darling rivers was never easy as both rivers are shallow, narrow and have numerous sandbars and frequent meanders. Because of the annual flow cycle, river operations were limited by water levels with most sailings being between April and November. During periods of drought, some stretches could dry up, stranding river boats for lengthy periods of time. Another constant problem, particularly on the Murray, was snags, trees that had been washed into the river and become a navigation problem. To clear the waterway, barges equipped with steam-driven winches patrolled the river. Sand banks were another navigational problem, made worse by their constantly shifting nature. Flooding also caused problems for captains of river boats. Without the access to metrological reports available to captains of vessels in the contemporary era, upstream flooding was a constant worry during the annual wet season.

During the 1870s, the number of paddle steamers grew and river ports underwent considerable expansion. However, during the 1880s the opening of railway lines to competing river ports resulted in a decline in the volume of river trade as less boats were required to carry cargo along the river system, and as wool growers were able to trans-ship their wool clip through the numerous railway sidings that were established. The recession of the 1890s and the associated decline in wool prices also contributed to the fall in demand for river boat transport. This decline accelerated in the 20th century as spur railway lines and a large road network were constructed, and when large numbers of men volunteered for service in the Army during World War I. By the 1920s, the river trade had almost ceased, but a brief resurgence of the river trade occurred during World War II when the nation faced a severe shortage of trucks, rubber and fuel because of the war effort. With their large carrying capacity and ability to use timber as fuel, river steamers enjoyed a competitive edge during the war years. A recent resurgence in interest in river boats as tourism attractions has created yet another chapter in the colourful history of this unique form of transport.

Heritage
Both natural and built aspects of heritage occupy important positions in the basin's heritage appeal. The earliest settlement of the region can be traced back to 45,000 BP when the forefathers of Australia's Aboriginal people first settled in the region. There are at least 10,000 identified Aboriginal sites in the basin including camp sites, axe-grinding rocks, rock paintings and middens (Murray–Darling Commission, www.mbdc.au/encyclopedia/heritage, accessed 12 March 2008). While a number of these sites have been listed on the National Estate register of important sites, many have not been listed and knowledge of their whereabouts resides with traditional owners. One of the most significant Aboriginal sites is Lake Mungo where evidence of occupation has been found dating back 40,000 years BP. Throughout this period and until the time that Europeans settled in the basin, the river dominated Aboriginal life yielding food as well as being central to their beliefs and culture (Hope, 2004).

European settlement occurred when the basin's extensive rangelands were opened up for cattle and sheep production. Numerous towns were established to support these rural industries and, from the 1850s, to support the gold mining industry. The associated development of the Murray–Darling as a major transport route made a significant contribution to the development of the region. The construction of irrigation systems resulted in a third wave of development based on agriculture. The changes to the landscape that occurred through the growth of pastoralism and agriculture, as well as mining, have created a rich mosaic of built heritage that has become an important tourism resource in the 21st century. The role of the Port of Echuca in the development of Victoria was recognized in 2007 when Echuca Wharf, discussed in detail later in the chapter, was added to Australia's National Heritage list.

Aside from built heritage, the basin contains a wide variety of natural heritage sites based on ecosystems that include alpine, forest and rangeland biota. These areas, particularly the Alpine region, have become popular recreational areas and support a number of national parks. In Victoria, Parks Victoria has established a number of parks in the vicinity of the Murray River organized into three designated Murray River Reserves: Mildura to Robin vale; Headwaters to Echuca; and Echuca to Robin vale (www.parkweb.vic.gov, accessed 12 March 2008).

Another aspect of the Murray–Darling's heritage is the literature that recorded the deeds and lives of the region's early settlers. One particular example that stands out from the many fine examples of stories and poems of life in rural areas and on the gold fields is 'Banjo' Paterson's poem, *The Man from Snowy River*. The ballad, which describes a wild horse ride down an almost impossible mountain slope, is woven around the history, places and people of the high country and, as the dust jacket of Tim Hall's (1992) excellent commentary on Banjo Patterson's High Country attests, has become 'almost an anthem to the pioneering history of (Australia)'.

The Port of Echuca

There are a number of significant heritage sites along the Murray–Darling including the Swan Hill Heritage Village, the Port of Echuca, former river ports, restored paddle steamers and numerous individual buildings and small heritage precincts. Of all the sites, the one that best conveys a sense of what the past may have been like is the Port of Echuca, a precinct that has preserved many of its original buildings and its original wharf area. To provide a context for the development of the Port of Echuca as a heritage attraction, the following discussion highlights aspects of the development of Echuca as a river port during the 19th century.

Located adjacent to the junction of the Gouldburn, Campaspe and Murray rivers, Echuca, an Aboriginal word meaning 'meeting of the waters', was established through the enterprise of two fearlessly competitive ex-convicts, Henry Hopwood and James Maiden. About 1845, Maiden established a punt service at Moama on the New South Wales side of the Murray River across from what is today the town of Echuca. In 1846, Maiden built an inn later followed by a cattle sales yard that by 1851 was the largest outside of Melbourne. In 1850, Henry Hopwood established a ferry crossing on the site of the present Victorian town of Echuca. Initially known as Hopwood's Ferry, the settlement prospered as a trading post serving the growing gold mining industry and pastoralists. Construction of a pontoon bridge across the Murray by Hopwood in 1858 gave him a stranglehold on cross-border trade between Victoria and New South Wales. The town was ideally positioned as the shortest point between the Victorian colonial capital and seaport of Melbourne and the Murray River, a location that facilitated its rapid emergence as Victoria's largest river port.

As the Port grew, interest turned to ship building and a number of ships were built creating a second stream of income for the town. The State Government Shipping Register for 1895 shows that out of the then 105 paddle steamers and 110 barges registered to operate on the Murray, 48 boats and 54 barges were built at Echuca-Moama. Aside from boat building, timber milling was also an important industry for the town. Because they do not float, Red River gums were transported by barge to Echuca, as well as other sites for milling.

The opening of the Echuca to Melbourne railway in 1864 consolidated Echuca's position as the most important river port on the Murray–Darling. The ability to ship wool to Melbourne's wool brokers at a lower cost and in a faster time than the alternative routes resulted in wool growers in the South Australia, Victoria and New South Wales sections of the Murray–Darling using Echuca as their main port. Resenting the loss of trade, the Governments of both South Australia and New South Wales built railways to connect with river ports in their respective sections of the Murray–Darling, breaking Echuca's monopoly from 1878 onwards. The construction of rail lines to Hay on the Murrumbidgee and Bourke on the Darling in the 1880s further weakened Echuca's role as the river system's major port in the latter part of the century.

The need for a wharf became urgent once the Melbourne to Echuca railway line opened and the Victorian railways was tasked with constructing a government wharf that could accommodate steamers at river levels ranging from the low river level encountered during droughts to the high levels encountered during floods. After five extensions to accommodate the growing river trade, the wharf eventually measured 332 m in length and was 13 m above low river level. Figure 10.3 illustrates the high and low levels of the wharf and several river steamers currently home ported at Echuca. The peak of the trade through the wharf was reached in 1880 when £2.5 million of produce was unloaded from 145 river steamers (Priestley, 1965). Over the next decade, the value of produce fluctuated as the number of steamers cleared declined and more wool was shipped through other ports connected to the

Fig. 10.3. The Port of Echuca c.2007 illustrating the restored section of the wharf to the left of the photo with three paddle steamers and a barge alongside. (Photograph courtesy Bruce Prideaux.)

South Australian and New South Wales railways. By 1890, the number of steamers cleared annually had declined to 74, down from a peak of 240 in 1872.

After 1890, the value of produce began a downward spiral from £20256 million in 1890 to less than £1 million by 1900 (Priestley, 1965). By 1910, the trade had declined to the extent that no records were kept (Coulson, 1995). A few cargo steamers continued to operate along the river during the first few decades of the 20th century with the last consignment of wool passing over the wharf in 1936 (Coulson, 1995). As the river trade declined, the wharf fell into disrepair, businesses folded and people left the town in search of employment. By 1911, the population of Echuca had fallen to a low point of 3745 persons (Coulson, 1995). As the river trade dwindled, many steamers were laid up as derelicts on 'Rotten Row' and the business centre of the town was relocated from the wharf area to Hare Street. Many of the buildings in the vicinity of the wharf area became derelict but fortunately were of little commercial value and were not demolished or otherwise redeveloped. The wharf was not as fortunate and a severe shortage of firewood during World War II (1939–1945) led to two-thirds of the wharf being demolished.

The Port of Echuca heritage project

By 1960, the wharf and its surrounding precinct were derelict but relatively intact because the centre of Echuca's commercial activity moved to Hare Street. The Echuca Historical Society became interested in the area and embarked on a Port of Echuca Restoration Project. In 1969, a feasibility study into restoring the port was commissioned by the Echuca City Council with some funding provided by local service clubs. In 1971, a project committee was established by the Council and later in the year a Port of Echuca Restoration Advisory Committee was approved by the Echuca City Council. Funding for the project was secured in 1972 based on a AUS$228,000 grant from the Victorian State Government, a AUS$100,000 grant from the Commonwealth Government and a loan taken out by the City Council for AUS$114,000 (Coulson, 1995). In 1973, restoration work commenced on Shackell's Bond Store and the Bridge Hotel and the remaining wharf was re-planked. Twelve additional freehold properties consisting of 17 buildings were acquired over the next 30 years and Committee of Management status was obtained over Crown land in the historic Port precinct (Ryan, n.d.). Local service clubs including Lions and Apex assisted in restoration work resulting in a project that had a high level of community ownership through the formal mechanism of ownership exercised via the City of Echuca and through voluntary contributions of funds and labour by a range of community organizations including the heritage society and service clubs.

The Port of Echuca opened for business in May 1974 with entry initially limited to the Bond Store, Bridge Hotel and the wharf. Over the next few years more of the site was opened and river cruises commenced. The first paddle steamer to commence operating short tours on the Murray was the PS *Pevensey* originally built in Echuca in 1911. What originally began as a

Fig. 10.4. A horse-drawn wagon passes the restored Star hotel on Main Street of the Port of Echuca. (Photograph courtesy of Bruce Prideaux.)

1 day a month operation in 1979 with a volunteer crew has become a tour that in 2005/06 operated 1893 trips carrying 57,500 passengers (Port of Echuca, 2006). In 1984, the PS *Pevensey* was joined by the PS *Adelaide* originally built in Echuca in 1866 and later by the PS *Alexander Arbuthnot*, the last river steamer to be built (1925). Interest in paddle steamers has been increasing and Echuca and its twin town of Moama now are home port for a fleet of 17 paddle steamers.

The aim of the Port of Echuca Authority is to recreate the atmosphere of the Port between the 1890s to the 1920s. Attractions opened in the Port precinct included a restored workshop where visitors can watch shipwrights and engineers restore a range of engines and other plant, as well as horse-drawn wagon rides (illustrated in Fig. 10.4), a museum and a number of commercial operations located in restored Port buildings. To recreate the atmosphere of the Port the original lighting, gutters and site artefacts have been retained although modern amenities such as running water, electricity and communications have been added (Ryan, n.d.). Other buildings and attractions opened included the Cargo Shed Museum, the Brothel, Murray Hotel, Railway Station, Star Hotel and the Freeman Foundry site.

The role of the Port of Echuca as a tourism attraction was given a considerable boost in the summer of 1982/83 when a television mini series, *All the Rivers Run*, was filmed in Echuca and shown on national television. Considerable interest in the Port was generated and the filming of a sequel in 1988/89 further stimulated tourism interest. By 1995, the tourism industry had grown to the extent that the Echuca-Moama region supported 30 motels, up from just

Fig. 10.5. Aspects of river cruising on the Murray River. (Photograph courtesy of Bruce Prideaux.)

four in the pre-tourism era of the 1970s. A significant new river-based industry that has emerged in parallel with the growth in interest in river heritage is river cruising based on purpose-built houseboats as well as refurbished paddle steamers as illustrated in Fig. 10.5.

This photo illustrates three forms of river cruising on the Murray. On the left, a modern cruise boat offering over night cruises is shown at a river birth. Behind it is an example of one of the numerous houseboats that are available for rental on the Murray. To the right is a refurbished 19th-century paddle steamer that offers day cruises. The photo also illustrates the narrow width of the river, a feature that creates continual problems for navigation.

Management of the Port

The Port is owned by the Shire of Campaspe (formed in 1994 and based on the previous City of Echuca) and operated by the Port of Echuca Authority established under section 86 of the Victorian Local Government Act of 1989. Under the Act, the Port of Echuca Authority has total control over the daily operations of the Port and is responsible for the future development of the area as a major tourism attraction. While the Shire of Campaspe retains all rights of control over the Port, it has empowered the Port of Echuca Authority to undertake management without constraints from the Council. To oversee the Authority, a nine-member board with eight of those members drawn from community nominations has been established. In recent years, the attention of the Board has been focused on the future direction of the Port.

The actual business of the Port is organized into six categories: boat and paddle steamer operations, museum, centres of the river trades, property management, retail and public affairs. Because entry to the heritage precinct is at no cost, revenue is raised from a number of sources including trips on the Port's paddle steamers, charters of paddle steamers, wharf weddings, sales from the Authorities' retail operations and rental income from businesses that lease restored buildings as shops, hotels and cafes. While some funds for development are generated by commercial activities, grants are actively sort from public sector-funding bodies. For example, in 2005, the Port obtained a grant of AUS$50,000 from the Australian Tourism Development Programme which was matched on a dollar-for-dollar basis by the Campaspe Shire Council and used to redevelop the Port's museum. In 2005/06, the Port generated an operating surplus of AUS$60,000 after loan redemption and capital works on total revenues of AUS$1.5 million (Port of Echuca, 2006).

Visitor numbers peaked in 1985/86 at just under 100,000, a direct result of the publicity generated by the television programme *All the Rivers Run*. After declining to a low point of about 50,000 in 1994/95, numbers have slowly grown to approximately 60,000 in 2005/06. According the 2006/07 Annual Report (Port of Echuca, 2006), the lack of growth in visitor numbers reflects the need for continual enhancement of the precinct. Looking to the future, the Authority has developed a Tourism Investment Strategy that is designed to add additional displays and attractions to the precinct in the near future.

Conclusion

At the beginning of the chapter, it was noted that many heritage sites have a commercial value and if not subject to some form of official protection may be redeveloped either as an adaptation of the existing site or demolished and used for other purposes. The Port of Echuca case study highlights a range of issues associated with river heritage in particular but also the wider issue of heritage and how it may be used as a tourist attraction. The value of sites such as the Port of Echuca can be measured from a number of perspectives: as an attraction that provides employment; its role as an iconic experience that underpins the sustainability of the regional industry; as an educational experience that connects present generations with the past; as an activity that has encouraged local participation and maximized local benefits (Swarbrooke, 1996); and as a significant heritage site that preserves significant elements of the past.

In the case of Echuca, the heritage value of the Port was not officially recognized for nearly 60 years after the river trade effectively finished. The buildings that comprise the heritage precinct of the old Port survived because there was no other use for them. After the decline of the river trade the relocation of the town's commercial centre spared this historic area from commercial redevelopment. However, recognition of its heritage values alone was not enough to preserve the site in its entirety. The sensitive refurbishment of the buildings in the precinct to suite their current use as tourism attractions has greatly enhanced their claim for preservation.

Another lesson that can be drawn from the Port of Echuca is that heritage precincts can operate without major public subsidies for running and maintenance costs provided that adaptive reuse of original buildings is allowed and that the precinct is managed from the outset as an enterprise that is given the task of running on commercial lines within the perimeters imposed on it by its heritage status. The purposeful creation of a tourism product managed in a way that allows it to be consumed by visitors may be criticized on the grounds that authenticity is lost as commodification becomes the dominant driver. However, as Ho and McKercher (2008) suggest the development of a cultural tourism product that offers a satisfactory tourism experience while retaining its cultural heritage value can be achieved, as is the case with the Port of Echuca. Without attractions such as a paddle steamer ride and the opportunity to shop and eat at a variety of outlets, the charm of restored buildings, even with museum standard interpretation and a claim of historical significance, is unlikely to excite a high level of visitor interest and support. From a wider perspective, the development of the Port of Echuca illustrates the value of heritage as a tourism attraction and also supports the case for heritage sites that offer life and celebration of the past in a contemporary context rather than heritage that offers interpretation but neglects to offer activity. It is through offering life and activity that community-supported heritage attractions are able to avoid the fate of heritage attractions that have failed.

Acknowledgements

The author wishes to acknowledge the assistance given by Frank Ryan, past Manager of the Port of Echuca.

References

Christopher, P. (2006) *Australian Riverboats A Pictorial History*. Axiom, Stephney, South Australia.

Coulson, H. (1995) *Echuca-Moama On the Murray*. Hyland House, South Melbourne, Australia.

Davidson, J. and Spearritt, P. (2000) *Holiday Business: Tourism in Australia since 1870*. University of Melbourne Press, Carlton South, Melbourne, Australia.

Geoscience Australia (2006) Deserts. Available at: http://www.ga.gov.au/education/facts/landforms/geogarea.htm

Gill, E. (1978) The Murray Darling River System. *Proceedings of the Royal Society of Victoria* 90(1), 1–4.

Hall (1992) *'Banjo' Patterson's High Country*. Cornstalk Publishing, Pymble, New South Wales, Australia.

Ho, P.S.Y. and McKercher, B. (2008) Managing heritage resources as tourism products. In: Prideaux, B., Timothy, D. and Chon, K. (eds) *Cultural and Heritage History in Asia and the Pacific*. Routledge, London, New York, pp. 178–188.

Hope, J. (2004) The Aboriginal people of the Darling River. In: Breckwoldt, R., Boden, R. and Andrew, J. (eds) *The Darling*. Murray-Darling Commission, Canberra.

McKercher, B. (2001) Attitudes to a non-viable community owned heritage tourism attraction. *Journal of Sustainable Tourism* 9, 29–43.

Port of Echuca (2006) *Port of Echuca Annual Report*, Port of Echuca Authority, Echuca.

Prideaux, B. and Timothy, D. (2008) Themes in cultural and heritage tourism in Asia and the Pacific. In: Prideaux, B., Timothy, D. and Chon, K. (eds) *Cultural and Heritage*

History in Asia and the Pacific. Routledge, London, New York, pp. 1–18.

Priestley, S. (1965) *Echuca: A Centenary History.* Jacaranda Press, Brisbane, Queensland, Australia.

Ryan, F. (n.d.) The Port of Echuca Recreating the Glory Days, Briefing Notes.

Swarbrooke, J. (1996) Towards sustainable future for cultural tourism: a European perspective. In: Robinson, N., Evans, P. and Callaghan, P. (eds) *Tourism and Cultural Change.* Sunderland, UK, pp. 227–256.

Thoms, M., Hill, S., Spry, M., Chen, X., Mount, T. and Sheldon, F. (2004) The geomophology of the Barwion-Darling basin. In: Breckwoldt, R., Boden, R. and Andrew, J. (eds) *The Darling.* Murray-Darling Commission, Canberra.

Young, W., Schiller, C., Roberts, J. and Hillman, T. (2001) The rivers of the basin and how they work. In: Young, W. (ed.) *Rivers as Ecological Systems: The Murray Darling Basin.* Murray Darling Basin Commission, Canberra.

11 White-water Tourism

R. Buckley

International Centre for Ecotourism Research, Griffith University, Australia

Introduction

Many rivers have rapids or white water in the terminology of river rafters, canoeists and kayakers. Most rivers start small and steep with rapids in their upper sections. Some cut through gorges which are steep or narrow enough to form rapids even if sections upstream and downstream are both slow-flowing. Some form rapids over gravel bars even in broad shallow reaches. Some even form rapids right at the ocean shoreline, as tidal movements augment the river's own flow to form races, whirlpools, waves or tidal bores.

White water attracts boaters, and this provides the basis for a large white-water tourism and recreation sector worldwide (Fig. 11.1). Commercial rafting trips are one of the archetypal components of the adventure tourism industry (Buckley, 2006), and sales of recreational white-water kayaks continue to rise year by year (Outdoor Industry Association, 2007). This chapter provides an overview of the commercial white-water tourism sector as it currently operates worldwide, picking out particular features which distinguish it from other forms of river tourism. The sector has received rather little attention in the academic literature to date, though case studies are provided in Buckley (2006).

Activities

At a global scale, the main commercial tourism activity associated with white-water rapids is simply looking at them from the river banks or bridges. Every day at Tiger Leaping Gorge on the Yangtze River in China, for example, thousands of Chinese tourists walk down concrete steps to look at the giant and legendary rapid where a number of rafters lost their lives in an ill-fated race to be first to boat the river end to end (Bangs and Kallen, 1987; Chapter 7, this volume). The spectacle supports an entire local economy of tourist services.

Fig. 11.1. Mekong River, China. (Photograph courtesy of Ralf Buckley.)

From a tourism perspective, however, this is more akin to waterfall tourism as at Niagara, Iguazu or Victoria Falls. This activity is not considered further in this chapter.

The principal participatory activity in the white-water river tourism sector is guided commercial rafting (Fig. 11.2). Tour operators may also offer kayak trips and so-called river-boarding or river-sledging using modified bodyboards. From an operational perspective most aspects of kayak and riverboard tours are similar to those for white-water raft tours. This chapter, therefore, focuses principally on rafting, with additional comments for other watercraft throughout the text as relevant. Apart from the type of boat, key features of any white-water tourism operation include the difficulty and danger of the rapids, the weather and terrain, the length of the trip and the degree of client participation. Other aspects, such as access and transport, accommodation if any, guides and equipment, safety practices and risk management, permits and liability releases, and marketing and financial aspects are also important, as for any form of adventure tourism, but are less specific to white-water river tours.

As with other forms of adventure tourism, the various types of white-water tours available can be thought of as forming a triangle or pyramid, with a broad base of high-volume, short-duration, low-skill, low-price tours in accessible areas; a narrow apex of low-volume, long-duration, high-skill, high-price trips in remote areas; and various intermediate combinations. High-volume white-water river tours are offered principally where there are major tourist gateway towns close to rivers with reliable flow, medium difficulty and easy access.

Fig. 11.2. Commercial rafting. (Wikipedia Commons, accessed 20 May 2008.)

Examples include the Tully River near Cairns, Australia; the Zambezi River near Victoria Falls, Zimbabwe; and the Shotover and Kawarau Rivers near Queenstown, New Zealand. At each of these sites, there are one or more relatively large rafting tour operators who each handle several large coachloads of clients every day, on a routine run which varies only slightly through the year, depending on river flow. For the rivers mentioned, these are: R'n'R and Raging Thunder in Cairns; Shearwater Adventures on the Zambezi; and Queenstown Rafting and Challenge Rafting on the New Zealand rivers. Detailed descriptions of these operations are given in Buckley (2006, pp. 90–92, 101–107).

Briefly, clients are picked up from their accommodation in the gateway town, by company buses, early each morning and driven to the river where they are allocated to boats and guides and receive a basic safety briefing (Fig. 11.3). For cold climate rivers such as those in New Zealand, there is an initial stop at an outfitting area where they are fitted out with wetsuits and/or paddle jackets. In warmer areas, clients are taken straight to the river where they are given helmets and life jackets. The rafts remain inflated throughout the season, usually stored in stacks on trailers which are parked overnight in a company compound. While the clients are receiving their safety briefing in the morning, the other guides and staff launch and check the boats. Most 1-day trips use paddle rafts where the boat is propelled by the clients using single-bladed paddles, under directions from the guide who steers with a long-bladed paddle at the rear. This provides greater opportunities for participation and excitement, which suits the generally younger clientele who predominate in the shorter and lower-priced trips. Paddle rafts are also quicker and easier

Fig. 11.3. River safety briefing. (Photograph courtesy of Ralf Buckley.)

to stack and launch than oar rafts rowed by the guide from a central seat, since oar rafts need a tubular aluminium rowing frame attached to the inflated walls or pontoons.

Once the clients get into their rafts, which may take from four to ten clients apiece depending on the size of the river and hence of the raft, the guides will give the clients some rapid basic training. This covers: paddle strokes and commands; how to balance the boat if it threatens to overturn; and how to get back on to the raft if flung out, either unaided or with assistance. On rivers where the first few rapids are easy, such briefings tend to be cursory; on those where the first few rapids carry significant safety risks, briefings may be more thorough. Either way, they are usually very quick, and the rafts soon move off downriver. Internationally, the principal guiding language is English, but many guides can also give instructions in Japanese because of the preponderance of Japanese clients at many destinations.

The practical details of running rapids are beyond the scope of this chapter. It is up to the guide to pick the line or route through each rapid, both by steering directly and by instructing the clients to paddle forwards, paddle backwards, or to turn left or right by paddling forward on one side and backward on the other. If the raft becomes caught in a stopper, a kind of standing wave which breaks continuously at a single point, the guide may yell 'high side' which is an instruction for all clients to move across the raft to the higher side, to prevent it tipping over. The same instruction is used if the raft becomes wedged against a rock in the river. Depending on the river and the individual rapids, there may be one regular route which all the rafts follow every day, or there may be multiple options which guides will select depending on water flow and the skills and enthusiasm of their clients on the day.

One of the guide's tasks and necessary skills is to reassure clients who are frightened, and take them down a safe 'dry' line with no spills; but to 'talk up' the risks to clients who seem unexcited, take them through 'wet' lines where they will get heavily splashed and will have to paddle hard, and sometimes to flip the raft deliberately at a safe spot so that the clients are tipped into the river and have to swim. Of course, flips often also happen by accident, and not always in the safest spots. Many raft tour operators use safety kayakers, often off-duty guides, who paddle alongside the rafts and can rescue 'swimmers', i.e. anyone who falls out. Guides may also have safety ropes which they can fling to swimmers who are in difficulties. If there is only one safety kayaker and several large rafts flip simultaneously, the task of the safety kayaker can suddenly become extremely energetic.

At the end of 1-day runs such as this, the guides may get the clients to help wash out the rafts roughly, and then load the rafts on to the trailers and the clients into the coaches as quickly as possible ready to depart. Some companies take their clients to a shop or café at this point, in order to sell them videos, souvenirs and other trips as well as food and drink. Both the two largest companies operating out of Cairns, for example, have their own purpose-built cafés near the take-out point specifically for this purpose, before driving back to the gateway city.

At the other extreme of the market are one-off expeditionary first descents of rivers in remote areas, where places are sold only to expert kayakers, and where food and camping equipment are carried either by a ground support team, on support rafts or catarafts, or in the kayaks themselves (Fig. 11.4). White-water kayaks come in different shapes and sizes, from extremely low-volume play

Fig. 11.4. Rangitata River, New Zealand. (Photograph courtesy of Ralf Buckley.)

boats which cannot carry any equipment, to larger craft which can carry food and minimalist camping gear for several days. The Fitzroy River Expedition in the Kimberley region of Australia in February 2006, for example, was an unsupported kayak trip with 12 overnight camps on the river. This, however, was in a tropical environment, and was not run as a commercial trip. Commercial multi-day white-water kayak tours offered in the Himalayas or the great rivers of China, for example, or on the Grand Canyon of the Colorado River in the USA, all have either ground or raft support (see Chapter 3, this volume).

Broadly, people run rivers wherever politics allow, with the volume of clients depending principally on the overall number of tourists in the area concerned. Some rivers experience a heavy level of private recreational use, e.g. in the eastern States of the USA. Some have a high level of locally purchased rafting tourism but relatively little international visitation, e.g. the rivers of Ecuador and Southern Siberia. Some have a high level of international but little local tourism, e.g. the Zambezi, or the White Nile in Uganda (see Chapter 5, this volume). Some have recreational users, domestic and international tourists all at once, e.g. many of the rivers in the South Island of New Zealand, east-coast Australia and North America. And some are run only occasionally by commercial groups but may well experience far greater use in future if political conditions permit, e.g. the rivers of the eastern Himalayan nations, western China and much of South-east Asia.

Structure

Like much of the adventure tourism industry, the commercial white-water sector is broadly structured in three tiers, albeit with some overlap between tiers. The core of the industry is the central tier, the on-ground operators who own the equipment, obtain access permits where required, operate all the logistic components, employ the river guides and are responsible for safety, insurance and for checking guide training and qualifications. For smaller operators, the owners may themselves work as guides; but more commonly, the tour operators hire qualified guides season by season or even trip by trip. The guides may work for the same company many years in a row, or they may move internationally from year to year or season to season to take advantage of demand, or they may simply live in an area with a strong white-water rafting industry, and work for different operators on different days. Indeed, in some cases different operators will actually run a single joint trip on a particular day, in the same way that airlines operate code-share agreements (Cater, 2006).

While most of these on-ground operators do carry out their own marketing, many of them gain the majority of their business through retail-level multiple-activity or multi-destination tour packagers and agents, who sell particular white-water tours under their own name, but subcontract the local operators to actually run the tours. Where an international company such as Sobek Mountain Travel in the USA, for example, offers a rafting tour on the Katun River in Russia, it uses a reputable local company such as Team Gorky to run the actual rafting section of the trip. Many other marketing models are also in use. For example, the major rafting tour operators in Cairns, Australia, sell their daily trips through several avenues: directly from their own offices; through brochures at tourist accommodation; and via a suite of small agencies along the waterfront who attract walk-in customers and sell a wide range of tours on commission. As in other adventure tourism sectors, there are also specialist white-water tour packagers who market through recreational paddling magazines and through the Internet, and offer white-water tours at a variety of destinations and rivers worldwide.

There are also on-ground tour operators such as Shearwater Adventures at Victoria Falls in Zimbabwe, who started solely as raft tour operators but now offer a range of different adventure activities at a single destination. A slightly different model operates in Queenstown, New Zealand, where a syndicate of independent tour operators jointly markets a package of different adventure activities, the so-called Awesome Foursome, of which white-water rafting is one. In tourist gateway towns which are known specifically as adventure destinations, there is also substantial cross-marketing between adventure tours such as white-water rafting, and evening activities such as nightclubs (Buckley *et al.*, 2006; Cater, 2006). Many companies add to their repertoire of rivers at intervals by exploring new options, and one or two companies also offer first descents of significant rivers in remote areas. For white-water rafters and kayakers, the first descent of a major river is a significant international event. Since most first descents are made by experienced private groups or sponsored professional teams, commercial tours offering first descents can command a price premium. From an operational perspective, however, a first descent is very different from a routine river-running tour. The river is unknown, the logistics are untested, and the tour is a one-off (Fig. 11.5).

Fig. 11.5. Salween River, Tibet. (Photograph courtesy of Ralf Buckley.)

Operations and Equipment

As with most adventure tourism activities, the keys to client safety and satisfaction are guides, equipment and logistics as well as the natural features of the site itself. The key role of the guide is common to most forms of ecotourism and adventure tourism. The clients rely on the guide for logistics, safety, information and even entertainment. The guide effectively has to choreograph the clients' experiences (Arnould and Price, 1993; Beedie, 2003); and especially on multi-day white-water river tours where the group camps each night on the river banks, working as a river guide involves considerable emotional as well as physical labour (Sharpe, 2005).

Not only must guides be skilled rafters or kayakers themselves; they also need to be able to train and coordinate a group of inexperienced paddlers so as to navigate their raft safely through a series of rapids, or to lead and encourage a group of kayakers who may be paddling close to the limits of their technical ability. On the river, the guides have to keep an eye on every client at all times. In most countries, river guides need qualifications in swift-water rescue as well as first aid or emergency medical technique (EMT). They must also have the ability to motivate, encourage and entertain the clients, dispel any disputes, and assess their clients' emotional states as well as their physical skills and well-being. To be a good guide is a highly skilled job.

In addition to hiring good guides, a successful river tour operator also needs to give them good equipment. The rafts need to be of appropriate size, design and construction, and in good repair. Indeed, the more reputable white-water raft tour operators will generally advertise the specific brand of rafts they use. The paddles used by most commercial white-water raft operators are of a relatively low-tech moulded plastic design and structure, but they need to be in good repair none the less, with undamaged shafts and T-pieces, a length appropriate for the size of raft, and a long-shafted steering paddle for the guide.

Paddles used by white-water kayakers, in contrast, are extremely high-tech carbon fibre constructions, with double concave-shaped and angled blades, and bent shafts with variable ovoid cross-sections for maximum grip and control. Most kayak tour operators expect their clients to bring their own paddles, and also their own helmets, life jackets, safety throw-ropes, sprayskirts, paddle jackets or drysuits, wetsuits or thermals, river sandals or bootees, and hoods and palmless mittens, known as pogies, for cold-water paddling. Many kayakers will also bring their own kayaks, especially on trips with raft or riverbank logistic support. Since the majority of kayakers own low-volume play boats, however, they may well prefer to use a higher-volume expedition boat provided by the tour operator for a trip where all equipment are carried in the kayaks. Higher-volume kayaks may also be preferred in large-volume rivers or by clients who may not be confident that their skills are adequate for the river concerned. There is an enormous range of different white-water kayak designs for different specialized purposes, but the details are beyond the scope of this chapter. One of the most interesting developments in recent years has been a rapid improvement in the design of inflatable kayaks. These may not yet constitute serious competition to hard-shell plastic designs, but they have advanced greatly from the punt-like constructions of a few years ago.

White-water rafts also come in a variety of different designs. Those most commonly used for commercial white-water tours are a relatively standard eight-sided ovoid polygonal design, with multiple independent compartments in the walls and an inflated floating floor. The floor is attached closely to the walls at numerous points, but is separated by small gaps or drain holes so that the raft is self-baling. Older designs had a fully sealed-in single-sheet floor and had to be baled manually when they shipped water. Rafts intended to be rowed using an oar rig need a number of heavy-duty integrated attachment points, usually stainless-steel D-rings with a hypalon strap welded into the wall construction, so as to attach the rowing frame using heavy-duty webbing. Hypalon is a wear- and cut-resistant waterproof reinforced plastic which is used in the construction of most white-water rafts. Rafts intended only for paddling, especially if only for day trips which do not need equipment to be tied in, do not need these attachment points and can hence be built to a somewhat cheaper design.

Oar rafts, rowed entirely by the guide with the clients acting purely as passengers, are only practical on relatively large, wide rivers with a high flow volume and low gradient so that there is ample room to manoeuvre and ample advance warning of each rapid. Oar rafts are used routinely, for example, on the Grand Canyon of the Colorado River, USA. Indeed, during the peak holiday season most tour operators use rafts which are too large to row and which are instead steered by a small outboard motor mounted in a well at the stern. A variety of even larger raft rigs are used specifically on the Grand Canyon, including some where several rafts are lashed together, and others made of enormous industrial pontoons. These, however, are not widely used outside the Grand Canyon.

For expedition raft tours in high-volume rivers where the rapids are unknown, companies such as Earth Science Expeditions (ESE) have successfully used oar-rig catarafts around 6 m in length, rowed by a single centrally seated guide. A cataraft consists of two separate double-ended pointed cylindrical pontoons held parallel by the rowing frame. Because of the much lower hull drag, these catarafts are much faster and more manoeuvrable than a conventional-floored raft of comparable size. Speed and manoeuvrability are important considerations in running technically complex rapids or unknown rivers. These catarafts do not carry as many passengers as the conventional-floored rafts, but they can carry a large load of food and equipment. The approach used by companies such as ESE and its subsidiaries is to take a combined group of kayakers and catarafts, with the kayakers scouting the river ahead in unladen kayaks and signalling back to the catarafts which carry the group's equipment. This approach has proved highly successful and ESE has a number of large-scale first descents to its credit.

On smaller and steeper rivers, where most of the rapids involve steep drops around and between rocks, oar rafts cannot safely be used, and only paddle rafts are feasible. The narrower and steeper the river, for example, the smaller the raft that can run it safely. On rivers such as the Franklin or Nymboida in Australia, for example, which include tight drops up to class V, tour operators such as World Expeditions use small four-person rafts. Except on large deep rivers such as the Grand Canyon, most commercial white-water raft tour operators supply their clients with helmets. These are of a relatively basic design, but sufficient to prevent a head injury if a client is washed head first into a rock or, as more often occurs, hit on the head by another client's wildly flailing paddle. In most countries, life jackets are mandatory, and it would be a foolish tour operator who did not provide them even if they are not. In some countries, for example Chile, white-water boating comes under the same regulations as offshore marine boating, and life jackets must meet marine standards and be equipped with whistles. More commonly, however, specialized white-water life jackets are used, designed to allow much greater freedom of movement than a standard marine life vest.

Experience

The client experience of a white-water river tour, as with many other forms of adventure tourism, depends as much on the client as the tour. Some people are interested in scenery, others in social opportunities; some want to take part, others to be looked after; and a rapid which is boring for one person may be terrifying for another, and vice versa. Guides have an important role in broadening the experience for all clients, by recognizing their different backgrounds, emotions and interests and treating them accordingly.

For example, some clients may not notice the scenery at all unless it is pointed out, but will appreciate it once they have noticed it. Many have no idea how to read a river, i.e. to use clues from the river surface to detect water flow patterns, depth and directions, and choose a safe route. Some clients do not care: as far as they are concerned, reading a river is the guide's job, and they will simply paddle when told. Most people, however, do indeed appreciate learning about the river as well as the raft, especially on longer multi-day trips. Clients on commercial white-water kayaking tours are generally much more experienced than clients of rafting tours: since a kayaker is necessarily a participant rather than a passenger, paddlers generally will not purchase a commercial tour, with the attendant expense, unless they are already sufficiently skilled to take full advantage of it. Many kayak tour operators also run training clinics, and less-experienced paddlers are more likely to purchase these.

For the more experienced paddlers, a commercial tour provides two main advantages over a private trip. First, it can provide invaluable assistance with logistics and language in an unfamiliar country; and second, it provides equally invaluable local knowledge of the river and rapids, including water flows, access points, permit requirements if any, scouting points before major rapids, and most importantly, the best route through each individual rapid. It is commonplace that after a few days on a difficult river with an experienced guide and group of fellow boaters, a kayaker will happily and competently run rapids which they would not have considered running on their own. Essentially, the guide is there to familiarize the clients with the river.

White-water rafting clients, on the other hand, tend to be much less experienced, and relatively few take multiple rafting trips. While a kayaker visiting a new country will look for as many rivers as possible to paddle, in the same way that a diver looks for many places to dive or a climber looks for many places to climb, a raft tour client will generally pick only one place to go rafting, using the rest of their visit for different activities. Broadly speaking, there are significant demographic differences between the clients of single-day white-water raft tours in well-known adventure tourism destinations, and multi-day tours on famous icon rivers. The former tend to attract a younger clientele, including the backpacker market. Typically they aim to provide thrills, spills and social interaction rather than scenic contemplation, and they are cross-marketed extensively with other activities which might appeal to the same clientele. Examples include: the Shotover and Kawarau Rivers near Queenstown, New Zealand; the Tully River near Cairns, Australia; the section of the Zambezi immediately below Victoria Falls, Zimbabwe; and the Itanda Falls section of the White Nile accessible from Kampala, Uganda (see Chapter 5, this volume).

Internationally, multi-day white-water rafting trips on icon rivers, which are of course considerably higher priced, tend to attract an older clientele for whom the trip is a long-planned or even lifetime experience rather than a quick adrenalin fix. The full-length raft trip on the Grand Canyon, for example, involves a significant investment of time and money even for domestic clients. Many of the clients are European, and the Grand Canyon trip may be the main component of their US holiday. Such clients are interested in scenery and environment as well as rapids. They have the time and opportunity to learn from the guides both on and off-river, since the rapids are quite widely spaced with long flat-water sections between them. There is also ample opportunity for conversation around the campfire in the evenings. Clients such as these expect to be treated as guests rather than participants, with guides to row the rafts and staff to cook and clean up.

The distinction outlined above, with backpackers taking the briefest tours and wealthier clients taking the more extended multi-day trips, runs counter to the general contrast between cash-rich, time-poor and time-rich, cash-poor clients across the adventure tourism sector as a whole; and in fact, appears to be driven by price alone. The reason backpackers do not buy Grand Canyon raft trips is simply that they are too expensive. The reason there are relatively fewer older clients on 1-day raft trips is simply that they are heavily outnumbered by younger customers. Relatively short multi-day white-water raft trips such as the Karamea in New Zealand, for example, attract a preponderance of older clients, because the helicopter access increases the price. Longer 10-day trips on the Sun Kosi in Nepal, in contrast, are relatively inexpensive and attract principally a younger clientele. This effect is even more pronounced for multi-day trips on the Karnali River in western Nepal, where access to the put-in point involves a 3-day trek.

An even better test of this hypothesis, i.e. that demographics are driven principally by price, is provided as follows. There are particular white-water raft tours in a number of developing nations which can be purchased directly, by domestic tourists and independent travellers who take time to discover them; and indirectly, at a significantly higher price, by international clients who go through a rafting or adventure tour operator in their own country of origin. Examples include the Luva River in Fiji, and the Chuya and Katun rivers in Siberia. These trips can be bought directly, through Rivers Fiji or Team Gorky respectively; or indirectly, through large international tour companies such as Mountain Travel Sobek. The clients who pay the higher price, in order to save time and gain assurance, are commonly older and wealthier than those who pay the lower price which involves more research and uncertainty.

Risk and Environmental Management

Routine financial, operational and personnel management for white-water tourism operations are broadly similar to adventure and outdoor tourism operations more generally, and need not be reviewed here. For operations in developing nations particularly, interactions of both staff and clients with members of local communities can also be an important component of overall operational management, but the issues are broadly similar for the entire range of adventure tourism activities. Risk and safety management aspects, however, are largely specific to the particular adventure activity concerned. There are safety and rescue techniques, training and qualifications which apply only for white-water rafting and kayaking, and these form a key component of guide skills. In addition, there are particular environmental management issues which apply for multi-day white-water trips with riverbank camping, especially in heavily used rivers. Here, therefore, only safety and environmental management issues are considered.

Safety and risk management for white-water rafting tours involves several separate components, all of them important. The first is the choice of river, section and rapids to run, which may vary from season to season and day-to-day according to water flow and the experience of the clients. Second is the skill of the guides, not only to steer the raft down the safest route but also to check equipment, coordinate clients, carry out safety briefings, and conduct rescue and emergency operations if they should be required. The skills of safety kayakers, if any, are also critical. Third is the selection and maintenance of equipment: rafts of appropriate size and configuration for the river and trip concerned; well-fitting helmets, life jackets, wetsuits and bootees for clients as well as guides; and safety throw-ropes, flip-lines and other gear properly stowed and ready for immediate use. Heavily worn or patched rafts, for example, are more likely to leak; life jackets may gradually lose buoyancy after extended use, and paddles with damaged shafts may break under load.

Next is the knowledge of what to do in an emergency: from the simplest flip to a difficult multi-client swift water rescue where people may be injured, hypothermic and/or hypoxic. In the event of severe injury or illness, guides need first aid or EMT skills, and the group needs an emergency communications and evacuation plan. This can be far from straightforward in extended multi-day trips in remote areas. On some rivers, the rapids are only one of the potential dangers. There may also be risk of crocodile attack, various diseases and pathogens, or altitude sickness. So, because things can go wrong even for the best-prepared group, a white-water tour company also needs appropriate insurance policies, and it needs a liability waiver for clients to accept before embarking on the trip.

Risks depend heavily on terrain, climate and the difficulty of the rapids. A client or guide swimming for several minutes in a river a few degrees above zero is at greater risk of hypothermia than one swimming in a warm tropical river. A person wearing more clothing for warmth in cold climates will find it more difficult to swim than one wearing only board shorts and a life jacket. A person gasping for breath at high-altitude rivers on the Tibetan Plateau may have greater difficulty fighting their way out of a dangerous rapid than at lower altitude. On the other hand, crocodiles, caiman and alligator, not to mention piranha or hippopotami, are only of concern in warmer waters; and rocks and rapids can be equally gnarly irrespective of water temperature.

White-water rapids are graded by degree of difficulty using an international scale from I to VI, where I is extremely easy and VI is essentially unrunnable, carrying an extreme and immediate risk of death. Class V rapids, the most difficult which can be run safely by suitably skilled paddlers, are often subdivided into Vi, Vii and Viii to recognize that rapids which may have been run once or twice by world-class kayakers can be very different from rapids which still qualify as class V under the international definition, but which are run repeatedly by kayakers and sometimes also by commercial rafters. On many wilderness rivers, there are also so-called float trips with few rapids, where the main attraction is scenery or wildlife. Commercial white-water trips in open canoes, especially for beginners, are largely confined to class I and II white water. Commercial raft trips intended for families with small children will generally raft only class II, or at most class III, white water. Commercial raft trips intended for fit young backpackers with good swimming skills run class IV white water, and in a few cases class V. Tour companies which offer trips for skilled kayakers will generally focus on class IV and V white water, sometimes denoted IV−, IV + or V− to indicate finer gradations in the degree of difficulty. In general, most tour companies running class V white water will select rivers where the class V rapids can if necessary be portaged; or at the very least, where individual clients can walk around the rapid if they wish, while the guides take the boats through. For some long and complex rapids such as Itanda Falls on the Zambezi, the upper part of the rapid may be portaged and only the lower part will be run.

Environmental management requirements for white-water raft tours differ greatly from country to country and river to river. For most single-day trips the main issue is simply to ensure that clients do not leave litter at lunch stops or throw anything into the river; and that there are adequate toilet facilities, and/or appropriate instructions for clients, at the put-in, take-out and lunch-stop sites. For extended multi-day trips with riverbank camping, appropriate environmental management practices depend upon surrounding land use and the volume of river traffic. On rivers which flow through national parks and protected areas in developed nations and which are heavily in demand for recreational and commercial rafting and kayaking, there are commonly park regulations which prescribe particular standards of behaviour. These may, for example: restrict camping to particular sites with a booking system; limit maximum group size;

ban campfires or require raft tour operators to bring their own firewood and firepits for campfires; require tour operators to bring sealable toilets which are later emptied at special pump-out stations off-river; ban hunting, fishing and wildlife feeding; and similar restrictions.

At the other extreme are white-water rivers running through areas of subsistence agriculture in developing countries, where there are already substantial organic inputs from villagers and livestock; empty containers are a valuable resource rather than a form of rubbish; and firewood is the principal fuel. In such locations, pit toilets are perfectly appropriate, as long as they are dug deep and sited discreetly. Campfires for cooking are also appropriate, as long as fuel wood is not in short supply for local residents. If it is, raft tours may sometimes be able to buy firewood from local villagers. Litter control remains an issue in developing as well as developed nations: many clients, for example, are likely to fling cigarette butts on the ground or in the water unless the guides ask them repeatedly not to do so.

Guidelines for best environmental practices in white-water rafting and kayaking tours were compiled by Buckley (1999) and compared against other such materials by Buckley (2002a). Actual environmental management measures for over 40 individual white-water raft and kayak tours in various environments are presented and compared in Buckley (2006). Those reports, however, reflect practices by industry leaders. More broadly, commercial raft and kayak adventure tour operators differ enormously in their environmental management practices. Many follow some or all relevant minimal-impact guidelines for wilderness travel and camping, but some do not. Performance tends to be better in national parks, in developed countries and for longer multi-day trips.

Environmental management performance also depends on the principal clientele for the particular tour concerned, and on the structure of the rafting industry. Best-practice environmental management is only achieved where: retail operators refer to minimal-impact practices in their marketing materials, generally because they perceive this as an aspect of their market niche; onground operators provide appropriate equipment, typically because this is prescribed by land managers or a local industry agreement; and guides practise and teach minimal-impact behaviours, generally because of their own personal convictions. The overall outcome is highly significant to the tourism industry. Best-practice environmental management in the white-water rafting industry is low cost and easy to implement, but it can increase the allowable maximum volume of commercial tourism by an order of magnitude or more.

Conclusions

White-water rafting is a very successful and widespread sector of the adventure tourism industry. Some of the likely reasons for its success may be summarized as follows. It is exciting but safe. There is a high probability that rafting clients will get wet, thrown around and occasionally frightened, but a rather low risk that they will actually suffer any significant injury. It allows active participation for unskilled clients. A complete neophyte can play an active role in paddling a white-water raft. For most other adventure tourism activities, there is a much longer learning curve before clients can take part so actively. Tandem skydiving, for example, does not require any prior skill for the client, but nor does it involve any active participation.

It is relatively inexpensive. White-water rafting tours are available in many countries for under US$100 per day, including food, transport and all equipment. Multi-day trips are available in some countries at around half this rate. These prices compare favourably with most other broadly available adventure tourism activities, and are within reach of most of today's backpackers. At the same time, there are more upmarket options available, with guides rowing the rafts and taking care of camps and catering, for older clients who are prepared to pay for a higher level of service.

It is something different. Unlike other relatively low-cost outdoor adventure tour options such as hiking and trekking, which involve a familiar activity in unfamiliar surroundings, white-water rafting generally involves a very new set of experiences for the average urban-dwelling tourist. Both the surroundings and activity are quite unfamiliar for the majority of clients.

It is a commonplace component of combination products at adventure tourism destinations. At icon adventure tourism sites such as Queenstown in New Zealand, Cairns in Australian, Victoria Falls in Zimbabwe, Moab or Bozeman in the USA, Banff in Canada, Kathmandu in Nepal or Pacific Harbour in Fiji, white-water rafting is one of a suite of standard adventure activities on offer, either as a stand-alone tour or as part of a multi-activity package (Buckley et al., 2006). Holidaymakers looking for adventure opportunities, whether families or backpackers, have come to expect white-water rafting tours as one of the options available.

Some of the more expensive multi-day tours are run on famous icon rivers. The Grand Canyon of the Colorado, the Franklin River in Tasmania, the Yangtze in China or the Alsek and Tatshenshini in Canada and Alaska have all been subject to controversy over conservation, and the subject of well-known art, literature and even music. For many raft tour clients on rivers such as these, the journey has many attractions in addition to adrenalin: the scenery has connotations of sculpture, and the journey itself may almost be akin to a pilgrimage or at least a lifetime experience.

Raftable rivers are widespread worldwide. By using different types, sizes and rigs for their rafts, white-water tour operators can run everything from tight technical creeks to giant rivers in flood; and by kitting their clients out with wetsuits and bootees, they can provide adequate comfort in cold as well as warm climates.

The market for commercial white-water kayak tours is somewhat different. The majority of clients are skilled and experienced kayak paddlers, who use a tour operator to provide local knowledge and logistic support in an unfamiliar area. Even though the number of recreational white-water kayakers is large and continuing to grow, especially in Europe and North America, it is still a much more specialized market than for white-water raft tours, which are available to any reasonably capable client. Currently, most kayakers are more likely to organize their own trips and travel than to sign up for a commercial kayak tour. As today's young playboaters begin to age, however, the market for commercial white-water kayak trips will increase in the same way as has happened already in the surfing sector (Buckley, 2002b).

Apart from purely market-related factors, there seem to be several significant constraints on the continuing growth of the white-water tourism sector. The most severe of these is the continuing loss of runnable rivers, principally through hydroelectric and irrigation dams, and various forms of industrial pollution. Few countries, it seems, especially in the developing world, have yet come to appreciate the economic significance of their rivers for tourism. The second constraint is the continually changing political climate for access to different rivers. In developing nations, sudden political changes can have drastic impacts on the international inbound tourism industry for the entire country. In developed nations, access to run particular rivers may depend on the priorities and permitting systems of particular land management agencies.

The third potential constraint is crowding. During peak season on popular rivers in many developed nations, it sometimes appears as though the entire water surface is covered in large multi-coloured bubbles of plastic and rubber. Rafts queue up to run the major rapids and tour operators send staff ahead to stake out preferred campsites. It is to manage these difficulties, of course, that many public land management agencies have introduced quota and booking systems for private as well as commercial raft and kayak trips, albeit with some severe shortcomings and continuing controversy in many cases.

Despite these difficulties, white-water tourism is one of the major components of river tourism more broadly, and the principal option available in the upper sections of most rivers. There is no reason to suppose that it will not continue to thrive.

References

Arnould, E. and Price, I. (1993) River magic: extraordinary experiences and the extended service encounter. *Journal of Consumer Research* 20, 24–45.

Bangs, R. and Kallen, C. (1987) *Riding the Dragon's Back*. Atheneum, New York.

Beedie, P. (2003) Mountain guiding and adventure tourism: reflections on the choreography of the experience. *Leisure Science 22*, 147–167.

Buckley, R.C. (1999) *Green Guide to White Water*. STCRC and Griffith University, Gold Coast Australia. Available at: www.griffith.edu.au/centre/icer

Buckley, R.C. (2002a) Minimal-impact guidelines for mountain ecotourism. *Tourism Recreation Research* 27(3), 35–40.

Buckley, R.C. (2002b) Surf tourism and sustainable development in Indo-Pacific islands.

I. The industry and the islands. *Journal of Sustainable Tourism* 10, 405–424.

Buckley, R.C. (2006) *Adventure Tourism*. CAB International, Wallingford, UK.

Buckley, R.C., Ollenburg, C. and Johnson, J. (2006) Adventure destinations. In: Buckley, R., (ed.) *Adventure Tourism*. CAB International, Wallingford, UK, pp. 411–428.

Cater, C. (2006) World adventure capital. In: Buckley, R., (ed.) *Adventure Tourism*. CAB International, Wallingford, UK, pp. 429–442.

Outdoor Industry Association (2007) *Active Outdoor Recreation Economy Report*. Available at: http://www.outdoorindustry.org/research.social.php?action = detail& research_id = 26

Sharpe, R. (2005) 'Going above and beyond': the emotional labour of adventure guiding. *Journal of Leisure Research* 37, 29–50.

12 Basin-based Governance for Integrated Water Resources Management: Prospects and Challenges

F.P. Fellizar Jr.

Ritsumeikan Asia Pacific University, Beppu, Japan

Introduction

'Water is life.' 'No water, no future.' 'Water is for all.'

These statements evoke lots of meaning and sentiments. They confirm the vital importance of water, in particular fresh water to human life. They also serve as clarion call – a warning to societies not to take the future of water less seriously and point to the need for collective action from individuals and nations to avert the impending global crisis in freshwater supply. Water is everybody's business. No wonder 2003 was declared as the International Year of Fresh water and there have been several 'critical' World Water forums since then.

Many countries are already experiencing serious problems arising from water scarcity. Some 2 billion people in the world are facing water shortages, at least half that number in the Asia Pacific Region. It has been noted that water is getting scarcer due to excessive unsustainable use; and that water quality is diminishing due to unsanitary human practices and poor management of household, industrial and agricultural wastes. The impacts of human interference in the cycling of water are enormous, leading to decline in both quality and quantity of freshwater supplies. It is estimated that by 2025 a number of countries will be too dry to maintain rates of current uses (CSD, 1997a). About one-third of the world's population lives in countries suffering from moderate-to-high water stress – where water consumption is more than 10% of renewable freshwater resources. Some 80 countries, constituting 40% of the world's population, were suffering from serious water shortages by the mid-1990s (CSD, 1997a) and it is estimated that in less than 25 years two-thirds of the world's people will be living in water-stressed countries (CSD, 1997b).

By the mid-1990s, it had been noted that already some 80 countries with nearly 40% of the world's population were suffering from serious water shortages and it has been estimated that by 2025 some countries will be too dry to support levels of current uses with about two-thirds of the world's population living in water-stressed countries in less than 25 years (CSD 1997a,b).

Given the ever-growing world population and the increasing demand for fresh water to serve a variety of uses, including tourism, the challenge that will confront nations is to maintain a balance between water demand and supply. The paramount concerns and imperatives of the 21st century are to ensure access to quality water and to protect the sources of fresh water from further degradation.

The latter is crucial considering that the volume of fresh water available is limited, distribution uneven and the location of sources remote from human population. The earth's total water volume is about 1400 million cubic kilometres. Of this only about 2.5% or nearly 35 million cubic kilometres is fresh water, which is either stored in deep groundwater aquifers or locked up as permanent ice or snow in Antarctica and Greenland. Fresh water for human consumption mainly comes from sources such as rivers, lakes, groundwater basins and soil moisture. Sadly, only about $200,000 \, km^3$ of water – less than 1% of all fresh water and only 0.01% of all water on earth – is available for human consumption (UNEP, 2002).

The critical factor at the bottom of freshwater issues is management. The lack of proper management of, and care for, water as a vital resource has allowed the diminution of freshwater resources all over the world, both in terms of quality and quantity. There is now a growing consensus that water crises can be directly linked to issues of governance. More explicitly, it was agreed in various conferences and forums on water that *the water crisis is mainly a crisis of governance*. Consequently, resolving the issues and problems in this area must be a key priority if we are to achieve sustainable water resource use (Update, 2002).

It is in the light of the foregoing arguments and observations that this chapter presents options for ensuring a sustainable 'water future' for tourism as much as for community and environmental water supplies. The discussion is centred on the Asia Pacific Region and focuses on river basins (catchments); however, the comments made apply to river basins across the world. The discussion revolves around the need to enhance river basin-based governance as a key to improved integrated water resources management and therefore of water availability for river tourism, by discussing the importance of river councils as a governance mechanism and the basin plan as an instrument for harmonizing collective efforts in a river/lake context.

The Asia Pacific Region: the Water Situation

It is worth noting that the Asia Pacific Region accounts for nearly one-third of the yearly global total runoff of approximately $13,269 \, km^3$ (ESCAP, 1997). In many developing countries in the region, the annual renewable water resources are considerable in absolute terms although not available for exploitation. The People's Republic of China, Indonesia and Pakistan are the countries with the highest absolute quantities of water resources available. However, this region also has the lowest per capita availability of fresh water, with renewable water resources amounting to about $3690\,m^3$ per capita per year in mid-1999 for the 30 largest countries in the region for which records are available (UNDP, UNEP, World Bank and WRI, 2000 and United Nations Population Division, 2001).

Sources of freshwater supply

Rivers, lakes and man-made reservoirs are the main sources of surface water abstraction in the Asia Pacific Region. The region has several important river systems, with 400 major rivers in India, 200 in Indonesia, 108 in Japan, 50 in Bangladesh and 20 in Thailand. There are also international rivers that include the Mekong, Indus, Ganges, Brahmaputra and Meghna river systems. Moreover, the region has substantial number of lakes. Among the largest and providing multiple uses are the Dongting-hu in People's Republic of China, Tonle Sap in Cambodia, Lake Toba in Indonesia, Kasumigaura and Biwa lakes in Japan, Laguna de Bay in the Philippines, Lake Songhkla in Thailand and Lake Issy Kul in Kyrgyzstan (ESCAP-ADB 2000).

The region also contains vast groundwater reservoirs that depend on abundant rainy season recharge such as those in Bangladesh, India, Indonesia, Nepal and Myanmar. Many countries in the region rely on groundwater to supplement scarce surface water resources at the rate of 30–35% of the total supply in Bangladesh, India and Pakistan (ADB, 1998).

Water scarcity and lowered quality: limits to growth

Growing population, urbanization and economic development are putting great pressure on the quantity and quality of the region's fresh water. Due to increasing population, the amount of per capita water resources available has been noted to be considerably less in 2000 compared to that in 1950. Increasing population coupled with economic expansion creates severe competition for water and exacerbates potential for conflicting demands between various sectors and uses. For instance, agriculture is the biggest consumer (86%), with relatively smaller amounts going to industry (8%) and domestic use (6%) (UNDP, UNEP, World Bank and WRI, 2000).

Serious imbalances between supply and demand were caused by massive withdrawals from rivers, lakes and underground reservoirs. Sector competition and conflicts have become critical and intense. Excessive abstractions for agriculture are depleting the volume of water in some rivers and lakes. Water tables in underground aquifers have sunk, leading to land subsidence and saltwater intrusion. In coastal cities such as Bangkok, Dhaka, Jakarta, Karachi and Manila, excessive use of groundwater has led to saline intrusion and ground subsidence.

It has been observed that countries in the region are either experiencing, or are predicted to suffer, water scarcity and stress in the near future based on the widely accepted threshold for water adequacy of $1600\,m^3$ of renewable fresh water per capita per year. The Republic of Korea is currently approaching water stress, Singapore is already water-scarce and the Maldives has chronic water scarcity, with a water supply figure of $114\,m^3$ per capita per year (FAO, 1999). India's water scarcity is expected to intensify as the country's population is predicted to exceed 1.4 billion by 2025 (United Nation's medium projection). According to United Nations projections, the People's Republic of China will only narrowly miss the water stress benchmark in 2025 (Das Gupta, 1996).

Unfortunately, pollution and environmental degradation aggravate the growing scarcity of water in the region. Many rivers, lakes and aquifers have been rendered unsuitable for human consumption due to waste discharges, sewage and effluents from domestic, industrial and agricultural sources. Among the rivers of the region, Yellow River (People's Republic of China), Ganges (India), Amu and Syr Darya (Central Asia) top the list of the world's most polluted rivers according to a report of the World Commission on Water (The Independent Newspaper, 1999). All these rivers are used in some form for river-based tourism, and all impact on their country's tourism if they are in any way unacceptable environmentally.

In many cases, organic matter has been the cause of most groundwater pollution. Pollution sources include leaching from refuse, other solid waste and excessive use of agricultural inputs such as fertilizers, pesticides and animal wastes. Pollution from agricultural activities is particularly true in the case of the People's Republic of China and the countries of South and South-east Asia. Increase in dairy farm and fertilizer use is intensifying pollution in the groundwater, shallow lakes and streams in New Zealand (Smith *et al.*, 1993). It is estimated that around 90% of rivers currently experience water quality problems due to excessive nutrient inflows in New South Wales, Australia. Overall, approximately 50% of the rivers of the region have exceedingly high levels of nutrients while another 25% have a moderate problem, with nutrient levels occasionally exceeding the desirable levels (ESCAP, 1998). In Central Asia, water resource contamination posing health hazards was due to nutrients from excessive use of fertilizers, herbicides, pesticides and defoliants (Kharin, 1996; Mainguet and Letolle, 1998).

The measured concentrations of heavy metals (such as arsenic, cadmium, mercury and lead) in many of the region's water bodies also exceed basic water quality standards. The concentrations of dichloro-diphenyl-trichloroethane (DDT), polychlorinated biphenyls (PCBs), industrial solvents and other toxic chemicals are likewise rising. These can be traced primarily from mining, oil refineries, chemical works and in textile, wood pulp and pesticide factories. In fact, the water bodies of the South-east Asian sub-region are noted to be the most heavily polluted with heavy metals and toxic chemicals (ADB, 1997, 1998).

Soil erosion due to reforestation and land conversion is also exacerbating the natural process of siltation of water bodies. As a result, greater quantities of sediment are accumulating in the rivers, dams and reservoirs of the region. For example, erosion is responsible for an annual sediment yield of over $1000\,t/km^2$ in the Ganges, Brahmaputra and Yellow River basins. Pakistan's Tarbela Dam on the Indus River accumulates 200 million cubic metres of silt each year filling the reservoir at a rate of 2% per year. Deforestation in the upper catchment of Lake Tonle Sap in Cambodia is significantly reducing the lake's depth, affecting the lake fisheries and the tourism industry.

The Asia Pacific Region has the world's greatest concentration of salt-affected soils (FAO, 1990). Due to poor drainage from agricultural areas, salinity levels in major rivers are becoming highly concentrated, making the water unsuitable for downstream users (Seckler *et al.*, 1999). Over-pumping in some coastal cities of the region has resulted in the movement of salty seawater inland, known as 'saline intrusion'. This occurs when water levels in freshwater aquifers are lowered to a point where saltwater can invade through the water-bearing beds in the direction of the wells (Das Gupta, 1996). For instance, seawater intrusion into aquifers presents a major problem in Metro Manila. Vietnam's major river basins and coastal plains experience rising salinity with an average of approximately 3000–4000 ppm, a level unsuitable for drinking (Asian Media Information and Communication Centre, 1997). In the Indian state of Gujarat, saline intrusion occurred in some areas where irrigators have heavily over-pumped local aquifers close to the coast (Postel, 1996).

Integrated Water Resources Management and Basin-based Governance: Overcoming the Limits to Available Water

Water scarcity and lowered quality are serious threats to the development of the Asia Pacific Region's river-based tourism as well as its overall survival. Water is essential to the region's growth and water-related problems will limit the region's options for the future. Traditionally, government policies and strategies on water management have been aimed at the expansion of supply in order to meet the ever-increasing water demands of the domestic, agriculture and industrial sectors. The largely fragmented approach that has traditionally been applied has allowed conflicts and competition, and has led to the over-exploitation of scarce water resources. The current challenge for many countries of the region is to overcome fragmented sub-sector approaches and to design and implement integrated mechanisms, particularly for the implementation of projects that transcend sub-sectors.

Integrated Water Resources Management (IWRM) is 'a process which promotes the coordinated development and management of water, land and related resources in order to maximize the resultant economic and social welfare in an equitable manner without compromising the sustainability of vital ecosystems' (GWP-TEC, 2003). It is a political process and involves mediation of conflicting interests. The three pillars of IWRM include management instruments, enabling environment and institutional framework. Encapsulated, analysis and understanding of IWRM begins at defining a spatial locus within which the critical components interact with and among each other. The locus of analysis and action most appropriate is the watershed, catchment or a basin area. The river/lake basin is a discrete unit of the earth's surface. More distinctly, it is a naturally defined territorial unit of a surface drainage system and, as such, is a clearly identifiable ecological unit for interface management between biophysical and human systems.

   The basin approach to IWRM refers to the formulation and implementation of courses of action involving the use of natural and human resources in a basin, taking into account the social, political, economic and institutional factors operating within it to achieve specific objectives. IWRM in the context of a river basin considers the basin as an ecosystem within which there is a dynamic interplay and interactions between and among the natural resources, population, institutions and technology as it responds to, and is influenced by, its external environment (Figure 12.1). The concept of water resources management within a river basin or water catchment area, focusing on the integration of land and water-related issues, has been applied in some countries including Australia, People's Republic of China and Japan. In India, the national water policy asserts that water resources planning be undertaken for a hydrological unit, such as drainage basin or sub-basin. In Indonesia, institutions for water resources management have been established for some river basins, although these are yet to become fully functioning (UN-ESCAP, 2000). The basin approach to IWRM has the following attributes:

1. It treats the basin as an ecosystem, requiring systems approach and perspectives.
2. It considers the basin area as the primary unit for integrating social, economic, administrative, institutional and environmental concerns.
3. It recognizes the man–environment interactions as the major focus of analysis for planning.

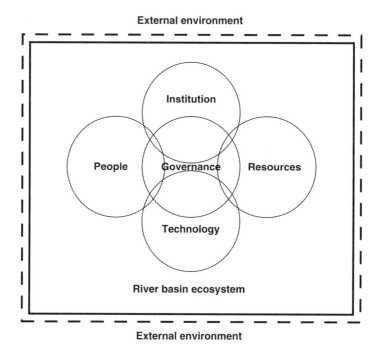

Fig. 12.1. Governance and integrated water resources management (IWRM). (From Fellizar, 2003.)

4. It recognizes the upstream–downstream continuum as well as other relevant off-site and on-site changes and impacts.
5. It considers water as the integrator and indicator of activities in the basin.
6. It recognizes the natural and functional linkages with national and regional development.
7. It requires application of specialized skills and methodologies from a multi-disciplinary team of experts.
8. It emphasizes the role of the local communities and other stakeholders in resources management.

Thus, the rationale for the basin approach to IWRM can be summarized as follows:

1. The basin is a functional unit established by physical relationships.
2. The basin approach is logical for evaluating the biophysical linkages of upland and downstream activities because within the basin they are linked through the hydrologic cycle (CSD, 1997a).
3. The basin approach is holistic, which enables planners and managers to consider many facets of resource development.
4. Land-use activities and upland disturbances often result in a chain of environmental impacts that can readily be examined within the basin context.
5. The basin approach has a strong economic logic. Many of the externalities involved with alternative land management practices on an individual farm are internalized when the basin is managed as a unit.
6. The basin provides the framework for analysing the effects of human interactions with the environment. The environmental impacts within the basin operate as a feedback loop for changes in the social system.
7. The basin approach can be integrated with, or be part of, programmes including forestry, agriculture, soil conservation, rural and urban development, river tourism, coastal resources management, infrastructure development and biodiversity conservation among others.

Indeed, the basin provides the context by which integration relevant to IWRM within the natural system and the human system is better understood. Integration within the natural system concerns, for instance, the integration of land and water management and use (including river tourism), surface water and groundwater supplies, and upstream and downstream water-related issues and concerns as they relate to and impact on the hydrologic cycle. Within the human system, integration relates to cross-sector interface of policies and strategies and transactions of all relevant stakeholders in the decision-making process. The integration of various sector views and interests relevant to IWRM becomes more tractable in the basin context (CSD, 1997b).

Another view of IWRM in the basin context is to consider the interaction of resources, population, institution and technology. At the core of the interactions, among the components is governance. Governance seen in this light is the hub that balances and harmonizes the interactions thereby ensuring that the demands of the population are being met without endangering the sustainability of the resources, because technologies, policies and organizational arrangements are applied and appropriately designed to meet the goals of IWRM. Governance comprises the complex mechanisms, processes and institutions through which citizens and groups articulate their interests, mediate their differences and exercise their legal rights and obligations. Good governance is, among other things, participatory, transparent and accountable. It is also effective and equitable and it promotes the rule of law. 'Good governance assures that political, social and economic priorities are based on broad consensus in society and that the voices of the poorest and the most vulnerable are heard in decision making over the allocation of development resources' (UNDP, 1997, 2000).

Examples of governance at the local level include a neighbourhood cooperative formed to install and maintain a standing water pipe, a town council operating a waste recycling scheme, a multi-urban body developing an integrated transport plan together with user groups (see Chapter 2, this volume, and the Port of Kolkata river tourism initiative), a stock exchange regulating itself with national government oversight and a regional initiative of state agencies, industrial groups and residents to control deforestation. At the global level, governance has been viewed primarily as intergovernmental relationships, but it must now be understood as also involving non-governmental organizations (NGOs), citizens' movements, multinational corporations and the global capital market. Interacting with these are global mass media of dramatically enlarged influence (The Commission on Global Governance, 2000).

With respect to water, 'governance refers to the range of political, economic and administrative systems that are in place to regulate the development and management of water resources and provision of water services at different levels.' Basin-based governance is simply the governance of water in a basin context. There are two key elements of basin-based governance: the organization or structure; and the basin plan. The following sections highlight the findings taken from a study of water governance in a basin context, with focus on 'River Councils' as governance mechanism, as well as the lessons and observations arising from actual basin planning conducted in one of the Philippine lakes. This study on River Councils focused on the understanding of the level of participation of the different actors, sectors and organizations and the manner by which efforts and resources are coordinated and harmonized through the Councils, as the governance mechanism for integrated water resource management in the Laguna de Bay Region of the Philippines. The discussions on the experiences in the planning conducted for Naujan Lake confirm the need for holistic, trans-disciplinary, integrated and participatory approaches.

River Councils as Governance Mechanism: a Glimpse at Participation and Coordination

Background

Laguna de Bay is a freshwater lake with a surface area of 900 km². It is the largest lake in the Philippines and one of the largest in the entire South-east Asia. The basin area is around 3730 km² and is home to over 10 million people.

The lake holds an average of 2.9 billion cubic metres of water and has an average depth of 2.5 m. The lake basin covers the provinces of Rizal and Laguna and is rich in biological resources including fish, mollusks and macrophytes. It serves multiple uses such as irrigation, fisheries, domestic water supply, navigation, reservoir of floodwater, power generation, recreation and tourism, and industrial cooling. The administration of the lake and its basin area is lodged with the Laguna Lake Development Authority (LLDA), a body organized by virtue of 'Republic Act 4850' as a quasi-governmental agency with regulatory and proprietary functions to lead, promote and accelerate the development and balanced growth of Laguna de Bay within the context of national and regional plans and policies for social and economic development. 'Presidential Decree 813' of 1975 and 'Executive Order 927' of 1983 expanded LLDA's authority to include environmental protection and jurisdiction over surface waters of the lake and to carry out the development of the basin with utmost regard for environmental management and control, preservation of the quality of human life and ecological systems, and prevention of undue ecological disturbances, deterioration and pollution.

Population growth, urbanization, extensive agriculture and industrialization continue to exert pressure on the lake and its basin areas, resulting to increased pollution load and reduced overall lake productivity. In 1995, LLDA embarked on a programme to rehabilitate and protect the 21 river systems flowing into the lake and adopted the basin or watershed approach to river rehabilitation. This led to the creation of 'River Rehabilitation Councils' in 1997. But it was only in 1999 that a formal resolution was duly approved duly institutionalizing the river rehabilitation councils/foundations for the 21 river basins in the lake region. Presently, the various Councils/Foundations are at different stages of development.

Functions and duties of the River Councils/Foundations

The River Councils/Foundations are expected to perform the following functions:

1. Vigorously pursue a comprehensive and sustained River Rehabilitation Programme for the specific river basin.
2. Mobilize various sectors in the community, towns and cities within the catchment/watershed of specific river systems in order to be intimately involved in the effort to protect our rivers and lakes.
3. Undertake information, education and motivation campaigns to raise the level of environmental and health awareness of the people in the communities.
4. Regularly conduct a physical survey of the river including flow measurements to assess its current condition, identify environmental problems and issues, pinpoint sources of pollution and other factors affecting its environmental quality, and, on the basis thereof, to formulate, prioritize and undertake appropriate measures to effectively address the identified problems and issues.
5. Formulate technically and environmentally sound Watershed Management Plans and/or project proposals and submit such plans and proposals to potential funding agencies and institutions.

6. Establish and maintain close linkages with LLDA for the necessary expertise, capability and know-how to undertake periodic water quality assessment, especially of identified establishments or entities discharging wastewater directly into the rivers.

7. Act as a network of environmental stewards and report to LLDA and other duly constituted authorities all cases of violations of environmental laws, regulations and standards.

8. Raise funds for the Watershed Management Plan, River Rehabilitation Programme and/or river protection, rehabilitation and/or development projects.

9. Undertake other functions and tasks in accordance with the main objectives set by the River Councils.

Nature and degree of participation

The members of the Councils are considered generally active. Participation is manifested through regular attendance in meetings and active participation in deliberations, membership in technical working groups/committees, exchange of ideas and information, resource-sharing, actual involvement in project implementation and resource generation. Council meetings are held monthly and members are also actively involved in the various working committees. In particular, all the Councils are able to raise financial support for their activities through different creative means of raising funds. The two most common and well-participated activities of the Councils are river clean-up projects and fund generation. For instance 'Limas Marina Council' is credited for launching the first municipal-wide clean-up drive called 'Pistang Linis Bayan' (or town clean-up festival). The same Council is also recognized as the first to have raised over PHP 500,000 through raffles and other fund-raising schemes. Two other councils, 'Sagip Ilog' and 'SaCRED' have also implemented their own river clean-up projects in addition to launching awareness campaigns and participation in local and international conferences.

All the Councils have undertaken strategic planning exercises where they have affirmed their commitment to pursue their vision and missions. Projects and other activities were also identified for future implementation. One of the indicators of strong partnership and participation is the sharing of resources and facilities in support of projects of the Councils. Office transport, equipment, spaces and supplies from many sources are volunteered to projects and activities. So far the Basin Councils' accomplishments and activities consist of the following: river and town clean-up drives; information campaign; fund-raising projects; strategic planning and visioning; formulating operations manuals; development of video, leaflets and other materials; attendance at conferences, educational trips, workshops, seminars and training programmes; technology dissemination; support to solid waste management; tree planting; and monitoring of polluting activities in the basin.

These may seem very modest activities and accomplishments, but what matters most is the interest and the quality of partnership established between and among individuals and organizations in each Council. Considering that the

Councils are relatively young, such accomplishments are signs of greater things to come. The issue now becomes sustaining the enthusiasm and the energies of the Councils and extending their work into areas like river tourism. Leadership, commonality of goals, mechanism/structure and authority are some of the key elements of coordinative capacity. There exist a high sense of commonality of, and commitment to, the objectives that are the keys to meaningful and effective coordination.

There are three tiers of coordination in the Council. These are: the Board of Trustees, which takes care of the policy-making functions and has a maximum of 15 members; the Executive Committee, headed by the President and which takes care of operational concerns; and, the Operational Committees which assist the President in planning and implementing projects and activities. These levels of coordination enable greater participation and involvement among members and facilitate the smooth functioning of the Council. Authority is shared and not something that arises from formal or legal basis but more out of mutuality and professional respect. Since Councils are by their nature voluntary, authority is manifested more in terms of influence and persuasion rather than by sanctions or dictates. This is so far one of the strong attributes of the Council arrangements. Of course, this is only possible when people prove themselves trustworthy, when there is openness and transparency and when people who lead have the moral authority to do so.

Hurdles and challenges

The Councils recognize that the road ahead may not be that level and smooth. Indifference of local government officials and the residents is one of the most difficult tests. For one, concern for the environment is not the top priority in most local governments, and two, politicians are more concerned about their personal careers. There are vital river basin environmental initiatives that may not be favourable to the interests of some politicians as a result. Resources to support the Councils' projects and activities are limited and there is therefore a need to explore more creative ways of raising money. While the Councils have undertaken fund-raising activities, the generated funds may not be sufficient to sustain the planned projects.

But perhaps more importantly, the technical capability of the Councils to plan, manage and monitor watershed development and protection programmes and projects is severely wanting. Indeed, the support of LLDA may not be adequate at this point since the organization itself needs to beef up its technical expertise for basin management. Due to the interdisciplinary nature of watershed management, technical expertise will have to be sourced from different organizations and institutions. Finally, conflicting schedules and demands of their own professional engagements are another limitation by Council members. Managing time and prioritization become a practical difficulty for members. There is apprehension that volunteerism may soon wane and fade among members. The challenge becomes one of sustaining the interests and enthusiasm of the members.

Amidst these actual and perceived difficulties, the Councils are none the less committed to pursue their goals and programmes. They see that the support and encouragement given to them by LLDA is one reason they can go on. There are also resources and services that are being made available to them by other individuals, organizations and especially academic institutions. The Councils also recognize the existence and willingness of other national, regional and international organizations with which they can establish linkages. The globalization of environmental concerns and most specially the campaign for water security is a strong support for each Council. They are also aware that technologies, information and expertise are available; how to connect and tap these sources is something they are currently exploring.

So far, the Councils as local governance mechanisms are able to complement the efforts and resources of the LLDA, promote healthy partnerships among sectors and community members, generate resources and expertise, and bring concern for the conservation of lakes and its basins closest to the community. Given these seemingly outstanding attributes and accomplishments of the Councils as governance mechanisms, there still remain areas for further improvement. These include the need to develop their technical capability for basin-wide planning and monitoring, to generate a stable financial base for both project and operational requirements and to obtain greater political commitments from local government units.

The Basin Plan: Blue Print of Interactions and Options

Another element of basin-based governance is the basin plan. In particular, the planning process enhances the appreciation of multiple-stakeholders and compels their participation not only in the planning process but more so in the implementation of the plan. The plan serves as the road map that enables stakeholders to commit time and resources to achieve the plan objectives. In this manner, conflicts and issues are understood in better light and their impacts may be minimized, priorities established, strategies properly harmonized and organizational relationships modified and adjusted.

This section examines the planning process conducted for one of the lakes in the Philippines, the Lake Naujan on Mindoro Island, but can equally be applied to the major rivers themselves. Naujan Lake's basin area includes four municipal government units. Declared as a national park in 1957, the area has largely retained its natural beauty and natural resources, but in the last few years has been experiencing the impact of human activities in its environment. Specific examples are declining fish catch, uncontrolled illegal fishing even within the designated fish sanctuary, destructive agricultural practices and highly polluting practices, and uncontrolled expansion of human settlements and tourism. For these reasons, Naujan Lake has been classified as a protected area under the National Integrated Protected Areas System (NIPAS) Act of 1992. Under NIPAS, protected areas are defined identified portions of land and water set aside by reason of their unique physical and biological significance, managed to enhance biological diversity and protected against destructive human exploitation. The NIPAS Act provides the legal framework for the effective and efficient management of all protected areas in the Philippines through the formulation of site-specific protected area Management Plans, which serve as the basic long-term framework in the management of each park or protected area, and thus guide park decision makers and managers in preparing, implementing and monitoring annual operational plans.

The following are the intrinsic and emergent issues addressed by the Naujan Lake National Park (NLNP) Management Plan based on the study led by the author in 1999/2000 commissioned by the Park and Wildlife Bureau of the Republic of the Philippines with funding from Ramsar Convention on Wetlands to the South-east Asian Ministers of Education Organization (SEAMEO) Regional Center of Graduate Studies and Research in Agriculture (SEARCA) with office in College, Laguna, Philippines. The plan shows how sector concerns are balanced through the participatory planning process.

Conservation and biodiversity concerns

Naujan Lake National Park has been designated as an Anatidae Site Network in May 1999. Anatidae (ducks, geese and swans) is a group of water birds ecologically dependent on wetlands for at least some part of their annual life cycle. Law enforcement with regard to poaching and hunting needs improvement. Other issues include overfishing using illegal fishing gear, fishing in the restricted fish sanctuary, destruction of forest resources and protected animal species (e.g. *Crocodylus mindorensis*), land degradation due to destructive farming practices and conversions, and conflicting demands for surface and underground water resources.

Habitat rehabilitation needs

There are three habitats that are under constant threat of destruction, namely: unregulated conversion of marshland and swamps into agriculture and human settlements, forest denudation due to slash-and-burn agriculture and over-exploitation and siltation of the Butas River, which is the only outlet of the lake leading to the sea.

Management constraints

There is a need to update and/or establish appropriate guidelines to enable the NLNP Protected Area Management Board (PAMB) to effectively manage and govern the park. The tenure of PAMB members should be rationalized to consider the elective tenure of local government officials. Upgrading the skills and resources of the Office of the Protected Area Superintendent (PASu) is critical towards effective and efficient enforcement of rules and regulations within the park, and the need for empowering local communities cannot be overemphasized.

Local interests, rights and concerns

The fish sanctuary, which occupies the northern half of the Naujan Lake, covers the municipality of Naujan and portions of Pola and Victoria. To fish legally, fishers from these municipalities (in particular those from Naujan) have to go to the southern end, thereby incurring high operational costs (e.g. boat depreciation, additional expenses for boat fuel and oil and longer labour hours). The present location of the sanctuary is therefore seen as inequitable. The basis for such delineation has also not been adequately explained to local communities. The major services provided by Naujan Lake include fisheries, irrigation, transportation, tourism and domestic uses, among others. Proposed development projects should carefully consider the equitable allocation and sustainable use of water from the lake.

Tenure and security is a highly contentious issue within NLNP at present. There is a need to identify valid claims among various stakeholders of the park, and for the Department of Environment and Natural Resource (DENR) to institute and apply the tenure instrument that will address the needs of tenured migrants within the park. Lack of supplemental/alternative livelihood and continued dependence of small fishers and lakeside communities on fishing as primary source of food and income intensify pressures on NLNP fishery and lake resources. The complexity of resource use conflicts brought about by the different sociocultural, economic and political backgrounds and affiliations of stakeholders can also be a problem. Recognition and protection of the rights of Mangyans (local indigenous communities) and other tribal peoples in the area must be recognized and protected.

Changes required in legal status

Most small farmers and fishers in NLNP have been occupying their residential and/or agricultural land without any formal claims. There is a need to thoroughly investigate reported fake land titles within the NLNP, as this undermines the integrity of the park and intensifies tenure conflicts in the area.

The NLNP Management Planning Process

The development of the NLNP Protected Area Management Plan (PAMP) involved a systematic process that was closely coordinated with, and involved, the two institutions that have direct authority over the area – DENR Regional Office IV and the NLNP PAMB. The process framework resulted from critical discussions and interactions between the same members of the Technical Team who produced the comprehensive profile of NLNP, utilizing the considerable information acquired through months-long data-gathering activities and extended field visits in 1997. Data and information generated by ocular inspection and observation visits, formal household surveys, sessions with key informants in the community, and laboratory and technical analyses, served as the focal and starting point of subsequent management planning for the lake and its basin area. A team of technical experts representing various disciplines such

Table 12.1. Strategic programmes for the NLNP management process.

NLNP strategic programmes	Title	Function
B. 1.1	Biota and Ecosystems Management Programme (BEMP)	Ecosystem conservation
B. 1.2	Land and Water-use Management Programme (LWUMP)	Sustain water resources
B. 1.3	Protection and Law Enforcement Programme (PLEP)	Compliance
B. 1.4	Stakeholders/Community Awareness Programme (SCAP)	Education
B. 1.5	Socio-economic Welfare Programme (SWP)	Livelihood options
B. 1.6	Land Tenure Programme (LTP)	Secure land tenure
B. 1.7	Regional and National Integration Programme (RNIP)	Regional integration
B. 1.8	Ecotourism and Visitor Management Programme (EVMP)	Community-based ecotourism and river basin tourism
B. 1.9	Database Management Programme (DMP)	Natural and socio-economic databases
B. 1.10	Policy and Institutional Development Programme (PIDP)	Continuous policy review
B. 2.1	Administrative, Monitoring, and Evaluation Programme (AMEP)	Develop administrative mechanisms
B. 2.2	Fiscal Management Programme (FMP)	Generate funds from public and private sources

as watershed and land-use planning, tourism, aquatic biology, hydrology, policy and institutions, sociocultural, economics and wildlife provided the technical knowledge and expertise to integrate various sustainable systems and methodologies to the stakeholders' concerns in protected area planning and management. The resulting strategic programmes are given in Table 12.1.

Several validation and consultation workshops were conducted to solicit the stakeholders' ideas, perceptions and views on the provisions of the NLNP Management Plan. Members of the PAMB, representatives from Protected Areas and Wildlife Bureau (PAWB), DENR, non-government organizations (NGOs), local government units (LGUs) and other stakeholders participated in these workshops and consultation meetings.

Lessons Learned and Implications/Impacts for IWRM

River Councils as a governance mechanism for river basins

Basin-based local governance mechanisms in whatever form are potent tools for effective integrated water resources management practice, but they must be central to IWRM. Local organizations and communities if properly motivated and empowered can make permanent and lasting difference in improving water resource management. Efforts must be directed at enhancing volunteer- ism and coordination capacity at the community/basin levels. Councils can serve as a self-policing mechanism among members as they allow internal checks and balances to be constructed within a spirit of mutual respect and confidence. Councils too can become effective means for resolving conflicts among and between members.

Resources for technical and organizational capability building for local councils/organizations must be made accessible. For instance, Councils often lack the technical expertise for basin-wide planning, as well as for monitoring activities that are detrimental to the quality of water and its sources. A healthy partnership between legally mandated organization such as LLDA and a River Council is an important factor to consider in IWRM. This largely depends on the level of trust and rapport established between them. Leadership ability and attributes of both the Councils and the agency make a whole lot of difference.

Intra-governmental and intergovernmental issues and problems *can* be handled at the Council level. The Councils serve as a venue for identifying and mitigating these problems. A lot, however, depends on the degree of openness and trust among members. Somehow, as long as the issues and problems are surfaced, at least they can be threshed-out objectively and eliminated. In this way, concerned parties are able to recognize relevant issues that may ultimately lead to corresponding adjustments and/or resolutions. Councils can also gener- ate resources, financial and otherwise in support of their activities. Such resources supplement the limited resources of government and other con- cerned agencies. This redounds to more programmes without depending on the other agencies for support.

River Councils, however, can be constrained by a lack of support from local governmental decision makers. They can also be hindered by the chang- ing personalities as representatives of local governments by virtue of election or non-re-election. Recommendations from the Councils may not be looked upon favourably by local law makers and therefore may not be considered for approval as local ordinances. River Councils may have to learn the art of advocacy for their findings and recommendation to be adopted by local govern- ments. Even if there are local government representatives in the Councils, there is no guarantee that proposals can be adopted and approved.

Basin planning

Mobilizing stakeholder's interests in the planning process and ensuring their commitment to sustain their active participation is the first and most crucial step in plan formulation. Making sure that every sector is represented and that they are heard are basic elements of successful planning. A team of facilitators and scientists who are willing to transcend their disciplinary biases is also needed to handle the process. Scientifically generated information can ensure holistic and integrative planning. Leadership in the team is also crucial. In addition to this, planning is an iterative process and is a means of enhancing awareness of all actors to issues in the basin area as well the interactions of these issues. So, crafting a common vision as the building block for the plan takes time and creativity as various actors have their own priorities and biases. This vision reflects the desires, preferences and commitment of the participants in the planning process.

Formulating a plan is one thing and implementing it is another. Acceptance and authorization by legally mandated authorities and institutions are needed. It is therefore important that these personalities are involved in the initial stages of the planning process.

Conclusions: a Practical Approach to IWRM and a Sustainable Water Future for the Asia Pacific Region

Basically, this chapter has highlighted one of the key elements for effective integrated water resource management: basin-based water governance. River Councils as governance mechanisms for IWRM have vast and yet untapped potentials for achieving the sustainability goal of IWRM and as a result, river tourism. Each basin however represents unique features and therefore must be managed differently. Formulation of a holistic and comprehensive basin-wide plan as the basis and spirit for collective governance is imperative. It is essential that this basin-wide plan be evolved with as broad participation as possible from all stakeholders. Drawing in the various actors in the planning process would be both educational and challenging. If and when the various participants commit themselves to the plan, there is great possibility that they too can align their organizational and individual priorities. A sound and science-based basin plan is a very potent tool for clarifying roles and expectations from stakeholders, thereby making governance more effective and responsive. This implies the following:

1. Promoting local organizations and/or Councils as integrated water resources managers. They have vast potential and at the same time they have vested interest in ensuring availability of cheap, safe and high-quality water.

2. Promoting a basin approach to IWRM and providing assistance to Councils in formulating sound and science-based comprehensive basin plans.

3. Providing education/training/capability-building opportunities for local councils to enhance their technical and organizational capabilities. A challenge to educational institution is to formulate/evolve a curriculum that would make possible trans-disciplinary sharing of knowledge and expertise. Basin-based governance, in particular basin planning and management, requires a distinct set of perspectives, attitudes, knowledge and skills from practitioners. Disciplinary borders must be overcome to avoid a rigidity leading to fragmented efforts.

4. Establishing a learning resource centre for river basin management in each region to support local councils, communities, scientists and policy makers in enhancing their capabilities. This learning resource centre can be a venue for training, information exchange and technology demonstration among others. A consortium of education and training institutions must be established.

5. IWRM requires financial and technological support or assistance to local communities and councils. Establishing support systems to provide for such needs is critical.

6. IWRM issues and concerns are greatly appreciated and better managed at the local level with corresponding supportive policy framework at the national and global levels. This is to emphasize that while water security is a global issue, its management remains local and so does its governance. National and global policies must recognize the peculiarities of each basin and therefore must reflect and accommodate these unique attributes and not the other way around. Bottom-up policy formulation must be adopted. This is worth a try.

7. Understanding/clarifying the interface between levels of governance and uses for water is an urgent concern. Which ones take precedence? This is a critical question to settle in the case of the use of rivers for river-based tourism.

8. Document 'best practice' in IWRM in each region for proper dissemination to relevant parties and organizations. There is no substitute for experience.

9. Political will and commitment from local and national leadership are critical elements for river basin-based governance. Basin-based governance critically needs leaders who can mobilize, harmonize and sustain efforts towards sustainable integrated water resources management.

In conclusion, the concern for sustainable quality water is woven in the fabric of everyday life in any community. Local actions need to be promoted and enhanced. Local or, more appropriately, 'basin-based governance', as it involves the participation of different stakeholders in the management of water as a precious resource, must be strengthened and supported. This is because IWRM is best done at the basin level within which there exist stakeholders who are willing to collaborate, actively participate and take responsibility for the sustainability of water for varied uses, and will do this most easily based on a sound, comprehensive and integrative plan that is scientifically and collectively formulated. In addition, a new paradigm in water education is critically needed. Basin-based governance builds a sense of ownership and accountability for the resource among the stakeholders that form the building block for sustainable IWRM. It is believed that solving the crisis of governance at the basin level is one step to solving the global water crisis, for 'river tourism' and any other use of this critical resource.

References

Asia Development Bank (ADB) (1997) *Emerging Asia: Changes and Challenges.* ADB, Manila.

Asia Development Bank (ADB) (1998) *The Bank's Policy on Water.* Working Paper. ADB, Manila.

Asian Media Information and Communication Centre (AMICC), 1997. Water: Asia's Environmental Imperative, Nanyang Technological University, Singapore. Cited in: UNESCAP-ADB (2000) *State of Environment in Asia Pacific.* United

Nations, New York. Available at: www.unescap.org/esd/environment/soe/2000

CSD (1997a) Comprehensive Assessment of the Freshwater Resources of the World. Report of the Secretary-General, United Nations Economic and Social Council. Available at: http://www.un.org/documents/ecosoc/cn17/1997/ecn171997-9.htm[Geo-2-117]

CSD (1997b) Overall Progress Achieved Since the United Nations Conference on Environment and Development. Report of the Secretary-General, Addendum – Protection of the Quality and Supply of Freshwater Resources. Application of Integrated Approaches to the Development, Management and Use of Water Resources, United Nations Economic and Social Council. Available at: http://www.un.org/documents/ecosoc/cn17/1997/ec

Das Gupta, A. (1996) *Groundwater and the Environment, Inaugural Lecture*. Asian Institute of Technology, Bangkok.

Economic and Social Commission of Asia Pacific and Asian Development Bank (ESCAP-ADB) (2000) *State of the Environment in Asia and the Pacific*. United Nations, New York. Available at: www.unescap.org/esd/environment/soe/2000.

ESCAP (1997) Implementation of Sustainable Development Programmes for Agenda 21 Chapter 18 – Freshwater Resources. Report of ESCAP on the Implementation of Freshwater-Related Recommendations of Agenda 21, Bangkok, Thailand.

ESCAP (1998) *Sources and Nature of Water Quality Problems in Asia and the Pacific*. United Nations, ESCAP, New York.

FAO (1990) *Problem Soils of Asia and the Pacific*. FAO RAPA Publication No. 1990/6, Bangkok.

FAO (1999) Irrigation in Asia in Figures, Water Reports.

Fellizar, F.P. Jr. (1994) Achieving sustainable development through community-based resource management. *Regional Development Dialogue* 15(1), 201–217.

Fellizar, F.P. Jr. (2003) Enhancing Local Governance for Integrated Water Resources Management. Paper presented at the *1st Southeast Asia Water Forum*, Chiang Mai, Thailand.

GWP-TEC (2003) *Integrated Water Resources Management*. GWP-Technical Committee (TEC) Background Paper No. 4.

Kharin, N. (1996) Strategy to combat desertification in Central Asia. *Desertification Control Bulletin* 29, 29–34.

Mainguet, M. and Letolle, R. (1998) Human-made desertification in the Aral Sea Basin: planning and management failures. In: Bruins, H.J. and Lithwick, H. (eds) *The Arid Frontier: Interactive Management of Environment and Development*. Dordrecht: Kluwer Academic, pp.129–142.

Postel, S. (1996) Forging a Sustainable Water Strategy. In: Brown, L.R. (ed.) *State of the World*. Worldwatch Institute, New York.

SEAMEO-Regional Center for Graduate Study and Research in Agriculture (SEARCA) (2000) Naujan Lake National Park Management Plan, Laguna, Philippines, 188 pp.

Seckler, D., Barker, R. and Amarasinghe, U. (1999) Water scarcity in the 21st century. *Water Resource Development* 15(1 & 2), 29–42.

Shiklomanov, I.A. (1999) *Assessment of Water Resources and Water Availability of the World*. World Meteorological Association, Geneva.

Smith, C.M., Wilrock, R.J., Vant, W.N., Smith, D.G. and Cooper, A.B. (1993) Towards sustainable agriculture in New Zealand: freshwater quality in New Zealand and the influence of agriculture, MAF Policy Technical paper 93/10. Ministry of Agriculture and Fisheries, Wellington. The Commission on Global Governance (2000). Available at: www.gdrc.org/u-gov/governance-define.html

The Commission on Global Governance (2000) Available at: www.gdrc.org/u-gov/governance-define.html

The Independent Newspaper (1999) *Headline: Half of the World's Rivers Polluted or Running Dry*. Byline by Mary Dejevsky in Washington, DC.

UNDP (United Nations Development Programme) (1997) Governance for Sustainable Human Development: A UNDP

Policy Document. Available at: http://magnet.undp.org/policy/default.htm

UNDP (2000) Internet Conference Forum on Public Private Interface in Urban Environmental Management. Available at: www.gdrc.org/u-gov/governance-define.html.

UNDP, UNEP, World Bank and WRI (2000) World Resources 2000–2001. World Resources Institute, Washington, DC.

UNEP (1999) *GEO-2000*. United Nations Environment Program, Earthscan, London and New York.

UNEP (2002) *Global Environment Outlook 3*. Earthscan, Bangkok.

UN-ESCAP (2000) *State of the Environment in Asia and the Pacific*. UN-ESCAP, Bangkok.

United Nations Population Division (2001) *World Population Prospects 1950–2050*. United Nations, New York. Available at: www.un.org/esa/population/publications/wpp2000/wpp2000h.pdf.

Update (2002) *Dialogue on Effective Governance*. UNDP, GWP; ICLEI, Bangkok.

WRI, UNEP, UNDP and World Bank (1998) *World Resources 1998–99: A Guide to Global Environment*. Oxford University Press, New York.

13 Sustainable Water Resources and Water Security

K. Nakagami[1] and K.M. Nwe[2]

[1]*Ritsumeikan University, Kyoto, Japan;* [2]*Ritsumeikan Asia Pacific University, Beppu, Japan*

Introduction: Sustainable Water Management

Today's environmental problems and their causes and impacts can easily be traced back directly or indirectly to human activity. The forces and processes that constitute 'human activity' have far-reaching and long-term effects not only inside immediate boundaries of settlements, but also on the entire region in which these are located. Environmental management is critical in this situation, and stands for the systematic and conscious effort on the part of city or municipal governments or any other public institution to influence human activities susceptible of damaging the environment. It must be perceived as a permanent framework for preventing and/or responding to the negative effects of man–environment interaction such as air pollution, traffic congestion, water pollution and waste (Amin, 2002). In particular, it is critically important for ensuring that both host communities and visitors can enjoy water-based environments such as rivers and lakes even if they are affected by the usual environmental problems found in human settlements. In practice, environmental management has come to be understood generally to mean two related things:

- Environmental management is concerned with creating a healthy and pleasant physical environment within which we can all enjoy our lives.
- Environmental management is concerned with ensuring that we look after our physical resources in a sustainable way and as far as possible eliminate, or at least minimize, pollution.

This means that environmental management is concerned with much of what communities are used to doing: providing and maintaining infrastructure, looking after public health, maintaining a pleasant ambience and creating and implementing plans to ensure an efficient and pleasant community environment into the future.

Over the past two decades, world population has increased by more than 42% (from 3800 to 5400 million) and the percentage of urban-based dwellers has reached nearly half of the total (Hangzhou, 2000). This has put sustainable environmental management under extreme pressure in many countries, and the countries of the Asia Pacific region are no exception, given their very high population growth rate and their people's expectations of constantly improving standards of living (IGES, 2005). There are however major disparities in the pace of change within the region. In Japan, urbanization proceeded rapidly in the 1950s, followed by South Korea during the 1960s; over 79% of the populations of both countries now live in urban areas. During the 1970s and 1980s, South-east Asia's urbanization started at a slower rate but has rapidly gained momentum since then.

Urbanization is closely linked to the growth of industrialization and an often catastrophic decline in the quality of environmental resources (note that industrialization also includes modern forms of agriculture). Japan's rapid industrialization started in the 1950s and 20 years later South Korea initiated a range of policies aimed at accelerating industrialization. China's open door policy was initiated in the late 1970s. This was followed by increasing economic openness and export-led growth models in Malaysia, the Philippines, Indonesia, India and Thailand. Average annual rates of economic growth of 10% and above were achieved and sustained by some of these countries. But this rapid economic development including urbanization has also been synchronous with severe environmental problems such as lack of water supply and sanitation, waste and wastewater generation, industrial water pollution, air pollution from industries and vehicles, inadequate urban infrastructures and new settlements/informal settlements in environmentally difficult areas.

CSD (1997) reported that the proportion of the global population suffering from water scarcity is expected to rise from one-third in 1995 to about two-thirds in 2025. Every year millions of people, most of them children, die from diseases associated with inadequate water supply, sanitation and hygiene. At least 1.1 billion people lack access to safe water and 2.4 billion lack access to basic sanitation across the world, most of these in Africa and Asia. High rates of population growth consequently generate demand well beyond the capacity of inadequate water and sanitation infrastructure and services and it is usually river basins that suffer. When the use of river water for tourism is overlain on this, it is possible to see that this industry may just exacerbate the problems rather than help to solve them. This last assertion is borne out by the situation regarding the Ganges in India, for example.

The 1992 Rio Declaration noted that human beings are at the centre of concerns for sustainable development, and that they are entitled to a healthy and productive life in harmony with nature. However, sustainable environmental management is a complex and difficult task. This conundrum can only be solved with a multidisciplinary approach, which needs to factor in the socio-economic and cultural and political contexts of environmental management as an integral part of the problem-solving process. There is a distinct need to take a good look at how effective historical efforts to resolve environmental problems have been and of particular concern are the scope and magnitude of these efforts in relation to the needs of a sustainable water environment. This chapter provides that background to the book's discussion of riverine systems and their associated tourism.

Sustainable Water Resources Management

Principles of water sustainability

Water is an important resource necessary for human survival, economic development and the functioning of the ecosystem. Organisms can live only where there is access to adequate supplies of water. Its depletion may impose heavy economic costs (Pearce *et al.*, 1994), health problems and consequences on future generations. Issues of water quality and quantity have forever troubled humans, characterized by the phenomena of floods and droughts. While several recent efforts have made progress in defining the issues (Golubev *et al.*, 1988; Koudstaal *et al.*, 1992; Plate, 1993; Raskin *et al.*, 1995), the sustainability issues of water resources have not been clearly defined.

Since the late 20th century, water use has been raised sharply by several major driving forces such as increasing population, economic development, climate change, etc. Misuse of water resources and poor water resources management practices have often resulted in depletion of aquifers, falling water tables, shrinking inland lakes and in-stream river flows diminished to ecologically unsecure levels. The availability of water sets the environment in which we live. Less than 1% of the world's freshwater resources are in rivers and lakes that are easily available as water on the earth. The allocation of water on earth also sits unfavourably with our population. The Amazon River accounts for 15% of the global runoff and 0.5% of the world population use, while China has 21% of the world population and 7% of the global runoff (World Resources Institute, 1994; PRB, 1998). Under these circumstances, the need for sustained and more efficient management of water resources is obvious.

Within concern over the global implications of water problems, sustainability of water supplies has been advanced as an important objective to be realized in water management. This concept is not new, it has been used in scientific literature for many centuries in fishery, forestry, groundwater, river transport and other areas indicating the rate of use of renewable natural resources to ensure the continuous supply of resources and their maximum use. In 1987, the World Commission of Environment and Development (WCED) reintroduced the sustainable development principle, which subsequently was turned into the UN action plan. The popular definition of sustainability in the Brundtland Commission Report entitled *Our Common Future* (WCED, 1987) is 'the ability to meet the needs of the present generation without compromising the ability of future generations to meet their needs'.

The concept of sustainable development in this context means the basic principle of harmonizing environment and development, but the practical issues in harmonizing development and the environment are difficult and controversial. Because the definition of sustainable development consists of three conceptual components: needs, generations and equity, this implies that the development is necessary because of human needs but that intra-generational and inter-generational equity should hold. In recent times, the concept of sustainable development with intra- and inter-generational equity has motivated various leading policy agencies to reconsider the environmental impacts of their projects and development activities. With these new policies, financial and other institutions, national and international, are now expressing support for the implementation of the sustainability principle.

In the context of freshwater resources academic discussion of sustainability requires that we understand both the physical resource and the service that those resources must provide. In particular, that water resource systems can satisfy the changing demands that will inevitably be placed on them, without significant system degradation (Loucks and Gladwell, 1999). However, their performance may vary at different times and under different environmental and sociocultural conditions. Dixon and Fallon (1989) provided a useful way of categorizing sustainability for water resources management with respect to the social-physical-economic concept. They clearly defined the *sustainability of water resources management as a set of activities that ensures that the social value of the services provided by a given water resources system will satisfy present societal objectives without compromising the ability of the system to satisfy the objectives of future generations.* This approach includes three considerations for water sustainability such as nature (rivers and their environment and ecosystems), current generation needs and future generation needs. Thus, water resource systems must be considered integral parts of our changing societal systems.

Further to this, we could say the main principle for the sustainability of water resources is that the rate of extraction from both ground and surface water sources should not exceed the rate at which the resource is renewed. In other words, extraction must not jeopardize the biodiversity of the ecosystem (ESCAP, 1998). Equity is thus an important objective of sustainability. It is often expressed as the equitable distribution of the benefits, as well as the mitigation of adverse impacts on people (such as residents of reservoir areas or downstream water users) affected by such development (Little and Mirrlees, 1968; UNIDO, 1972; Cernea, 1988). Indeed, factors that affect temporal and spatial equity in water resources development can be either anthropogenic or natural or both. Temporal equity is associated with resource depletion and long-term cumulative effects that may lead to disasters in the future, while spatial equity refers to the conflict between upstream and downstream areas in a river basin and often concerns the conflict between various water users (Cai et al., 2001). Water quality is also considered an equity issue. Conflicts arise when upstream users release excessive pollutants into the river and downstream users suffer damage resulting from the poor water quality. It is reflected in the widespread consideration of environmental impacts on water sustainability. In addition, upstream land use ranging from forest, agricultural and mining to urban and industrial uses may degrade downstream land, surface water and groundwater resources via runoff of sediments (pesticides, fertilizers, organic and toxic wastes). These effects are clearly shown in the loss of useful reservoir storage capacity in dams caused by sedimentation from upstream, the eutroph-ication of lakes and reservoirs from nutrients, the salinization of downstream rivers and the pollution of groundwater aquifers by seepage or injection of organic and non-organic substances to the aquifer from urban and industrial sources. But even if there is no environmental deterioration such as erosion, sedimentation, salinization and/or pollution, the finite amount of water availa-ble is highly variable both seasonally and annually. Consideration of this varia-bility must be undertaken in the management of sustainable water resources.

A more fundamental issue with the philosophy of sustainability is the flawed logic of comparing a finite resource with exponential population growth. Sustainability is ultimately impossible for critical uses. At some point in the Malthusian argument (first espoused in 1798), population demand will outstrip resource supply (Wood, 2004). Therefore, there should be an obvious desire to minimize waste and misuse through maximizing efficiency for finite resources of water. Efficiency can be enhanced in several ways. Technology advances from time to time to enhance delivery systems, utilization techniques and extraction methods in such ways as to advance the sustainable use of water. Prendergast (1993) wrote that 'sustainable development is an effort to use technology to help clean up the mess it helped make, and engineers will be central players in its success or failure'. He believes that future technology and professionals will use natural resources more efficiently through conservation measures and switch to renewable sources, waste minimization, greater recycling and reuse of resources and material. Thus, education and knowledge-based transactions can also facilitate further improvements for efficient use of water resources where water efficiency is the long-term ethic of conserving water resources through the employment of water-saving technologies. Whatever is done to increase the level of sustainability of our water resources, we will ensure that water will be available for future generations through efficiency. A good understanding of these aspects of finite resources of water, including quantity and quality of sup-ply water, is required for long-term planning, especially of river basins and their associated uses (see Chapter 12, this volume). It reflects on the future impact of the economy, on the environment, on ecology and on society that will result from decisions and actions taken in the present.

Therefore, there are needs enabling conditions that all parties can be involved in so as to be aware of the 'rules of the game'. This condition focuses on the changes within the framework of legal, institutional and economic develop-ment. All these three pillars are related to one another and each presents its own specific practices for directing resource distribution. The laws governing the use of water and the institutions created to manage them are a product of a country's history, society and economy (Winpenny, 1994). Hence, water resources management institutions should promote or at least not constrain the achievement of the multiple objectives of water resources management plans, in particular, their development, equity, environmental quality and sustainability objectives (Hufschmidt and McCauley, 1988). These should be channelled to allow efficient and equitable use of water resources on a sustainable basis, with appropriate accountability for unavoidable adverse environmental and social consequences. Demographic, societal, economic and political factors interact to often create an unfavourable environment for sustainability. The transition to new technologies, new management practices and new institutions (or institutional leadership) must proceed in an orderly and equitable manner (Loucks and Gladwell, 1999). The roles of people must be changed for sustainability of water resources, the main actors will be individuals and groups in households and communities with new responsibilities for their use of water and water-related services, as part of a cooperative strategy. One way is that planning must provide information that helps the public make judgements about which 'needs' and 'wants' can and should be satisfied. The principles of sustainability and equity can help bridge the gap between such diverse and competing interests (Gleick, 1998).

Therefore, 'sustainability' itself can be viewed as the maintenance of positive rate of improvement. While development changes by improving a situation or condition over time, sustainability implies the continuance or maintenance of a certain situation or condition over time. In order to achieve the positive rate of improvement, water resource sustainability is not simply a scientific question of how to conserve water but a social construct involving decisions over when, why and where to do so.

Sustainable water resources management

The paradox of water is that although it is one of the most common substances on earth only a fraction is suitable for human consumption. Most of the fresh water is underground water, ice caps, glaciers, and only 1% can be used or is available for human consumption (Serageldin, 1995). These figures suggest that water in fact is a scarce resource and should be treated accordingly. The problem with water is that it is a 'two faced' resource. On one hand, water is a *scarce resource* and on the other hand it is a *public good*. The essence of public goods is that they should be accessible to everyone (Gleick *et al.*, 2002). However, the management of scarce resources is governed by market forces (EDI of the World Bank *et al.*, 1995). From a managerial point of view, it is difficult to find a method, strategy or plan to combine these two aspects in a satisfactory way.

Historically, water resources management, development and policy have evolved in a variety of ways, which differ from country to country. Water resources management and development is the responsibility of national or city authorities in many countries. Therefore, these authorities should pay careful attention to water resources management because lack of it can affect all sectors of society in the country. Each country, developed or developing must put together their own plan of action suitable for their hydrological conditions and needs. The plan and management for water must not only be developed in theory but should be feasible and carried out in reality.

In reality, there is no universal handbook on water resources management but some managerial strategies and guides are more useful than others. Water resources management aims at managing the tasks required to generate water and produce water-related goods and services for the benefits of the society as a whole. The holistic management of fresh water as a finite and vulnerable resource, and the integration of sectoral water plans and programmes within the framework of national economic and social policy are of paramount importance for the objectives of integrated water development and management from here to beyond (UN, 2003). This approach creates a sustainable blueprint for water resources management. In 1977, the United Nations Water Conference in Mar del Plata, the International Conference on Water and the Environment in Dublin, and in 1992, the Earth Summit in Rio de Janeiro articulated a set of principles for good water resources management. These are:

1. The ecological principle, which requires that water be treated as a unitary resource within river basins, with particular attention to ecosystems.
2. The institutional principle, which recognizes that water management requires the involvement of government, civil society and the private sector, and that the principle of subsidiarity is respected. It also gives special emphasis to the role of women in water management.
3. The instrument principle, which requires that water be recognized as a scarce economic good and that greater use be made of 'user pays', 'polluter pays' and other market-friendly instruments.

Within ideologist thinking of good water resource management, water resources management planning should start at the macro level, the national level, with a clear definition of the 'rules of the game' but must find its way to the lowest levels (Wnukowska, 2004). Water resources management starts to address resources issues with often-conflicting interests of the different beneficiaries. This means that new approaches and new concepts must be introduced. Thus, policies should be formally stated or they must be only implicit in an agency's actions. For example, although data collection may be inadequate to measure and assess environmental conditions or even to devise sound projects no policy is enforced to remedy the situation (Frederikksen *et al.*, 1994). Therefore, it is favourable to look at the issues and problems from a centralized point of view, but solve them on a decentralized level. This statement does not suggest however that a country should apply centralized water management schemes with a top-down approach. The authorities should acknowledge that a general nationwide agenda for resources management must exist as a blueprint for provincial and local management schemes. Such approach cannot be achieved by a single organization in isolation. It requires a sound framework for environmental management and requires the coordinated efforts of the local, provincial and national government agencies as well as NGOs, community organizations and people.

The function of water resources systems

Generally, water resources systems include various components such as the natural system, human-made infrastructure and the institutional arrangements to regulate and control the availability and access of users to these components. Jain and Singh (2003) defined the water resources system as a set of water resources elements linked by interrelationships into a purposeful whole. For example, a water supply reservoir for a small city, linked with a water distribution network, would constitute a system. To an engineer, these systems may be dams and weirs, tunnels, levees, pipelines, electrical power plants, water treatment and reclamation and similar physical works, which have been constructed to provide certain benefits. An economist's views include economic efficiency, income redistribution and stimulation of economic growth. To a lawyer, a water resources system is a device for the implementation of water rights. To those living in an arid environment, water resources systems mean food and fibre, homes and jobs, laws and politics. To many conservationists, water resources systems are unwanted interventions, responsible for the destruction of wild rivers, scenic beauty and wildlife habitat. And to river tourists the water resource of the river covers almost all these components. Indeed, the water resources system includes all these points of view, which could be physical, technological, sociological, biological, legal, geological and agricultural.

In order to better understand the assessment, development and management of water resources system then, Ertuna (1995) presented the fundamental function of a water resources system in his article 'Water resources development and management in Asia and the Pacific' (Table 13.1).

Water security and Integrated Water Resources Management (IWRM)
Water security involves the sustainable use and protection of water systems, the protection against water-related hazards (floods and droughts), the sustainable development of water resources and the safeguarding of (access to) water functions and services for humans and the environment, including water-based tourism (Schultz and Uhlenbrook, 2007). IWRM is a logical and intuitively appealing concept in its simplest form. Rationally, promoting IWRM process is in fact due to the increasing world population pressure, securing water for food production, trans-boundary conflicts, increasing economic activities and improved standards of living that lead to increased competition for, and conflicts over, the limited freshwater resources. However, IWRM is still an evolving

Table 13.1. Functions of the water resources systems. (From Ertuna, 1995.)

Functions	Description	Examples
Subsistence functions	Local communities make use of water and water-based products which are not marketed	– Local drinking water supply – Traditional fishing – Subsistence irrigation
Commercial functions	Public or private enterprises make use of water or water-based products which are marketed or otherwise given a monetary value	– Urban drinking water supply – Industrial water supply – Irrigation – Hydropower generation – Commercial fishing – Transportation – River tourism
Environmental functions	Regulation functions, non-consumptive use	– Purification capacity – Prevention of salt intrusion – Recreation and tourism
Ecological values	Values of water resources systems as an ecosystem	– Integrity – Gene pool diversity – Nature conservation value

---

Box 13.1. Some definitions of Integrated Water Resources Management (IWRM). (From Moriarty *et al.*, 2004.)

---

1. IWRM is a process, which promotes the coordinated development and management of water, land and related resources, in order to maximize the resultant economic and social welfare in an equitable manner without compromising the sustainability of vital ecosystems (GWP, 2000).
2. IWRM is a process of assignment of functions to water systems, the setting of norms, enforcement (policing) and management. It includes gathering information, analysis of physical and socio-economic processes, weighing of interests and decision making related to availability, development and use of water resources (van Hofwegen and Jaspers, 1999).
3. IWRM involves the coordinated planning and management of land, water and other environmental resources for their equitable, efficient and sustainable use (Calder, 1999).

IWRM expresses the idea that water resources should be managed in a holistic way, coordinating and integrating all aspects and functions of water extraction, water control and water-related service delivery so as to bring sustainable and equitable benefit to all dependent on the resource.

---

concept. The following Box 13.1 presents some definitions of IWRM among the many. The three key concepts: equity, efficiency and sustainability, are formed in one and are present in all definitions of the IWRM process.

Indeed, the concept of IWRM is as concerned with the management of water demand as with its supply as the many different uses of finite water resources are interdependent. Obviously, high irrigation demands and polluted drainage flows from agriculture mean less usable fresh water for drinking or industries or environmental flows in rivers; contaminated municipal and industrial wastewater pollutes rivers and threatens ecosystem; and conversely if water has to be left in a river to protect fisheries, tourism, transport and ecosystems, less can be diverted to grow crops. Thus, IWRM is an essential management tool. Although it is not a goal in itself, IWRM is a flexible tool for addressing water challenges and optimizing water contribution to sustainable development. For this reason, GWP (2000) documented the IWRM framework and approach regard with complementary elements of an effective water resources management system that must be developed and strengthened concurrently. These complementary elements are shown in Fig. 13.1 below and include the three pillars for implementing an IWRM process.

This figure illustrates the whole implementation process of IWRM, moving towards an enabling environment of appropriate policies, strategies and legislation for securing water resources development and management in sustainable way.

Emerging challenges and opportunities for IWRM in Asia and the Pacific

The emerging challenges of water management in the present day world are how to achieve sustainability in the face of continuous expansion of population and economic activities and the pervasive problems of poverty and environmental degradation (Hufschmidt, 1993). The most serious problems that are

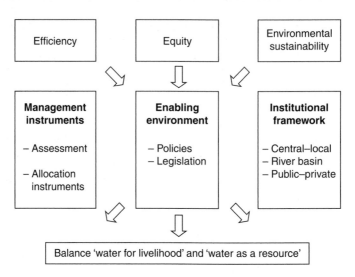

Fig. 13.1. The three pillars of integrated water resources management. (From Global Water Partnership, TEC paper No. 10, 2004.)

likely to strike in developing countries are that high rate of population growth (both urban and rural), poverty and environmental degradation are persistent, while major economic development activities are taking place simultaneously.

The world population is increasing as discussed earlier. At the same time, Asia and the Pacific region are increasing in economic development and the annual growth rate of gross domestic product (GDP) for all of the developing Asia Pacific is over 7%. The growth of populations and the subsequent expansion of industry mean that the demand for water is exceeding supply in several regions of the world (Postal, 1999). The quantity of water consumed in Asia alone is 2.85 trillion cubic metre per year, more than any other region in the world. Consumption is expected to rise 150% by the year 2025. However, the countries of the Asia Pacific region have made great strides in managing their water resources. There is an increasing concern for water resources availability, not only about the importance of water resources sustainability but also of the impending shortages of water in the future due to excessive withdrawal. Numerous studies pointed out the factors responsible for the steady increase in water use and shortages (see Jeffrey, 1989; Gleick, 1993). In the Asia Pacific region, the per capita availability of water was 3760 m³/year in 1995, which is naturally decreasing with the growth of population. The estimation for changes in water availability per capita by subregion over the period from 1950 to 2000 is presented in Table 13.2. Simultaneously, pollution is rising to such an extent that it is reducing the amount of usable water in river basins like the Ganges–Brahmaputra–Meghna in India and Bangladesh (Chapter 2, this volume). Suffice it to say there will be an immense demand on the developing Asia and the Pacific nation's water resources and a challenging task in demand management to reduce consumption and conserve precious water resources, as well as efficiency improvements to combat the waste of water.

Table 13.2. Estimated water availability per capita in Asia and the Pacific (1950–2000) in 1000 m³/year. (After Shiklomanov, *The world's water resources*. International Symposium to Commemorate the 25 years of IHD/IHP, UNESCO, Paris, 1991.)

Subregion	Area (million km²)	1950	1960	1970	1980	2000
North China and Mongolia	9.14	3.8	3.0	2.3	1.9	1.2
South Asia	4.49	4.1	3.4	2.5	2.2	1.1
South-east Asia	7.17	13.2	11.1	8.6	7.1	4.9
Central Asia	2.43	7.5	5.5	3.3	2.0	0.7
Australia	7.62	35.7	28.4	23.0	19.8	15.0
The Pacific	1.34	161.0	132.0	108.0	92.4	73.5

Water resources management has been traditionally supply-oriented without sufficient attention to options for influencing water demand and increasing water-use efficiency, despite the level of water losses from public water supply systems exceeding 50% in some large cities in Asia. High level of water losses in water supply system seriously affects the financial viability of water utilities through lost revenues and increased operational costs. At the same time, engineering and environmental costs are much higher for new water supplies than for sources already tapped. As a result, new challenges call for a new approach. The emerging challenges are the needs of concerted policies for integrated management on their water resources and action towards conservation of water resource that should be undertaken in order to achieve sustainability of water vis-à-vis the water conservation is to be enhanced by incorporating demand management activities and water-use efficiency measures.

On the other hand, governments are hard-pressed in many countries but they must become more directly responsible for infrastructure and basic services. The provision of wastewater and sewerage infrastructure is very poor in the low- and middle-income countries of the region, with over a third of all urban residents and almost all rural residents still lacking adequate sanitation services. Only 10% of the region's population is connected to public sewers, with the remainder either without facilities at all or served by septic tanks or illegal connections to storm water drainage systems and open water bodies (SOE in Asia and the Pacific, 2000). In recent years, the provision of sanitation infrastructure has been the focus of considerable multilateral and bilateral investment and many urban centres are in the process of improving their wastewater and sewerage facilities due to water pollution and shortage of water resources around the urban areas.

Managing water sustainability is extremely complex because of the cross-sectoral and cross-jurisdictional nature of urban and national political economies. Governments have often misallocated and wasted water as well as permitted damage to the environment, due to institutional weakness, market failures, distorted policies and misguided investments. The spatial planning, pricing, service levels and management of all of these may have impacts on the secure water

---

Dublin Principles and Key Concepts

Principles

1. Water is a finite, vulnerable and essential resource, which should be managed in an integrated manner.
2. Water resources development and management should be based on a participatory approach, involving all relevant stakeholders.
3. Women play a central role in the provision, management and safeguarding of water.
4. Water has an economic value and should be recognized as an economic good, taking into account affordability and equity criteria.

Key Concepts
1. Integrated water resources management, implying an intersectoral approach, representation of all stakeholders, all physical aspects of water resources and sustainability and environmental considerations.
2. Sustainable development, which is sound socio-economic development that safeguards the resource base for future generations.
3. Emphasis on demand-driven and demand-oriented approaches.
4. Decision making at the lowest possible level.

Fig. 13.2. Dublin Principles and Key Concepts for water resources management. (From Savenije and van der Zaag, 1998.)

resources environment. Most of the countries in the region are rationalizing their institutions dealing with water resources development, management and protection. The result shows that many countries have developed relatively sophisticated water management institutional machinery comprising sometimes a dozen of governmental agencies dealing with various aspects in water sector. However, many governments lack the technical knowledge or the staff to adequately enforce environmental regulations, fixing and collection of charges.

Yet, all described situations are not all this bleak. Many innovative and effective approaches to water resources management have been taken or are being taken around the world, increasingly in response to demands for water-based tourism. A globally accepted water management principle for water sustainability is contained in the *Dublin Principles* (see Fig. 13.2). A balanced set of policies and institutional reforms should be sought that will both harness the efficiency of market forces and strengthen the capacity of governments to carry out their essential roles because each situation has its own unique circumstance. Hence, policy options for sustainability of water management should be city-specific and river basin-specific.

Case Study: Water Quality Management and River Tourism in Myanmar

Myanmar is located on the mainland of the South-east Asia region, has an approximate land area of 677,000 km² and is administratively divided into seven divisions and seven states. The country shares borders with China, India, Bangladesh, Thailand and Lao PDR. In the south and south-west, the country has a long coastline of 2832 km in total length along the Bay of Bengal and the Andaman Sea. Yangon City is highly urbanized and the designated economic centre as well as the former capital city of the Union of Myanmar, and is located 34 km inland from the mouth of the Yangon River. The city is influenced directly by the tropical monsoon climate and has an average rainfall in excess of 100 in. (2500 mm) during the 6 months period May through October. The city population was estimated at 5 million in 2004 by the Human Resources Development Indicators project (UNFPA, 2005). Yangon has a population density of 1622 people per square mile.

The river basin characteristics of Myanmar are quite variable due to differences in physiographic features. The principal watercourses comprise four major rivers: the Ayeyarwady (Irrawaddy), Sittoung, Thanlwin, Bago, plus their major tributaries such as the Chindwin, Myittha, Mu, Zawgyi, Panlaung, Samon, Myitnge, Mone, Man, Salin, Yaw and Mindon. All rivers, with the exception of the Thanlwin are within Myanmar territory and can be considered nationally owned water assets. Their drainage area is spread widely over the country, amounting to some 876.73 million acre/feet (1082 km³) of water volume per annum from a drainage area of about 284,800 square miles (737,628.6 km²). The monthly distribution of river flows closely follows the pattern of rainfall, i.e. about 80% during the monsoon season (May–October) and 20% in the dry season (November–April). The estimated groundwater potential in Myanmar is around 495 km³ in eight principal river basins.

There are about 200 gauging stations installed by the Department of Irrigation for water level recording and discharge measurement. Some 70 hydrological stations have been installed along the Ayeyarwady, Chindwin, Myitnge, Sittoung, Thanlwin, Bago and Kalandan rivers since 1965 by the Department of Meteorology and Hydrology. This department controls about 30 discharge stations and 20 sediment discharge stations on main rivers and big tributaries as well as about 15 water quality stations on rivers of Ayeyarwady delta area for measuring discharge and sediment flows, and monitoring salt intrusion. These measurement data are valuable for national planning related to water management and, in August 2003, the Myanmar National Committee for the International Hydrology Programme for cooperation with the United Nations Education, Scientific and Cultural Organization (UNESCO) was established for strengthening these activities.

In Yangon City, the Yangon River is formed by the junction of the Panhlaing and Hlaing rivers at a point about 8 miles upstream of Monkey Point. The Panhlaing River is a distributary of the Ayeyarwady River, while the Hlaing River is a true river rising in the Bago Yomas and having a drainage area of about 5000 square miles. Pazundaung Creek, named Ngamoyeik Creek in the northern part of the city, joins the Yangon River at Monkey Point, the southeastern extremity of the city. Pazundaung Creek has a drainage area of about 574 square miles. The Bago River, with a drainage area of 2000 square miles, also joins the Yangon River just east of the city, from which point the Yangon River flows south some 28 miles into the Gulf of Bengal.

The country of Myanmar is generally blessed with abundant water resources. Yangon City's water resources are also abundant; however, water resources for city water supply are far from the city area. Near the city area, there is natural saline water intrusion and tidal effects, and all the rivers and creeks adjacent to Yangon are known to be tidal within and beyond the limits of the city. During low tide, the tidal water recedes way out into the sea, transporting the river water with all its contents of wastewater away from the vicinity of the city. Such tidal influence keeps the ecological system of the Yangon River in a healthy balance. However, untreated domestic wastewater and industrial effluent are being disposed of into the Yangon River and this volume of wastewater and its potential pollution loading are expected to increase with the modernization and expansion of the city.

The water quality management system in Myanmar

The mission statement for the water sector is 'to establish a beneficial framework and effective mechanism for managing, developing and protecting water and related resources in an environmentally and economically sound manner in order to meet the needs of the people of Myanmar'. This statement, if adopted by the Government, will provide a guiding light towards establishing national strategies for both short- and long-term efforts by all agencies, people and stakeholders towards the common goals of national socio-economic development and environmental conservation.

There is no single umbrella law covering all aspects of water resources; the laws of Myanmar deal with the subject in one way or another. The Ministry of Forestry is responsible for the rehabilitation and conservation of forests and watersheds and for maintaining the stability of the environment, in order to develop the social and economic conditions of the nation, especially in rural areas. The National Commission for Environmental Affairs (NCEA) was formed in February 1990 to deal with all environmental matters. In March 2004, the Environmental Conservation Committee was set up with the aim of carrying out environmental conservation activities in the country effectively and systematically.

With respect to water quality evaluation, water quality testing in rivers is carried out as part of investigations for new water development projects, for special purposes and in emergencies, when disease outbreaks are reported. The Irrigation Department and the Water Resources Utilization Department (WRUD) under the Ministry of Agriculture currently undertake analysis of impounded or storage water at some existing reservoirs and lakes through surface water sampling. The WRUD is responsible for evaluation of water quality in rivers and streams for development projects and surface water sampling as well as analysis of the mixing conditions of saline fronts along some major tributaries in the Ayeyarwady River system. Until recently, there was no regular water test for any streams and rivers in Myanmar.

At present, there is no specific national law and regulation on sewerage system management in Myanmar. However, Order No. 2/96 of Law 33(2) YCDC has been enacted to control the systematic disposal of sewerage from household, commercial activities and factories responsible by the Yangon City Development Committee. By-Law No. 6/99, Water Supply and Sanitation covers effluent standard of sewerage, source of sewerage, types of sewer and connection of sewer pipelines permits and permission for latrine construction. Emission standards for water and air pollutions were formulated by Ministerial Standing Order No. 3/95 of Ministry of Industry but only refer to those generated from industrial activities; there is no specific standard for domestic wastewater discharge in Myanmar. Similarly the Emergency Provisions Act (1950), Canal Act (1905), Yangon Water Act (1885), Ports Act (1908), Yangon Port Act (1905), Private Industrial Enterprises Law (1990), Petroleum Act (1934) and the Myanmar Insurance Law (1993) are also related to wastewater management.

The NCEA has initiated the drafting of a framework environmental law. Entitled Myanmar Environmental Protection Law, it will soon be submitted to the Cabinet. For the moment, environmental pollution control is written in the Water and Sanitation Related Order No. 2/96 issued by the YCDC; however, the specific content of this Order cannot fully be implemented by the Sanitation Division (SD) because there are no specific standards for domestic wastewater pollution control and a lack of commitment from the city authority. There is no discussion concerned with environmental pollution control management in the annual meeting and official report to be submitted by the sewer division to the National Commission for Environmental Affairs (NCEA) for the purpose of quality of environment within Yangon City.

The sewerage system in Myanmar

The sewerage network system covers only the downtown area of the former capital city, which is located 34 km inland from the mouth of the Yangon River. It is situated at the southern part of the city lying between the present railroad and the Yangon River. Botathaung, Kyaukthada, Lanmadaw, Latha, Pabedan and Pazundaung Townships are included in the downtown area. Usually, wastewater includes sanitary sewage, industrial sewage and storm water; however, the central sewerage network system in Yangon collects only domestic sewage particularly human excreta. The centralized sewer network system in Yangon was constructed in 1888, for population of about 40,000. At present, the population in the downtown area of Yangon is about 350,000 (2005–2006). Domestic wastewater and the storm water are disposed through open surface drains. The discharge of wastewater from centralized sewerage ejector stations was collected through a network of cast iron pressure mains and discharged straight into the Yangon River without any treatment until 2004 when a wastewater treatment plant was constructed in Yangon. This facility has cleaned up the river to some extent and has allowed river tourism to commence (Fig. 13.3).

River tourism

River cruise vessels were introduced on a Yangon–Twante Canal–Yangon day return tour from November 2006. These cruises include the river and sightseeing around Twante with horse carts and lunch on the boat. The vessel depicted in

Fig. 13.3. The RV *Mahaythi* on Yangon River cruise. (From http://www.rvmahaythi.com/.)

Fig. 13.3 caters to travellers and business persons alike as a passenger-carrying vessel and is also licensed as a floating restaurant. Based on a former rice and sand-carrying barge, *Mahaythi* can accommodate up to 20 clients for dining. The RV *Mahaythi 2* entered service in 2007 and covers not only the day trips to Twante and sunset and dinner cruises along the Yangon River but has also allowed operations between Yangon and the Ayeyarwady Delta and Meinmahla Kyun (Island) Wildlife Sanctuary. A number of other vessels and tour companies offer a range of cruises in the same mode as the above, and gradually these are extending out from Yangon as the growth of tourism to the country begins to speed up. Tourism represents a major source of foreign currency for the city although the actual number of foreign visitors has always been quite low (about 250,000 in recent years) by South-east Asian standards. Yangon's international standard hotels, built with foreign investment in the 1990s, still await the influx of tourists for which they were built.

In the western headwaters of the Ayeyarwady River, there are also now some white-water rafting opportunities. Suitable for most age groups, the Nam Lang River combines Class 3 and 4 white water through thickly forested canyons, with a closer insight into a people and their way of life unchanged for centuries (http://www.indochinaexploration.com/).

The problem of water quality management in Myanmar

Many issues in the law, particularly the roles and responsibilities of various agencies for specific activities in water pollution control and integrated water resource management, need to be developed in order that the basic resource for river tourism is maintained. There is an urgent need for the formulation of further legislation or decrees for proper management. The Central Law Organization (CLO) and the Attorney-General have the final responsibility for issuing decrees. The water sector faces several problems including unusual rainfall patterns in some years, flooding and drought in some of the main agricultural areas of country, the impact of shifting cultivation, illegal logging in water resources areas as well as management conflicts of interest and a lack of coordination within the agencies. The most important challenges for water quality security in Myanmar include:

1. Strengthening the legal framework to ensure effective and harmonious integration of water resources management, development and protection activities into the socio-economic development process of the country;
2. Enhancing and consolidating the existing systems;
3. Operating, maintaining and rehabilitating of facilities safely, reliably and efficiently;
4. Prioritizing capacity-building needs in order to enhance organizational capacity and effectiveness of the water quality management and water resources coordination system.

Water quality and river management under development pressure

Water of adequate quality and quantity is central to the existence of every life form everywhere. Water pollution therefore has the potential to become a limiting factor for growth. Pollution may have adverse effects on drinking water supply, on the use of water for the production of food and by other industries, on the environment and on activities such as fishing, recreation and tourism. Tourism is not that important in the Myanmar context at present; the freshwater resources are mainly used by the agriculture sector; with small quantities being used for domestic, industrial and other purposes. Although Myanmar has abundant water resources and no scarcity of water at present, proper management and a strong policy on sustainable and continuous development of the economy and the conservation of the environment are required for the security of future generations.

Present organizational arrangements at the national and provincial levels generally support the achievement of national policies, but the current institutional problems in the water sector are mainly related to: (i) the lack of coordination and collaboration between agencies within the sector and with those of other sectors; and (ii) inadequate communication and coordination between the national agencies and authorities. The NCEA has attempted to provide the environmental management laws and regulation necessary to prevent the environmental pollution and promote pollution control programme but the follow-up action was not yet implemented because of the political commitment.

Despite the many Acts, laws and regulations related to the water sector, most require modification. Therefore, they should be reviewed with a view to enacting a unified water resources law in order to promote a more effective legal framework for coordination and management of water resources. Some Acts (such as the Burma Groundwater Act of 1930) are still weak as their jurisdiction was greatly limited when they were first passed and no attempts have been made to amend them. In fact, some Acts are no longer applicable or suitable to the present and changing situation. Other weaknesses in the water sector are limited trained workforce, scarce financial resources, a lack of appropriate monitoring facilities, proper and systematic record keeping and irregular monitoring and surveillance of water quality. As for water quality control, basic standards of quality for drinking water were recommended in 1990, but have not yet been approved. As a result, the current water resources policies and legislation of all water-related agencies in Myanmar need to be reviewed and modified. Further policies and legislation should be developed for efficient water resources management and environmental protection. The following policy proposals are designed to achieve the sustainable management of Myanmar's water resources by protecting or enhancing the qualities while allowing for sustainable development in accordance with the mission of the water sector in the Country.

Policy proposals for water quality management

To secure water quality any system must manage the discharge of pollutants from all sources to waters (point or non-point sources) on a watershed basis to ensure the physical, chemical and biological integrity of those waters now and in the future. Thus, the objective of policy is to achieve sustainable use of the nation's water resources by protecting and enhancing their quality while maintaining the economic and social development of Myanmar. To implement this water quality management plans should incorporate:

- national consistency in methods for setting goals, objectives and standards;
- clear and explicit administrative processes;
- clear and explicit assignment of responsibilities for the water sector administration and operation;
- accountability and matching of administrative structures;
- involvement of stakeholders in definitions of goals, development of plans and implementation of strategies;
- opportunities for harnessing market forces to the water quality management task.

Policy proposals for river tourism

Tourism can be considered one of the most remarkable socio-economic phenomena of the 20th and 21st centuries. Tourism as an economic activity has an inevitable effect on the environment of the visitor destination. However, the environment is often regarded as the major pull factor of visitor movement, contributing to the desirability and attractiveness of a tourist destination (Lim and McAleer, 2003). As the environment is an indispensable asset to the tourism industry, the protection and conservation of environmental resources (which include natural, cultural and historic resources) are prime considerations for the tourism industry. For this reason, a suitable tourism policy will propose for secure water resources the following: *Sustainable Tourism Development to meet the needs of present tourists, host regions while protecting and enhancing secure natural water resources development opportunities for the future.* To achieve this, the National authorities in Myanmar should adopt such strategies as:

- formulation of national and regional strategies for sustainable tourism and river development;
- promotion of regulatory mechanism and economic instruments for tourism management plan and promotion that address environmental sustainability;
- initiation of voluntary activities and embark on intensive education and mass awareness programmes to promote community participation in water resources conservation and environmental protection in sustainable tourism management;
- promotion of tourism that protects conserves and manages the environment and natural resources of the country in a sustainable manner;
- establishment of environmental focal points in the institution responsible for tourism that will constantly liaise with the environmental affairs institutions.

Conclusions

This chapter has shown that water is an important resource necessary for human survival, economic development and the functioning of the ecosystem. We can live only where there is access to adequate supplies of water, and its depletion may impose heavy economic costs, health problems and consequences on future generations. Issues of water quality and quantity have forever troubled humans, characterized by the phenomena of floods and droughts and our difficulties with waste management. The degradation in the environment of the World's and the Asia Pacific's major rivers is of particular concern, especially as river tourism is becoming one of the most attractive forms of tourism throughout the world. The paradox of water is that although it is one of the most common substances on earth only a fraction of available fresh water is suitable for human consumption. Most of the fresh water is underground water, ice caps, glaciers and only 1% can be used or is available for human consumption. These figures suggest that water in fact is a scarce resource and should be treated accordingly.

Historically, water resources management, development and policy have evolved in a variety of ways, which differ from country to country. Water resources management and development is the responsibility of national or city authorities in many countries, therefore, these authorities should pay careful attention to water resources management because it can affect all sectors of society in the country. Each country, developed or developing must put together their own plan of action suitable for their hydrological conditions and needs. The plan and management for water must not only be developed in theory but should be feasible and implementable in reality. Tourism and river tourism in particular may provide the impetus for otherwise parochial national and regional organizations to address these requirements speedily and more efficiently.

References

Amin, A.T.M.N. (2002) *Sustainable Urbaniza-tion Policy Lecture Handouts*. UEM, AIT, Bangkok.

Cai, X., Mckinney, D.C. and Rosegrant, M.W. (2001) *Sustainability Analysis for Irrigation Water Management: Concepts, Methodology, and Application to the Aral Sea Region*. EPTD Discussion Paper No. 86, Environment and Production Technology Division, International Food Policy research Institute, Washington, DC.

Calder, I.R. (1999) *The Blue Revolution, Land Use and Integrated Water Resources Management*. Earthscan, London.

Cernea, M.M. (1988) *Involuntary Resettle-ment in Development Projects: Policy Guidelines in World Bank-Financial Prospects*. World Bank Technical Paper No. 80, Washington, DC.

CSD (1997) Comprehensive Assessment of the Freshwater Resources of the World. Report of the Secretary-General, United Nations Economic and Social Council. Available at: http://www.un.org/documents/ewsoc/cnl 7/1997/ecnl71997-9.htm [Geo-2-117].

Dixon, J.A. and Fallon, L.A. (1989) The con-cept of sustainability: origins, extensions, and usefulness for policy. *Society and Natural Resources* 2(2), 73–84.

Economic and Social Commission for Asia and the Pacific (ESCAP) (1998) *Towards Efficient Water Use in Urban Areas in Asia and the Pacific*. United Nations, New York.

Economic Development Institute (EDI) of the World Bank (1995) *The Economic Appraisal of Environmental Projects and Policies: A Practical guide*. Organization for Economic Co-operation and Develop-ment, Paris.

Ertuna, C. (1995) *Water Resources Develop-ment and Management in Asia and the Pacific*. Environmental Soil and Water Management: Past Experience and Future Directions, pp. 1–36.

Frederikksen, H.A., Berkoff, J. and Barber, W. (1994) *Principles and Practices for Dealing with Water Resources Issues*. World Bank Technical Paper No. 233, Asia Technical Department Series, The World Bank, Washington, DC.

Gleick, P.H. (1993) *A Guide to the World's Fresh Water Resources*. Pacific Institute for Studies in Development, Environment, and Security, Stockholm Environment Institute, Oxford University Press, Stockholm.

Gleick, P.H. (1998) Water in crisis: paths to sustainable water use. *The Ecological Society of America, Ecological applica-tions* 8(3), 571–579.

Gleick, P.H., Wolff, G., Chalecki, E.L. and Reeves, R. (2002) The new economy of water: the risks and benefits of globalization and privatization of fresh water. Available at: http://www.pacinst.org/reports/new_ economy_of_water.pdf

Global Water Partnership (GWP) Technical Advisory Committee (TAC) (2000) *Inte-grated Water Resources Management (IWRM)*, TAC Background Paper No.4. Global Water Partnership, Stockholm.

Global Water Partnership (2004) Intergrated Water Resources Management and Water Efficiency Strategies by 2005: Why, What and How? TEC paper No. 10, Colombo, Sri Lanka: International Water Management (IWMI).

Golubev, G.N., David, L.J. and Biswas, A.K. (1988) Sustainable water development: special issue. *Water Resources Development* 4(2), June, pp. 77–144.

Hufschmidt, M.M. (1993) Water policies for sustainable development. In: Biswas, K. A., Jellali, M. and Stout, G.E. (eds) *Water for Sustainable Development in the Twenty-first Century.* Oxford University Press, New York, pp. 60–69.

Hufschmidt, M.M. and McCauley, D.S. (1988) Strategies for integrated water resources management in a river/lake basin context. *International Journal of Water Resources Development* 4(4), 224–231.

IGES (International Global Environmental Strategies), Japan (2005) Urban Environmental Management Challenges in Asia.

Jain, S.K. and Singh, V.P. (2003) *Water Resources Systems Planning and Management.* Elsevier Science, BV, Amsterdam.

Jeffrey, D. (1989) Water rights in the occupied territories. *Journal of Palestine Studies* 19(1; 73), 46–71.

Koudstaal, R., Rijsberman, F.R. and Savenije, H. (1992) Water and sustainable development. *Natural Resources Forum* 16(4), 277–289.

Lim, C. and McAleer, M. (2003) *Ecologically Sustainable Tourism Management.* Available at: http://www.e.u-tokyo.ac.jp/cirje/research/03research02dp.html

Little, I.M.D. and Mirrlees, J.A. (1968) *Manual of Industrial Project Analysis in Developing Countries.* Social Cost-Benefit Analysis, Vol. 2. Organization for Economic Cooperation and Development, Paris.

Loucks, D.P. and Gladwell, J.S. (1999) *Sustainability Criteria for Water Resource Systems.* UNESCO/IHP Project M-4.3.

Moriarty, P., Butterworth, J. and Batchelor, C. (2004) *Integrated Water Resources Management and Domestic Water and Sanitation Sub-Sector.* Thematic Overview Paper. IRC International Water and Sanitation Centre, The Netherlands. Available at: www.irc.nl/page/10431

Pearce, D., Turner, R.K., O'Riordan, T. and Adger, N. (1994) *Measuring Sustainable Development (Blueprint 3).* Earthscan, London.

Plate, E.J. (1993) Sustainable development of water resources. *Water International* 18, 84–94.

Population Reference Bureau (PRB) (1998) *World Population Data Sheet Wall Chart.* Population reference Bureau, Washington, DC.

Postal, S.L. (1999) *Pillar of Sand.* W. W. Norton, New York.

Prendergast, J.B. (1993) A model of crop yield response to irrigation water salinity: theory, testing and application. *Irrigation Science* 13(4), 157–164.

Raskin, P., Hansen E. and Margolis, R. (1995) *Water and Sustainability: A Global Outlook.* Polestar Series Report No. 4, Stockholm Environment Institute, Boston, Massachusetts.

Savenije, H.G. and van der Zaag, P. (1998) Conceptual framework for the management of shared river basins; with special reference to SADC and EU. *Water Policy* 2(1–2). Elsevier, The Hague.

Schultz, B. and Uhlenbrook, S. (2007) *Water Security: What Does It Mean, What May It Imply?* Discussion Draft Paper for the session on water Security, Delft, The Netherlands.

Serageldin, I. (1995) *Toward Sustainable Management of Water Resources.* The World Bank, Washington, DC.

Shiklomanov, I.A. (1991) The world's water resources. *International Symposium to Commemorate the 25 years of IHD/IHP.* UNESCO, Paris.

State of the Environment (SOE) in Asia and the Pacific, 2000.

The United Nations (UN) (2003) *Agenda 21-Chapter 18.* Available at: http://www.thewaterpage.com/agenda_21.htm

United Nations Industrial Development Organization-UNIDO (1972) *Guidelines for Project Evaluation.* United Nations, New York.

United Nations Population Fund (UNFPA) (2005) The Human Resources Development Indicators, Myanmar.

Van Hofwegen, P.J.M. and Jaspers, F.G.W. (1999) *Analytical Framework for Integrated Water Resources Management: Guidelines for Assessment of Institutional*

Frameworks. Balkema, Rotterdam, The Netherlands.

Winpenny, J. (1994) *Managing Water as an Economic Resource*. Routledge, London.

Wnukowska, K. (2004) *Management of Urban Water Resources in Hanoi, Vietnam*. Master thesis, Minor Field Study, Royal Institute of Technology, KTH, Stockholm.

Wood, W.W. (2004) Water sustainability: science or science fiction? Perspective from one scientist. In: Alsharhan, A.S. and Wood, W.W (eds) *Development in Water Science 50 – Water Resources Perspectives: Evaluation, Management and Policy*, Elsevier, Amsterdam, 385 p.

World Commission on Environment and Development (WCED) (1987) *Our Common Future*. Oxford University Press, Oxford.

World Health Organisation (2000) Issue Paper on Urban Environment Management in Asia and the Pacific, Regional Office for Western Pacific of the World Health Organization, Hangzhou, China.

World Resources Institute (1994) *World Resources Report (WRR)*, 1994–1995, World Resources Institute. Oxford University Press, New York.

Internet Resources accessed:

http://www.rvmahaythi.com/ (16 May 2008)

http://www.indochinaexploration.com/ (16 May 2008)

14 'The River City'? Conflicts in the Development of a Tourism Destination Brand for Brisbane

G. Marzano,[1] E. Laws[2] and N. Scott[1]

[1]School of Tourism, The University of Queensland, Ipswich, Australia;
[2]James Cook University, Cairns, Australia

Introduction

Tourism destinations are characterized by coexistence within the same geographical space of multiple private business and public sector organizations of varying scale and sophistication that offer a variety of target markets a range of services 'necessary to make the space maximally attractive to consumers of the tourism space' (Judd, 1995, p. 179). The complexity of the tourism destination as an amalgam of products, facilities and services that together comprise the travel experience (Buhalis, 2003) is enhanced by a lack of centralized control over destination marketing and development activities that characterizes commercial organizations (Laws et al., 2002). While, generally, tourism destinations support a body that coordinates marketing and image-building activities, research shows that the major challenge to the ability of tourism destination to build positive destination brand equity (Konecnik and Gartner, 2007) is the achievement of a collaborative environment among the different stakeholders that all together contribute to the delivery of destination experience.

The creation of a destination image that is shared among stakeholders is none the less a problematic issue. While this need for collaboration among stakeholders in the image building of a tourism destinations seems, at least from a normative perspective, inherent to the complex nature of tourism, several studies (Ryan and Zahra, 2004; Marzano, 2007) show that each stakeholder or coalitions of them tend to try to exert influence and seek to push forward a favourite destination image in their own interest. The choice of a destination image able to encompass and satisfy different stakeholders' needs emerges therefore as a result of conflicts and mediations about choosing the appropriate set of organic images of the destination (Gartner, 1993) to match its preferred marketing positioning. The agreement on the defining features of a destination has been a matter of concern not only in tourism destination marketing, but also more broadly in the area of city planning. Describing the problems related with the building of an identity for Shanghai in the 19th century, Yeh (2006, p. 304) observes that the city was interpreted and framed:

> As people were drawn to this enclave for different reasons and with different vision for its future, their minds were far from unified in their understanding of the city's defining features. Yet for all this broad variety, the Shanghai Foreign Settlements were seen from the beginning through a limited set of conflicting but interwoven myths
>
> Yeh (2006, p. 304)

The analysis of how different interests and conflicts characterize the development of a city image is at the core of this chapter, which examines how the idea of having the Brisbane River as the source of identity for the city of Brisbane, Australia, has been favoured and disputed over time. The case of Brisbane and the controversial 'River City' tag that has characterized the marketing of the city offers a significant example for the discussion of the issue of leadership in promoting destination areas through marketing partnerships. As previously observed there are relatively few destinations where one major commercial organization can take this role. Typically, this occurs only in purpose built resort areas, and is unlikely in cities or dispersed and varied regions where an official marketing organization is usually established and partly funded by the Government. In the latter case, some local tourism organizations may be resistant to the policies or direction which the lead organization wishes to promote, and subsidiary or local levels of government often have objectives which conflict with the official tourism policy. In the case of capital cities, tourism is one of many facets of policy making, and may not be seen as a priority. Furthermore, the boundaries of the visitor's interest and experience are unlikely to coincide with the geopolitical administration area which, as is the case in Brisbane, both encompass a much wider geographic area (South-east Queensland) and disregard many of the suburbs of the city itself.

Destination authorities are now seen as responsible for making decisions about their images, brands and product and market portfolios, choosing facilities to offer, trying to anticipate the demands and changing tastes of their visitors, and attempting to influence the nature of their experiences, in contrast to the often ad hoc, opportunistic entrepreneurial responses which have characterized the early development of many of the original mass-market resorts (Laws and Cooper, 1998). But these decisions are taken within the framework of much broader government (or council) policy regarding social and economic priorities, infrastructure development and budgetary realities.

This chapter draws on the political underpinnings of destination marketing and explores how the image of the Brisbane River produced a controversy that allows a better understanding of the problems that relates organic and inorganic images of a destination. While the Brisbane River flows through the city and symbolically and geographically connects many of its suburbs, the argument presented in the chapter outlines the theoretical context by which this complexity may be better understood. It then gives an empirical account of events and issues in the evolution of a river tourism policy for Brisbane, and provides an initial analysis of these.

The Making of the City Image: a Political Task

Cities are complex and multifaceted places (Bramwell and Rawding, 1996). Pile (1999), describing the essence of a city, considers that things, institutions and architectural forms together with people living together and a network of communication that allows residents to move around and beyond the space are the constituent elements of a city. Cities are places of work, consumption, circulation, play, creativity, excitement, boredom (Amin and Thrift, 2002). Cities however exist not as simple and tangible urban environments but also as metaphors, metonyms, symbols that all together not only account for a variety of representations of city life, but (are) also a crucial aspect of the material experience of the urban (Highmore, 2005). From this perspective, cities require symbols, and symbols nurture the city's identity by proving immediate clues to its personality. However, while symbols can be found in the organic images that the city offers, it is marketing that builds a bridge between the tangible dimensions that architectural landscapes and people give to the city and the images of the city that cities create and project with the aim of creating an exchange that satisfies both the individual (the visitor) and the organization (in this case, the city and its citizens; Kolb, 2006).

Consistent with the description of destination branding as a complex activity which involves multiple stakeholders (Morrison and Anderson, 2002; Kaplanidou and Vogt, 2003; Morgan, 2003; Morgan *et al.*, 2003), city marketing has been described as a 'a complex endeavour that demands a wide view on its goals, effects and general approach' (Kavaratzis and Ashworth, 2007, p. 17). To survive well, bigger cities must play on varied stages – from the immediately local, through the regional and national, to the widest global platform. These mixed targets, goals and audiences each demand something different. Often they pull and stretch in different directions (Landry, 2006). As a consequence, the challenge for city marketers is to synthesize the multifaceted places and different and sometimes contrasting interests (Morgan *et al.*, 2002) in a simple overall marketing message (Bramwell and Rawding, 1996).

Kavaratzis and Ashworth (2007) suggest that the concept of an 'action net' allows a greater understanding of city marketing as a process that involves plurality of stakeholders. The concept of action net was first elaborated by Czarniawska (2002) who proposed that city management consists of many collective and interconnected actions, which can be conceptualized as an action net and engage many and varied organizations. Taking a similar perspective, Hankinson (2004) proposes that place branding, and the marketing of a city within it, may be understood by using a network paradigm and proposes that a group of stakeholders contributes to the creation and enhancement of four

different types of relationships – media, primary services, consumer and brand
infrastructure – that all together contributes to the creation of the core values
of the brand.

The need for such a perspective is inherent to the nature of a city. A city,
in fact, cannot be conceptualized as a single product but as van den Berg *et al.*
(2002, p. 45) observe:

> a city provides a 'line of products' that are difficult to isolate completely from
> their environment and are, moreover, highly interdependent. Although the city as
> such is not a clearly defined product, the various target groups base their decision
> to locate in or visit a city on their own conception of a city; the city is then a
> 'brand name'.

The art of city making (Landry, 2006) is therefore not only limited to amalga-
mation in a cohesive social structure of different neighbourhoods and suburbs,
parks and dumps, shopping centres and recreation facilities, parks and gardens, warehouses and parking spaces (Amin and Thrift, 2002) as city market-
eers face the challenge of understanding how the different parts of the city
contribute to the overall urban experience. In this context, place is both a con-
tainer and stage for activity-based products as well as being a product in itself
(Ashworth and Voogt, 1994). Within this context, districts, neighbourhood precincts, natural and human-made attractions contribute with their distinctiveness
and individuality to the image of the city (Fig. 14.1).

The complexity of city marketing as a multi-stakeholder decision-making
process is enhanced by the fragmentation and the preponderance of small
businesses in the tourist sector. This often leads to a lack of management

Fig. 14.1. River and city, Brisbane. (Photograph courtesy of Tourism Queensland. With
permission.)

expertise, a divergence of aims between the public and commercial sectors and a short-term planning horizon which in part is driven by public sector, 12-monthly budgeting cycles, but also by the tactical operating horizon of small businesses (Athiyaman, 1995). Furthermore, for some cities and Brisbane is a case in point, the administrative boundaries are not congruent with the realities of the tourism industry. These difficulties of collaboration among stakeholders and control of their marketing-related activities have the potential to undermine marketing because promotional campaigns can be undertaken by a variety of tourist businesses with no consultation or even agreement on the prevailing message or the destination values being promoted. This can result in conflicting or contradictory policies and images being promoted. Thus, a political dimension becomes important in the evolution of tourism policy as various alliances form to take advantage of, or to propose or oppose new ideas about, image, target markets and infrastructure development. The foregoing also implies at least the potential for a lack of customer-focused marketing as product-based perspectives dominate. This point is significant for those promoting a destination because, as Levitt (1960) has shown, managers should focus on understanding what their clients want. People do not buy products; they buy the expectation of benefits. It is the benefits that are the products.

Within this theoretical context, the case study presented in this chapter is a clear example of how Brisbane's image was built not as a result of an understanding of tourist perception but as a way of fulfilling the political agenda of Brisbane's City Council. With these theoretical propositions as background, this chapter charts the course of the development of the image of Brisbane over a period of 30 years. It begins by providing an extended case study of the main events involved in development of the destination image (or brand) for Brisbane, Australia.

A Brief History of Brisbane

Brisbane was initially established as a penal settlement in 1825 later becoming the capital of Queensland when it was established as a separate British colony in 1869. By the time of Australian Federation in 1901, Brisbane was the economic hub of Queensland, then the fastest-growing state in the new nation. After World War I, Brisbane became the largest local authority in Australia when the 1924 City of Brisbane Act amalgamated the two city councils, six town councils and ten shire councils that collectively administered the city creating a single council that governed $1220\,km^2$. Brisbane is located in South-east Queensland (see Fig. 14.2) and in 2007 had a population of 1.84 million people and was Australia's third largest city after Sydney and Melbourne. Surrounding Brisbane are two major coastal leisure destinations: the Sunshine Coast to the immediate north and the Gold Coast to the south. Brisbane has become the commercial centre for South-east Queensland with extensive domestic and international air links. Residents and visitors to Brisbane enjoy a subtropical outdoors lifestyle with the amenities of a capital city, and with

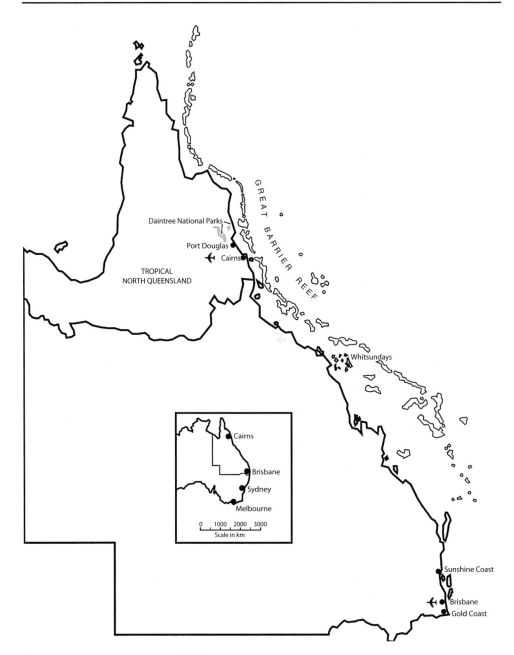

Fig. 14.2. Location of the city of Brisbane.

leisure destinations nearby suitable for day trips. The inner city, metropolitan Brisbane, is surrounded by leafy, sometimes very hilly, suburbs. Further out in the suburbs, the traditional Australian house on a large block or even acreage dominates. Brisbane is a city where tourism is now vital to the economy as shown in Table 14.1.

Table 14.1. Regional tourism profiles – South-east Queensland. (From Tourism Queensland, 2007.)

Tourism flows	Brisbane	Gold Coast	Sunshine Coast
International overnight visitor nights ('000) – year ending December 2005	9,827,000	6,740,000	1,993,000
Domestic overnight visitor nights ('000) – year ending December 2005	15,332,000	16,260,000	10,965,000
Domestic day-trip visitors ('000) – year ending December 2005	8,601,000	6,254,000	3,980,000
Tourism share of gross regional product (%)	3.8	14.5	16.0
Tourism-related employment (full-time equivalents), 1998–1999	30,200	27,700	14,500

Emergence of a Modern Tourism Structure and Policy for Queensland

Early development

The Queensland Government adopted tourism as an agent of economic development for its regionally diverse state prior to World War II. At that time, Queensland had a network of Government Tourist Bureaus in regional centres of Queensland and southern states directed at encouraging interstate visitors. After World War II, the Queensland Government had set up a board of inquiry to make recommendations in regard to the development of Queensland's tourist resources (Ferguson, 1947). A number of regional tourism attractions were noted, and these became the centre of regional tourism clusters, including Brisbane, the Sunshine Coast, the Gold Coast and Cairns, in the North. Despite this, in the 1970s, Queensland was regarded as 'The Cinderella State' and Brisbane was seen as 'a city with its jacket off and its sleeves rolled up – hot, languorous, at times sensuously, indolent, just a branch manager town, a city of also-rans, a man's city-matey, slow to change and a bit rough around the edges' (Garnsey, 1984, p. 2). Table 14.2 summarizes the main events in the evolution of a tourism policy for Brisbane. These events are discussed in more detail in the following case study.

Triggers for Brisbane's modern tourism development

The 1982 Commonwealth Games are generally considered to have begun the emergence of Brisbane as a modern international destination. This event brought new sports and cultural facilities to Brisbane, as well as a renewed identity. In 1988, World Expo was held in Brisbane and hailed as another major international success for the city and for Australia with 15.8 million attendances. Expo 88 encouraged overseas visitation and residents of Brisbane experienced many different cultures for the first time. This was also the first

Table 14.2. A selected chronology of events in the marketing of Brisbane for tourism.

1947	Board of Enquiry to make recommendations in regard to the development of Queensland's tourist resources
1979	QTTC founded by State Government to provide leadership and guidance for tourism industry
	BVCB established to promote Brisbane as a tourism destination
1980	Commonwealth Games awarded to Brisbane. The city of Brisbane introduces 'leisure' regulation
1982	Commonwealth Games
1984	Expo proposed in Brisbane – at South bank Parklands. Urban redevelopment near the Brisbane River begins
1985	Brisbane council set up Economic Steering Committee
1986	'Get into Brisbane' campaign
1987	River Strategy notes Brisbane's River also has potential as a tourism resource
1988	Expo 15.8 million attendances
1988	Resident survey finds negative views of city
1989	Tourism Strategy Review identifies four issues
1989	'Beautiful Brisbane River City' campaign
1990	QTTC reduces number of Regional Tourism Associations to gain regional focus
1991	Pacific Gateway strategy
1996	Queensland's developed tourism regions promoted
1996	Report finds Brisbane 'has no defined image'
1997	'City of Sundays' campaign
1999	Capital City policy identifies eight issues
2000	Brisbane Marketing established
	Meet in Brisbane
	Experience Brisbane
2000	Completion of upgraded Brisbane–Gold Coast motorway – The Pacific Highway?
2001	Southern Queensland campaign: 'Southern Queensland, you'll love every piece'
2002	'Brisbane its happening' campaign

free enterprise Expo, meeting costs through sponsorship, ticket sales, rental of exhibition space and the resale of the site. Brisbane's image is considered to have been positively and significantly affected by Expo 88 and to have become more 'friendly' (Stimpson, 1991). Both events were strongly supported by the then newly established Queensland Tourist and Travel Corporation (QTTC), which was charged with promotion and marketing of Queensland as a tourist destination. Both QTTC and the Brisbane Visitors and Convention Bureau (BVCB) were established in 1979 in the lead up to these two major international events, and were instrumental in their success.

Tourism Queensland
As an instrument of the Queensland State Government, QTTC and its successor Tourism Queensland (TQ) provide leadership and guidance to the State's tourism industry while at the same time delivering the Queensland Government's tourism programme through its integrated approach to tourism policy, destination development and marketing. One of the first actions of the QTTC after

being established in 1979 was to expand the network of Government Tourist Bureaus in regional centres into a series of industry-based Regional Tourism Associations (RTAs), including the BVCB. In 1990, BVCB received AUS$ 135,000 in funding from the Queensland Government via the QTTC and other RTAs were allocated AUS$100,000.

From 1979 to 1990, the number of RTAs in Queensland increased to 17 but consolidation occurred in 1990 for financial reasons and the introduction of a zonal marketing system resulted in a reduction to 12 RTAs. The aim of the zonal marketing system was to group geographically and psychologically similar regions together and to market each of them as one unit (Laws et al., 2002). In this process, Brisbane was combined with its surrounding hinterland area (excluding the separate coastal areas of the Gold and Sunshine Coasts). In 1994, the features and attractions of Brisbane as reported to the QTTC by the BVCB were colonial heritage, sporting facilities, natural attractions and shopping/restaurants.

The Emergence of 'The River City'

Brisbane river strategy

The BVCB was established in February 1979 as the official marketing authority for the City of Brisbane with 205 members. The success of the 1982 Commonwealth Games confirmed the potential of tourism to the Brisbane City Council. In March 1985, the Lord Mayor established an Economic Steering Committee to analyse the city's economy and to prepare an Economic Development Strategy for the City. In turn, the Committee appointed a Tourism Subcommittee to develop a detailed action plan to maximize the social and economic value of the tourism industry to Brisbane. This plan was to be implemented through the BVCB and QTTC (Tourism Strategy Review Committee, 1989).

In 1987, another committee of the Council, the Brisbane River Strategy Committee, began to examine the environmental quality of the Brisbane River. The final report of this committee found that: 'Brisbane's unique winding river, its subtropical climate and its position near other tourist resorts all give our "city a more" realistic chance of achieving a tourist image than most other river "cities"' (Balkin and Camden, 1987, p. 69). In this report, and for the first time, the Brisbane River was seen as a tourist resource.

The Brisbane River Strategy had as its primary economic objective to make the river a focal point of tourism by promoting realization of its leisure and tourism potential both for Brisbane residents and visitors from interstate and overseas. The Council's action plan resulting from the Economic Development Strategy identified four operational objectives:

- to promote Brisbane internationally and domestically as a tourist destination in its own right;
- to maximize visitation levels and tourist expenditure in the region;

- to encourage existing and potential tourism developers to identify opportunities for providing the necessary tourism infrastructure for Brisbane;
- to realize the Lord Mayor's objective to establish Brisbane as the Sporting and Convention Capital of the southern hemisphere (Brisbane City Council, 1985).

Get into Brisbane

During the period 1986–1989, an advertising campaign designed to enhance residents' awareness of the variety of attractions Brisbane had to offer was aired using television and radio media. This campaign, called: 'Get into Brisbane!', won the 1988 Queensland Award for Regional Tourism Authorities. However, more than just advertising needed to be done to improve the attractiveness of the city; in February 1988, a study of residents' needs indicated Brisbane was strongly associated with a casual atmosphere, warm and friendly to visitors and a safe place. The same study identified a need for 'attractions' that could contribute to the variety and quality of life in Brisbane as well as enhancing Brisbane's appeal as a tourist destination. Some particular needs identified were:

- new open air restaurants with longer opening hours;
- more live entertainment and a higher standard of entertainment;
- greater focus on the river for restaurants, entertainment and tours; and
- a Brisbane casino and poker machines in hotels.

Beautiful Brisbane – River City

In 1989, a new review of the tourism strategy for Brisbane identified four major issues. These were: marketing (especially convention marketing); the Brisbane River (both as a tourism resource and a transport artery); the need for a new international air terminal; and the need for a convention/exhibition centre (Brisbane City Council, 1989). The marketing issue related to the image of the city, with a consultation process, identifying that the marketing and promotion of South-east Queensland was too fragmented. Brisbane especially was not given the exposure it warranted by tourist organizations promoting Australia to overseas markets. It suggested that Brisbane should be promoted with the rest of South-east Queensland (in international markets). At this time, a number of image problems for Brisbane were identified. The Brisbane River (Fig. 14.3) was seen either as an eyesore with the wrong colour water (brown not blue), a wasted recreational and entertainment resource or an underutilized transport resource. This was problematic since in 1989 the slogan adopted for Brisbane was *Beautiful Brisbane – River City*.

In 1991, a draft Brisbane Strategic Plan was developed. One chapter of this report is devoted to the topic of 'City Image'. As part of this study it was concluded 'that people feel their city does have an image and that it should be projected. This image is about Brisbane's lifestyle and the charm of the city's environment' (Stimson, 1991). This report also advocated a convention centre as being central to further development of Brisbane as a 'Pacific gateway' and complimenting its new international airport terminal.

Fig. 14.3. Brisbane River and the central business district (CBD), Queensland. (Photograph courtesy of Tourism Queensland. With permission.)

In 1996, the QTTC proposed to market Queensland as a series of developed regions, based on the Gold Coast, Whitsundays, Sunshine Coast, Cairns and Far-north Queensland, and Brisbane. As part of this programme, it was decided to allow the marketing of destinations within Queensland. This had not previously been part of the brief of the QTTC. However, a study by Brian Sweeney and Associates (1996) found the following:

- Brisbane has an ill-defined image and lacked a common identity.
- Knowledge of what Brisbane had to offer to holiday makers is vague in the extreme.
- Brisbane is largely overshadowed in Queensland by close-by coastal holiday destinations.

The study noted that '[t]here appear to be many misconceptions based on a lack of information..."a big country town"..."slow and boring"..."a retirement centre"..."nothing to see or do"' (Brian Sweeney and Associates, 1996, p. 2).

City of Sun Days
As a result, the QTTC developed a new advertising programme, *City of Sun Days*, that targeted the short-break market defined as the area that lay within a 400 km drive radius of the city. Little coordinated marketing effort had been focused on this primary source region although Brisbane experiences intense competition for short-break leisure visitors from the nearby Gold and Sunshine Coasts. For these reasons, the main thrust of an initial 3-year marketing programme was focused on the regional drive market. Forays into secondary interstate markets were specifically designed to enhance the potential of special

events such as the local *River festival*, a week-long festival held in September each year from 1998 to celebrate the Brisbane River.

Integrated city marketing

In January 1999, the Queensland Government and the Brisbane City Council launched the Capital City Policy programme, a joint partnership initiative designed to address key policy issues facing the development of the city. Integrated City Marketing was one of eight salient issues; others included the Integrated Regional Transport Plan, co-originating major sport and entertainment facilities and festivals and events strategies. Nevertheless, an opposition Brisbane councillor said: 'We've had the Australian Tourism Exchange and are having the Goodwill Games in the city, but there is no branding of Brisbane. We've got some serious concerns' (Retschlag, 2001, p. 9). In 2001, a new Chief Executive Officer (CEO) was appointed. He said efforts to put Brisbane on the tourism map had been hampered by a lack of coordination and short-term vision (Anonymous, 2001, p. 4). In the same article, the then Chairman of Brisbane Marketing confirmed that the city slogan, City of Sun Days, which had been launched 2 years ago and was now virtually forgotten, would be replaced (Anonymous, 2001, p. 4).

In 1999, the Lord Mayor of Brisbane announced his intention to restructure local government marketing and promotion entities – including Brisbane City Council (BCC) interests in Brisbane Tourism. This more active involvement in tourism destination marketing by the Brisbane City Council was led in part by an interest in increasing international visitors to Brisbane. This again focused attention on the iconic attraction of Brisbane city. The reaction of tourism operators was to focus attention not on the political debate but the opportunities for successful promotion of Brisbane internationally. In May 2000, key players stated that international travel writers '*may not find Brisbane a place worth visiting*' (Retschlag, 2000, p. 11). In the same article, the Australian Federation of Travel Agents CEO was reported as saying Brisbane was not currently sold as a destination in its own right. '*When you pick up the brochures they relate to Queensland.*' Also in the same article, the Queensland Backpacker and Independent Travellers Industry Association chairman said while Brisbane was a 'liveable' city, it lacked 'wow', and the Brisbane Tourism General Manager said his organization lacked the funds to aggressively market Brisbane.

Integrated marketing for South-east Queensland

In 2000, Brisbane's Lord Mayor proposed a unified approach to South-east Queensland's promotion of tourism in response to the QTTC's regional policy and the recent upgrading of the Brisbane–Gold Coast motorway. The unified approach provoked negative reactions from the nearby Sunshine and Gold Coast civic leaders. The city, its 12 surrounding shires, Moreton Bay and its islands, the Gold Coast and Sunshine Coast and their hinterlands were to be presented as a single, integrated destination, a stylized jigsaw map of the region with the slogan: '*Southern Queensland – You'll Love Every Piece.*' This suggestion created controversy and the response from the Gold Coast reported in the local paper *The Gold Coast Bulletin*, called Brisbane 'a transit lounge' for coast tourists. The Gold Coast Mayor commented: 'If you did a survey in virtually any Asian country and asked people to name two Australian cities, they'd say Sydney and the Gold Coast. . . . We have a high recognition factor overseas which we have built up over many years' (Wright, 2001, p. 19).

The tourism peak body attempted to provide a positive interpretation. 'The (Brisbane) mayor's suggestions were very positive', said the Queensland Tourism Industry Council chief executive (Wright, 2000), 'This is not about a take-over attempt by Brisbane. It's about inclusiveness and about creating business for everybody – growing the pie, not slicing it up differently'. The Queensland Tourism Industry Council also supported the mayor's idea that to create a successful tourism marketing strategy for the south the region has to 'punch through by connecting its combined tourism assets' (Wright, 2000). The Gold Coast theme park Warner Bros Movie World, which is listed in the national tourism hall of fame as one of the best attractions Australia has developed, is a paid-up member of Brisbane Tourism and an industry prize winner for the city. So are Dreamworld, Sea World and Wet 'n' Wild, the other main theme parks on the Gold Coast. Other south and north coast and hinterland Brisbane Tourism members include Sanctuary Cove, Binna Burra Mountain Lodge, O'Reilly's Rainforest Guesthouse, Couran Cove Resort (South Stradbroke Island), Australia Zoo (Caboolture) and Sunshine Coast-based company, Coachtrans. These attractions are already being promoted overseas as components of a single southern Queensland destination by Brisbane Tourism and its counterparts on both coasts with Tourism Queensland support.

The Brisbane Marketing chairman has also commented: 'We have to get people into the much bigger picture, to convince them that the sum is greater than the parts and that everybody will win from it. Dreamworld is 30 min from central Brisbane . . . you can get to it quicker from Brisbane than from Coolangatta. Is it part of the Gold Coast, or a part of Brisbane or part of a greater region?'

'The River City': a tired image?

During the winter of 2007, the search for a new slogan to represent Brisbane city has revealed the passion and the humour of Queenslanders and the fierce pride they have in their city. *The Sunday Mail* reported on 7 October 2007 that it had received hundreds of suggestions as to how the city could be promoted, many of them good. Brisbane Marketing launched a 12-month project to discover the 'essence of Brisbane'. The idea was to find a new slogan and branding to promote the city here and overseas in the same way *I Love NY* is associated with the Big Apple, and New Zealand's *100% Pure* campaign. The idea caught the imagination of readers in Queensland, all over Australia and even some living overseas. The 'River City' featured heavily in suggestions, but one Brisbane resident living overseas pleaded: 'Please don't use "The River City" because it is a dreadful soapie over here.'

The case study effectively stops at this point in time, but tourism marketing and policy have continued to evolve. Most recently, BVCB has been placed more firmly under the control of the Brisbane City Council. During this reorganization, tourism marketing responsibilities as well as the role of the marketing of the main central business district shopping precinct have been combined. This has to some extent focused the attention of the newly named 'Brisbane Marketing' on residents of Brisbane rather than tourists.

Discussion

This case study has highlighted the increasing attention given to tourism in Brisbane and summarized in Table 14.2 (above). There have been a number of areas of emphasis over the period of the case. A first factor was the establishment of relevant organizations such as the QTTC and BVCB. Next, the staging of major events proved to be the catalyst for increasing interest in tourism and for involvement of local residents. Later attention focused on developing the tourist image of Brisbane. The Brisbane River, arguably not an international icon, was seized upon by the Brisbane City Council as the image of Brisbane, but primarily for domestic marketing purposes. This led to contention between the QTTC and BVCB over the effectiveness of this brand image. Similarly, the growing interest of Brisbane city in the promotion of tourism began to challenge the established tourism resort areas of the Gold Coast and the Sunshine Coast. This was evidenced by debate regarding promotion of South-east Queensland in international markets.

This interpretation of the case material will now be discussed in terms of theoretical concepts. Schumpeter (1934, 1943, 1966) has noted that economic development consists primarily in employing existing resources in different ways. Organic images such as a river are an example of the resources available to city such as Brisbane and that can be used to transform a physical place into a tourism destination. The case study clearly reveals that translating organic images into a destination brand is a political process. While most of the destination branding literature argues that destination branding is a collaborative process (Morgan *et al.*, 2002; Hankinson, 2004), the conflicts aroused around using the river as the brand image of Brisbane reveal that the 'creative and synergistic outcomes, which many writers associate with collaboration, may also follow from conflictual interorganizational relationships' (Hardy and Phillips, 1998, p. 218). The case of the River City is an example of how problems domain such as destination branding are 'objectively given' entities (Trist, 1983). In fact, Brisbane River was just the starting point of the creation of a destination brand for Brisbane which, as the case demonstrates, is a socially constructed entity created through shared appreciation, and mutually agreed rules and structures, and conflicts among different stakeholder views.

This case study also reveals the fallacy of those deterministic models that describe tourism marketing as a rationale decision-making process. The development of the events that underpin the creation of a destination brand for Brisbane allows us to describe tourism destinations as continuously changing entities where the redeployment of resources challenges existing orders. Such disruption, as Faulkner has shown (Faulkner and Russell, 2001; Faulkner and Vikulov, 2001) whether caused by entrepreneurs or disasters, leads to change and indicates there is no optimal solution to tourism systems. From this perspective, the tourism destination is in a chaotic state (Gleick, 1988; Waldrop, 1992), constantly transforming itself, undergoing changes that are increasingly complex and irreversible (Selin and Chavez, 1995). These changes may be caused by shifting internal conditions, or be in response to external opportunities and threats.

However, out of the chaos can develop new structures and increased fitness for survival. A dynamic system may appear to be chaotic, but its identity, history and sense of purpose define its boundaries and guide its evolution and growth (Bechtold, 1997). In this sense, chaos in such tourism destinations has a purpose. It is a symptom of struggle for survival rather than an end in itself. From this perspective, evolution, seen as a struggle for survival through increased 'fitness', provides a better metaphor for longer-term change in a tourism destination.

From an academic perspective, the question of change and mechanisms of change has been a central point of debate in the social sciences. A number of paradigms of social change have been adopted including classical scientific determinism, complexity theory (Faulkner and Russell, 1997) and the focus of this chapter, evolutionary theory (Alderson, 1965; Van Parijs, 1981; Hallpike, 1986; Tremblay, 1999). These paradigms directly or indirectly influence research investigations and questioning their appropriateness is important for theory building (Kuhn, 1981). From a practical perspective, this chapter has addressed central issues related to the tourism planning and management of a city and the difficulty of destination image development in the face of multiple stakeholders.

Limitations of this study

Many of the details of Brisbane's marketing have necessarily been excluded from this chapter due to length limitations. In selecting the material to present the authors have attempted to provide empirical evidence which illuminates the main theoretical issues considered above. In so doing we have excluded other important material, notably the spectrum of political views and actions within the various organizations involved in Brisbane's tourism, preferring instead to emphasis the different positions these organizations have taken at various times. We have also omitted any discussion of the roles of the Australian Commonwealth government in setting and funding tourism policy. Methodologically, we have drawn only on published sources including Council documents and the views expressed in local newspapers by some of participants in these decisions. Further understanding of the politicized nature of the evolution of tourism policy may be obtained in future research by conducting interviews with these decision makers and others involved at the time.

A final conclusion

Despite the great progress made in tourism research, particularly in the study of a range of destination issues under the broad umbrella of sustainability, the limitations on improving the understanding of tourism policy result from two main weaknesses:

- the restricted analytical approaches applied to destination management issues; and
- the lack of recognition of the interdependencies and complexities of tourism systems.

Developing such policy requires an understanding of the character of change in tourism systems. This chapter provides an underpinning theoretical mechanism for change in tourism that embraces the chaos and complexity theory of Faulkner as part of longer-term evolution of the destination. While speculative, such an approach is considered attractive by the authors as it resonates with the desire for tourism operators to survive.

References

Alderson, W. (1965) *Dynamic Marketing Behavior.* Richard D. Irwin, Homewood, Illinois.

Amin, A., and Thrift, N. (2002) *Cities: Reimagining the Urban.* Polity, Cambridge.

Anonymous (2001, 3 August) Sun sets on boring city image. *The Courier Mail.* p. 4.

Ashworth, G.J. and Voogt, H. (1994) Marketing and place promotion. In: Gold, J.R. and Ward, S.V. (eds) *Place Promotion.* Wiley, Chichester, UK, pp. 39–52.

Athiyaman, A. (1995) The interface of tourism and strategy research: an analysis. *Tourism Management* 16(6), 447–453.

Balkin, G. and Camden, D. (1987) The potential for tourism on the Brisbane River. In: Council, B.C. (ed.) *The Brisbane River. A strategy for our future.* Brisbane City Council, Brisbane, Australia, pp. 69–70.

Bechtold, B.L. (1997) Chaos theory as a model for strategy development. *Empowerment in Organizations* 5(4), 193–201.

Bramwell, B. and Rawding, L. (1996) Tourism marketing images of industrial cities. *Annals of Tourism Research* 23(1), 201–221.

Brian Sweeney and Associates (1996) *Brisbane Image Research.* Queensland Tourist and Travel Corporation, Brisbane, Australia.

Brisbane City Council (1985) *A Tourism Strategy for Brisbane – A New Beginning 1986–1989.* Brisbane City Council, Brisbane, Australia.

Brisbane City Council (1989) *Review of the Tourism Strategy.* Brisbane City Council, Brisbane, Australia.

Buhalis, D. (2003) *e-Tourism: Information Technologies for Strategic Tourism Management.* Financial Times Prentice-Hall, New York.

Czarniawska, B. (2002) *A Tale of Three Cities or The Globalization of City Management.* Oxford University Press, Oxford.

Faulkner, B. and Russell, R. (1997) Chaos and complexity in tourism: in search of a new perspective. *Pacific Tourism Review* 1(2), 93–102.

Faulkner, B. and Russell, R. (2001) Turbulence, chaos and complexity in tourism systems: a research direction for the new millennium. In: Faulkner, B., Moscardo, G. and Laws, E.

(eds) *Tourism in the 21st Century: Lessons from Experience*. Continuum, London, pp. 328–349.

Faulkner, B. and Vikulov, L. (2001) Katherine, washed out one day, back on track the next: a post-mortem of a tourism disaster. *Tourism Management* 22(4), 331–344.

Ferguson, E.A. (1947) *Report of the Queensland Tourist Development Board*. Queensland Government, Brisbane, Australia.

Garnsey, J.M. (1984, 19–20 March) Queensland and Brisbane as a focus for advertising strategies and the games. Paper presented at the 1982 Commonwealth Games: A Retrospect, Brisbane, Australia.

Gartner, W.C. (1993) Image formation process. In: Fesenmaier, D.R. and Uysal, M. (eds) *Communication and Channel Systems in Tourism Marketing*. Haworth Press, New York, pp. 191–215.

Gleick, J. (1988) *Chaos: Making a New Science*. Cardinal, London.

Hallpike, C.R. (1986) *The Principles of Social Evolution*. Clarendon Press, Oxford.

Hankinson, G. (2004) Relational network brands: towards a conceptual model of place brands. *Journal of Vacation Marketing* 10(2), 109–121.

Hardy, C. and Phillips, N. (1998) Strategies of engagement: lessons from the critical examination of collaboration and conflict in an inter-organizational domain. *Organization Science* 9(2), 217–230.

Highmore, B. (2005) *Cityscapes: Cultural Readings in the Material and Symbolic City*. Palgrave Macmillan, New York.

Judd, D.R. (1995) Promoting tourism in US cities. *Tourism Management* 16(3), 175–187.

Kaplanidou, K. and Vogt, C. (2003) *Destination Branding: Concept and Measurement*. Department of Park, Recreation and Tourism Resources, Michigan State University, Michigan.

Kavaratzis, M. and Ashworth, G.J. (2007) Partners in coffee shops, canals and commerce: marketing the city of Amsterdam. *Cities* 24(1), 16–25.

Kolb, B.M. (2006) *Tourism Marketing for Cities and Towns: Using Branding and Events to Attract Tourism*. Elsevier/Butterworth-Heinemann, Amsterdam.

Konecnik, M. and Gartner, W.C. (2007) Customer-based brand equity for a destination. *Annals of Tourism Research* 34(2), 400–421.

Kuhn, T. (1981) *What Are Scientific Revolutions?* The MIT Press, Cambridge.

Landry, C. (2006) *The art of City Making*. Earthscan, London.

Laws, E. and Cooper, C. (1998) Inclusive tours and commodification: the marketing constraints for mass-market resorts. *Journal of Vacation Marketing* 4(4), 337–352.

Laws, E., Scott, N. and Parfitt, N. (2002) Synergies in destination image management: a case study and conceptualisation. *International Journal of Tourism Research* 4(1), 39–55.

Levitt, T. (1960) Marketing myopia. *Harvard Business Review* 38(July–August), 45–56.

Marzano, G. (2007) The effect of stakeholder power on a destination branding process: the Gold Coast VeryGC brand. Unpublished PhD, The University of Queensland, Brisbane, Australia.

Morgan, N. (2003) Destination branding: creating the unique destination proposition. *Journal of Vacation Marketing* 10(1), 87.

Morgan, N., Pritchard, A. and Piggott, R. (2002) New Zealand, 100% pure. The creation of a powerful Niche destination brand. *Journal of Brand Management* 9(4/5), 335–354.

Morgan, N., Pritchard, A. and Piggott, R. (2003) Destination branding and the role of stakeholders: the case of New Zealand. *Journal of Vacation Marketing* 9(3), 285–299.

Morrison, A.M. and Anderson, D.J. (2002) Destination branding. Paper presented at the Annual Meeting of the Missouri Association of Convention and Visitor Bureaus.

Pile, S. (1999) What is a city? In: Massey, D., Allen, J. and Pile S. (eds) *City Worlds*. Routledge, London, pp. 3–52.

Retschlag, C. (2000, 13 May) City liveable not loveable – Visitors face search for the 'wow' factor. *Courier Mail*. p. 11.

Retschlag, C. (2001, 8 June) Brisbane campaign shapes as non-event. *Courier Mail*. p. 9.

Ryan, C. and Zahra, A. (2004) The political challenge: the case of New Zealand's tourism organizations. In: Morgan, N., Pritchard, A. and Pride, R. (eds) *Destination Branding: Creating the Unique Destination Proposition,* 2nd edn. Butterworth-Heinemann, Oxford, pp. 79–110.

Schumpeter, J. (1934) *The Theory of Economic Development.* Harvard University Press, Cambridge.

Schumpeter, J. (1943) *Capitalism, Socialism and Democracy.* Allen and Urwin, London.

Schumpeter, J. (1966) *Innovation and Economic Growth.* Harvard University Press, Cambridge.

Selin, S.W. and Chavez, D. (1995) Developing an evolutionary tourism partnership model. *Annals of Tourism Research* 22(4), 814–856.

Stimpson, R.J. (1991) *Brisbane – Magnet City.* Brisbane City Council, Brisbane, Australia.

Stimson, R.J. (1991) *Draft of the Brisbane Plan: A City Strategy.* Brisbane City Council, Brisbane, Australia.

Tremblay, P. (1999) The future of tourism: an evolutionary perspective. Paper presented at the Ninth Australian Tourism and Hospitality Education Conference, Adelaide, South Australia.

Trist, E.L. (1983) Referent organizations and the development of interorganizational domains. *Human Relations* 36, 247–268.

Tourism Queensland (2007) *Queensland – Regional Update: Year Ended December 2005.* Queensland Government, Brisbane, Australia.

Tourism Strategy Review Committee, BVCB (1989). *Get into Brisbane! Focus on the Nineties: A Tourism Strategy for Brisbane.* Brisbane Visitors and Convention Bureau, Brisbane, Australia.

van den Berg, L., Braun, E. and Otgaar, A.H.J. (2002) *Sports and City Marketing in European Cities.* Ashgate, Aldershot, UK.

Van Parijs, P. (1981) *Evolutionary Explanation in the Social Sciences: An Emerging Paradigm.* Tavistock Publications, London.

Waldrop, M. M. (1992) *Complexity: The Emerging Science at the Edge of Order and Chaos.* Penguin Books, London.

Wright, J. (2001, 9 November) Jigsaw puzzle's missing pieces. *Courier Mail.* p. 19.

Yeh, C.V. (2006) *Shanghai Love: Courtesans, Intellectuals, and Entertainment Culture, 1850–1910.* University of Washington Press, Seattle, Washington.

15 Conclusions and Challenges

M. Cooper[1] and B. Prideaux[2]

[1]*Ritsumeikan Asia Pacific University, Beppu, Japan;* [2]*James Cook University, Cairns, Australia*

Introduction

The fact that rivers are among the most significant outdoor assets for tourism and recreation, coupled with their ubiquity, made it difficult to choose between them in presenting the material in this book. Nevertheless, certain rivers pick themselves: the Nile, Amazon, Rhine, Volga, Danube, Colorado, Mississippi, Ganges, Yangzi and Mekong had to be covered; and certain types of tourism associated with them are equally as obvious. Like many other water bodies, these rivers have become important locations for travel, cultural tourism, sports tourism and other water-related activities that many people travel long distances to experience, but they are particularly iconic for the reasons outlined in the chapters devoted to them. In addition, the tourism based on the rivers chosen for this book provides a descriptive concept map (Moscardo *et al.*, 2006) of the main elements of river tourism that can be applied to most if not all rivers.

We noted in the introduction to the book that since the beginnings of recorded history, rivers have played a critical role in human survival, the progression of civilization, and more recently, economic development. In ancient times, rivers facilitated long- and short-distance travel, trade and hunting. They were also instrumental in powering ancient and modern empires and the first stages of the Industrial Revolution in Europe, and featured in many transportation innovations still utilized throughout the world today. Rivers are also central to localized recreational opportunities wherever they occur.

Several direct relationships between tourism and rivers have been identified in this book. First, rivers provide a wealth of attractions and aesthetic appeal for tourists and provide a unique venue in which tourism can take place. In some parts of the world, the physical morphology of rivers results in amazing natural landscapes that draw visitors from all parts of the globe. Perhaps less impressively, but no less importantly, rivers can provide solitude, beauty and interesting history that appeals to locals and tourists alike. The second relationship of importance comes about through rivers used as transportation corridors. Navigable rivers are a valuable asset to any region or country for the transportation of raw materials and manufactured products. However, in a post-Fordist economy where services are becoming more important than primary resource extraction and manufacturing, as is the case in most of the developed world, rivers are taking on an additional element to their uses for commerce and trade: that of transporting tourists on sightseeing cruises or as a long-distance mode of transportation. Third, rivers are an important resource for tourist destinations in three ways: to provide water supplies for domestic and resort use; to facilitate the development of intense tourism-oriented environments such as viewing historic, cultural and industrial remains; and to fill swimming pools. These are especially important considerations in arid regions (e.g. Egypt and Nubia, Arizona in the USA), where local residents are often required to sacrifice their own water use for the broader benefit of tourism. Finally, river water is necessary to grow many of the agricultural products and generate the electricity needed to sustain tourism in all regions of the world.

In summary then, rivers are complex ecosystems that are noticeably influenced by many human activities, including tourism and recreation. The tourist use of the world's rivers must be monitored and well managed to be able to conserve the natural and cultural wealth of these unique ecosystems for present and future generations. And a distinction has to be made between tourism *beside* the river and tourism *on* the river. Many of the world's major tourism destinations are located beside rivers and use riverside settings as a tourism resource. On the river, major activities include cruising, sailing and white rafting.

River Tourism in Retrospect

As we have seen through the chapters of this book, rivers are an important but surprisingly neglected aspect of the global tourism industry. Yet rivers form the basis for many of the ecosystems that underpin ecotourism and other recreational activities, in addition to providing water to sustain urban growth, farming, agriculture-related experiences such as viticulture and the transport of goods and people (as outlined in the chapters by Francisco Fellizar Jr. (Chapter 12, this volume) and Ken'ichi Nakagami (Chapter 13, this volume), but also forming a consistent theme throughout). Compared to the research and industry attention that ocean cruising has attracted recently, rivers have apparently been of little interest to tourism academics although the same cannot be said for leisure and recreation scholars who have demonstrated considerable interest in fluvial systems as outdoor recreation resources in recent years. The aim of this book was to explore issues related to river tourism, raise awareness of the role that rivers play in tourism and identify areas that require further research.

The main component of river tourism is the natural feature of water, one of the most popular natural settings for rest and recreation. Even short periods near water have a beneficial soothing effect on most people, which explains why tourist destinations offer water features in various forms of rivers, canals, lakes, waterfalls, hot springs and beaches. If water is not available in a natural state, man-made landscaping including fountains, ponds, swimming pools and artificial waterfalls are provided to appeal to tourists. The potential of a river is even greater, due to the changing scenery and different natural and urban settings along its shores. But this is not their only attraction. Malcolm Cooper (Chapter 2, this volume) shows that the rivers of South Asia are equally as important for their religious value (to the Hindu people rivers in India are considered as Gods and Goddesses and for the international tourist they provide the possibility for insights into the historical, cultural and traditional aspects of India, Pakistan and Bangladesh/Assam) as for their transportation value. Patricia Erfurt's discussion (Chapter 6, this volume) of rivers and canals in Europe shows that they are valued for their relaxing way of travel and their associated riverbank activities and for the exceptional scenery and culture they traverse. In the European context, river tourists have the opportunity to engage with local communities, go shopping, sightseeing and take up any offer that might suit them to enjoy during their holiday.

The management and sharing of water which crosses international borders is a matter of concern in relation to river tourism – because a river can be a transboundary environmental resource that does not recognize national borders. Given the geography, demographics and politics of human settlement in river basins (such as the Mekong river basin as discussed by Eric Laws and Peter Sermone in Chapter 4, this volume), regional cooperation over the use and distribution of water will be decisive for the sustainable development of river tourism. The bases of cooperation must be developed even though the lingering barriers of history and the problems of the present stand as hurdles. It is important to accept that river tourism needs cooperation for its development. All that is needed for the emergence of significant river tourism in South Asia is a genuine dedication of its partner countries towards attaining this goal. For this to happen, the tourism sector must be considered in the context of the economic and geopolitical situation. All the physical and cultural attractions in the world cannot bring river tourists to an area in a situation of political conflict over the very resource that it requires for its continuation.

As a river that is not in a basin which crosses national boundaries, but one which has nurtured several divides in the political and economic history of the USA, the Mississippi remains a vital transportation corridor and source of water for agriculture and human consumption, and is increasingly vital for the riverine tourism (based on cruises and gambling in the most part) that may be able to improve local standards of living along its length. Chapter 3 (this volume) by Dallen Timothy examines this river and the Colorado; showing that several tourism and recreation corridors have been delimited and planned in recent years in the Mississippi river basin. The history of the river with its nostalgic elements (e.g. plantations, gambling and steamboats) creates an important heritage product that focuses on white and African-American historic settlement and socio-economic activities of the past. Similarly, the tourism resources of the riparian countries along the Nile largely stem from that river's long association with human settlement. As Chapter 5 (this volume) by Malcolm Cooper shows, the Nile valley is deserving of its reputation as the world's largest open-air museum.

In Chapter 10 (this volume), Bruce Prideaux noted that heritage sites have a commercial value and if not subject to some form of official protection may be redeveloped either as an adaptation of the existing site or demolished and used for other purposes. His description of the Port of Echuca case study on the Murray River in Australia highlights a range of issues associated with river heritage in particular but also the wider issue of heritage and how it may be used as a tourist attraction. The value of sites such as the Port of Echuca can be measured from a number of perspectives: as an attraction that provides employment; as the iconic experience that underpins the sustainability of the regional tourism industry; as an educational experience that connects present generations with the past; as an activity that has encouraged local participation and maximised local benefits; and as a significant heritage site that preserves significant elements of the past.

In addition to human heritage, rivers are rich in natural heritage, particularly aquaculture, bird migrations and various natural landscapes. Owing to these characteristics, many of the major rivers forming the core of river tourism world-wide are protected in various public forms, such as municipal waterfront parks, nature preserves and National Parks. One of the most impressive of these environments is that of the Colorado River and the canyons and other geophysical landscapes it helped create, including the Grand Canyon and Glen Canyon (as described by Dallen Timothy in Chapter 3, this volume). The Grand Canyon (Arizona) is the second most visited National Park in the USA and draws people from around the globe to witness its spectacular scenery, much of which was created over millions of years by the Colorado River. Since the late 1800s, the Grand Canyon and the Colorado River at large have been a major attraction for hikers, rafter, trekkers, poets, artists, sightseers and nature 'pilgrims'. They were also a major impetus for the development of tourism in the American West before and after the beginnings of the interstate highway system in the 1950s.

What gambling is to the Mississippi, white-water rafting is to the Colorado, Ganges, Indus and many other major rivers around the world. Rafting is probably the most unique aspect of recreation and tourism on the upper reaches of any of the important rivers for tourism. Ralf Buckley describes the growth and importance of this form of adventure (sometimes extreme) tourism in Chapter 11 (this volume). The canyon-like landscapes in their upper valleys that the rivers create are at the root of this appeal, and set the upper reaches of any river apart from the lower (see also Dean Carson's description of the Daly River in Australia's Northern Territory in Chapter 8, this volume). The Grand Canyon portion of the Colorado River is the longest stretch of recreational water within a national park in the world, for example, and provides some of the world's best white water, attracting people from many countries. White-water rafting is thus a very successful and widespread sector of the adventure tourism industry. The reason for this is that it is exciting but (usually) safe. While there is a high probability that rafting clients will get wet, thrown around and occasionally frightened, there is a rather low risk that they will actually suffer any significant injury. For most other adventure tourism activities, there is a much longer learning curve before clients can take part so actively. Tandem skydiving, for example, does not require any prior skill for the client, but nor does it involve any active participation.

The natural environment

The impact of the riverine environment on river tourism must also be seen in the context of the other uses that rivers are put. And sadly, this does not make good copy for a book on river tourism! As Patricia Erfurt notes in Chapter 6 (this volume), a rather dark part of European river history includes the abuse of natural freshwater streams by a range of industries and agriculture, and pollution from municipalities. The rivers in Europe were used as a giant waste water disposal facility, flushing toxic waste from chemical factories, pesticides and herbicides from adjoining plantations and fields, as well as effluent from urban sewers downstream for some 200 years, before being very recently cleaned up. The more recent industrial development of China has also resulted in major pollution problems for earth, air and also water. As Wolfgang Arlt and Feng Gequn show in Chapter 7 (this volume) swimming in the Yangzi River is not advisable! But perhaps more sadly visitors coming for wildlife experiences to this river system are almost certainly too late: of the two major species indigenous to the river, the Chinese or Yangzi Alligator is down to about 200 animals and features on the list of highly endangered species. However, even with this status, it is still better off than the Yangzi River Dolphin which was last sighted in 2004 and declared as 'functionally extinct' in 2007.

But perhaps the most difficult form of human impact on a major river system that limits its safe use for river tourism is that shown by the religious use of the Ganges and associated river systems in India. The sheer size of the problems of waste disposal are outlined by Malcolm Cooper in Chapter 2 (this volume). The result is that the Ganges is essentially toxic, especially in and around the religious centre of Varanasi, where some 50 million pilgrims attempt to continue their religious observances tied to the river (bathing, drinking and disposal of the dead) among the virtually untreated waste water flowing into the river.

River-based ecology is also of special interest for aquatic ecotourists and geotourists. Seasonally flooded wetlands along many rivers dominate the landscape and offer rare flora and fauna, and many have been designated as a protected natural area. For the river tourism industry, of special importance are the spectacular wetlands of the Danube Delta as it meets the Black Sea, said to be unique in the world and increasingly one of Europe's favoured tourist destinations. At the other end of the scale the Himalayan region, which generates and nurtures many of the rivers described in this book, has equally important mountainous landscapes now being frequented by an increasing number of tourists. Often, the rivers of the region provide the only means of access and travel through these areas, a fact of increasing importance to both local communities and to tourists alike and marketed strongly to the potential river tourist.

Creation of branding and marketing of river tourism resources are discussed by Giuseppe Marzano, Eric Laws and Noel Scott in their chapter on the Brisbane

River in Australia (Chapter 14, this volume). They note that tourism destinations are characterized by the coexistence within the same geographical space of multiple private business and public sector organizations of varying scale and sophistication that offer a variety of target markets and services. The complexity that this situation creates is amply illustrated by the case of Brisbane and the controversial 'River city' tag that has characterized the marketing of the city.

The Contribution of this Book

Rivers have been developed in the past century beyond their natural systems to include dams for reservoirs, wildlife preserves, national parklands and regions of cultural heritage. The purpose of this book was to describe the current situation of tourism and recreation on the major rivers listed in Chapter 1 (this volume) in line with this change. The book highlights the unique forms of river tourism associated with each river, and examines how the water resource they represent is used in contemporary society to form regional and local tourism products.

The book also provides readers with an introduction to each region in which the rivers are situated, sets tourism policy in the broader context of regional, social and economic development initiatives and summarizes the recent emergence of a cohesive regional approach to river tourism in many countries and regions. This is not limited to use of the river only, the German term, *bootwandern* (Chapter 6, this volume), for example, refers to sharing the mode of travel between the use of a boat and hiking on land beside the river, with the convenience of having the major part of personal luggage on the boat which serves as accommodation during the night. The same principle works for bicycles and canoes which may be provided by a cruise company or be privately owned, offering the river tourist exercise on demand instead of inactivity on board.

Although the main aspects of river tourism are related to the aquatic environment, other tourism types such as event tourism are frequently integrated with this to reach a wider range of potential customers. Conference visits and cultural festivals at cruise destinations or functions such as seminars and presentations on board are examples of an extended range of activities available to river tourists. Aspects of wellness tourism are also offered by large cruise companies in the form of first-class facilities and qualified staff for spa facilities as part of a river cruise holiday.

Importantly, the book also discusses in a number of contexts the fact that recent attention in river governance has focused on the issue of whether states that share a given resource can cooperate effectively in its use and management. Makim (2002, p. 5), in discussing the Mekong region notes that '[t]here is now considerable evidence to suggest that, in matters of transboundary resource use, states are often able to establish and sustain collective action'. This appears to be particularly true of river tourism, as evidenced by the joint attempts by Pakistan and India, and Bangladesh and India to jointly develop river tourism (see Chapter 2, this volume). We note that River Councils as governance mechanisms for integrated water resources management have vast and as yet largely untapped potentials for achieving sustainability goals, and as a result coherent river tourism. Each basin however represents unique features and therefore must be managed differently, and it is essential that basin-wide plans be developed with as broad participation as possible from all stakeholders. A politically, socially and science-based river basin plan can be a very potent tool for clarifying roles and expectations from stakeholders, thereby making governance for river tourism more effective and responsive.

Nevertheless, water resources management, development and policy have evolved in a variety of ways from country to country. Water resources management and development is usually the responsibility of national or city authorities in many countries; therefore, these authorities should pay careful attention to water resources management because this can affect all sectors of society, not just river tourists. Each country, developed or developing, must put together their own plan of action suitable for their hydrological conditions and needs, and incorporate river tourism wherever appropriate. These plans for water management must not only be developed in theory but should also be feasible and implementable in reality. Tourism and river tourism in particular may provide the impetus for otherwise parochial national and regional organizations to address such requirements speedily and more efficiently.

Gaps and Challenges

Despite the great progress made in tourism research recently, the fact that this book represents one of the very first attempts to document *river tourism* means that the editors must acknowledge that their choices of subjects and geographical areas may be overtaken by new research in the short- to medium-term, particularly in the study of a range of destination issues for river tourism under the broad umbrella of sustainability. In this context the limitations on improving the understanding of river tourism policy in this book result from two main weaknesses:

- the restricted analytical approaches applied to destination management issues in river tourism; and
- a lack of recognition of the interdependencies and complexities of river and river tourism systems.

In particular, for river tourism governance this implies the following gaps and challenges:

1. Local tourism organizations and local water authorities must become integrated water resources managers. Each has a vested interest in ensuring availability of cheap, safe and high-quality water for both locals and visitors.

2. A basin-based approach to integrated water resource management would provide assistance to both water supply authorities and tourism authorities in the formulation of sound and science-based comprehensive usage plans, as well as assisting governments to solve transboundary issues where these exist.

3. Understanding/clarifying the interface between levels of governance and uses for water is an urgent concern. Which ones take precedence? This is a critical question to settle in the case of the use of rivers for river-based tourism.

4. Documenting 'best practice' in river tourism in each region for proper dissemination to relevant parties and organizations is critical if this is to be achieved. There is no substitute for experience, whether it be in white-water rafting or in waste water disposal.

5. Finally, political will and commitment from local and national leaderships is a critical element for river basin-based governance and therefore river tourism. Basin-based governance critically needs leaders who can mobilize, harmonize and sustain efforts towards sustainable integrated water resources management.

Future Research Directions

This book has highlighted the opportunities that exist for developing tourism using rivers for cruising and adventure pursuits, and for access to rural and urban locations. The book has also used such models as the Destination Development Matrix to illustrate the relationships that exist between the demand and supply sides of river tourism and the central position occupied by the policy and marketing sectors in its development. The importance of the relationships between the public and private sectors in the development of this form of tourism has been shown, but needs further work.

One question that has often not been adequately addressed in the limited amount of previous research on this topic is the *sustainability* of river tourism. As several of the chapters in this book testify, further work needs to be done on prudent approaches to river tourism development to avert future problems in many regions. In specific areas and for specific forms of river tourism there may also be issues that will need to be addressed locally. For example, in sensitive environmental areas, there may need to be specific visitor number levels established and/or controls placed on tourism involving indigenous populations. Our hope is that the material presented in this book has set the scene for a much more vigorous debate on the benefits and costs of river tourism while enhancing the capacity of researchers to undertake this task.

References

Makim, A. (2002) Resources for security and stability? The politics of regional cooperation on the Mekong, 1957–2001. *The Journal of Environment Development* 11(1), 5–52.

Moscardo, G., Prideaux, B. and Laws, E. (2006) Researching and managing tourism and hospitality service: challenges and conclusions. In: Prideaux, B., Moscardo, G. and Laws, E. (eds) *Managing Tourism and Hospitality Services*. CAB International, Wallingford, UK.

Index